THE CANADIAN CONSTITUTION IN TRANSITION

The year 2017 marked the 150th anniversary of Confederation and the 1867 *Constitution Act*. Anniversaries such as these are often seized upon as opportunities for retrospection. While re-examining topics that have long concerned scholars and students of constitutional law and politics, this volume takes a forward-looking approach as well. Featuring essays from both emerging and established scholars, *The Canadian Constitution in Transition* reflects on the ideas that will shape the development of Canadian constitutional law in the decades to come. Moving beyond the frameworks that previous generations used to organize constitutional thinking, the scholars in this volume highlight innovative approaches to perennial problems and seek new insights on where constitutional law is heading.

Featuring fresh scholarship from contributors who will lead the constitutional conversation in the years ahead – and who represent the gender, ethnic, linguistic, and demographic make-up of contemporary Canada – *The Canadian Constitution in Transition* enriches our understanding of the Constitution of Canada and uses various methodological approaches to chart the course towards the bicentennial.

RICHARD ALBERT is a professor of law at the University of Texas at Austin and, in 2017–18, Distinguished Visiting Professor at the Faculty of Law, University of Toronto.

PAUL DALY is a senior lecturer in public law at the University of Cambridge and the Derek Bowett Fellow in Law, Queen's College, Cambridge.

VANESSA MACDONNELL is an associate professor in the Faculty of Law at the University of Ottawa.

The Canadian Constitution in Transition

EDITED BY
RICHARD ALBERT, PAUL DALY,
AND VANESSA MACDONNELL

UNIVERSITY OF TORONTO PRESS
Toronto Buffalo London

Toronto Buffalo London
utorontopress.com

ISBN 978-1-4875-0394-9 (cloth) ISBN 978-1-4875-2302-2 (paper)

Library and Archives Canada Cataloguing in Publication

The Canadian Constitution in transition / edited by Richard Albert, Paul Daly, and Vanessa MacDonnell.

Includes bibliographical references and index.
ISBN 978-1-4875-0394-9 (hardcover). – ISBN 978-1-4875-2302-2 (softcover)

1. Canada. Constitution Act, 1867. 2. Constitutional law – Canada. I. Albert, Rich-ard (Law professor), editor II. Daly, Paul, 1983–, editor III. MacDonnell, Vanessa, 1981–, editor

KE4219.C345 2019 342.71 C2018-904116-1
KF4482.C366 2019

This book has been published with the help of a grant from the Federation for the Humanities and Social Sciences, through the Awards to Scholarly Publications Program, using funds provided by the Social Sciences and Humanities Research Council of Canada.

University of Toronto Press acknowledges the financial assistance to its publishing program of the Canada Council for the Arts and the Ontario Arts Council, an agency of the Government of Ontario.

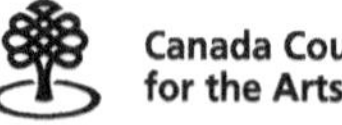

Funded by the Government of Canada
Financé par le gouvernement du Canada

Contents

THE CANADIAN CONSTITUTION IN TRANSITION

Introduction: The Constitution of Canada in a New Key

RICHARD ALBERT, PAUL DALY, AND VANESSA MACDONNELL

Charting the Road Ahead

The year 2017 marked the 150th anniversary of Confederation and the *Constitution Act, 1867*. Anniversaries such as these are often seized upon as opportunities for retrospection. This volume, by contrast, is more forward looking in its approach. While the contributors draw from the frameworks that have organized our constitutional thinking for generations, they are not constrained by them. The result is a volume that offers fresh ways of thinking about perennial problems and new insights into where constitutional law is heading in the years ahead.

What are these frameworks, and how does this collection build upon them in some respects and upend them in others? A quick glance through the leading textbooks and treatises on Canadian constitutional law suggests that the field has come to be described in predictable ways.[1] Federalism, constitutional rights, and Aboriginal and treaty rights are presented as prominent subcategories of the discipline and

1 See, e.g., Peter C. Oliver, Patrick Macklem, and Nathalie Des Rosiers, eds., *Oxford Handbook of the Canadian Constitution* (New York: Oxford University Press, 2017); Peter Hogg, *Constitutional Law of Canada*, 5th ed., loose-leaf (Scarborough, ON: Thomson Carswell, 2007); Constitutional Law Group, *Canadian Constitutional Law*, 5th ed. (Toronto: Emond Montgomery, 2016); Joseph Magnet, *Constitutional Law of Canada*, 9th ed. (Edmonton: Jurileber, 2009); Leonard Rotman, Bruce Elman, and Gerald Gall, eds., *Constitutional Law: Cases, Commentary and Principles* (Toronto: Thomson Carswell 2008); Guy Régimbald and Dwight Newman, *The Law of the Canadian Constitution*, 2nd ed. (Markham, ON: LexisNexis Canada, 2017).

are the focus of most constitutional law courses.[2] The institutions of government are also central,[3] although less time is spent teaching law students about them. Constitutional conventions, constitutional principles, and constitutional amendment round out the field.[4]

Canadian constitutional law is also framed by debates about the proper allocation of authority between the political and judicial branches of government. In the modern era, the outright rejection of judicial review is not often contemplated, although there continue to be debates about the appropriate intensity of judicial review and "comparative institutional competence."[5] Distinctions between administrative and constitutional law remain firmly entrenched, as does the division between public and private law.

While other edited collections have examined discrete aspects of Canada's constitutional law, including the monarchy,[6] institutional reform,[7] the impact of the *Canadian Charter of Rights and Freedoms*,[8] constitutional

---

2 See Oliver, Macklem, and Des Rosiers, *supra* note 1; Hogg, *supra* note 1; Constitutional Law Group, *supra* note 1; Régimbald and Newman, *supra* note 1; Rotman, Elman, and Gall, *supra* note 1.

3 See sources cited, *supra* note 1.

4 Oliver, Macklem, and Des Rosiers, *supra* note 1; Hogg, *supra* note 1; Constitutional Law Group, *supra* note 1; Nicole Duplé, *Droit constitutionnel: principes généraux* (Montreal: Wilson and Lafleur, 2014).

5 See, e.g., Sujit Choudhry, "So What Is the Real Legacy of *Oakes*? Two Decades of Proportionality Analysis under the *Charter*'s Section 1," *Supreme Court Law Review* 34 (2006) 501; Dennis Baker, *Not Quite Supreme: The Courts and Coordinate Constitutional Interpretation* (Montreal and Kingston: McGill-Queen's University Press, 2010); F.L. Morton and Rainer Knopff, *The Charter Revolution and the Court Party* (Peterborough, ON: Broadview Press, 2000).

6 Michael D. Jackson and Philippe Lagassé, eds., *Canada and the Crown: Essays in Constitutional Monarchy* (Montreal and Kingston: McGill-Queen's University Press, 2014).

7 Nadia Verrelli, ed., *The Democratic Dilemma: Reforming Canada's Supreme Court* (Montreal and Kingston: McGill-Queen's University Press, 2013); Jennifer Smith, ed., *Democratic Dilemma: Reforming the Canadian Senate* (Montreal and Kingston: McGill-Queen's University Press, 2009).

8 Grant Huscroft and Ian Brodie, *Constitutionalism in the Charter Era* (Markham, ON: LexisNexis, 2004); Errol P. Mendes and Stéphane Beaulac, *Canadian Charter of Rights and Freedoms*, 5th ed. (Markham, ON: LexisNexis, 2013); Benjamin L. Berger and James Stribopoulos, eds., *Unsettled Legacy: Thirty Years of Criminal Justice under the Charter* (Markham, ON: LexisNexis, 2012); James B. Kelly and Christopher P. Manfredi, eds., *Contested Constitutionalism: Reflections on the Canadian Charter of Rights and Freedoms* (Vancouver: UBC Press, 2009); Dwight Newman, ed., *Religious Freedom and Communities* (Markham, ON: LexisNexis, 2016).

change,[9] the legacy of individual judges,[10] and views from abroad,[11] fewer collections openly question the established frameworks that structure how we think about constitutional law. (Contributions that deal with the resurgence of Indigenous legal orders are a prominent exception.[12]) In our view, doing so is a worthwhile exercise.

The chapters in this volume show that while some of the existing ways of describing and demarcating Canadian constitutional law continue to be important, others are limiting. Until the *Charter* was enacted in 1982, federalism provided the major basis for judicial review of government action. It is unsurprising, then, that it was the focus of most constitutional law courses and treatises.[13] While federalism may have fallen temporarily out of fashion as a subject of academic enquiry in the first decades of the *Charter*, it is once again receiving renewed attention, this time with more nuance. For example, in his contribution to this volume, Wade Wright argues that provinces should not enforce federal criminal laws of questionable constitutionality. In doing so, his piece "complicates two competing visions of Canadian federalism":

> The first (increasingly beleaguered) vision focuses on the protection of exclusive, independent allocations of federal and provincial jurisdiction; the other (now more popular) vision eschews this emphasis on exclusivity and independence, focusing on coordinating the overlapping, interdependent allocations of jurisdiction thought to typify Canadian federalism

---

9 Emmett Macfarlane, ed., *Constitutional Amendment in Canada* (Toronto: University of Toronto Press, 2016).

10 Dwight Newman and Malcolm Thorburn, eds., *The Dignity of Law: The Legacy of Justice Louis LeBel* (Markham, ON: LexisNexis, 2015); Peter C. Oliver and Graham Mayeda, eds., *Principles and Pragmatism: Essays in Honour of Louise Charron* (Markham, ON: LexisNexis, 2014); Adam Dodek and Daniel Jutras, eds., *The Sacred Fire: The Legacy of Antonio Lamer (Chief Justice of Canada)* (Markham, ON: LexisNexis, 2009); Jamie Cameron, ed., *Reflections on the Legacy of Justice Bertha Wilson* (Markham, ON: LexisNexis, 2008); Lionel D. Smith, *Ruled by Law: Essays in Memory of Justice Sopinka* (Markham, ON: LexisNexis Butterworths, 2003).

11 Richard Albert and David R. Cameron, eds., *Canada in the World: Comparative Perspectives on the Canadian Constitution* (Cambridge: Cambridge University Press, 2017).

12 See, e.g., John Borrows and Michael Coyle, eds., *The Right Relationship: Reimagining the Implementation of the Historical Treaties* (Toronto: University of Toronto Press, 2017).

13 See Albert Abel, *Laskin's Canadian Constitutional Law: Cases, Text, and Notes on Distribution of Legislative Power*, rev. 4th ed. (Toronto: Carswell, 1975).

> in the service of "cooperative federalism." The account offered here of provincial non-enforcement reveals an arrangement where jurisdiction is not clearly demarcated, but fluid and contested.[14]

Thus, while federalism remains an important constitutional category, contemporary scholars understand it quite differently than their predecessors.

Paul Daly's piece on s. 96 of the *Constitution Act, 1867* (which establishes the provincial superior courts) also complicates existing constitutional categories. He explains that while the Supreme Court has secured the "core jurisdiction" of the superior courts against incursions by government, it has also allowed a range of dispute resolution bodies and processes to exist alongside the courts to promote access to justice.[15] Daly's chapter challenges the divide between public and private law by showing that the Court's interpretation of s. 96 has very real consequences for the resolution of private disputes. His chapter also emphasizes the inextricable link between constitutional and administrative law, links that are barely visible in conventional accounts of Canadian constitutional law.

In his contribution, David Milward explains that the Supreme Court's Aboriginal rights jurisprudence has failed to mitigate or redress the impact of colonization on Indigenous peoples. He argues that justice will be achieved only through "the recognition of a right of Aboriginal communities to internal autonomy under s. 35(1)" – that is, "the right to govern the conduct of their own members in accordance with their traditional laws and customs."[16] He notes that there is a particularly acute need for self-government in the area of criminal justice. Milward's chapter demonstrates that Canadian constitutional law has not yet weeded out its colonial dimensions. Only a fundamental reorientation of Canada's Aboriginal rights jurisprudence – one that begins and ends with Indigenous approaches to justice – will suffice to dismantle the legacy of colonialism. Here it is obvious that existing frameworks for thinking about constitutional law have failed.[17] "New" frameworks for governing the relationship between Indigenous peoples and the

---

14 Wade K. Wright, chap 4 in this volume at 106.
15 Paul Daly, chap 3 in this volume.
16 David Milward, chap 9 in this volume at 264.
17 Sujith Xavier, chap 10 in this volume.

Canadian state, which Indigenous scholars have in fact been thinking about for some time, are required.

The Nature of This Anniversary

For many scholars, the 150th anniversary of Confederation and the *Constitution Act, 1867* inspires mixed feelings. Consider the act's treatment of Indigenous people. Rather than including Indigenous communities as partners to Confederation,[18] s. 91(24) of the *Constitution Act, 1867* granted the federal government jurisdiction over them. As Xavier emphasizes in his contribution to this volume, it is impossible to isolate this defining aspect of Canada's constitutional chronology from the larger history of colonialism and domination that defined European settlement of North America.[19]

The constitutional compact was deficient in other respects as well. It was negotiated by the "Fathers" of Confederation. Membership in the Senate was predicated on one's status as a landholder.[20] And the constitution implied, wrongly, that Canada's population could be divided into two religious traditions, Protestant and Catholic.[21]

It is trite to say that much has changed since 1867. Canada's population is now infinitely more diverse than it was at Confederation.[22] While women continue to experience disadvantage, it is now recognized that they must be extended the full benefits of citizenship. And there is a slow but growing movement to restore Indigenous legal traditions to their proper place in the constitutional order.[23] It will, therefore, not

18 Asha Kaushal, chap 7 in this volume.

19 Sujith Xavier, *supra* note 17.

20 S 23(3) of the *Constitution Act, 1867*.

21 Howard Kislowicz, chap 6 in this volume; s 93 of the *Constitution Act, 1867*; Lorraine Weinrib, "Canada's Constitutional Revolution: From Legislative to Constitutional State," *Israel Law Review* 33, no. 1 (1999) 13 [Weinrib, "Constitutional Revolution"]. On some of these factors serving as an impetus for constitutional change leading up to the enactment of the *Charter*, see Lorraine Weinrib, "Canada's *Charter*: Rights Protection in the Cultural Mosaic," *Cardozo Journal of International and Comparative Law* 4 (1996) 395 [Weinrib, "Cultural Mosaic"].

22 Kaushal, *supra* note 18; Efrat Arbel and Eileen Myrdahl, chap 14 in this volume; Weinrib, "Cultural Mosaic," *supra* note 21.

23 Milward, *supra* note 16; John Borrows, *Canada's Indigenous Constitution* (Toronto: University of Toronto Press, 2010); Sarah Morales, "*'a 'lha'tham'*: The Re-Transformation of s 35 through a Coast Salish Legal Methodology," *National Journal of Constitutional Law* 7, no. 2 (2016) 145.

surprise the reader to learn that many of the contributors to this volume approach this anniversary with a critical rather than a celebratory eye.

The challenges Canada faces today are both similar to and different from the ones it has faced in the past. The recurrence of familiar problems has been one consequence of Canada's constitutional endurance. Since Confederation, the challenge of internal reconciliation – between English and French, east and west, federal and provincial, First Peoples and settlers – has remained unresolved and, in some ways, has been exacerbated. As Canada approached its centennial in 1967, political scientist Dale Thomson wrote of these challenges:

> Burdened by history with a permanent internal tug-of-war between the two main ethnic groups and between the different geographical regions, and exposed over 4,000 miles of open frontier to the influence of a giant neighbor, [Canadians] have become almost morbidly introspective. The national pastime, says the Transport Minister, Mr. J. W. Pickersgill, apparently is to pull up the delicate young plant of nationhood at regular intervals to see if it is still growing.[24]

Thomson then raised a question that Canadians have asked themselves many times since, most recently when Quebec nearly voted to leave Canada in 1995: "Why, it might well be asked, is Canada in danger of falling apart at this time, when no external issue divides the population and the country is enjoying the greatest period of growth and prosperity in its history?"[25]

The deputy high commissioner for Canada to the United Kingdom, Geoffrey Murray, made the same diagnosis, only more concretely in connection with Confederation. He observed in 1967 that, "to a surprising degree and certainly in some essential respects, the major influences to-day are not unlike those which faced Canadians at the time of Confederation, one hundred years ago."[26] He then listed five categories of problems that had endured unresolved for a century: what he described as "the urgent demand for economic and social development throughout the country," the threat of the United States to Canadian nationhood, the "compelling need for effective co-operation between

24 Dale C. Thompson, "Crisis in Canada," *World Today* 20, no. 10 (1964) 431.
25 *Ibid.*
26 Geoffrey S. Murray, "The Meaning of Confederation," *Journal of the Royal Society of Arts* 115, no. 5136 (1967) 953, 958.

Federal and Provincial Governments," the "central problem of national unity deriving from our duo-national origin and the multi-cultural composition of our present population," and what he identified as "the drawbacks of pluralism in Canadian politics at [the] national level and in some provinces."[27] Many, if not all, of these words could apply today about Canada at the country's sesquicentennial.

But this anniversary is also different from the centennial in important ways. Then, Canada was in the midst of a fifty-five-year internal struggle to find a domestic amending formula; today, Canada has patriated the constitution, which is now fully amendable by Canadian political actors. Then, Canada had recently adopted the 1960 *Canadian Bill of Rights*, a mere statute that offered little reassurance to Canadians about the security of their rights; today, Canada enjoys an entrenched *Charter of Rights and Freedoms*. Then, Canada hewed more closely to the model of parliamentary supremacy inherited from the United Kingdom; today, with the advent of the *Charter* and a strong culture of constitutional review, Canada more closely resembles our neighbour to the south. And then, there was very little discussion of the role of Indigenous legal orders in the Canadian constitutional framework; today, the work of reconciliation and of proper recognition of Indigenous legal orders is viewed as a first priority of Canadian constitutional law. Canada has, therefore, changed in significant ways over the past fifty years.

Change versus Stability

The theme that binds this volume together is a familiar tension in domestic constitutional law: change versus stability. For all their differences, modern democratic constitutions have had to find ways of responding to demands for constitutional change, particularly from groups and interests that had been excluded from the initial compact.[28] However, such change inevitably disrupts public institutions and legal relationships that have found stability in the old constitutional infrastructure. The challenge for constitutional law is therefore to strike a balance between the need for constitutional evolution and constitutional durability.[29]

27 *Ibid*.
28 Kaushal, *supra* note 18.
29 See Dwight Newman, chap 11 in this volume.

Few constitutions are older than Canada's. The average historical lifespan of a national constitution is nineteen years,[30] about half the age of the *Charter*, adopted in 1982 to modernize the constitution. The endurance of Canada's constitution is something that sets it apart from most others. We would argue that what has made it possible for the constitution to endure for 150 years is also what has allowed Canadian constitutional law to successfully strike a balance between change and stability – a culture of constitutional contestation. From Confederation to the present day, Canadians have contested their most fundamental constitutional norms. In so doing, Canada has developed a culture of self-interrogation and introspection. Neither the structure of federalism nor the classes of and grounds for rights have been spared from scrutiny. Everything has been fair game in our collective effort to reconcile our aspirations for the future with the unresolved questions of our past.

Unlike countries whose constitutions that have produced a political settlement, Canada remains in search of its own. As Peter Russell has observed about Canadians, "so deep are their current differences on fundamental questions of political justice and collective identity that Canadians may now be incapable of acting together as a sovereign people."[31] Yet there is an upside to the absence of any political settlement in the conventional sense: Canadians can look ahead to a constitutional future unbounded by the constraints that many other constitutional states experience.

This Collection

This edited collection is the product of a symposium held at Yale University in December 2015. Participants were asked to use the 150th anniversary of Confederation and the *Constitution Act, 1867* as an opportunity to reflect upon the current state of Canadian constitutional law and, more importantly, its future directions. We felt strongly that this discussion should be led by emerging scholars. Many edited collections on Canadian constitutional law lean heavily on established scholars and methodologies. This collection features the voices of scholars

30 Zachary Elkins et al, *The Endurance of National Constitutions* (Cambridge: Cambridge University Press, 2009), 2.

31 Peter Russell, *Constitutional Odyssey: Can Canadians Become a Sovereign People?* (Toronto: University of Toronto Press, 1992), 5.

whose work and approaches will shape the future development of Canadian constitutional law.

This volume takes the 150th anniversary of Confederation as a starting point for reflection on the future of Canadian constitutional law. The essays that follow take up this challenge in a variety of ways. Some focus on concrete legal problems and on how courts and legislators might better respond to them. Others take a more theoretical approach, identifying frameworks for future analysis or explaining how a more critical lens on constitutional law and practice would improve constitutional doctrine. Whatever the approach, the common thread that binds the collection together is a willingness to examine Canadian constitutional law through fresh eyes, unencumbered by the "truths" about this area that so many of us have internalized.

The essays in this collection also employ a diversity of methodologies. Political science features as a particularly prominent sister discipline, appearing in the contributions of Mary Liston, Emmett Macfarlane, Michael Pal, and Dwight Newman, but critical theory (Vrinda Narain and Sujith Xavier), demography (Asha Kaushal), and philosophy (Emily Kidd White) also appear. Strikingly, there is easy interdisciplinarity throughout the collection. A notable example is Efrat Arbel and Eileen Myrdahl's contribution, which moves fluidly from doctrinal critique to insights drawn from sociology to provide a convincing analysis of the shortcomings of judicial protection of equality rights.

The subjects covered by this volume emerged organically. They were driven by the expertise of the authors and by a desire for linguistic, demographic, and methodological diversity. The collection therefore makes no claim to comprehensiveness. Rather, it represents the considered views of experts on topics that will preoccupy scholars and practitioners of constitutional law in the decades to come. The contributors take stock of developments in Canadian constitutional law, usually by examining contemporary challenges. To some extent, the collection is shaped by these challenges – reconciliation with Indigenous peoples is squarely on the national agenda,[32] for example, in a way that, at the moment, language rights are not. Together, the essays provide a starting point for future litigation, law reform, intergovernmental negotiation, and scholarly discussion.

---

32 Truth and Reconciliation Commission, *Honouring the Truth, Reconciling for the Future: Summary of the Final Report of the Truth and Reconciliation Commission of Canada* (Ottawa: Truth and Reconciliation Commission of Canada, 2015).

In chapter 1, Mary Liston renews the call for problems of executive dominance to be dealt with head on. She questions how it is that "power [has] simultaneously become more concentrated in parts of the executive, while more diffuse and unaccountable overall."[33] She suggests that the other branches of government have an important role to play in reigning in the executive, although she acknowledges that implicating courts in this project is "controversial."[34] Like other contributions, Liston's is notable for its focus on extradjudicial arenas as sites of constitutional interpretation and change. In Canada, as in the Westminster tradition more generally, constitutional law is not simply "what the courts do" but has a broader political dimension.[35]

Macfarlane's contribution in chapter 2 argues that Canada's framework for constitutional amendment has rendered most efforts at constitutional change impossible.[36] He demonstrates that the challenges associated with amendment flow not simply from the amendment formula itself but also from political factors, such as past unsuccessful attempts at "mega-constitutional reform"[37] and from recent judicial interventions into when the amending formula – and the general amending formula, in particular – is engaged. This suggests that the avenues available for making good on proposals to reform or modernize institutions are limited.

But even perennial problems plaguing the constitutional state take on new dimensions in this collection. In his contribution in chapter 3, Paul Daly sidesteps the "tortuous history of the judicial treatment"[38] of s. 96 of the *Constitution Act, 1867* and examines the tension between preserving the core constitutional jurisdiction of the superior courts and facilitating institutional and interpretive pluralism, which creates an important space for the emergence of new forms of administrative justice as well as for new modes of governance, some of which are explored in other contributions. There is an interesting contrast

33 Mary Liston, chap 1 in this volume at 57.

34 *Ibid* at 58.

35 On the constitution "outside the courts," see, generally, Mark Tushnet, *Taking the Constitution Away from the Courts* (Princeton: Prince University Press, 1999).

36 Emmett Macfarlane, chap 2 in this volume.

37 Peter Russell, *Constitutional Odyssey: Can Canadians Become a Sovereign People?* 3rd ed. (Toronto: University of Toronto Press, 2004), speaking of "mega-constitutional politics"; Macfarlane, *ibid*.

38 Daly, *supra* note 14 at 86.

between the contributions made by Daly and Macfarlane. Where Daly applauds judicial doctrine for opening up space for political experimentation, Macfarlane is critical of how the courts have constrained the already limited scope for innovation in constitutional amendment.

Wright offers a new take on federalism in chapter 4, suggesting that provincial attorneys general are under an obligation not to prosecute offences that they believe to be unconstitutional.[39] That Canadian constitutional issues do not come marked "federal" or "provincial," to be inserted into the appropriate watertight compartment is, of course, now well understood; and the challenge of squaring the existence of a national criminal law with decentralized administration of the *Criminal Code* by the provinces is also familiar. Wright innovates by using the *Charter* to accord the provinces a legitimate role in constitutional interpretation and enforcement, a role that permits them to challenge views formed at the federal level about the constitutionality of criminal law. As with Liston, Wright's focus is often on what happens on the ground, not what is recorded in the law reports. Indeed, a major theme running through these contributions is the need for constitutional scholars to look beyond courts and appreciate that constitutional law may be made in many different fora.

Noura Karazivan offers surprising observations about the impact of cooperative federalism on Quebec's provincial interests in chapter 5.[40] Despite the logical risks that cooperative federalism might pose to Quebec's autonomy, the Supreme Court's application of the concept has had relatively little deleterious impact, leading her to conclude that cooperative federalism is a much less divisive concept from Quebec's standpoint than might be thought. Her conclusion is based in part, however, on the emptiness of "cooperative federalism," which, in her view, is manifested not in judicial rhetoric but in concrete cooperation between different levels of government. Karazivan's chapter thus picks up a thread running through other chapters by suggesting that cooperative federalism is to be found in political action, not judicial decisions.

In chapter 6, Howard Kislowicz shines a light on two key points of contest in the religious freedom jurisprudence.[41] The first is the apparent

---

39 Wright, *supra* note 15.

40 Noura Karazivan, chap 5 in this volume.

41 Kislowicz, *supra* note 21.

inconsistency between the non-establishment branch of the Supreme Court's s. 2(a) jurisprudence and the special provisions for minority religious education for Catholics and Protestants guaranteed by s. 93 of the *Constitution Act, 1867*. He implicitly questions whether minority religious education for Protestants and Catholics continues to deserve constitutional protection. This right appears increasingly anomalous in light of Canada's growing secularization and religious diversity. The second point of contest probes whether religious freedom should be characterized as an individual or a collective right or, perhaps more accurately, when the collective dimensions of religious freedom should be recognized and protected. While the courts were traditionally very reticent to depart from the traditional liberal conception of religious freedom, the Supreme Court's more recent jurisprudence has affirmed some of religious freedom's collective aspects.[42]

Kaushal contrasts the "narrative[s]" that have historically been used to describe the "constitutional population" with the reality of Canada's contemporary make-up.[43] Not only did Canada gain several provinces after 1867, but Indigenous peoples were also not partners to Confederation. Moreover, "It is increasingly obvious that, from the French fact in Canada to the creation of Nunavut to the political backlash against the niqab, heterogeneity is part of the Canadian constitutional landscape."[44] She argues that minority communities have more to gain from jurisdictional autonomy than from judicially enforceable rights. There is some tension between her contribution and that of Kislowicz: where Kislowicz sees the broadening of religious rights as a means of including new communities, Kaushal places the emphasis on giving those communities the tools to govern themselves (a proposition consistent with the legal pluralism advocated by Daly in his chapter as well as Milward's call in chapter 9 for self-government).

In her contribution in chapter 8, Narain analyses recent, mostly failed attempts by Canadian politicians and courts to regulate minority cultural communities, especially Muslim women.[45] She advocates for a more "critical" approach to multiculturalism policy,[46] to be formulated

42 *Alberta v Hutterian Brethren of Wilson Colony*, 2009 SCC 37, Abella J, dissenting; *Loyola High School v Quebec (Attorney General)*, 2015 SCC 12; Kislowicz, *supra*.
43 Kaushal, *supra* note 18 at 193, 194.
44 *Ibid* at 193.
45 Vrinda Narain, chap 8 in this volume.
46 *Ibid* at 218.

inside and (picking up on a theme exposed in earlier chapters) outside the courts, one that does not "other" these communities but instead focuses on remediating the disadvantage that women, and particularly racialized women, face in society.[47] Rather than regulating minority women and their attire,[48] the state would be better off extending appropriate social supports to women[49] and removing barriers to their full participation in society. That Narain's contribution follows those of Kislowicz and Kaushal permits the reader to reflect on whether expanding rights or jurisdictional autonomy would be a better means of advancing multiculturalism in contemporary Canada.

In chapter 9, Milward takes on the constitution's failure to bring about reconciliation between Indigenous and non-Indigenous peoples.[50] Milward traces this failure partly to the Supreme Court's interventions on Aboriginal rights, noting that the test the Court has developed for recognizing Aboriginal rights under s. 35 has dramatically and inappropriately limited the scope for successful claims, particularly as it relates to self-government.[51] Milward suggests that the jurisprudence and government negotiations must make way for comprehensive self-government claims. He points to criminal justice as one area in which restoring self-government to Indigenous communities could have a significant and positive impact on communities that have been victimized by the uneven application of the criminal law.[52] Milward's chapter complements Daly's contribution on legal pluralism and Kaushal's chapter on the value of jurisdictional autonomy for different communities.

In chapter 10, Xavier reminds us that constitutionalism is rooted in Western, colonial modes of governance.[53] The constitution provided the

47 *Ibid* at 228.

48 Ruthann Robson, *Dressing Constitutionally: Hierarchy, Sexuality, and Democracy, from Our Hairstyles to Our Shoes* (Cambridge: Cambridge University Press, 2013); Natasha Bakht, "In Your Face: Piercing the Veil of Ignorance about Niqab-Wearing Women," *Social and Legal Studies* 24, no. 3 (2015) 419.

49 Narain, *supra* note 44.

50 Milward, *supra* note 16.

51 *Ibid.*

52 *Ibid.* See also Jonathan Rudin, "Aboriginal Over-Representation and *R. v. Gladue*: Where We Were, Where We Are and Where We Might Be Going," *Supreme Court Law Review* (2d) 40 (2008) 687; Jonathan Rudin, "Looking Backward, Looking Forward: The Supreme Court of Canada's Decision in *R. v. Ipeelee*," *Supreme Court Law Review* (2d) 57 (2012) 375.

53 Xavier, *supra* note 17.

regulatory machinery for federal control over the destiny of Indigenous peoples in Canada, and it made possible some of Canada's most horrific human rights violations as part of the residential school system. Placed to be read in conjunction with Milward's contribution, Xavier's essay will provoke scepticism on the part of the reader about the appropriateness of applying national (and, indeed, necessarily Western) norms to Indigenous communities.

Dwight Newman's contribution in chapter 11 strikes a cautionary note about approaches that venerate the flexibility and open-endedness of constitutional law.[54] Newman also challenges the simplistic narrative around property rights that most scholars of Canadian constitutional law blithely accept and propagate. While it is true that the *Charter of Rights and Freedoms* does not secure private property rights, the constitution has important things to say about public property ownership at the provincial level as well as about Aboriginal title.[55] The difficulty, he explains, is that these two variants of property rights have developed in somewhat different ways: while provincial property is subject to "reasonably clear"[56] rules, the jurisprudence on Aboriginal title remains murky and erratic. This, Newman concludes, suggests that "how property is and is not entrenched in the Canadian constitution might give rise to significant future instability."[57]

Newman's chapter acts as a bridge between contributions that emphasize questions of jurisdiction and the remaining contributions, where the emphasis is mostly, though by no means exclusively, on rights. Emily Kidd White's contribution in chapter 12 explores where human dignity fits in the broader *Charter* jurisprudence.[58] She rejects the now-familiar critique that human dignity is insufficiently precise to be of use as a concept in Canadian constitutional law, and she explores "the three functional features of human dignity as a *Charter* value,"[59] thus opening up new avenues for exploring the concrete ways in which human dignity shapes constitutional adjudication. Juxtaposing Newman's and Kidd White's contributions should again prompt critical reflections on the part of the reader: on the one hand, stability is an

54 Dwight Newman, chap 11 in this volume.
55 *Ibid*.
56 *Ibid* at 289.
57 *Ibid* at 308.
58 Emily Kidd White, chap 12 in this volume.
59 *Ibid* at 312.

important constitutional value; but on the other hand, making sense of broadly drawn constitutional rights might inevitably require courts and commentators to have recourse to abstract notions such as dignity that do not lend themselves to easy definition.

Michael Pal's contribution in chapter 13 is on the "emergence of the permanent campaign,"[60] a new challenge whose solutions are still very much to be worked out. Pal argues that relatively modest – although not constitutionally uncontroversial – amendments to existing election law can effectively preserve Canada's egalitarian model of elections without unduly hampering freedom of speech. Pal's contribution focuses on values, but it builds on a theme advanced in the opening chapters: some of the solutions to the problems Pal identifies would require action by those outside the courts.

Finally, Efrat Arbel and Eileen Myrdahl take issue with the Supreme Court's use of immutability as the touchstone for determining analogous grounds of discrimination under s. 15 of the *Charter*.[61] They argue that the problems with this requirement become obvious when one considers the cases on whether immigration status constitutes an analogous ground of discrimination. The courts have generally refused to find immigration status to be an analogous ground, Arbel and Myrdahl explain, despite the tangible disadvantage suffered by claimants in these cases. Arbel and Myrdahl's contribution implies an important role for courts in addressing some of the demographic challenges highlighted by Kaushal and Narain. In this respect, there is some affinity between Arbel and Myrdahl's contribution and that of Kislowicz.

Enduring Tensions

What emerges from the volume as a whole is a sense that the constitutional project remains unfinished. The tensions the chapters identify are unlikely to disappear. Nor is there a single way of remedying them; existing constitutional shortcomings must be addressed through a combination of formal constitutional amendment,[62] political action,[63]

60 Michael Pal, chap 13 in this volume at 340.

61 Arbel and Myrdahl, *supra* note 22.

62 Macfarlane, *supra* note 34; Newman, *supra* note 53.

63 Wright, *supra* note 14.

judicial interpretation and the balancing of interests,[64] intergovernmental negotiation,[65] and citizen engagement,[66] perhaps in the spaces that several contributors would carve out for diverse groups to create their own norms of governance.[67] And throughout, constitutional actors must be guided by the core values and "principles [that] inform and sustain the constitutional text,"[68] carefully balancing the need for "continuity" and "stability"[69] with the need for a constitution to remain relevant.[70]

---

64 Hugo Cyr, *Canadian Federalism and Treaty Powers: Organic Constitutionalism at Work* (Brussels: PIE Peter Lang, 2009), 222.

65 Milward, *supra* note 16; Karazivan, *supra* note 39.

66 Pal, *supra* note 58.

67 See, especially, Daly, *supra* note 15; Kaushal, *supra* note 18; and Milward, *supra* note 16.

68 *Reference re Secession of Quebec*, [1998] 2 SCR 217. See, especially, Newman, *supra* note 52; Pal, *supra* note 57; and Kidd White, *supra* note 55.

69 Newman, *supra* note 52.

70 *Ibid*. See also Richard Kay, "Examining Constitutional Transitions," *National Journal of Constitutional Law* 37 (2017) 35.

1 The Most Opaque Branch? The (Un)accountable Growth of Executive Power in Modern Canadian Government

MARY LISTON*

Living across the Atlantic, and misled by accepted doctrines, the acute framers of the Federal constitution, even after the keenest attention, did not perceive the prime minister to be the principal executive of the British Constitution, and the sovereign a cog in the mechanism.[1]

Introduction: The Most Opaque Branch

Canada's system of government is composed of a legislature that operates as the least effective and most marginalized branch of government,[2] a judiciary that is arguably either the least or the most dangerous branch, according to one's ideological predispositions,[3] and an

* I would like to thank Richard Albert, Paul Daly, and Emmett Macfarlane for their helpful comments. I would also like to thank Dustin Chelen for excellent research assistance. Finally, I acknowledge the helpful assistance of the editors and external reviewers.

1 Walter Bagehot, *The English Constitution*, ed. and with intro. by Paul Smith (1867; repr., Cambridge: Cambridge University Press, 2001), 48 [Bagehot, *English Constitution*].

2 *The Least Examined Branch: The Role of Legislatures in the Constitutional* State, ed. Richard W. Baumann and Tsvi Kahana (New York: Cambridge University Press, 2006). See also media columnist Andrew Coyne's critical assessment, "Repairing the House: How to Make Members of Parliament Relevant Again," *Walrus*, October 2013, https://thewalrus.ca/repairing-the-house/.

3 A notable proponent of the first position is Alexander M. Bickel, *The Least Dangerous Branch: The Supreme Court at the Bar of Politics* (New Haven, CT: Yale University Press, 1986); and of the second, Robert I. Martin, *The Most Dangerous Branch: How the Supreme Court of Canada Has Undermined Our Law and Our Democracy* (Montreal and Kingston: McGill-Queen's University Press, 2005).

executive long characterized as a "friendly dictatorship."[4] The twentieth century has indeed seen the enormous change in, and growth of, the executive branch's role and functions in Western liberal democracies like Canada's, including the political executive, the civil service, administrative agencies, and a variety of supervisory watchdogs.

This chapter examines Canada's federal executive,[5] looking back 150 years to the constitutional theory that prevailed at Confederation and forward to the creation of a constitutional democracy with the patriation of the constitution in 1982,[6] to glean insights into how this branch of government has been transformed through formal and informal change. By contrasting the past with the present in theory and in practice, I hope to underscore how the trajectory from our 1867 parliamentary democracy to our post-1982 constitutional democracy has been salutary, modernizing, but not without serious concerns. I will do this by invoking then-contemporary British constitutional theorists Walter Bagehot, Albert Venn Dicey,[7] and Frederick Maitland,[8] who, in their time, railed against earlier medieval theories that maintained unhelpful legal fictions in the face of grim political reality. From today's vantage point, however, these thinkers are also guilty of participating in the fictions of Westminster government, and their language, still used by Canadian courts and governments, has gone beyond unhelpful to positively pernicious. As Peter Oliver writes, speaking particularly of Dicey, these thinkers comprise "a sort of intellectual Empire of [their] own" from which Canadian public law needs to be freed.[9]

---

4 Jeffrey Simpson, *The Friendly Dictatorship* (Toronto: McClelland and Stewart, 2002); and H.D. Munroe, "Style within the Centre: Pierre Trudeau, the *War Measures Act*, and the Nature of Prime Ministerial Power," *Canadian Public Administration* 54, no. 4 (2011), 531.

5 Provincial executive branches will not be considered. Federalism as a legal constraint on executive power will also not be considered, nor will specific *Charter* rights (e.g., *Charter* rights to democratic essentials like access to information).

6 *Constitution Act, 1982* being Schedule B to the *Canada Act 1982* (UK), 1982, c 11 [*CA, 1982*].

7 A.V. Dicey, *Introduction to the Study of the Law of the Constitution*, 10th ed. (London: Macmillan, 1959) [Dicey, *Law of the Constitution*].

8 F.W. Maitland, *The Constitutional History of England* (Cambridge: Cambridge University Press, 1926) [Maitland, *Constitutional History of England*].

9 Peter C. Oliver, *The Constitution of Independence: The Development of Constitutional Theory in Australia, Canada, and New Zealand* (Oxford: Oxford University Press, 2005), 56. Oliver provides an excellent analysis of Canadian constitutional theory from the time of Confederation until patriation.

Despite the fundamental import of this growth in power for public law, it has been Canadian political scientists who have largely provided the overall leadership in studying and scrutinizing the problem.[10] Political science has largely provided the analysis of how power in the executive branch has become excessively concentrated as a global phenomenon in modern liberal democracies.[11] The problem is more acute in Canada, and, given the country's proximity to the United States, we commonly call the concentration of executive power the "presidentialization" of our parliamentary system.[12] If we remained true to our traditions, as Philippe Lagassé suggests, this process of centralization might be better termed "regalization" due to its origin in royal authority.[13] Simultaneously, and on the other hand, we are witnessing the dispersal of executive power without corresponding oversight mechanisms – changes often described as "democratic deficits."[14] The combined effect of these

---

10 The seminal work on the modern concentration of executive power is Donald J. Savoie's *Governing from the Centre: The Concentration of Power in Canadian Politics* (Toronto: University of Toronto Press, 1999). For an acute analysis of power wielded by ministers and Cabinets, see Graham White, *Cabinets and First Ministers* (Vancouver: UBC Press, 2005). And for a discussion of the domination of parliamentary democracy by prime ministers, see Donald J. Savoie, *Court Government and the Collapse of Accountability in Canada and the United Kingdom* (Toronto: University of Toronto Press, 2008).

11 Presidentialization of the role of the prime minister is a concern shared among common-law Westminster systems; see Thomas Poguntke and Paul Webb, eds., *The Presidentialization of Politics: A Comparative Study of Modern Democracies* (Oxford: Oxford University Press, 2005), 199–220 [Poguntke and Webb, eds., *Presidentialization of Politics*].

12 See Herman Bakvis and Stephen B. Wolinetz, "Canada: Executive Dominance and Presidentialization," in *The Presidentialization of Politics: A Comparative Study of Modern Democracies*, ed. Thomas Poguntke and Paul Webb (Oxford: Oxford University Press, 2005), 199–220. See also Tom Ginsburg, Jose Cheibub, and Zachary Elkins, "Beyond Presidentialism and Parliamentarism," *British Journal of Political Science* (2013), http://works.bepress.com/tom_ginsburg/58/, for a sceptical take on the validity of too strong a distinction between the two systems and, indeed, an argument for similarities in executive-legislative institutional relations.

13 Philippe Lagassé, "The Crown and Royal Power," *Canadian Parliamentary Review* 39, no. 2 (2016) 17.

14 Sanford Levinson provides a pithy definition: "A democratic deficit occurs when ostensibly democratic organizations or institutions in fact fall short of fulfilling what are believed to be the principles of democracy"; see "How the United States Constitution Contributes to the Democratic Deficit in America," *Drake Law Review*

two contemporary dynamics undermines the ability of our parliamentary system to ensure accountability and responsible government. The result is that the underlying structural commitments of our constitutional democracy – principles such as the rule of law, the separation of powers, and adherence to constitutional rights and values – have become imperilled. Older theories of Westminster governance do not describe this reality, nor can they act as a source for remedial prescription.

Legal scholarship needs to catch up with these transformative changes. Two deficiencies characterize current legal scholarship in this area. First, and on the one hand, Canadian legal scholarship remains piecemeal in its focus on executive power.[15] For the past thirty years, Canadian constitutional scholars have concentrated on the *Charter*[16] and the "rights revolution" it has precipitated. Consequently, this stream of scholarship has largely neglected a comprehensive examination of the fundamental changes in the modern executive branch. Second, and on the other hand, more recent legal scholarship focusing on a critical treatment of executive power has tended to concentrate on the constituent nature of sovereign power and the pervasive problems wrought by post-9/11 states of exception.[17]

Of note, however, is David Schneiderman's recent overview of the shifts in Canadian constitutional practices towards American-style governance and how Canadian constitutional culture and norms have

---

55 (2007) 859, 860. For Canada, see Patti Tamara Lenard and Richard Simeon, eds., *Imperfect Democracies: The Democratic Deficit in Canada and the United States* (Vancouver: UBC Press, 2012) [Lenard and Simeon, *Imperfect Democracies*].

15 Many articles focus on the issue of the centralization of power within the executive branch, but do so in relation to one particular issue, crisis, or policy area such as prorogation, judicial and other executive appointments, national security, policing and prosecution, electoral reform, and so on.

16 *Canadian Charter of Rights and Freedoms*, Part I of the *Constitution Act, 1982* being Schedule B to the *Canada Act 1982* (UK), 1982, c 11 [*Charter*].

17 See Martin Loughlin, *The Idea of Public Law* (Oxford: Oxford University Press, 2003); and Thomas Poole, *Reason of State: Law, Prerogative and Empire* (Cambridge: Cambridge University Press, 2015). In Canada, see Craig Forcese and Kent Roach, *False Security: The Radicalization of Canadian Anti-terrorism* (Toronto: Irwin Law, 2015). Concerns voiced about executive power in this scholarship are symptomatic of the problem of executive power writ large and in general.

become less distinctive as a result.[18] His comparative analysis focuses on the two prorogation episodes, Senate reform, and the Supreme Court of Canada's appointments process. Each of these moments, Schneiderman argues, provided the Conservative Party with an opportunity to not only separate and enhance executive authority but also to shift, successfully in part, Canadian constitutional culture and public perceptions about our system of government.[19] These changes, Schneiderman wryly observes, "fly somewhat under the constitutional radar" of most citizens.[20]

Schneiderman's book examines the following trajectory: "What emerges over time is a robust species of parliamentary self-government that is constrained by bicameralism, the federal division of powers, and a charter of rights – meaningful constraints, to be sure – but otherwise unlimited. This enables Canadians to better translate their preferences into law. It also gives rise to troubling centralization of authority in the executive."[21] His astute and insightful institutional lens, then, rests on the constitutional constraints provided by federalism, our bicameral system of government, the *Charter*, and some legislative initiatives aiming to tame executive authority. Missing from the picture he draws – since part of his focus is on the restraints created or implemented by democratic legislatures – is an analysis of the constraints imposed by other forms of public law – such as administrative law – and how the judiciary remains a central institution through its function to provide oversight of the executive branch.

This chapter, therefore, takes a complementary, court-centric approach to expand on Schneiderman's legislature-centric picture by examining the common law of judicial review of executive action (i.e., administrative law), which pays heed to the whole "mass of discretion inherited by the prime minister"[22] and the executive branch. Here it is the constitutional duty of the courts – not the Senate or the legislature or the division of powers – to ensure that any part of the executive branch could come under rule of law scrutiny for unlawful behaviour.

---

18 David Schneiderman, *Red, White, and Kind of Blue? The Conservatives and the Americanization of Canadian Constitutional Culture* (Toronto: University of Toronto Press, 2015) [Schneiderman, *Red, White, and Kind of Blue?*].

19 *Ibid*, 3, 20–1.

20 *Ibid*, 4.

21 *Ibid*, 20.

22 *Ibid*, 294.

Given these gaps in Canadian public law scholarship, as well as recent efforts at reforming the executive undertaken in the United Kingdom,[23] this moment provides an opportune time to examine the strengths and weaknesses of the constraints on executive power as a general problem for contemporary Canadian government. To do this, the chapter does a "full body scan" of the executive branch to capture its parts and complexity. This scan permits me to diagnose and convey the numerous accountability problems that continue to plague the body politic 150 years on, to provide a comprehensive picture that ties the political and legal literature together, and to fill in some of the legal gaps that exist regarding executive power.

To do this, the chapter first examines the executive branch in terms of its actors, functions, and powers. The section "From Responsible to Irresponsible Government?" considers the range of constraints within Canada's broad constitutional framework – political and legal, internal and external, written and unwritten – that aim to guide and control the exercise of executive power. This section highlights current weaknesses, gaps, and other accountability problems such as omnibus legislation, the governor general's powers, prime ministerial abuse of prerogative power, Cabinet irrelevancy, declining ministerial responsibility, and the erosion of neutrality and independence in government. These problems will be examined through the dual lenses of the rule of law and democratic deficits, with an eye to highlighting how, in many of these examples, courts may or can provide an appropriate and beneficial accountability function. Two emerging, new forms of accountability are discussed, and finally, the chapter concludes with a brief diagnosis of the current conditions of our modern, Westminster-styled constitutional democracy.

The Non-ideal Executive: Institution, Actors, Functions, and Powers

> The English Constitution, in a word, is framed on the principle of choosing a single sovereign authority, and making it good; the American [and

23 For an overview of these fundamental changes, see Robert Hazell, "Constitutional Reform in the UK: Past, Present and Future," in *Reconstituting the Constitution*, ed. Catherine Morris, Jonathan Boston, and Petra Butler (Heidelberg: Springer, 2011), 83–98. See also the work of the Constitution Unit at University College London, https://www.ucl.ac.uk/constitution-unit.

> now the Canadian], upon the principle of having many sovereign authorities, and hoping that their multitude may atone for their inferiority.[24]

When viewed realistically, and not according to the idealized constitutional theory, the executive has always lain at the heart of the Westminster system. While it is true that the judiciary has long been an effective, independent branch and that the democratic will expressed by Parliament is (supposedly) supreme, the executive's role, powers, and place are undoubtedly central, whether they have taken the form of a monarch or a prime minister and Cabinet.

Despite the institutional centrality of the political executive, in traditional British constitutional theory, it was "barely known to the law" because common law courts considered it an extra-legal organization composed of a multiplicity of constituent parts.[25] This conclusion was made despite the fact that these courts also simultaneously held that *the Crown* was indivisible.[26] Indeed, it was so opaque that the prime minister, Cabinet, and early administrative state were not explicitly mentioned in our first constitution, the *British North America Act, 1867*.[27]

The closest that our British-derived legal system has come to recognizing the "executive as a whole" is in the concept of the Crown. Canada has retained this metaphorical shorthand, but, depending on the legal area, one will find the *executive as a whole* referred to as either the *Crown* or the *executive branch*. In this sense, Canadian public law has acknowledged an entity called *the executive*, unlike in the United Kingdom. In the Westminster system, Parliament usually confers powers on the components of the executive – ministers, departments, and other executive actors – rather than the executive as a whole. Over time, courts came to recognize that the executive (including the Crown) had a legal personality as a corporate, *heterogeneous* body, and therefore the courts could grant common law remedies for unlawful executive action.

---

24 Bagehot, *English Constitution*, 154. In Bagehot's constitutional theory, the single sovereign authority was the House of Commons, as represented by the principle of parliamentary supremacy when housed in a representative democracy.

25 See *Town Investments Ltd v Department of the Environment* [1978] AC 359, 398 (Lord Simon) [*Town Investments*]. See also Maitland, *Constitutional History of England*, 387–8.

26 *Town Investments*, 400 (Lord Simon).

27 See sec III, "Executive Power," *British North America Act, 1867*, SS 1867, c 3 (UK), now *Constitution Act, 1867*, 30 & 31 Victoria, c 3 (UK) [*CA, 1867*].

An Inferior Complex?

The primary function of the executive branch is to create, administer, and implement policy as the governing body of the state. As discussed above, strictly speaking, the executive is not a single entity, but a varied assortment of institutions and political actors. While the executive is what one normally thinks of as *the government*, the government in reality consists of what is called the *political executive*, the bureaucracy (or civil service), and the administrative state. So, while one can quickly grasp the essential features of executive power in terms of basic constitutional theory, the executive branch must necessarily be complexified to glean an accurate picture of it in the modern public law landscape. The full political executive includes the Queen, the governor general, Privy Council, the prime minister, and Cabinet. According to Peter Hogg, Cabinet is the formal locus of the supreme executive authority in Canada.[28] But, and as we will see later, the influence of Cabinet has substantially waned in the modern executive.

When we look at our system of government, and contrast it with a presidential system, Canada's separation of powers is not "bright line": the executive branch is always partially fused with the legislative branch, particularly when the party in power has a majority of the seats in the House of Commons.[29] In many other ways, the executive has always overlapped with and often impinged on the other two branches. For example, the extensive appointments power – which is not examined in this chapter – permits executive control of both the judiciary and the administrative state.[30] These overlaps work to enhance the centralizing power dynamic in the political executive and the role of the prime minister.

---

28 Peter W. Hogg, *Constitutional Law of Canada*, student ed. (Toronto: Carswell, 2015), 9.4(b) [Hogg, *Constitutional Law*].

29 See *Wells v Newfoundland*, [1999] 3 SCR 199, paras 52–3: "On a practical level, it is recognized that the same individuals control both the executive and the legislative branches of government. … The separation of powers is not a rigid and absolute structure. The Court should not be blind to the reality of Canadian governance that, except in certain rare cases, the executive frequently and *de facto* controls the legislature."

30 Recall, for example, the widespread public controversies over the Conservative government's (non-)appointment of Federal Court Justice Marc Nadon to the Supreme Court as well as its interference in Statistics Canada's long-form census, leading to the resignation of then chief statistician Munir Sheikh. For an examination of the appointments process and the Nadon affair, see Schneiderman, *Red, White, and Kind of Blue?*, chap 5.

Over time, and with the entrenchment of a written bill of rights, Canada's executive has become more legally constrained than it was at Confederation. Most important, the judiciary has become a true third branch of government because of the *Charter*, our entrenched bill of rights.[31] Our separation of powers, then, is much less "cavalier"[32] than what currently still prevails in the United Kingdom.[33] Nevertheless, problems with the separation of powers in relation to the executive branch are a recurring theme in this paper. For example, it is not uncommon to see the sources and constraints on executive authority described as "utterly opaque," "imprecise," "difficult to determine," and even inevitably "disappearing into the mists" of the unwritten constitution, thus foiling the accountability mechanisms entailed in our separation of powers.[34] The problems associated with our constitutional constraints on executive power will be discussed below.

What Is Seen and Overseen

THE (IN)VISIBLE MONARCH

Clearly, one of the most significant changes since Confederation concerns the diminution of the role and powers of the monarch. Historically, only the Crown exercised executive power as ministers were

---

31 Contrast Canada's doctrine with this forceful claim: "The English judiciary is not the third branch of the State, separate yet equal. … In England the judiciary is, properly conceived, neither entirely separate nor entirely equal: it is not fully separated (even now) from the Crown, and it remains subservient to it as a source of authority. This is a controversial analysis"; see Adam Tomkins, *Public Law* (Oxford: Oxford University Press, 2003), 55 [Tomkins, *Public Law*].

32 This is how Mark Elliott and Robert Thomas describe the United Kingdom's doctrine of the separation of powers in *Public Law*, 2nd ed. (Oxford: Oxford University Press, 2014), 97 [Elliott and Thomas, *Public Law*].

33 Some commentators have even called it a "not particularly important" doctrine in English public law; see Andrew Le Sueur et al, *Public Law: Text, Cases, Materials*, 2nd ed. (Oxford: Oxford University Press, 2013), 119. For a historical and theoretical overview of the concept of the separation of powers, see Schneiderman, *Red, White, and Kind of Blue?*, chap 3.

34 Quotes are taken from expert testimony provided to the United Kingdom's House of Commons Political and Constitutional Reform Committee and reproduced in its report, *Role and Powers of the Prime Minister*, http://www.publications.parliament.uk/pa/cm201415/cmselect/cmpolcon/351/351.pdf, 34, 7, and 4.

subservient to the British monarch. These powers, capacious in scope, are best described by Bagehot: "I said in this book that it would very much surprise people if they were only told how many things the Queen could do without consulting Parliament. ... In a word, the Queen could by prerogative upset all the action of civil government within the government."[35] The redistribution of power to the executive and legislature in the United Kingdom (one result of the revolutionary Bill of Rights of 1689[36]) meant that royal power has substantially diminished over time.[37] Conventions of responsible government ensured that the exercise of actual political power, and accountability for that exercise, clearly remained with elected executive actors such as the prime minister and the body of ministers comprising the "government of the day."[38] Today the Queen reigns, but truly does not rule.

Section 9 of the *Constitution Act, 1867* declares that the entire executive government and its authority are formally vested in the Queen.[39] As is well known, although our actual head of state is the Queen, the Queen has delegated all powers to the governor general (except for power to appoint and dismiss the governor general), and the governor general now stands as the effective head of the Canadian state.[40] The personal influence of the Queen and the sovereign's representative is also minimal in Canada. The governor general, for example, possesses the following *personal* or *reserve* prerogative powers of the Queen on an exclusive basis (i.e., without the advice of the prime minister or Cabinet): (1) appoint the prime minister, (2) appoint and dismiss ministers,

---

35 Bagehot, *English Constitution*, 210.

36 For a brief history of the end of the sovereign's personal influence over the administration of affairs and judges in Britain, see Locke J's judgment in *Boucher v the King*, [1951] SCR 265.

37 This statute eliminated the monarch's ability to use prerogative powers to suspend a law for a period of time or to dispense with a law in a particular case; see *Bill of Rights* [1688] 1688 c 2 (Regnal 1 Will and Mar Sess 2); and Hogg, *Constitutional Law*, 1.9.

38 Lord Diplock held that the *Crown* is synonymous with *government* and embraces "both collectively and individually all of the ministers of the Crown and parliamentary secretaries under whose direction the administrative work of government is carried on by the civil servants employed in the various government departments"; see *Town Investments*, 381.

39 Ss 9–16 of the *CA, 1867* set out executive power.

40 Article II of the Letters Patent constituting the office of the Governor General of Canada (1947), RSC 1985, App II, No 31 instructs that the governor general is "to exercise all powers and authorities lawfully belonging to Us in respect of Canada."

(3) dissolve Parliament (implicitly recognized in s. 50 of the *Constitution Act, 1867*), and (4) prorogue Parliament (implicitly recognized in s. 5 of the *Constitution Act, 1982*[41]). Normally, these powers are exercised under the constitutional convention that the Queen (or her representative) acts on her ministers' advice – in reality, the prime minister's command. This ensures that accountability for the exercise of personal prerogative power resides with the democratically elected government of the day, thus satisfying the constitutional demands of responsible government. As in the United Kingdom, the monarchical element of our constitutional democracy appears to exercise no real power at all and has very little political influence on the day-to-day activity of executive government.

Recollect from the beginning of this section that the executive branch is also called *the Crown* in public law. Traditionally, the concept of the Crown referred to the actions taken by the queen or king in the exercise of governmental authority, rather than in her or his personal capacity as a monarch. At one time, of course, all executive power was prerogative and housed in the monarch.[42] Historically, though, it was the primary type of power exercised by government.[43] Since the Victorian era, statutes have "tamed," or supplanted, the majority of types of this monarchical power, but "unfettered" pockets of prerogative power remain and continue to be recognized by the common law.[44] In our jurisprudence, the *royal, or Crown, prerogative* is therefore usually described as "the residue of discretionary or arbitrary authority, which at any given time is left in the hands of the Crown" and consists of "the powers and privileges accorded by the common law to the Crown."[45] Public

41 Enacted as Schedule B to the *Canada Act 1982*, 1982, c 11 (UK) [*CA, 1982*].

42 The best elaborator of this form of government remains Thomas Hobbes; see "Of the Rights of Soveraignes by Institution," in *Leviathan*, ed. Richard Tuck (Cambridge: Cambridge University Press, 1996).

43 Lord Nolan of Brasted and Stephen Sedley, *The Making and Remaking of the British Constitution: The Radcliffe Lectures at the University of Warwick for 1996–97* (London: Blackstone Press, 1997).

44 Orders in Council, for example, are a rare example of executive prerogative, exercised by a minister on behalf of the Crown. Most are now made under statutory authority. But it remains possible for a responsible minister of the Crown to make a recommendation in the form of an Order in Council, which would take legal effect only when signed by the governor general.

45 A.V. Dicey, quoted by Laskin JA in *Black v Chrétien*, (2001) 199 DLR (4th) 228 (Ont CA), para 25 [*Black*].

law constraints on these prerogative powers take two forms: external constraints imposed by courts and constraints imposed by legislatures through statutes. These constraints and their effectiveness will be discussed further below.

Crown prerogative power may, in theory, belong to the monarch, but it is the political executive – especially the prime minister – who exercises it in practice. In *Black v Chrétien*, the Ontario Court of Appeal confirmed that prerogative powers were exercisable not only by the Queen/governor general but also by the prime minister.[46] These Crown powers, not personal but executive in nature, include such residual powers as declaring war, signing treaties,[47] heading the armed forces, and granting mercy and honours. The prime minister also exercises the royal prerogative to select (or dismiss) ministers as well as to advise the governor general.

These powers are not governed by constitutional conventions, nor have they been displaced by and controlled by statutes. Increasingly, their appearance as legally unfettered has been challenged in litigation on *Charter* and other constitutional grounds such as the unwritten constitutional principle of the rule of law. In a recent judgment, the Supreme Court of Canada underscored the important institutional role of the courts to constrain executive power: "In exercising its common law powers under the royal prerogative, the executive is not exempt from constitutional scrutiny. … It is for the executive and not the courts to decide whether and how to exercise its powers, but the courts clearly have the jurisdiction and the duty to determine whether a prerogative power asserted by the Crown does in fact exist and, if so, whether its exercise infringes the *Charter* … or other constitutional norms."[48]

Outside of a statutory basis, and the established categories of prerogative power, the executive branch may be said to operate on the basis of prerogative power implicitly recognized by the common law. This broad and controversial interpretation of prerogative power, first put forward by Dicey, means that it is not just special governmental powers that are prerogative in nature (such as declaring war) but also

46 *Black*, para 39.

47 Note that the signing of treaties in the United Kingdom is subject to the statutory requirement that Parliament has a right to veto any entry into treaty obligations. See *Constitutional Reform and Governance Act 2010*, Pt 2.

48 *Canada (Prime Minister) v Khadr*, 2010 SCC 3, [2010] 1 SCR 44, para 36 (citations omitted).

authorizations of other, more ordinary actions such as the power to enter into contracts. The opposing view is that the government is not exercising prerogative power (which should be narrowly construed), but is, rather, permitted to do anything that is not unlawful or unconstitutional, just as an ordinary person can do.[49]

Whatever the basis for this residual legal authority – since it has not been resolved and cannot be pursued further in this chapter – the executive can exercise implicitly authorized common law powers in contract and property just as an ordinary person does. A statute will often empower a government to enter into a contract. A government can also "contract out" services that were formerly delivered on a statutory basis. This area raises a number of crucial issues that are beyond the scope of this paper, including privatization, the growth of contracting out for public services, public-private partnerships, and Crown liability.

Despite its "invisibility" to ordinary Canadians, the Crown remains an important symbol of the historical continuity of royal authority and, to some extent, our national identity. As David Smith argues, "Although Canadians are willing to ignore it and depreciate its importance, the monarchical principle is the organizing principle of Canadian government."[50] It would be a grave mistake to underestimate the structural and functional role of the Crown in modern Canadian public law: the Crown is not a natural person, but a vital metaphorical figure, a key legal concept, and an important symbol of the constitutional order.[51]

FROM FIRST AMONG EQUALS TO SOVEREIGN COMMANDER: "PRESIDENTIALIZATION"

Constitutional convention requires that the leader of the political party that can command the confidence of the legislature – typically, but not always, the party with the overall majority of seats in the House following a general election – should be appointed as prime minister

49 See *McDonald v Anishinabek Police Service*, 2006 CanLII 37598 (ON SCDC), paras 61–9. The Court does not resolve the issue, but suggests that it need not because both prerogative powers and powers relating to natural persons can be judicially reviewed. In the United Kingdom, see Carnwath LJ in *Shrewsbury and Atcham Borough Council v Secretary of State for Communities and Local Government*, [2008] EWCA Civ 148, para 44.

50 David E. Smith, *The Invisible Crown: The First Principle of Canadian Government* (Toronto: University of Toronto Press, 1995), 5 [Smith, *Invisible Crown*].

51 *McAteer v Canada (Attorney General)*, 2014 ONCA 578 at para 52.

by the governor general. The prime minister then selects his or her Cabinet, usually from among the party's elected members of Parliament, or caucus. Traditionally, the prime minister acts as "first among equals" in Cabinet. Graham White argues that although this equality obtained pre-Confederation and still does provincially, at the federal level, this has not been the case since Sir John A. Macdonald.[52] Today this convention faces even more stress as a result of the role's growing presidentialization.[53]

The prime minister is now *the* most important politician in our political system, commanding the confidence of the legislature, heading the government, appointing (shuffling, removing) ministers, overseeing the political executive as well as the civil service and the administrative state, appointing judges, and being ultimately responsible for the government's policies and decisions at the ballot box. In a survey of prime ministers in twenty-two countries, Canada's prime minister ranked as the most powerful (8.24 on a scale from 1 to 9) and by the widest margin overall.[54] The prime minister exercises prerogative powers (discussed above), delegated statutory powers, and informal, or soft, power, which is styled according to the particular personality of the leader and whether he or she has a majority or minority government.[55] Several of the democratic and rule of law deficits examined below are a direct consequence of this corrosive dynamic.

Traditionally, the exercise of prerogative power was not subject to judicial review at all. Recent case law has expanded the scope of judicial review to cover (theoretically) all exercise of prerogative power by actors such as the prime minister and perhaps even the governor general. But, although courts can review the prerogative, the lack of clarity about what *is* a prerogative power renders judicial review weak. In some respects, Canada has not moved very far from Dicey's observation that "[e]very act which the executive government can lawfully do without the authority of an Act of Parliament is done in virtue of

52 Graham White, "The Centre of the Democratic Deficit: Power and Influence in Canadian Political Executives," in *Imperfect Democracies: The Democratic Deficit in Canada and the United States*, ed. Patti Tamara Lenard and Richard Simeon (Vancouver: UBC Press, 2012), 231 [White, "Centre of the Democratic Deficit"].

53 See notes 11 and 12 and text *infra.*

54 For this data set, see Eion O'Malley, "The Power of Prime Ministers: Results of an Expert Survey," *International Political Science Review* 28, no. 1 (2007), 17, table 3.

55 Note that Canada does not have a strong tradition of coalition governments.

this prerogative."[56] Judicial interpretation of the courts' role creates an incoherent and uneasy state of legal affairs: courts arrogate to themselves the ability to determine the types of and limits on prerogative, but continue to insist that some matters of prerogative are either legally inappropriate (i.e., not justiciable) or have limits that are impossible to determine (i.e., too political).[57]

THE EXECUTIVE IN OUR SIGHTS

It is tempting to think of *the executive* in monolithic terms, as a single coherent and cohesive body. In contrast to the legislative and judicial branches, the executive branch is highly heterogeneous, and, as discussed above, this heterogeneity of actors and functions is also complicated by the concurrent centripetal and centrifugal dynamics in modern government. Several key actors are visible to widely varying degrees. While *Privy Council*, for example, can easily be identified in our constitution,[58] it rarely meets (usually only for ceremonial occasions) and does not have a current governance function.[59] The active and visible executive actors are the prime minister, the Office of the Prime Minister (more commonly known as the PMO), Cabinet, ministers, ministerial staff and advisers, the public service, and executive agencies.[60]

The *PMO* exercises considerable power around government appointments, messaging, and policy advice. It is a partisan body composed of the prime minister and the prime minister's top political staff as well as speechwriters, strategists, and communications personnel. Pierre Trudeau is generally credited with turning the PMO into a central body, taking power away from Privy Council. Increasingly, the PMO is a competitor with other parts of the executive including Privy Council,

---

56 Dicey, *Law of the Constitution*, 425.

57 See *Operation Dismantle v The Queen, Supreme Court Reports* 1 (1985), 441 on non-justiciability and political questions.

58 See ss 3 and 11–13 of the *CA, 1867*.

59 Originally the central advisory body to the monarch, Privy Council includes not only current Cabinet members but also many other individuals such as past ministers and honorary members.

60 Other executive actors include Crown corporations, the military, enforcement bodies such as the police and Crown prosecutors, and municipalities (which are creatures of provincial statutes). Crown corporations usually perform a particular public function and separately exercise this function on behalf of the Crown. Unadulterated Crown corporations are now rare, and many executive corporate bodies take the form of public-private partnerships.

Cabinet, the civil service, and even the attorney general. The growth of the PMO may be seen as a counterpart to the rise of a more presidential-style prime minister (both in Canada and in the United Kingdom), mirroring on a smaller scale the Executive Office of the President of the United States.[61] It also assists in the centralization of power in the highest echelons of the executive branch.

In theory, *Cabinet* is the supreme decision-making body in the executive branch. It is also a creature of convention, remaining implicit in the words of the *Constitution Act, 1867.* Because only ministers hold powers, Cabinet has no legal powers per se. Cabinet functions as an integrating and coordinating decision-making body, chaired by the prime minister, and focused on policy formation and implementation. Cabinet exercises collective responsibility for policy decisions, and all ministers must agree to and defend those decisions despite their personal views (or else resign). Whether Cabinet possesses a large scope of decision-making power autonomously from the prime minister depends on the style and strength of the prime minister. Increasingly, it also depends on whether decisions have already been taken in the PMO.

The Crown (on the advice of the prime minster) appoints and dismisses *ministers*. Depending on their rank, ministers may sit in Cabinet and/or on Cabinet committees. Canadian practice (which differs from that found in Australia and the United Kingdom) is for the prime minister to admit all ministers to Cabinet. Because ministers, who exercise executive functions, must also be members of the House of Commons, Canada's separation of powers does not strictly separate individuals by *personnel* form, unlike presidential systems. Although considered part of the Crown (as discussed above), ministers are, in fact, servants of the Crown and do not enjoy Crown immunities.[62]

One minister is singled out for special consideration in this chapter: the federal minister of justice, who is also the attorney general. By convention, this minister usually has a legal education or qualifications because he or she serves an important function as the chief legal

---

61 Graham White cautions that the power of the PMO may look different and considerably less robust when viewed from the inside rather than the outside and that some ministers are more equal than others in relation to prime ministers; see White, "Centre of the Democratic Deficit," 236, 238.

62 See *Canada (Attorney General) v Saskatchewan Water Corporation*, 1991 CanLII 3951 (SK CA), where Bayda CJ adopts H.W.R. Wade's comments on the House of Lords' decision in *R v Transport Secretary, ex p. Factortame Ltd.*, [1990] 2 AC 85.

adviser to the government, the official responsible for the criminal justice system, and the guardian of the public interest in ensuring a lawful administration.[63] The attorney general is a member of Parliament and, in Canada (but not the United Kingdom), is also a member of Cabinet. These legal and political responsibilities can conflict when the legality of the advice given to the government is questioned or in decisions not to investigate or to halt investigation of specific criminal matters.

Last, ministers can employ *other ministerial staff* using public funds. These individuals provide ministers with political support and advice that the non-partisan public service cannot because of the overlap between party priorities and modes of policy implementation. In addition, they often communicate the government's views to the media and the general public. Ministerial staff and special advisers are exempt from the constitutional requirement to be impartial, neutral, and objective, but must still uphold the obligation to act honestly and with integrity.

Most modern executive powers are delegated to executive actors through statutes passed by Parliament. Parliament, through theses statutes, sets down in legislation rules, principles, and values that both enable and constrain the exercise of executive power. This type of legislative action exemplifies the principle of parliamentary sovereignty. A common example is a statute that grants a minister (and/or her statutory delegates, like administrative officials) discretionary powers to make decisions in a particular policy area. Delegated authority is a necessity in modern government and also implicitly conveys expertise. A decision about particular matters over particular individuals requires consideration of specific facts and often a balancing of various factors, functions that cannot be carried out by Parliament.[64] Government departments are better equipped both to handle specialized decision making and to provide fair procedures for persons affected by those decisions.

Last, because Parliament cannot itself enact all the legal rules needed for effective governance, it needs executive rule-making. Statutes delegate power so that the executive – Governor-in-Council – can make

63 See ss 4 and 5 of the *Department of Justice Act*, RSC, 1985, c J-2.

64 Just like, as a practical matter, much of administrative mass adjudication cannot be undertaken by the courts.

subordinate legislation like regulations.[65] Most ordinary powers of government, subject to relatively few exceptions, are conferred by statute upon ministers and not upon the Crown.[66] Public law remedies, including compulsory common law remedies like *mandamus*, are therefore potentially available against ministers.[67]

Decolonizing the Sovereign

Unlike the United Kingdom, the Canadian Crown is divided, due to its bifurcation by the federalism principle, into provincial and federal units.[68] Because of its role in relation to Indigenous peoples, and its division by the federalism principle, the Crown has become "Canadianized" rather than remaining in the same form as the British Crown.[69] From an imperial perspective, full Canadianization of the Crown occurred only with the patriation of the constitution in 1982, thereby removing the last vestiges of British colonial authority.[70] Canada is no longer a subordinate colony and has become fully independent.

The Canadian Crown also fulfils a different constitutional and administrative function in relation to Indigenous peoples. The *Royal Proclamation, 1763*[71] is a key, quasi-constitutional document, and it

---

65 For a history of delegated authority and the growth of executive rule-making, see Michael Taggart, "From 'Parliamentary Powers' to Privatization: The Chequered History of Delegated Legislation in the Twentieth Century," *University of Toronto Law Journal* 55 (2005) 575.

66 In public law, the composite nature of the political executive has significant consequences for litigation. For example, two entities (e.g., the minister of citizenship and immigration and the minister of public safety and emergency preparedness) may be part of the Crown, but they may constitute different parties in law, even in relation to the same legal matter. Issue estoppel will therefore not apply. See, e.g., *Dhaliwal v Canada (Public Safety and Emergency Preparedness),* 2015 FC 157.

67 Ministers can be held to account through remedies sought under s 24 of the *Charter* or through the common law (e.g., traditional prerogative writs such as *habeas corpus*, quashing, and prohibition).

68 See Hogg: "[f]or nearly all purposes the idea of the Crown as one and indivisible is thoroughly misleading," *Constitutional Law*, 10.1.

69 Smith, *Invisible Crown*, 28.

70 For recent judicial consideration of the Canadianization of the Crown, see Weiler JA in *McAteer*, paras 47–51, and the larger historical discussion, paras 33–54.

71 *Royal Proclamation 1763* (UK), reprinted RSC 1985, App II, No 1. For a contemporary analysis of the import and effects of the British Empire's constitutional dimensions domestically and internationally, see Dylan Lino, "Albert Venn Dicey and the Constitutional Theory of Empire," *Oxford Journal of Legal Studies* 36, no. 4 (2016) 751.

set out the sovereign-to-sovereign relationship that structured legal relations between the Crown and Indigenous peoples before Confederation. It represents the main legal source for the *sui generis* fiduciary duty that lies on the Crown at all times and that is embedded in the principle of the honour of the Crown; this principle regulates the relationship between the government and Indigenous peoples. Courts review executive decision making affecting Indigenous peoples to uphold the honour of the Crown and the underlying fiduciary duty characterizing this legal relationship. The courts are especially empowered to hold the executive to account to ensure non-arbitrary exercises of Crown discretion over Indigenous interests and to encourage good-faith consultation, negotiation, and reconciliation among the parties.[72] The current judicial track record in this area is uneven at best.[73] While Canada no longer exists as a colony of the United Kingdom, true decolonization – as several chapters in this collection argue – remains an unfulfilled project in which the executive branch plays a crucial role.[74]

Undersighting Oversights

When considering arbitrary executive power, our historical gaze has mistakenly focused on the irrelevant monarch rather than the core executive. Only recently have we asked ourselves how well the executive controls its own exercise of public power or even considered how well our system of responsible government, in conjunction with external oversight mechanisms like courts, ensures that this power is limited and made accountable. The amount of delegated authority exercised by the post–Second World War executive is enormous – and remains so, despite decades of cutbacks to reduce the size of government. The scale and complexity of government raises concerns about accountability gaps, a problem that will be addressed throughout the next section.

That section canvases a range of constraints – political and legal, internal and external, written and unwritten – that aim to guide and control the exercise of executive power, with a special focus on the

72 See *Haida Nation v British Columbia (Minister of Forests)*, [2004] 3 SCR 511, 2004 SCC 73.

73 See David Milward, chap 9 in this volume, for further discussion of this constitutional failing.

74 On the potential for greater institutional space for legal pluralism in Canada, see also Paul Daly, chap 3 [Daly]; Asha Kaushal, chap 7; and Howard Kislowicz, chap 6.

political executive. To understand the constraints placed on the executive branch, it is essential to place it within a broad network of constitutional arrangements; otherwise, the executive would appear much less fettered and sometimes unfettered. That said, in many respects, the executive is not nearly fettered enough, as will be shown by the consideration of a current democratic and rule of law deficit in each subsection.

From Responsible to Irresponsible Government? Weaknesses, Gaps, and Other Accountability Problems

> It is the duty of the courts to be as alert now as they have always been to prevent abuse of the prerogative.[75]

The executive is held to account both politically and legally. Without a doubt, a key difference in Canada's system of government is that the executive is now explicitly governed by constitutional or legal principles rather than solely by the democratic will or political imperatives.[76] The United Kingdom's executive still operates largely under the political constitution; Canada, conversely, operates under both a political and a (positive) legal constitution. Courts also continue to review government action on procedural fairness and substantive grounds through administrative law.[77] From a public law perspective, Canada participates in two traditions. Peter Cane argues that, in the American administrative law tradition, the judiciary's main task is to constrain and legitimize the exercise of power, especially executive power and rule-making. Conversely, the British tradition of administrative law exhibits a tension between the view that administrative law is a "law of rights," whose purpose is to protect citizens against the state, and a "law of wrongs," whose purpose is to ensure that government acts within the law.[78]

---

75 Wilson J (dissent) in *Operation Dismantle v The Queen*, [1985] 1 SCR 441, para 61 citing Lord Devlin in *Chandler v Director of Public Prosecutions*, [1962] 3 All ER 142, 159.

76 Contrast this with Elliott and Thomas's discussion of the United Kingdom's executive in the political constitution in *Public Law*, 108–9.

77 See Daly for a discussion of the constitutional role of superior courts and administrative law.

78 Peter Cane, "Review of Executive Action," in *Oxford Handbook of Legal Studies*, ed. Peter Cane and Mark Tushnet (New York: Oxford University Press, 2005), 153.

Canada, as usual, lies in between the two traditions and attempts to do all at the same time – nurturing new, American-style, constitutional legalism, with its separation of powers concerns, while maintaining the traditional, British, political constitutionalism, with its focus on the evolving relationship between the Crown/government and its legal subjects. The case law discussed in this chapter reflects these unresolved tensions. Moreover, and increasingly problematically, the constraints regulating the executive and its relationship with other branches of government generally take the form of constitutional conventions rather than positive legal rules written down in legislation or a constitution. We are not without recourse, and a range of remedial options will be discussed in this section. In keeping with the theme of this chapter, some recommendations involve a stronger role for the courts and judicial review.

Diminishing Constraints

THE RISE AND MISUSE OF OMNIBUS LEGISLATION

Formally, Parliament plays a key political oversight role in a Westminster system. It does so – imperfectly and sometimes ineffectually – in two ways. First, the House of Commons provides principal and principled opposition to the government. Her Majesty's Loyal Opposition plays an essential role in holding the executive to account in the legislature by scrutinizing its actions. A typical example would be criticism of the executive's policy choices concretized in the form of a bill. Structured discussion over proposed legislation ensures that the executive does not have its own way because it has to persuade the legislature of a bill's merits, then potentially negotiate or make changes or amendments to that bill. But, where a strong majority government prevails, political constraints weaken since the executive has both *de jure* and *de facto* control of the legislature. Question Period may thereby be rendered otiose as legislation can be pushed through more quickly and ministerial accountability resisted. Second, Parliament exercises control over supply issues around budgets, administrative costs, and funding policy alternatives – the constitutional importance of which cannot be denied.

Parliament's general oversight of legislation, however, remains wanting: "Of the functions here we have identified it is the one over which Parliament actually has the least control. ... Public lawyers ... have tended to overplay Parliament's contribution to law-making."[79] Adam Tomkins points out that blame for this blind spot rests in part with Dicey's overly robust interpretation of the sovereignty of Parliament. In truth, parliamentary sovereignty means no more than legislative supremacy of acts of Parliament over the common law and executive prerogative power. The most obvious criticism of this constitutional theory from a Canadian perspective is that parliamentary supremacy is now subordinate to constitutional supremacy.[80] But, more important, we should neither idealize parliamentary sovereignty through the lens of deliberative or republican democratic theory nor view the system as a happy hybrid form because it is subject to a written bill of rights with concomitant, heightened judicial oversight.

Current parliaments are not functionally capable of robustly scrutinizing legislation. The oversight function originally exercised by Parliament (and supported by an outmoded constitutional theory) has to be internally reproduced within the executive to be made effective (see "the Decline of Ministerial Responsibility"). Alternatively, when legal problems emerging from omnibus legislation come before the courts, and given the reality of a lack of legislative oversight, it may be permissible for courts to engage in more intensive judicial review of the statutory language, exercise of discretion, or scope of an executive actor's jurisdiction.

Perhaps the crux of the problem is that Parliament is not the key institution through which government actually legislates; rather, it is the executive branch. A prime example of this phenomenon is the recent overuse of omnibus legislation, which frustrates parliamentary oversight.[81] The term *omnibus* now has mostly negative connotations and

---

79 Tomkins, *Public Law*, 93. Criticisms of the traditional depiction of parliamentary contributions to law-making also emphasize the reductive nature ascribed to the principle of parliamentary sovereignty. Law is, in fact, made by many powers – including the executive and the judiciary – and when Parliament delegates authority to make rules, it necessarily lessens the purchase of parliamentary sovereignty.

80 The continued saliency of Diceyan-derived theories of parliamentary sovereignty can be seen in Jeffery Goldsworthy's *The Sovereignty of Parliament* (Oxford: Oxford University Press, 1999). For a different Canadian analysis, see Lebel J's (in dissent) discussion of how the implied bill of rights contained in the common law has always necessarily limited the principle of parliamentary sovereignty, *R v Demers*, [2004] 2 SCR 489, 2004 SCC 46, paras 78–86.

81 Canada, Parliament, *House of Commons Debates*, 41st Parl, 1st Sess, Vol 146, No 133 (4 June 2012), 1200 (Ms Elizabeth May). An omnibus bill is a multi-part bill that

is often used by opposition parties to indicate that a bill impacts too many diverse issues at once or raises suspicions that the government is attempting to conceal or shield the true scope and purpose of amendments from scrutiny (often successfully). Despite these concerns, omnibus bills are considered an acceptable practice. Although the Speaker could theoretically demand a bill to be divided, this has never happened, with the preferred approach being to leave such issues to be determined by the House (and, on a few notable occasions, a bill has successfully been divided).

Omnibus bills are not unique to Canada. The United Kingdom and Australia, however, exercise stricter control over their use. And, while the use of omnibus bills is also commonplace in the United States, the current trend towards overly large and complex omnibus legislation appears to be a distinctly Canadian phenomenon. As Andrew Coyne has noted, "the scale and scope are on a level not previously seen, or tolerated. ... There is no common thread that runs between them, no overarching principle; they represent not a single act of policy; but a sort of compulsory buffet."[82] In short, omnibus bills gut the remaining vestiges of parliamentary oversight of government legislation. It is entirely within the jurisdiction of both houses of Parliament (subject to executive influence or direction, of course) to more strictly control the (mis)use of omnibus legislation.[83] Such a reform would not be difficult to implement and would sidestep an enhanced role for the judiciary.[84]

---

concurrently amends, repeals, or enacts multiple acts that are purportedly related through a central unifying theme or basic purpose. Omnibus bills may extend to several hundred pages in length and may impact as many as seventy acts at one time.

82 Andrew Coyne, "Bill C-38 Shows Us How Far Parliament Has Fallen," *National Post*, 30 April 2012, http://news.nationalpost.com/full-comment/andrew-coyne-bill-c-38-shows-us-how-far-parliament-has-fallen.

83 See Adam Dodek, "The Constitutional Problems of Omnibus Budget Bills" (paper presented to the Symposium on the State of Canada's Constitutional Democracy, David Asper Centre for Constitutional Rights, February 2016). See also the report of the Special Senate Committee on Modernization, *Senate Modernization: Moving Forward* (Ottawa: Senate of Canada, 2016), http://www.parl.gc.ca/content/sen/committee/421/MDRN/Reports/MDRN_FINAL_FirstReport_webversion_e.pdf.

84 In the 2015 Speech from the Throne, the Liberals promised to not employ omnibus bills; see http://www.cbc.ca/news/politics/read-and-watch-the-full-speech-from-the-throne-1.3351400.

THE EXISTENCE AND (NON-)USE OF THE GOVERNOR GENERAL'S RESERVE POWERS

Constraints on the governor general remain largely political in nature. Therefore, continued recognition and acceptance of constitutional conventions is essential for keeping this part of the executive legitimate and in check. Until recently, things ran relatively smoothly here. But, with the 2008 and 2009 "prorogation crises," the stability of some conventions has become unsettled, and the scope of the governor general's powers has come into question.

In the 2008 prorogation crisis, then prime minister Stephen Harper's minority government faced a proposed Liberal-NDP coalition and the subsequent threat of losing a confidence vote. In this context, the prime minister advised then governor general Michaëlle Jean to prorogue Parliament. This context seemed to undermine the constitutionality of the prime minister's advice and seemed to weaken the efficacy of our constitutional conventions. In 2009, Prime Minister Harper sought another prorogation of Parliament – very shortly after the first – so that his government could avoid a House Standing Order to provide unredacted documents regarding the Canadian practice, during the mission to Afghanistan, of handing over Afghan detainees to prisons where they were tortured. Actual disobedience of the Standing Order would, of course, have been unconstitutional and would surely have led to a lost confidence vote. Again, concerns about a potential abuse of executive power arose.

From these crises, the following questions took centre stage: (1) Does an imminent or anticipated loss-of-confidence vote undermine the constitutionality of a prime minister's advice to prorogue Parliament? and (2) If the answer is yes, does this affirm the ability of the governor general to invoke the Crown's reserve power to reject the proffered advice? Two clear camps emerged in the aftermath.[85]

The first camp[86] approved of the potential exercise of the governor general's discretionary reserve powers to reject the prime minister's advice. The common rationale for this argument was: (1) the governor general should generally follow the advice given by the prime minister

---

85 For full arguments on this issue, see Peter Aucoin et al, *Democratizing the Constitution: Reforming Responsible Government* (Toronto: Emond Montgomery, 2011).

86 Experts in this camp included Eugene Forsey, Andrew Heard, Jean Leclair and Jean-François Gaudreault-DesBiens, Peter Russell, Brian Slattery, and Lorne Sossin.

or follow it only when the prime minister has the confidence of the House; (2) the governor general should reject the prime minister's advice only when it is necessary to protect parliamentary democracy/ responsible government/the constitutional order from serious abuses of power by the government and for which there is no other remedy (including a potential judicial remedy); (3) the governor general is also empowered by the unwritten principles of democracy and the rule of law to "second-guess" the prime minister's potentially arbitrary advice and therefore act as a necessary check on executive power (subject to point 2); and (4) the governor general should provide a public justification for the resulting decision. Less consensus existed on two points: (1) whether the governor general should be able to reject advice on this basis for both dissolution and prorogation and (2) whether the courts should be able to review prerogative decisions about prorogation to enquire into their propriety.

The second camp rejected the governor general's potential use of reserve powers – and some even questioned the very existence of reserve powers.[87] Their arguments were simpler and began with the observation that we still need to protect parliamentary democracy from monarchical control because the potential exists as much for an authoritarian monarch as for an authoritarian prime minister. The strongest argument here is for continued acceptance of the general rule: the governor general is constitutionally obliged to accept advice – even if it is bad advice – and maintain a dignified distance from politics.

In my view, the governor general's first prorogation decision appears to be a reasonable exercise of discretionary decision making based on the fragility of the proposed alternative coalition as well as several other factors.[88] The second decision, however, is not so clearly based on

---

87 Experts in the second camp included Henri Brun, Robert Dawson, Ned Franks, Peter Hogg, and Guy Tremblay.

88 See Schneiderman, *Red, White, and Kind of Blue?*, chap 2 for the results of Schneiderman's excellent media analysis of this controversy, where he shows how Prime Minister Harper and the Conservative Party won the "war of words" (108) because, since the media remained steadfastly uninterested in educating Canadians about their system of government, public opinion polling showed that the claim had taken hold that the prime minister is directly elected (like the American president), such as when a fresh election needs to be called when a government is overturned. Schneiderman argues that the governor general rightly agreed to the prime minister's request, but that, in her and any subsequent decision, she should not insist on "stability" as a criterion for approving another governing party or coalition

legitimate advice. The second prorogation crisis, therefore, remains a potentially viable example of a case that could be amenable for judicial review of the abuse of prerogative power by the prime minister and/or the governor general.[89] Although Parliament created the solution, the remedy devised by then speaker Peter Milliken is exactly the sort of process-oriented public law remedy that a court might have conceivably constructed if called to step in.[90] I would suggest that this is one future remedial possibility, and its limited nature and scope would not threaten our separation of powers.

Overall, clearer constitutional rules are necessary to recognize, legitimize, and/or constrain the reserve powers of the governor general.[91] We need no longer fear the discretionary exercise of the monarch's prerogative power, which still retains the three core "rights" that Bagehot initially identified: to be consulted, to encourage, and to warn.[92] Such prerogative power remains dependent on the political executive and constitutional culture.[93]

---

as it is too vague a concept and the governor general is in no better position than parliamentarians to judge the stability of any minority government (112).

89 See Schneiderman, *Red, White, and Kind of Blue?*, chap 3 for his assessment of the 2009 prorogation. He focuses on the concept of the separation of powers and how the prorogation pitted the executive's prerogative powers over foreign affairs and national security against the parliamentary privileges grounded in responsible government. He argues that the Harper government attempted to create a protective zone around the political executive by arguing that our separation of powers is more bright-line and therefore the executive is not accountable to the legislative branch in all matters.

90 The Speaker recognized parliamentary privilege as a near-absolute constitutional power underpinning the order to produce relevant documents and disclose information so that the government could be held to account. In turn, the government/executive could request that sensitive information remain secret and confidential; the House would then determine whether the executive's reasons for refusing to share and/or disclose were justified. Subsequent to this ruling, three of the main parties (the Conservatives, Liberals, and Bloc Québécois; the New Democratic Party declined) signed a memorandum of understanding establishing an ad hoc parliamentary committee, which would review sensitive documents to determine whether information should be disclosed.

91 The larger constitutional issue concerning the monarchy's abolition seems some ways off on the political horizon.

92 Bagehot, *English Constitution*, 60.

93 For further constitutional analysis of ministerial "advice," see Mark Walters, "Judicial Review of Advice to the Crown," *Constitutional Forum* 25, no. 3 (2016) 33. Walters concludes that when ministerial advice is publicly given or can otherwise

THE PRIME MINISTER'S ABUSE OF EXECUTIVE PREROGATIVE

In Dicey's constitutional theory, Crown prerogative survives as a wide discretionary authority exercised by a prime minister and Cabinet. For Dicey this augments, rather than detracts from, the authority of the House of Commons (and ultimately electors) because the political executive tends to carry out (as a matter of discretion) the democratic will. This conclusion rested on Dicey's key assumption that "the House of Commons has become by far the most important part of the sovereign body."[94] But, as David Smith counters, "Canadian experience demonstrates no easy congruence between the action of the executive and the will of the legislature. Instead, concerns abound about the space that exists between them, and at the executive's predominance."[95] We therefore still need to be concerned about the abuse of prerogative powers by the political executive generally and the prime minister in particular, especially given the presidentialization dynamic.

In countries with Westminster systems, a key concern is whether the role of the prime minister has evolved (or devolved) into a presidential role without explicit constitutional authorization or the coterminous development of appropriate checks and balances.[96] Some scholars, however, and contrary to Donald Savoie and Jeffrey Simpson, do not locate the growth of prime ministerial power and the corresponding decline of Cabinet with the Trudeau, Mulroney, and Chrétien years. Indeed, they argue that one can go all the way back to Borden, Bennett, and Mackenzie King: "Nothing could be clearer or blunter. Canada has a long history of prime ministers who dominated, sometimes even ignored, the cabinet over which they presided."[97]

A cautionary example is provided by the fixed-election-dates case, *Conacher v Canada (Prime Minister)*.[98] This case illustrates judicial reticence to review a prerogative power that fuses the roles of the governor

---

be established through evidence, it may legitimately be judicially reviewed for constitutional compliance. This may happen rarely, but it comports with a larger culture of legality. Courts may properly defer to justified and justifiable ministerial advice.

94 Dicey, *Law of the Constitution*, 466.

95 Smith, *Invisible Crown*, 36.

96 See, generally, Poguntke and Webb, eds., *Presidentialization of Politics*.

97 R.A.W. Rhodes et al, *Comparing Westminster* (Oxford: Oxford University Press, 2009), 79–80.

98 *Conacher v Canada (Prime Minister)*, 2008 FC 1119 [*Conacher*] (application for leave to the Supreme Court of Canada denied).

general and the prime minister in the giving of advice about dissolution for the purpose of calling a snap election. It therefore highlights an "outer limits" problem for judicial review and raises the concomitant problem of too much judicial deference or restraint when examining a possible abuse of executive power.[99] On review, federal courts found that fixed election dates could amount to only a statutory "expectation" – unless further evidence pointed to the development of an actual, crystallized convention. Even then, the courts cautioned that they could not award a remedy, other than to recognize an expectation of obeying the legislation or crystallized convention. At Federal Court of Appeal, Stratas JA remained circumspect about whether stronger parliamentary intent, communicated through clear and specific wording, would be an acceptable constitutional constraint on the advice-giving power of the prime minister to call a snap election.[100]

One political remedy would be to put prerogative powers on a statutory basis (assuming that we know which prerogative powers currently exist) to guarantee that positive limitations are placed on their exercise.[101] This would have the added benefit of helping parliamentary oversight of executive action because Parliament would know the actual basis for ministers' prerogative decisions. If, however, interpretation of s. 9 to s. 16 of the *Constitution Act, 1867* concludes that the executive's prerogative functions are, in fact, constitutionally entrenched, these powers can never be fully abolished or displaced by statute.[102] The legal remedy would be a judicial rethinking of the role of the courts in reviewing prerogative powers and providing better access to remedies.[103] All prerogative powers should be subject to judicial review, but

99 Lorne Sossin provides a comprehensive examination of the scope of and limits on judicial decision making in *Boundaries of Judicial Review: The Law of Justiciability in Canada*, 2nd ed. (Toronto: Carswell, 2012).

100 *Conacher*, para 5. Nevertheless, fixed election dates do appear to be an emerging, voluntarily accepted constraint on federal and provincial executive prerogative power.

101 See, e.g., the United Kingdom's House of Commons Public Administration Select Committee report *Taming the Prerogative: Strengthening Ministerial Accountability to Parliament* (HC 422 2003–04).

102 See Dale Gibson, "Monitoring Arbitrary Government Authority: Charter Scrutiny of Legislative, Executive, and Judicial Privilege," *Saskatchewan Law Review* 61, no. 2 (1998) 297.

103 Philippe Lagassé provides an insightful examination of judicial ambivalence about reviewing prerogative powers as well as the reluctance to impose robust remedies;

those that engage politically sensitive matters, such as foreign affairs, may be shown more deference, and the government of the day may be given a greater margin of appreciation in terms of potential legal sanctions.

THE GROWING IRRELEVANCY OF CABINET

Cabinet is now less relevant, the core executive is more fragmented, and clear lines of accountability or responsibility remain in abeyance. This has produced a clear democratic deficit.

One cannot look at Cabinet without also considering the multitudes of Others (e.g., PMO, ministerial staff, and special advisers) who have replaced it – but, again, without a corresponding increase in the accountability of the executive branch. Not only, as Martin Smith argues, has decision making "moved beyond the parliamentary arena," this development ensures that "cabinet is now almost universally accepted as nothing more than a rubber stamp."[104] The constitutional implications are profound because, without Cabinet, conventions concerning individual and ministerial responsibility become real fictions. Formal, collective decision making and oversight is replaced by a host of informal, non-constitutional bodies whose functions are developed in an ad hoc, unconstrained way and with weak or no lines of accountability, save possibly the media.

So, although ministerial staff and special advisers serve an important function in a modern government, their presence does not come without some legal discomfort. Because they are political, and their special positions exist apart from the civil service, they are not directly "captured" by the doctrine of ministerial responsibility, although ministers and the prime minister still retain responsibility for their management and conduct. Concerns about their accountability or their ethical conduct have grown. That said, special advisers and other like staff are not protected from the consequences of bad advice or bad behaviour and are, unlike public servants, politically expendable.

The growth of these unaccountable personnel generates further anxieties that their use and presence may also undermine the neutrality and

---

see "Parliamentary and Judicial Ambivalence toward Executive Prerogative Powers in Canada," *Canadian Public Administration* 55, no. 2 (2012) 157.

104 Martin J. Smith, *The Core Executive in Britain* (Houndmills, UK: Macmillan Press, 1999), 253.

non-partisan advice given by public servants, particularly if they are able to exercise power over public servants by issuing instructions and controlling the advice that is given to them.[105] Overlap with the public service concerning advice provision and other functions also leads to a lack of clarity and perhaps unnecessary duplication.[106]

The blurry lines of accountability remain troubling. Creating external watchdogs (discussed below) may address some of these concerns.

THE DECLINE OF MINISTERIAL RESPONSIBILITY

By convention, ministers are accountable to both houses of Parliament and are usually members of the legislature.[107] This means that they are formally accountable to Parliament through the convention of ministerial responsibility. Ministers are responsible in two ways: (1) they are individually responsible for the exercise of their power, and (2) they are institutionally responsible for the administration of their particular department. Ministers are also subject to the prime minister's unfettered discretionary power to reorganize the executive, move and dismiss ministers, create new departments, and reallocate functions.[108] These operational changes are not subject to scrutiny by parliamentary committees or to a vote in Parliament. A mechanism is needed to ensure that government explains and justifies such changes to Parliament.[109] This would also permit Parliament to have control over

---

105 In less neutral terms, this is called "spinning."

106 One example is the Harper government's decision to appoint a special adviser and legal counsel to the prime minister to provide personal legal advice to the prime minister and the PMO; it paralleled or possibly replaced the attorney general and Department of Justice.

107 Note that in the United Kingdom, the *House of Commons Disqualification Act* 1975 contains a rule (s 2(1)) that there can be no more than ninety-five holders of ministerial office in the House of Commons, a measure that prevents executive dominance in the House.

108 See Alissa Malkin, "Government Reorganization and the Transfer of Powers: Does Certainty Matter?," *Ottawa Law Review* 39, no. 3 (2007) 537. Malkin argues that when statutory authority is transferred from one minister to another, it is difficult to trace and therefore determine which ministers have legal responsibility for the exercise of power. She argues that this offends the constitutional principles of the rule of law and responsible government.

109 But see Nicholas d'Ombrain, who argues that first ministers should not have their powers reduced; rather, they should pay more heed to their duties under the convention of ministerial responsibility. See "Ministerial Responsibility and the Machinery of Government," *Canadian Public Administration* 50, no. 2 (2007) 195.

not just government, but Cabinet itself, thereby reducing the scope of a prime minister's discretionary power.

The delegation of powers by statutes to ministers also entails a form of checks and balances. When the legislature delegates power to ministers or other administrative actors, common law courts serve an essential constitutional oversight function by examining whether those powers have been lawfully exercised in accordance with legislative intent or constitutional limits and values. Under administrative law, reviewing courts place great weight on legislative intent. They also follow a variety of principles and presumptions that support giving deference to other branches. Because ministerial responsibility is a fiction, legal oversight of ministers and their delegates remains a crucial oversight function performed by courts in public law. Courts can, of course, compel a statutory delegate to do what the statute requires them to do when it takes the form of an express or implied public law duty. Courts can also, using statutory interpretation, go beyond the grammatical and ordinary meaning to imply purposes, restraints, and values that shape the exercise of power. And courts can, through the duty to give reasonable reasons, which mirrors the justificatory demands contained in s. 1 of the *Charter*, compel the executive to explain the choices made under delegated authority to uphold or limit fairness, rights, proportionality, and *Charter* values. Over the past twenty years, though, Canadian administrative law has seen the rise of judicial deference to executive interpretations of statutes. While generally viewed as a positive development in public law, anxieties have recently arisen that too much deference to legal interpretations made by executive actors could lead to judicial abdication of the oversight function on questions of law.[110]

Statutes may also permit certain ministers to make law on an as-needed, emergency basis. While always a possibility in "ordinary" times, this type of delegated authority and rule-making raises heightened concerns during states of emergency such as 9/11 and its aftermath.

110 See the vigorous discussion about the relationship between the separation of powers and the administrative law standard of review in *Canada (Fisheries and Oceans) v David Suzuki Foundation*, 2012 FCA 40. In this case, Mainville JA rejected a deferential approach to review the interpretation by the minister for fisheries and oceans of a question of law in his home statute on the basis that expertise did not include legal or interpretive expertise. This is a currently controversial area in Canadian administrative law. Also see Daly on this point, *supra*, in his chapter's discussion of institutional and interpretive pluralism in the Canadian legal system.

The basis for this power is that the ordinary legislative process is too cumbersome to facilitate an appropriate and flexible response in times of crisis. Enabling a minister to make emergency regulations to prevent, mitigate, or control the effects of a crisis best allows the executive to respond. At its broadest, this type of law-making permits an executive actor to amend current or future legislation based on a discretionary evaluation of the circumstances and required purposes. Courts may not be able to exercise their oversight function due to constraints on information or deference to security imperatives, leading to legal "black" and "grey" accountability holes.[111]

In addition to worries about the general decline of ministerial responsibility in the legislature, the fused role of the minister of justice/attorney general has come under recent strain.[112] Canada, unlike the United Kingdom, has not engaged in conversations about how the fusion of the legal and political rules may lead to bias issues or concerns about the lack of independence in this office.[113] The Edgar Schmidt case illustrates the potentially problematic overlap between the political and legal functions in the role of the minister of justice/attorney general.[114] Edgar Schmidt worked as general counsel in the Department of Justice, where he came to believe that pre-legislative statutory examination

---

111 David Dyzenhaus, "*Schmitt v. Dicey*: Are States of Emergency inside or outside the Legal Order?," *Cardozo Law Review* 27 (21 August 2008) 2005, http://ssrn.com/abstract=1244562.

112 See also Wade K. Wright's discussion of provincial attorneys generals' discretionary power of non-enforcement of federal criminal note, chap 4 in this volume. Note that, at the provincial level, it is permissible for the premier, the minister of justice, and/or the attorney general to be the same individual. See *Askin v Law Society of British Columbia*, 2013 BCCA 233, where the Court of Appeal concluded that BC's attorney general need not be a member of the local bar or even qualified to practise law.

113 For an exemplary treatment of the institutional significance of the attorney general and government lawyers, see Adam Dodek's work "The 'Unique Role' of Government Lawyers in Canada," *Israel Law Review* 49, no. 1 (2016) 23; and "Lawyering at the Intersection of Public Law and Legal Ethics: Government Lawyers as Custodians of the Rule of Law," *Dalhousie Law Journal* 33 (2010) 1. Note that, in 2006, the Public Prosecution Service of Canada (PPSC) was moved out of the Department of Justice to better fulfil the role of external adviser and public prosecutor in matters prosecuted by the attorney general of Canada on behalf of the Crown.

114 At Federal Court, Noël J rejected Schmidt's arguments outright, stating that the examination provisions did not call for a different, stricter mechanism – no matter

provisions legally required the minister of justice to make a report to Parliament whenever he or she formed the opinion that, on a balance of probabilities, draft legislation was inconsistent with *Charter* rights. The attorney general countered that this duty was activated only when the minister formed the opinion that "no credible argument" existed to defend the legislation against a court challenge.

Although not claiming bad faith behaviour, Schmidt came close to arguing that the minister of justice actively permitted the passing of poor-quality legislation that very likely violated *Charter* rights without being accompanied by a compelling justification. In his view, this violated the constitutional duties of the minister as well as the unwritten principles of the rule of law, democracy, and responsible government since, without a report, Parliament might not be made aware of the potential problems with the legislation. The minister, on the other hand, argued that constitutional duties were not avoided and that responsibility for legislative scrutiny was not improperly transferred either to litigious citizens or to the courts.

Regardless of the parties' arguments, it is clear that Canada should give some thought to dividing up the responsibilities for the different functions currently housed in the fused role of the minister of justice/attorney general. It may be appropriate to also shift the oversight function originally exercised by Parliament so that it is internally reproduced within the executive as a stricter form of pre-legislative scrutiny. Alternatively, and in the United Kingdom, it is the minister responsible for a bill who is obligated to assess and publicly justify its constitutionality.

Finally, a fundamental aspiration remains unrealized in delegated legislation: when Parliament confers powers on the executive through statutes, one hopes that it also seriously considers the scope of delegated authority, the precise terms and limits on that authority, and the purposes of the proper exercise of those powers. Systemic scrutiny of the appropriate type and scope of delegated authority is largely a fiction. Where possible, a parliamentary committee[115] can examine

---

how laudable a result this might be. See *Schmidt v Canada (Attorney General)*, 2016 FC 269 (CanLII). Schmidt appealed the trial decision, but his appeal was dismissed, with the Federal Court of Appeal judges largely agreeing with the lower court's decision. See *Schmidt v Canada (Attorney General)*, 2018 FCA 55. It remains open to the government to amend the statute and create a stricter standard.

115 For instance, in the United Kingdom, the House of Lords' Delegated Powers and Regulatory Reform Committee. In Canada, we have the Standing Joint Committee for the Scrutiny of Regulations.

legislation that delegates imprecise powers and rule-making to ministers to recommend clarifications, preambles, definitions, purpose statements, and/or amendments to constrain the conferral of unduly wide discretionary powers.

THE EROSION OF NEUTRALITY AND INDEPENDENCE IN THE CIVIL SERVICE AND EXECUTIVE AGENCIES

Civil servants are accountable to ministers and are managed by them under the royal prerogative. This accountability is required by both the principle of public service neutrality and the conventions of ministerial responsibility as part of the principle of responsible government. The public service (or *bureaucracy*) serves the party in power (or government of the day), but is ultimately loyal to the Queen as servant of the Crown. The public service model relies on an impartial and relatively permanent staff that serves and advises present and future governments. But, because the growth of executive power mirrors the development – since the First World War and especially since the Second World War – of the modern welfare state, the civil service is massively bigger than it was in the early twentieth century.

Civil servants, despite their lower constitutional status, often exercise a great deal of power to make, implement, and advise on policy. They may even appear to run the show (as in the television shows *Yes Minister* and *Yes, Prime Minister*). The doctrine of ministerial responsibility is therefore quite thin for, in reality, ministers may not really supervise civil servants. Parliament will therefore not be able to hold ministers responsible for the policy choices made by their staff. Ministerial responsibility in the context of large-scale government with big bureaucracies is, once again, a fiction.

Several principles structure the relationship between the civil and elected political officials.[116] The principle of ministerial responsibility means that the presiding minister must be held politically responsible for all matters arising in the department. In the context of modern government, this principle appears as a fiction that is truly tested only in the courts on judicial review. The principle of political neutrality requires civil servants to carry out their responsibilities loyally to the government in power, regardless of their own political views. A traditional

---

116 For judicial elaboration of the principle of public service neutrality, see *Fraser v PSSRB*, [1985] 2 SCR 455.

model dictates that civil servants should be restricted in their ability to engage in partisan political activities and that they cannot express publicly their personal views on policy issues. Last, the principle of public service neutrality entails that civil servants should be accountable to their ministerial overseers, but are not directly answerable to Parliament.

The principle of public service neutrality was tested as civil servants sought to exercise their freedom of expression and openly criticize,[117] or run against,[118] the outgoing Harper government. In a recent op ed piece, Donald Savoie stated that this malaise has indeed worsened, but it is not new, and the civil service has been "in the process of decomposing for some time. Survey after survey of federal public servants going back to the 1980s consistently revealed a widespread and deepening morale problem."[119] Savoie provided no easy answers to the fundamental problems of the civil service other than to recommend that civil servants continue to remain non-partisan and impartial, and that a new government structure a House of Commons committee to pursue these questions about how best to organize government.

The Supreme Court of Canada has also ruled that executive agencies – commonly known as agencies, boards, and commissions

117 Former Environment Canada scientist Tony Turner drew criticism when he wrote and uploaded the *Harperman* song, which openly called for a change in government. Turner was suspended from his job after releasing the song and chose to retire rather than wait for an investigation. The federal information commissioner's office began an investigation after receiving complaints from other federal scientists, who had been denied permission to speak to the media unless they conformed to pre-approved government talking points.

118 Emilie Taman, a prosecutor with the PPSC, took an "unauthorized" leave without pay from the public service to run in an Ottawa riding. PPSC turned down her request because of the conflict among neutrality, political office, and the role of a public prosecutor. Taman sought judicial review. At Federal Court, Kane J ruled that while Taman's *Charter* rights were limited, the Public Service Commission had struck the right balance by upholding the principle of political impartiality in the public service and denying leave. See *Taman v Canada (AG)*, 2015 FC 1155. This decision was overturned at Federal Court of Appeal, which agreed with Taman that the PPSC was not justified in refusing to grant her permission to seek elected office and therefore its decision was unreasonable. See *Taman v Canada (Attorney General)*, [2017] 3 FCR 520, 2017 FCA 1.

119 Donald Savoie, "A Change in Government Alone Won't Fix the Malaise," *Globe and Mail*, 28 November 2015, http://www.theglobeandmail.com/globe-debate/a-change-in-government-alone-wont-fix-the-malaise/article27509697/.

(or ABCs) – "may be seen as spanning the constitutional divide between the executive and the judicial branches of government" and primarily serve an executive policy function, unless the home statute indicates otherwise.[120] They therefore attract strong guarantees of independence from the executive only if that is what the legislature has intended – even if they primarily serve an adjudicative or investigatory function. This renders appointments to administrative bodies vulnerable to purely partisan motives and the potential abuse of the timing of a prime minister's discretionary power.[121] In public law, it remains legally permissible for a new government to "clean house" by dismissing from office members of ABCs (except those whose appointment can be terminated only by the legislative assembly) made by a previous government, even when they fulfil an adjudicative function, and for purely ideological reasons.[122] Statutory reform protecting ABC appointments in the form of guaranteed terms, termination for cause only, and other structural guarantees of independence would enable reviewing courts to play a larger, protective role through administrative law.

Finally, the sheer size of the administrative state, as noted above, raises fundamental concerns about accountability and oversight.[123] In the past, Parliament shared an oversight function with common law courts, but this traditional role has been eclipsed by the courts due to

---

120 *Ocean Port Hotel Ltd. v British Columbia (General Manager, Liquor Control and Licensing Branch)*, [2001] 2 SCR 781, 2001 SCC 52, para 24. ABCs generally do not attract the same constitutional guarantees of independence as courts, and the unwritten principle of judicial independence does not extend to their members.

121 See Carl Baar and Peter Russell, "Why Won't the Liberals Act on Harper's Overreach on Appointments?," *Globe and Mail*, 28 March 2016, http://www.theglobeandmail.com/opinion/why-wont-the-liberals-act-on-harpers-overreach-on-appointments/article29388808/. Baar and Russell controversially suggest that constitutional conventions (i.e., the "caretaker" convention) and unwritten principles do not support the ability of a prime minister to make executive appointments to fill vacancies that do not become vacant until after an election. The Trudeau government, elected in 2015, only requested their voluntary resignation.

122 See *Saskatchewan Federation of Labour v Government of Saskatchewan*, 2013 SKCA 61 for judicial confirmation that appointments to a labour tribunal are not protected by the constitutional principle of independence, unlike the judiciary.

123 For deeper and comparative analysis of this problem, see Benedict Sheehy and Donald Feaver, "Re-thinking Executive Control of and Accountability for the Agency," *Osgoode Hall Law Journal* 54, no. 1 (2016) 175. Sheehy and Feaver's study presents this as a simultaneous, worldwide shift to a less accountable, "hyper-powered" executive in both republican and responsible government models.

the growth of administrative law and also because of the *Charter*. When the executive controls the legislature, Parliament *will* confer the types of delegated power the executive wants and on the terms (broad, discretionary, vague) it wants. This result again underscores the crucial role of the courts through judicial review and statutory interpretation to place limits on the exercise of delegated power to actors in executive agencies.

Newer Mechanisms of Accountability and Oversight

Newer mechanisms of accountability complement the existing "webs of accountabilities" but also contribute to the sense of "government overload."[124]

CODES AND CODIFICATION OF CONSTITUTIONAL CONVENTIONS

The political constitution can be written down. Codes can make conventions positive, concrete, and clearer. Many parliamentary systems have "officialized" various constitutional conventions in Cabinet manuals that are politically enforceable.[125] Other examples would be ministerial codes,[126] civil service codes,[127] and codes of conduct for special advisers.[128] Technically soft law, and so not legally binding, these documents are interpreted against the background political and legal norms of accountability, integrity, and the rule of law. Many contain explicit statements about core values and principles. Breaches of codes may be

---

124 R.A.W. Rhodes, "Executives in Parliamentary Government," in *Oxford Handbook of Political Institutions*, ed. R.A.W. Rhodes et al (New York: Oxford University Press, 2008), 333. As befits the silos that can exist among academic disciplines, Rhodes does not discuss the courts as part of the accountability network.

125 Three examples are the *Manual of Official Procedure of the Government of Canada*, the United Kingdom's *The Cabinet Manual: A Guide to Laws, Conventions and the Rules on the Operations of Government*, and New Zealand's *Cabinet Manual*.

126 See the United Kingdom's recent Ministerial Code, https://www.gov.uk/government/uploads/system/uploads/attachment_data/file/468255/Final_draft_ministerial_code_No_AMENDS_14_Oct.pdf.

127 See the Values and Ethics Code for the Public Sector, http://www.tbs-sct.gc.ca/pol/doc-eng.aspx?id=25049.

128 See the Code of Conduct for Special Advisors (London, 2010). Because of s 8(1) of the *Constitutional Reform and Governance Act* 2010, this code is statutorily required to exist.

enforced internally by Cabinet or the prime minister and may lead to resignation. Codes may also be enforced externally by so-called watchdogs, which may (if empowered) launch independent investigations.

Codes of conduct can also be upgraded to statutory form. In Canada, the adoption of the *Federal Accountability Act* put standards of ethical conduct for ministerial staff into law, brought into force the *Conflict of Interest Act*, and made significant amendments to the *Lobbying Act* – statutes that have effectively constrained executive power in these areas.[129]

Last, attempts to actually codify unwritten conventions as legally enforceable statutes have not met with success in Canada. They have even been criticized as exacting a detrimental, paralyzing effect on our constitutional system.[130] Canada has similarly resisted codification of the remaining royal prerogatives through soft law or statutes.[131]

WATCHDOGS, NOT LAPDOGS

Agencies, auditors, commissioners, and ombudspersons exist as watchdogs or advisers that operate at arm's length from the government. Examples include the chief electoral officer, the parliamentary budget officer, the ethics commissioner, the information commissioner, the privacy commissioner, the public sector integrity commissioner, and the military police complaints commissioner. Many are officers of Parliament – for example, the information commissioner, whose appointment both the House of Commons and the Senate approved – who provide much stronger independence from the executive than ordinary administrative bodies. The downside of creating these types of watchdogs is

129 *Federal Accountability Act*, SC 2006, c 9. See the United Kingdom's *Constitutional Reform and Governance Act 2010*, s 7(4); it provides a statutory basis for the civil service so that core principles and values are enshrined in law.

130 James W.J. Bowden and Nicholas A. MacDonald, "Writing the Unwritten: The Officialization of Constitutional Convention in Canada, the United Kingdom, New Zealand and Australia," *Journal of Parliamentary and Political Law* 6, no. 2 (2012) 365. The authors discuss the failed attempts to codify conventions in Canada in 1978 (*Constitutional Amendment Bill*) and Australia in the 1970s and 1980s (*Resolutions of the Australian Constitutional Convention* of 1985). See also Emmett Macfarlane, chap 2 in this volume, for a similar plea to retain the flexibility of unwritten constitutional mechanisms.

131 See Schneiderman, *Red, White, and Kind of Blue?*, 168–72, for a brief discussion of the United Kingdom's efforts at codifying prerogative authority and several Canadian proposals to do so.

threefold: (1) they have contributed to the complexification, fragmentation, and non-transparency of the executive branch; (2) they have taken over the kind of oversight that should be shared with Parliament and so provide no incentives to improve the House of Commons; and (3) they suffer from the same lack of accountability and legitimacy problems that other executive actors in the administrative state face. Nevertheless, some argue that these executive institutional actors are essential to achieving accountability in democratic responsible government and may constitute an imminent fourth branch of government.[132]

Micropsia: The Constitution Is Bigger Than What We See

The first part of this section described how large our accountability problem in public law is. Although executive hegemony has not been realized, we have and always have had a problem with this branch of government. How have we reached the point where this power has simultaneously become more concentrated in parts of the executive, while more diffuse and unaccountable overall? How can we remedy these deficiencies? Do we even have the political will to do so?

Our governance problems may be dire, but they are not intractable. What I hope this chapter also discloses is that the range of our constitutional correctives is even bigger if one looks beyond a piece of paper. Both so-called presidentialization and democratic deficits can be addressed through a range of options, not all of which involve rights and the courts (for those who are leery of the court-centric nature of this chapter).[133] New legislation, for example, can be introduced to better constrain broad ministerial discretion. Parliamentary rules can change to control or discourage the use of omnibus legislation. Constitutional conventions, such as those surrounding prorogation, can be written down. New watchdogs with real teeth can be created. Control over administrative appointments can be removed from the political executive and given to an independent body, and adjudicative tribunal members can have independence extended to them through ordinary legislation. Last, key actors in the executive can willingly participate in a constitutional culture through voluntary and informal behavioural

132 Karine Azoulay, "Making the Case: Canada's PBO, the Courts and the Fourth Branch of Government," *Journal of Parliamentary and Political Law* 8, no. 1 (2014) 107.

133 For a similar approach, see Michael Pal's contribution in chap 13 on how to effect egalitarian reform in our elections law.

change. Nevertheless, this chapter has argued that courts – often in partnership with legislative reform – can also take a firmer lead in reviewing different forms of executive action.

Conclusion: "Ottawa, We've Had a Problem Here"

> The language of public law has not kept pace with the evolution of modern executive power in democratic times.[134]

This chapter provided a comprehensive overview of the nature, sources of, and constraints on executive power in Canada, with a focus on how courts (not legislatures) have traditionally sought to control, constrain, and tame the heterogeneous forms of executive power and how they may do so in the future. To do this, it looked back at late nineteenth- and early twentieth-century constitutional theories to chart where we were 150 years ago at Confederation and where we are now. From this, it concludes that a "golden era" never existed for Westminster constitutionalism. Our system of government is fraught with tensions resulting from competing traditions – the older English constitution overlapping and in competition with a newer, written constitution; the American system with the British – like tectonic plates subducting.[135]

Taking notice of these strains, my overview of the executive's sources of power and the problems with the current constraints on that power recommends a more court-centred approach to holding the executive in check. This remains a controversial position because of the inherent tension for courts in judicial review between controlling and legitimizing both government action and their own power. In particular, the prospect of diminishing constraints presented in the previous section was countered with an exploration of where judicial review could play an enhanced role, especially in areas where tradition has counselled extreme deference or even non-justiciability, such as with prerogative

134 Elliott and Thomas, *Public Law*, 103.

135 For an optimistic view of a happier fusion between presidential and parliamentary values in the doctrine of the separation of powers, see Richard Albert, "Presidential Values in Parliamentary Democracies," *International Journal of Constitutional Law* 8, no. 21 (2010) 207. In giving an example of a constrained parliamentary system with both a central positioning of Parliament and a strong judiciary, Albert places Canada on the intermediate site along the spectrum of democratic systems.

powers. Nevertheless, it remains an approach that can work in harmonious partnership with legislative efforts to tame executive power.

Alternatively, as suggested in the Introduction, Canada could look to the United Kingdom's constitutional undertakings such as the House of Commons' Political and Constitutional Reform Committee[136] (and other select committees) to consider ways to improve Parliament and further tame the executive branch. Or, following Patrick Diamond's recommendation, the political remedy of a royal commission charged with examining constitutional issues concerning the core executive, the *de facto* centralization of (unaccountable) power, the role of the civil service and special advisers, the decline of parliamentary and ministerial accountability, and the abuse of prerogative powers could also be considered.[137] Last, following Andrew Coyne and others, we might focus on improving Parliament to prove wrong the view that it is more than a "cowed and supine body, the mere instrument of the government's will."[138] Regardless of the precise prescription, looking only to the *Charter* to solve our democratic woes will not suffice, and we will need to examine a fuller range of potential responses encompassing the breadth of public law – from the judicial to the political and from the formal to the informal constitution.

So, while we may have come a long, long way from the perceived deficiencies of the old English constitution, it might be even more apt to conclude that we have a significantly enduring democratic debt as a result of these deficits and that a crucial question therefore remains before us – how can we ensure that the next 150 years are constitutionally better than what we have now?

---

136 A good example of this committee's work would be the report on the role and powers of the prime minister, http://www.publications.parliament.uk/pa/cm201415/cmselect/cmpolcon/351/351.pdf.

137 Patrick Diamond, *Governing Britain: Power, Politics and the Prime Minister* (London: IB Tauris, 2014), 284.

138 Colin Turpin and Adam Tomkins, *British Government and the Constitution*, 7th ed. (Cambridge: Cambridge University Press, 2011), 158.

2 The Future of Constitutional Change in Canada: Examining Our Legal, Political, and Jurisprudential Straitjacket

EMMETT MACFARLANE*

Canada's relationship with constitutional change is a story of challenge, complexity, and contestation. Efforts to develop a domestic amending formula, something the *Constitution Act, 1867*[1] lacked, spanned decades and is regarded as a cornerstone of the country's "constitutional odyssey"[2] that was finally entrenched in 1982.[3] Two failed attempts at mega-constitutional reform – sweeping packages of amendments thought necessary by some actors in the aftermath of the 1982 agreement – have arguably had a chilling effect on political actors' willingness to engage in major constitutional change. More recently, two Supreme Court reference opinions expounded on the amending formula in the context of Senate reform[4] as well as the Court's own constitutional status.[5] This new jurisprudence makes certain changes to the constitutional order more difficult to accomplish than previously thought. Much doubt is also cast on the extent to which informal constitutional change remains a practicable option.[6]

* I would like to thank Paul Daly and Mary Liston for helpful comments on an earlier draft of this paper.

1 *Constitution Act, 1867* (UK), 30 & 31 Vict, c 3, reprinted in RSC 1985, App II, No 5.

2 Peter Russell, *Constitutional Odyssey: Can Canadians Become a Sovereign People?* (Toronto: University of Toronto Press, 2004).

3 *Constitution Act, 1982*, being Schedule B to the *Canada Act 1982* (UK), c 11.

4 *Reference re Senate Reform*, 2014 SCC 32 [2014] 1 SCR 704.

5 *Reference re Supreme Court Act, ss 5 and 6*, 2014 SCC 21 [2014] 1 SCR 433.

6 For an in-depth examination of issues surrounding constitutional amendment, see Emmett Macfarlane, ed. *Constitutional Amendment in Canada* (Toronto: University of Toronto Press, 2016).

This chapter examines the future of constitutional change in light of the constitution's 150-year history and this contemporary context. It is, in some ways, less optimistic about the flexibility that political actors enjoy to exercise discretion under the constitution than other contributions to this volume. For example, Wade K. Wright's chapter (see chapter 4) emphasizes the complementary role that the political branches of governments can play in constitutional interpretation, and his analysis focuses specifically on opportunities for provincial non-enforcement of constitutionally suspect federal criminal laws. Similarly, Mary Liston's chapter (see chapter 1) examines the power of the executive (including an acknowledgment of the relative deference that the judiciary gives to certain aspects of executive powers, like the exercise of prerogatives[7]).

I argue that the obstacles to achieving future constitutional change are daunting and that they derive from more than the amending formula itself. Two significant challenges confront Canada as it regards future constitutional change: the politics of federalism and the Supreme Court's recent jurisprudence. These obstacles represent a significant hindrance to maintaining the flexibility and vitality of Canada's constitutional order. The chapter then briefly examines possible ways that we Canadians might extricate ourselves from this constitutional straitjacket, including opportunities for informal constitutional change.

History

When the Dominion of Canada was created in 1867, the product of a confederation of the colonies of Canada (formerly Upper and Lower Canada), Nova Scotia, and New Brunswick, its principal written constitution was passed as an ordinary statute of the Parliament of the United Kingdom. That document, the *British North America Act* (*BNA Act*) of 1867, did not include a section outlining general procedures for amending the constitution. As Samuel LaSelva notes, the Confederation debates of 1865 contained almost no discussion of constitutional amendment.[8]

---

7 See also Philippe Lagassé, "Parliamentary and Judicial Ambivalence toward Executive Prerogative Power in Canada," *Canadian Public Administration* 55, no. 2 (2012) 157.

8 Samuel V. LaSelva, *The Moral Foundations of Canadian Federalism: Paradoxes, Achievements, and Tragedies of Nationhood* (Montreal and Kingston: McGill-Queen's University Press, 1996).

William Renwick Riddell, writing in 1919, suggests that the reason for the lack of an amending formula was that Lower Canada (Quebec) did not favour a straightforward super-majoritarian requirement that would allow English Canada to act without its consent.[9] Allowing the Imperial Parliament to enact amendments on the new country's behalf seemed logical, not only because of the strong colonial attachments to the United Kingdom among many of the Fathers of Confederation, but also because "no one feared that the Imperial Parliament would make any Amendment which was not desired by a practically unanimous Canada – French Canadians had and have the same implicit faith in the justice of the Home Parliament as English Canadians."[10] Riddell states that all parties to Confederation recognized the *BNA Act* as a compact and that "it would naturally follow that no change should be made in this compact without the consent of all the contracting parties."[11] While it is not clear whether all parties to Confederation shared this view with great confidence – indeed, as discussed below, a number of amendments would be passed by the Imperial Parliament without provincial consent – it is clear that there was little concern about the lack of a domestic amending formula in the new constitution. The notion that unanimous consent was required for all changes would be a source of conflict in discussions about constitutional amendment in Canada for most of its history.

A number of important amendments were passed by the UK Parliament. The *British North America Act* of 1871 created Manitoba and granted the Canadian Parliament the power to establish new provinces, administer territories, and alter provincial boundaries (with the consent of the relevant provincial legislature).[12] A 1915 amendment to senatorial divisions for Manitoba, Saskatchewan, Alberta, and British Columbia was made without provincial consultation, leading some scholars to conclude that "during this early period, there was no constitutional convention requiring the consultation of the provinces before a constitutional amendment, even when the amendment had a direct

9 William Renwick Riddell, "Constitutional Amendments in Canada," *Yale Law Journal* 28 (1919) 314.

10 *Ibid*, 317.

11 *Ibid*, 317–8.

12 Guy Favreau, *The Amendment of the Constitution of Canada* (Ottawa, February 1965), in *Canada's Constitution Act 1982 & Amendments: A Documentary History*, vol. 1, ed. Anne F. Bayefsky (Toronto: McGraw-Hill Ryerson, 1989), 25–6.

impact on provincial or regional interests."[13] A 1940 amendment, conducted after negotiations with the provinces, gave the federal government exclusive jurisdiction over unemployment insurance.[14]

Parliament was given new authority over constitutional amendments through the *British North America Act (No. 2)* of 1949, which inserted s. 91(1) into the *BNA Act*. The federal Parliament was free to make changes, with the exception of anything relating to provincial powers or rights, minority education, and languages. Until this time, only minimal changes to the original *BNA Act* could be made domestically. A handful of specific provisions authorized Parliament to make "housekeeping" changes to the Senate or House of Commons, such as increasing the number of members of Parliament (s. 52), establishing and changing electoral districts (s. 40), changing quorum in the Senate (s. 35), and amending the privileges and immunities of MPs (s. 18). Section 92(1) allowed provinces to make changes to provincial constitutions so long as these did not affect the lieutenant governor.[15] The 1949 changes broadening the scope of federal amending authority were made without provincial consent:

> The federal position was that provincial consent was unnecessary because the new amending power was of concern to the federal government alone and could not be used to affect provincial powers. The provinces rejected this justification and claimed that section 91(1) could nonetheless operate to permit the federal government to enact amendments that would indirectly affect provincial interests in the federation.[16]

In 1965, Parliament would use its new amending authority to impose a retirement age of 75 on senators, an issue that the Court would later address on separate occasions in two major reference opinions.[17]

The UK Parliament never refused to act on a request from Canada to pass an amendment (although there was substantial debate in the United Kingdom when Pierre Trudeau announced his intention to seek

13 Patrick J. Monahan and Byron Shaw, *Constitutional Law* (Toronto: Irwin Law, 2013), 176–7.

14 Favreau, *supra* note 12, 25–6.

15 Monahan and Shaw, *supra* note 13, 169–71.

16 *Ibid*, 171.

17 *Re: Authority of Parliament in relation to the Upper House*, [1980] 1 SCR 54; *Reference re Senate Reform*.

unilateral reform in the run-up to the 1982 patriation process), and it only ever acted to amend the constitution on Canada's request (notably, it would not act on a request of a province).[18] In David Smith's view, the role of the UK Parliament vis-à-vis Canadian constitutional amendment has reinforced the idea that it is a matter for lawyers and judges, and not the people. He writes, "If in Canada there is no sense of the people as a constituent power and if at the same time there is no sense of limits in the constitution, then part of the explanation is found in the remoteness of Westminster, which for so long played a central role in the development of the Canadian constitution."[19] Also reinforcing the remoteness of constitutional amendment, from the perspective of citizens, is the nature of the debate leading up to the 1982 agreement, conducted almost entirely in the context of intergovernmental meetings.

Widespread interest in the development of a home-grown amending formula did not emerge until the release of the Balfour Report in 1926, which declared the equality of the dominions and the United Kingdom (and which would be enshrined in the *Statute of Westminster, 1931*). It was recognized that to exercise meaningful independence and sovereignty, Canada needed full domestic control over changes to its own constitution. The history of Canada's attempts to reach agreement on a new amending formula has been well documented, so only a brief account is required in this paper.[20]

Attempts to develop amending procedures in a dominion-provincial conference in 1927 failed, as did later conferences in 1931, 1935, 1950, and 1960.[21] A 1964 proposal, the Fulton-Favreau formula, would have seen the unanimous consent of all provinces and the federal government required for any amendments affecting provincial jurisdiction, education, and the use of the French and English languages. If the matter affected some provinces but not others, only those affected needed to consent. Any other matters required the consent of two-thirds of the provinces representing at least 50 per cent of the population (the "7/50

18 *The Canadian Constitution and Constitutional Amendment* (Federal-Provincial Relations Office, 1978), in *Canada's Constitution Act 1982 & Amendments: A Documentary History*, vol. 1, ed. Anne F. Bayefsky (Toronto: McGraw-Hill Ryerson, 1989), 468.

19 David E. Smith, *Federalism and the Constitution of Canada* (Toronto: University of Toronto Press, 2010), 50.

20 For a more detailed examination, see Nadia Verrelli, "Searching for an Amending Formula: The 115-Year Journey," in *Constitutional Amendment in Canada*, ed. Emmett Macfarlane (Toronto: University of Toronto Press, 2016).

formula"). This latter procedure would become the general amending formula in the *Constitution Act, 1982*; however, at the time, Quebec withdrew its support for Fulton-Favreau because it regarded the unanimity requirements as too rigid and it feared that this would prevent major reforms (such as decentralization).[22]

The next major round of negotiations resulted in the Victoria Charter proposal of 1971, which was premised on regional considerations. Major changes would require agreement of the federal Parliament and a majority of provincial legislatures, including any provinces that, at any time, contained 25 per cent of the country's population (Ontario and Quebec), at least two Atlantic provinces, and at least two western provinces that, combined, had at least 50 per cent of the population of all the western provinces (meaning the support of Alberta or British Columbia would be required). As with the 1964 agreement, Quebec backed out, and its decision scuttled the deal. There were further attempts to negotiate a new constitutional package through the 1970s, but these proved unsuccessful.

The key issues regarding a new constitutional amending formula included a Quebec veto versus the principle of provincial equality, a provincial versus regional structure to the formula, and rigidity versus flexibility, which focused largely on how many issues would require unanimity versus some lower threshold. When negotiations failed again in 1980, Trudeau announced his intention to seek unilateral patriation of a new constitutional package, including a charter of rights and an amending formula. According to Webber, before 1980, "it was generally assumed that any formula should have the support of all, or virtually all, provinces."[23] Trudeau's resolution was referred to the courts of appeal in Manitoba, Newfoundland, and Quebec, which rendered opinions that were appealed to the Supreme Court in 1981; the Court issued a divided opinion that while, legally, the federal government could seek unilateral patriation, a convention existed that "a substantial degree of provincial consent" was required.[24] This compelled the parties back to the negotiation table.

21 *The Canadian Constitution and Constitutional Amendment, supra* note 18, 466–8.

22 Jeremy Webber, *Reimagining Canada: Language, Culture, Community, and the Canadian Constitution* (Montreal and Kingston: McGill-Queen's University Press, 1994), 94.

23 *Ibid*, 82.

24 *Re: Resolution to amend the Constitution*, [1981] 1 SCR 753.

By 1981, the provinces and federal government had staked out their positions. The Gang of Eight (provincial governments excluding Ontario and New Brunswick, which supported the federal government) favoured the 7/50 rule for most amendments, sought financial compensation for provinces that chose to opt out of amendments implicating provincial powers or rights, and argued for a limited number of issues requiring unanimity (the Crown, parliamentary representation, language, and the composition of the Supreme Court).[25] This agreement among the Gang of Eight came to be known as the "Vancouver formula," and it led from the principles articulated by Premier Lougheed of Alberta, which included provincial equality, no province having a veto, and the need for more than one method of amendment.[26] Significantly, Quebec signed on to the Vancouver formula, marking the first time it had abandoned its traditional claim of a veto over constitutional change.[27] As Webber notes, "the PQ government had effectively decided to trade the veto for opting out, even though there were many amendments (especially concerning the reform of central institutions) from which opting out was impossible."[28]

By contrast, the federal government was of the view that it was "inevitable" that Quebec get a veto.[29] The federal position also favoured the regionally based formula found in the Victoria Charter proposal (largely as a way of ensuring Quebec's veto). In November 1981, the federal government continued to advocate along these lines, but surrendered its position during final bargaining. The parties agreed to a revised version of the Vancouver formula, with some opt-out but without financial compensation, making Quebec's initial agreement to the Vancouver formula, in which it had abandoned its claim to a veto in

25 "Premiers' Conference, Ottawa, Ontario, April 16, 1981," in *Canada's Constitution Act 1982 & Amendments: A Documentary History*, vol. 2, ed. Anne F. Bayefsky (Toronto: McGraw-Hill Ryerson, 1989), 804.

26 "Federal-Provincial First Ministers' Conference, Ottawa, Ontario, February 5–6, 1979 – (a) 'Amending Formula for the Canadian Constitution, Alberta Proposal, Presented by Premier Lougheed,'" in *Canada's Constitution Act 1982 & Amendments: A Documentary History*, vol. 2, ed. Anne F. Bayefsky (Toronto: McGraw-Hill Ryerson, 1989), 556.

27 Webber, *supra* note 22, 110–1.

28 *Ibid*, 111.

29 Howard Leeson, *The Patriation Minutes* (Edmonton: Centre for Constitutional Studies, 2011), 22.

return for opting out with financial compensation, "fateful."[30] As Webber notes, some compensation for provinces opting out of changes to education or culture was later included as part of the final deal, but this was not enough to satisfy Quebec. The province famously rejected the agreement, but on the basis of the Supreme Court's articulation of the substantial provincial (as opposed to unanimous) consent requirement, the federal government and the other nine provinces proceeded with the package, resulting in the *Constitution Act, 1982*.

The final version of the amending formula contains five core procedures. The general or default procedure is the 7/50 rule. The unanimity procedure of s. 41 requires resolutions passed by the House of Commons and the Senate and the legislatures of all ten provinces in order to enact amendments in relation to several key issues, including changes to the office of the Queen, the governor general, or the lieutenant governor of a province; changes to minimum seat guarantees for provinces in the House of Commons; the use of the English or French language; the composition of the Supreme Court; and changes to the amending formula itself. The bilateral procedure of s. 43 allows for changes that affect one or more, but not all, provinces. Section 44 allows Parliament to make amendments in relation to the executive or the Senate and House of Commons. Finally, s. 45 allows individual provinces to make changes affecting their own constitutions.

The Politics of Federalism and Constitutional Change

A defining aspect of the impact of the 1982 constitutional package, and one that continues to act as a significant constraint on the prospects for future constitutional change in Canada, has been the fallout over Quebec's dissatisfaction. From Quebec's perspective, its lack of veto in the amending formula, coupled with the late-night compromise reached among the other parties (and to which it was not a party),[31] has meant a refusal to accept the constitutional status quo. Quebec even brought a reference to the Quebec Court of Appeal, appealed to the Supreme Court, on whether it had, by convention, a veto over major constitutional change. The Court's unanimous answer was no, in large part due

30 Webber, *supra* note 22, 114.

31 Many others have told the tale of the famed "kitchen accord." See Russell, *supra* note 2, 120–3.

to the fact that neither the federal government nor the other provinces had ever formally recognized such a veto.[32]

Doubts among some in Quebec and federalists elsewhere about the 1982 act's political legitimacy led to renewed attempts at constitutional change to accommodate Quebec or encourage Quebec to "sign on" to the 1982 act.[33] Efforts were made in the late 1980s and early 1990s by Prime Minister Brian Mulroney to pass new constitutional packages in an effort to satisfy Quebec's demands. A key component of both the Meech Lake and Charlottetown Accords was constitutionally entrenched recognition of Quebec's distinctiveness, but major institutional and other reforms were also part of the sweeping packages.

A discussion of the substantive content of the two accords is beyond the scope of this chapter, and they have been analysed at length elsewhere.[34] What is pertinent for the purposes of this analysis is the nature of their failure. With respect to Meech, two key issues relating to the process arose. The first was the closed nature of the negotiation process, conducted through executive federalism and largely without input from the public. First Nations leaders opposed the package as a direct consequence of their having been excluded from the process.[35] The public (outside Quebec) had input only after the amendment had been agreed upon by political leaders, and no changes were permissible.[36]

The second issue was the procedure for passing the package as an amendment. Although some of Meech Lake's provisions could be passed by the 7/50 rule, the entire agreement was to be passed as a single package, and so it was quickly determined that the unanimity procedure would be required. A complicating factor was the three-year period for ratification, with some suggesting that such a long term permitted "consensus to unravel: elections can and will occur, governments may change, partisan politics will continue, and extraneous issues and events may occur which, while legally unrelated to the

32 *Re: Objection by Quebec to a Resolution to amend the Constitution*, [1982] 2 SCR 793.

33 The language sometimes used in this regard risks implying not only that the *Constitution Act, 1982* suffers from a problem relating to its political or symbolic legitimacy but also that its *legal* legitimacy is questionable. As a matter of constitutional law, Quebec's refusal to sign the 1982 act does nothing to affect its legitimacy.

34 See, e.g., Russell, *supra* note 2; Webber, *supra* note 22.

35 Webber, *supra* note 22, 147.

36 Katherine Swinton, "Amending the Canadian Constitution: Lessons from Meech Lake," *University of Toronto Law Journal* 42, no. 2 (1992) 152.

amendment proposal, could reflect attitudes and derail the ratification process."[37] James Hurley notes that there is "nothing to prevent governments from reaching agreement on a much shorter ratification period," although there are risks with that if they are unsure about public consensus in support of the amendment.[38] Katherine Swinton notes that we can risk drawing too many lessons from a single failed reform, but three intervening elections during the ratification period (in New Brunswick, Manitoba, and Newfoundland) were likely significant, and two of them occurred in the first year of the process.[39] It cannot be too glib to note that obtaining unanimity in such a context – particularly when a divisive issue like a distinct society clause is at issue – is difficult.

The Charlottetown Accord was developed in the context of an even more expansive process and included a referendum on the final deal. Here, too, the idea of a distinct society clause for Quebec (embedded in a slightly more ambiguous "Canada Clause") proved divisive, although with such sweeping constitutional changes, ranging from Aboriginal self-government to Senate reform, it would be simplistic to peg any one item as the reason for the public's firm rejection of the deal. It is worth noting that a referendum procedure was included in draft versions of the amending formula during negotiations in 1981 and as part of the plan that Trudeau sought to unilaterally patriate.[40] Further, some commentators have argued that, after Charlottetown, a referendum was regarded as a requirement for future constitutional change and that any "Meech-like attempt at reform through pure executive federalism is now unthinkable."[41] It would go much too far to suggest the Charlottetown process has established a convention requiring popular consent for constitutional amendment; however, one of the predominant criticisms of Part V of the *Constitution Act, 1982* is that it treats amendment as the sole domain of governments and legislatures.

---

37 James Ross Hurley, *Amending Canada's Constitution: History, Processes, Problems and Prospects* (Ottawa: Minister of Supply and Services Canada, 1996), 163.

38 *Ibid.*

39 Swinton, *supra* note 36, 146.

40 "Proposed Resolution for a Joint Address to Her Majesty The Queen Respecting the Constitution of Canada, as Amended by the Committee (moved in the House February 17, 1981)," in *Canada's Constitution Act 1982 & Amendments: A Documentary History*, vol. 2, ed. Anne F. Bayefsky (Toronto: McGraw-Hill Ryerson, 1989).

41 Patrick James, *Constitutional Politics in Canada after the Charter: Liberalism, Communitarianism, and Systemism* (Vancouver: UBC Press, 2010), 101.

In the aftermath of the failure of Meech and Charlottetown, a 1995 referendum on Quebec sovereignty came within a sliver of succeeding, with voters rejecting the question by a margin of only 50.6 per cent to 49.4 per cent. The federal Liberal government's response to the close call included two things, with important implications for constitutional amendment in Canada. One was a reference posed to the Supreme Court on whether Quebec could secede from Canada unilaterally. In 1998, the Court rendered a controversial decision reminiscent of the *Patriation Reference* due to its reliance on unwritten principles of constitutionalism. In a unanimous opinion, the Court stated that neither Canada's constitutional law nor international law permitted Quebec to secede unilaterally, but added that in the event of a "clear majority" of Quebeckers expressing a desire for secession on a "clear question," the rest of Canada would have a duty to negotiate.[42]

Remarkably, the Court eschewed any specific analysis of the amending formula in Part V of the *Constitution Act, 1982* – indeed, no section in Part V is referred to, nor do the words "amending formula" or "Part V" appear in the opinion – for a focus on the principles of federalism, democracy, constitutionalism and the rule of law, and minority rights. The most pertinent passage of the opinion as it relates to the amending formula is as follows:

> It is of course true that the Constitution is silent as to the ability of a province to secede from Confederation but, although the Constitution neither expressly authorizes nor prohibits secession, an act of secession would purport to alter the governance of Canadian territory in a manner which undoubtedly is inconsistent with our current constitutional arrangements. The fact that those changes would be profound, or that they would purport to have a significance with respect to international law, does not negate their nature as amendments to the Constitution of Canada.[43]

The Court explicitly refused to state which procedure might effect secession, should negotiations ever commence.[44] It referred twelve times in its opinion to "the other provinces" as parties to theoretical negotiations along with the federal government and Quebec, never

42 *Reference re Secession of Quebec*, [1998] 2 SCR 217.
43 *Ibid*, para 84.
44 *Ibid*, para 105.

using the phrase "all parties" to imply unanimity or indicating any sort of threshold of provincial consensus.[45] However, most constitutional scholars expect that unanimity would be required.[46] Others note that it is not even clear whether Part V would ultimately apply given the force of the Court's unwritten principles.[47]

Following the Court's decision, the federal government passed the *Clarity Act*, which sets out the conditions by which Parliament would recognize the clarity of a question and of an expression of a clear majority of a province wishing to secede. It also indicates that a constitutional amendment would be required for any province to secede and that negotiations would involve "at least" all the provinces and the government of Canada.[48]

The federal government also passed the regional veto law, which prohibits federal government ministers from proposing constitutional resolutions unless consent is first obtained from Ontario, Quebec, British Columbia, at least two Atlantic provinces representing at least 50 per cent of the Atlantic populations, and at least two Prairie provinces representing at least 50 per cent of the Prairie populations (in effect, giving Alberta a veto).[49] The regional veto law effectively uses the federal government's inherent veto under most of Part V's amending procedures to establish a system of regional vetoes for constitutional amendment.[50] The law was passed to fulfil

---

45 The Court was also clear that the duty to negotiate did not translate into a legal entitlement to secession by Quebec; see *Reference re Secession of Quebec*, para 97. The Court attempted to reconcile this claim with its assertion, "The rights of other provinces and the federal government cannot deny the right of the government of Quebec to pursue secession, should a clear majority of the people of Quebec choose that goal, so long as in doing so, Quebec respects the rights of others," para 92. It is not clear that it succeeds.

46 See, e.g., Patrick Monahan, "The Law and Politics of Quebec Secession," *Osgoode Hall Law Journal* 33, no. 1 (1995) 1; Kate Puddister, "'The Most Radical Amendment of Them All': The Power to Secede and the Secession Reference," in *Constitutional Amendment in Canada*, ed. Emmett Macfarlane (Toronto: University of Toronto Press, 2016).

47 Donna Greschner, "The Quebec Secession Reference: Goodbye to Part V?," *Constitutional Forum* 10, no. 1 (1998) 19.

48 *An Act to give effect to the requirement for clarity as set out in the opinion of the Supreme Court of Canada in the Quebec Secession Reference*, SC 2000, c 26, ss 3(1).

49 *An Act respecting constitutional amendments* (SC 1996, c 1).

50 It would not appear to apply to certain amendments under s 38, where provinces can opt out, and presumably not to those that require only the federal government acting alone; see Monahan and Shaw, *supra* note 13, 217.

the government's commitment to Quebec federalists, but by giving Ontario, British Columbia, and (in effect) Alberta a veto, it makes future constitutional reform – including reform desired by Quebec federalists – considerably more difficult.[51]

It remains a matter of debate whether the amending formula achieves the appropriate balance between rigidity and flexibility from a normative perspective, although it is undeniable that its structure makes Canada's one of the most difficult constitutions in the world to formally amend. Significantly compounding this difficulty is the context of intergovernmental relations and federalism described here, in addition to what Richard Albert has described as "extra-textual restrictions on formal amendment," including the regional veto law and populist measures in British Columbia and Alberta requiring binding referenda before their respective provincial legislatures can pass amending resolutions.[52]

The long-standing position of successive Quebec governments on major constitutional change is perhaps the most difficult obstacle to future reform. Quebec will not accede to major constitutional changes absent the inclusion of either more power or autonomy for the province or the entrenchment of recognition of its distinct society, something the current premier, Philippe Couillard, has reiterated in the context of Senate reform.[53] Canada thus faces not only the normal challenge many federal countries face of obtaining substantial – in some contexts, unanimous – consent from its sub-national units to achieve significant constitutional change but also the second largest of its sub-national units refusing to consider virtually any change without support for its unique demands. The fact that previous efforts to deal with Quebec's demands arguably led to the near break-up of the country in 1995 adds to the dilemma; most political actors have demonstrated an unwillingness to entertain the thought of intergovernmental negotiations over broad-based packages of constitutional reform ever since.

---

51 Monahan and Shaw, *Ibid.*

52 Richard Albert, "The Difficulty of Constitutional Amendment in Canada," *Alberta Law Review* 53, no. 1 (2015) 85.

53 Joan Bryden, "PM Disappointed, but Will Heed SCC on Senate Reform," CTV News, 25 April 2014, accessed 1 November 2015, http://www.ctvnews.ca/politics/pm-disappointed-but-will-heed-scc-on-senate-reform-1.1792243.

Jurisprudence

In 2014, in two separate cases, the Supreme Court addressed substantive provisions of the 1982 amending formula for the first time. This jurisprudence has significant implications for both the balance and the dividing line among the various amending procedures in Part V and, from a practical perspective, the level of consensus required for certain types of reform. Both cases make clear that the Supreme Court's interpretation of Part V can have the important effect of raising the threshold required to achieve constitutional amendments. In contrast to other areas of executive and legislative authority, such as those explored in this volume by Wright and Liston, in the context of constitutional amendment, judicial decisions act as a significant constraint. If matters falling under the unanimity or general amending procedures are given a broader interpretation (relative to Parliament's authority for unilateral amendment under s. 44, for example), then the constitutional amending formula may be even more rigid than previously thought.

The Supreme Court Act Reference

Controversy erupted in 2013 when then prime minister Stephen Harper selected Federal Court judge Marc Nadon to fill one of the three Supreme Court seats designated by law for Quebec. Section 6 of the *Supreme Court Act*,[54] which outlines specific eligibility requirements for Quebec seats on the Court, states that they "shall be appointed from among the judges of the Court of Appeal or of the Superior Court of the Province of Quebec or from among the advocates of that Province." Complicating the interpretation of the eligibility requirements is the general application of s. 5 of the act, which specifies that eligibility requires "at least" ten years' standing at the bar of a province. The lack of explicit reference to the Federal Court or Federal Court of Appeal in s. 6 suggested that judges from those benches might not be eligible unless it was assumed that the phrase "or from among the advocates of that Province" was not limited to *current* advocates and that it should be read in tandem with the general requirement in s. 5 of at least ten years of experience.

54 RSC, 1985, c S-26.

When the issue was referred to the Court, the federal government also asked whether Parliament had the authority to amend the provisions relating to eligibility in the *Supreme Court Act* (or insert declaratory provisions ensuring its preferred interpretation, as it had attempted to do). The key issue here was whether eligibility requirements in the act fell under "composition of the Supreme Court" under s. 41(d) of Part V of the *Constitution Act, 1982* and would therefore require the unanimous consent of the provinces.

Until this point, the constitutional status of the Supreme Court had itself been an open question among constitutional experts. The Court was created by ordinary statute in 1875, as authorized by s. 101 of the *Constitution Act, 1867*. When provisions relating to the Supreme Court were included in the amending formula in the *Constitution Act, 1982*, some scholars believed that they were limited by the fact that the "Constitution of Canada" as defined in s. 52(2) did not include the *Supreme Court Act*. Hogg, for example, writes that the "amending procedures are not required for the amendment of statutes or instruments that are not part of the Constitution of Canada; anything that is not part of the Constitution of Canada can be amended by the ordinary action of the competent legislative body."[55] Hogg's contention was that future amendments to the constitution (such as those proposed in the Meech and Charlottetown processes) would see the Court formally entrenched, at which point the relevant provisions in the amending formula would become operative. Other scholars disagreed.[56]

The key issue for the Court was how broadly to interpret "composition of the Supreme Court," from two perspectives: whether eligibility requirements were essential features of the Court, and should thus be included in the *Constitution Act, 1982*, and whether the *Supreme Court Act* was effectively part of the constitution. In a 6–1 opinion, the Court determined that Federal Court judges were not eligible under the s. 6 requirements, firmly establishing the importance of preserving up-to-date knowledge of Quebec's civil law system for the three seats on the Court reserved for that province. Moreover, the majority determined that any changes to these requirements required the unanimous consent of the provinces under s. 41(d):

55 Peter W. Hogg, *Constitutional Law of Canada* (Scarborough, ON: Thomson Canada, 2003), 73.

56 Monahan and Shaw, *supra* note 13, 191; Stephen A. Scott, "Pussycat, Pussycat or Patriation and the New Constitutional Amendment Process," *University of Western Ontario Law Review* 20, no. 2 (1982) 272.

> Requiring unanimity for changes to the composition of the Court gave Quebec constitutional assurance that changes to its representation on the Court would not be effected without its consent. Protecting the composition of the Court under s. 41(*d*) was necessary because leaving its protection to s. 42(1)(*d*) would have left open the possibility that Quebec's seats on the Court could have been reduced or altogether removed without Quebec's agreement.[57]

The Court also noted that a general reference to the Supreme Court of Canada under the general amending formula in s. 42(d) related to the Court's "essential features" rather than to all the provisions of the *Supreme Court Act*. Without elaborating in great detail, the majority noted that "these essential features include, at the very least, the Court's jurisdiction as the final general court of appeal for Canada, including in matters of constitutional interpretation, and its independence."[58]

The Court's decision to include eligibility requirements as part of "composition" is certainly broader than what might be the narrowest (but still plausible) reading, which would be limited to the number of justices on the Court and, perhaps, the designation of three seats for Quebec. This is not to say that the Court necessarily read s. 41(d) too broadly. Nevertheless, the interpretation has an important consequence for future Supreme Court reform, including the standing policy of the federal Liberal Party and New Democratic Party in favour of instituting mandatory bilingualism for Supreme Court judges. It is apparent that inserting a new eligibility requirement like that one – especially one that departs from past practice, given the many unilingual judges who have served in recent history and the fact that at least one of the current judges remains unilingual – now requires a constitutional amendment through the unanimity procedure under s. 41.[59] Indeed, it would be

---

57 *Reference re Supreme Court Act*, *supra* note 5, para 93.

58 *Ibid*, para 94.

59 For a dissenting view on this, see Hugo Cyr, "The Bungling of Justice Nadon's Appointment to the Supreme Court of Canada," *Supreme Court Law Review* 67 (2014) 73, 105. Cyr's view is that a bilingualism requirement would reflect legitimate capacity requirements (like mental competency or criminal innocence). He goes so far as to say that a linguistic requirement "may already be present in the Constitution." I am of the view that imposing a formal bilingualism requirement would constitute the addition of a new eligibility requirement that is distinct from unstated requirements like mental competency because it would, in fact, be a departure from past practice, where unilingual judges have often been appointed to the Court.

very difficult to logically distinguish between altering existing eligibility requirements and inserting new ones for the purposes of including eligibility as an element of "composition" in Part V. It is possible that this is an unintended consequence of the Court's opinion; regardless, the effect is to make future reform in some contexts extremely difficult.

The Senate Reform Reference

Following failed efforts in Parliament to pass a long-promised bill implementing consultative elections for the Senate and term limits for senators, the Conservative government referred to the Court a series of questions about whether Parliament had the authority to make such changes unilaterally or whether provincial consent under the general amending procedure was required. The Court was also asked whether abolition of the Senate could be accomplished using the general procedure or required unanimity.

Section 42(1)(b) of the *Constitution Act, 1982* requires that changes to "the powers of the Senate and the method of selecting Senators" be made according to the general amending procedure. The federal government argued that, under the proposed consultative elections, the prime minister would retain ultimate discretion to make the final appointment (formally by advising the governor general); hence, the reform would not constitute a formal change to the method of selection. The Court dismissed this argument, noting that the very purpose of implementing consultative elections was "to bring about a Senate with a popular mandate. We cannot assume that future prime ministers will defeat this purpose by ignoring the results of costly and hard-fought consultative elections."[60]

In determining that bringing in consultative elections would constitute a change to the method of selecting senators, the justices thus pointed to two elements: first, such a change in the selection process would be likely to bind future prime ministers to the new process; and second, the reform itself would alter the very nature of the Senate. The Court's opinion, however, lacked clarity on both points.[61] Most important, it was not clear whether the presence of *either* of these potential

60 *Reference re Senate Reform, supra* note 4, para 62.

61 For a more detailed critique of the reference, see Emmett Macfarlane, "Unsteady Architecture: Ambiguity, the Senate Reference, and the Future of Constitutional Amendment in Canada," *McGill Law Journal* 60, no. 4 (2015) 883.

factors mandated recourse to the general amending formula or *both*. In the justices' view, after all, the democratic mandate itself was what would effectively bind future prime ministers to appointing senatorial candidates who won an election. But the Court's emphasis on the democratic nature of the proposed reform risks obscuring the nearly unfettered discretion that prime ministers have historically enjoyed to alter the front end of the senatorial selection process. Until now, prime ministers have theoretically been free to collect names for selection by consulting whatever source they wished, be it partisan staff in the Prime Minister's Office, Cabinet colleagues, the list of recipients of the Order of Canada, or by flipping a coin. It would seem an absurdity if the prime minister were free to consult with whomever he or she wished except members of the public.

As it relates to consultative elections, then, it would seem that the combination of formality – the proposed process would have been set out in legislation – and a change that would alter the "constitutional architecture"[62] or nature of the Senate would, in the Court's view, indirectly but in practice bind the prime minister and therefore constitute a change to the "method" of selection and generate a requirement for provincial consent under the amending formula. It is much less clear whether other potential changes to the senatorial selection process would generate the same requirement. Prime Minister Justin Trudeau has introduced a new merit-based, non-partisan process to advise him in filling Senate vacancies.[63] Implementing such a change by statute might be seen as an attempt to bind future prime ministers, but the prime minister is free to appoint a committee informally.[64] Nevertheless, the goal of the change is to increase the legitimacy of the Senate.

Would reducing patronage and altering the partisan nature of the Senate constitute a fundamental change to the constitutional architecture?

---

62 The Court explains that the constitution's basic internal structure, or architecture, reflects the fact that its individual elements are linked; see *Reference re Senate Reform*, *supra* note 4, para 26. Importantly, changes to the constitution's architecture are not limited to textual changes to the written constitution, as the Court states, para 27.

63 I was asked by the Liberal Party to advise it on the constitutionality of this proposal in 2014. Following the 2015 election, I was asked by the transition team to develop a proposal for a new process and an advisory committee that would recommend names to the prime minister for appointment. This advisory committee was established in early 2016.

64 At the time of this writing, no one has launched a legal challenge questioning the legitimacy of the reform.

Senators whose appointment was the product of a "merit-based" process might be regarded with greater legitimacy in the eyes of the public, something that could conceivably alter their behaviour. Further, if the current prime minister is successful in effecting some change along these lines, he might establish a new convention surrounding appointments, thus indirectly binding future prime ministers to this new advisory process. It is not clear that prime ministers would be any more likely to ignore the recommendations of an independent advisory body than they would the results of a consultative election.[65] The Court's opinion in the Senate reform reference fails to provide any guidance about whether such a change might require recourse to the formal amending procedure.

The Court also found that instituting term limits for senators would require provincial consent under the general amending procedure. Term limits, unlike the method of selecting senators, are not mentioned in the amending formula, and the government argued that Parliament enjoyed the authority to implement them under s. 44, which permitted it to "exclusively make laws in relation to the executive government of Canada or the Senate and House of Commons." The justices responded that any changes affecting the "fundamental nature or role" of the Senate required provincial consent under the general procedure.[66]

There is little question that short term limits or renewable terms could significantly alter the role and behaviour of individual senators, either by transforming an appointment that has traditionally come at the end of an individual's working life into a mid-career stint or, in the case of renewable terms, making senators compliant or beholden to the wishes of the prime minister. Less clear, however, is why lengthy, non-renewable terms would affect the role of senators or the Senate itself. In fact, the justices appear to acknowledge this dilemma, noting,

> [i]t may be possible, as the Attorney General of Canada suggests, to devise a fixed term so lengthy that it provides a security of tenure which is functionally equivalent to that provided by life tenure. However, it is difficult to objectively identify the precise term duration that guarantees an equivalent degree of security of tenure.[67]

65 I have advised the government that the prime minister is free to make such changes so long as they are informal (not implemented by legislation) and there is no attempt to alter the essential features of the Senate (individual senators are free to organize how they wish by joining an existing Senate caucus or party affiliation, etc.).

66 *Reference re Senate Reform*, *supra* note 4, para 78.

67 *Ibid*, para 81.

The justices' refusal to engage in the line-drawing exercise is problematic, both because of the fact that line drawing is precisely what was being asked of them and also because they refused to explain why Parliament was free to enact a mandatory retirement age unilaterally (something affirmed by the Court in the 1980 Upper House reference and acknowledged by the Court in the 2014 reference),[68] but not lengthy term limits. Further, a term limit of twelve to fifteen years would be consistent with the average term length that senators have historically enjoyed in practice.[69] The failure of the Court's reasoning on term limits raises the question whether s. 44, which should permit Parliament to make certain changes to its two houses or the executive, has been unreasonably limited. Indeed, the Court's narrow reading of s. 44 and the lack of clarity embedded in the constitutional architecture concept has already raised uncertainty in the context of electoral reform, leading to claims from some commentators that Parliament may not be free to enact electoral reform without provincial consent.[70]

The Future of Constitutional Change

The politics of constitutionalism and federalism in Canada, coupled with recent Supreme Court jurisprudence on the amending formula, raises the prospect of a constitutional paralysis. In this final section, I will briefly argue that the potential for significant constitutional change will depend on one of three things: political leadership capable of navigating the extremely difficult politics of federalism involved, an ability to find informal methods of reform in a context in which the Court's jurisprudence seems to hamper or cloud when and whether such informal changes are permissible, or an exogenous shock involving a particular aspect of the constitution that effectively makes an amendment compulsory.

68 *Re: Upper House*, *supra* note 17, 77.

69 See Macfarlane, *supra* note 61, 895–8.

70 Michael Pal, "Why Canada's Top Court Must Weigh In on Electoral Reform," *Globe and Mail*, 15 January 2016, http://www.theglobeandmail.com/opinion/why-canadas-top-court-must-weigh-in-on-electoral-reform/article28198932/. For an in-depth examination of why Parliament is free to implement electoral reform, see Emmett Macfarlane, "Constitutional Constraints on Electoral Reform in Canada: Why Parliament Is (Mostly) Free to Implement a New Voting System," *Supreme Court Law Review* 76 (2016) 375.

The climate of Canadian constitutional politics makes it apparent that sweeping packages of broad-based reform are unlikely to succeed. It is Canada's history of mega-constitutional politics that, to some extent, obscures the fact that major constitutional change might be implemented on an issue-by-issue basis, rather than as the product of comprehensive intergovernmental negotiations like those in Meech or Charlottetown. Indeed, any of the eleven partners of Confederation listed as actors under the general amending procedure can pass a resolution in their legislature and call on the others for a vote on the same. Any legislature that refused to consider even voting on a resolution would need to justify that to its constituents. Political will to attempt to deliver change on specific measures should not be so difficult to find.

Yet even targeted reform measures still face the political and institutional roadblocks described above. One of these – the federal regional veto act – is perhaps much easier to dispense with in the aftermath of the reference on Senate reform. By the Court's logic, any attempt to alter the constitutional architecture without recourse to formal amendment is impermissible. As described in the previous section, the regional veto act effectively acts as a unilateral amendment by Parliament to the amending formula itself. The law binds future governments to a regionally based formula not contemplated by the existing constitutional text, which can be altered only using the unanimity procedure, as stated in s. 41(e). In effect, the regional veto act ought to be regarded as unconstitutional.[71] Even if it is not found to be unconstitutional, the act sets rules only for when ministers can introduce resolutions; any other MP is thus free to initiate a resolution. In this respect, the regional veto act is less of a hindrance than might otherwise be thought.

The most significant obstacle to single-issue constitutional reform remains Quebec, where political leaders have consistently insisted that they will not support amendments absent the consideration of a distinct society clause or increased powers for the province. Formally, this presents a real constraint only on amendments that require unanimity. If Quebec refuses to take part in constitutional change that requires only the general amending procedure's 7/50 rule, Canada's other political leaders need to consider whether they are willing to pay the price of constitutional stasis in contexts where broad consensus exists about desired changes simply because a single province objects.

71 A number of constitutional experts adopted this position at the time the bill was being debated; see Rainer Knopff, "U2: Unanimity vs. Unilateralism in Canada's Politics of Constitutional Amendment," in *Constitutional Amendment in Canada*, ed. Emmett Macfarlane (Toronto: University of Toronto Press, 2016).

Given the lack of consensus over Quebec's long-standing demands, particularly the entrenchment of a distinct society clause, everything from adding rights to the *Canadian Charter of Rights and Freedoms* to relatively minor changes like senatorial term limits are off the table unless the other partners of Confederation are willing to act without Quebec. Some might argue that doing so would risk inflaming the alienation that some Quebeckers feel from the Canadian constitution. Yet there is evidence that this elite-level political resentment over the 1982 deal does not necessarily translate to the average Quebec voter. For example, public opinion polls have shown that the Canadian *Charter* is more popular in Quebec than in any other province.[72] Moreover, a willingness evinced by the rest of Canada to engage in issue-specific constitutional change might by itself generate pressure on Quebec's political leadership to engage in good faith; once certain constitutional changes become feasible, the rest of Canada might be more willing to consider and negotiate the difficult constitutional matters that the country has debated in the past.

Political leadership may not be sufficient to overcome the politics of constitutionalism in Canada. Even if political leaders were willing to propose resolutions on specific matters without entering into broader negotiations, and to dispense with the regional veto act requirements, they would still need to confront the general expectation for popular input into constitutional change. While the Charlottetown referendum has not necessarily created a precedent, policies in British Columbia and Alberta requiring their own votes before the introduction of resolutions in those provincial legislatures are another hurdle. Further, where s. 35.1 of the *Constitution Act, 1982* entrenches a "principle" of consultation with representatives of the Aboriginal population on constitutional changes directly affecting them,[73] a broader political understanding might require consultation with Canada's Indigenous peoples before *any* major constitutional changes were contemplated.[74]

---

72 Canwest News Service, "Canadians Love Their Charter of Rights and Freedoms – Even If They Don't Know Much about It," *Canada.com*, 15 April 2007, accessed 3 November, 2015, http://www.canada.com/story_print.html?id=a2c727e4-2767-485b-aff3-5271f4d8b86c.

73 The principle specifically applies to Class 24 of s 91 of the *Constitution Act, 1867* and s 25 and Part II of the *Constitution Act, 1982*.

74 Christa Scholtz, "Part II and Part V: Aboriginal Peoples and Constitutional Amendment," in *Constitutional Amendment in Canada*, ed. Emmett Macfarlane (Toronto: University of Toronto Press, 2016).

These political constraints are considerable, but not necessarily insurmountable. Failure to achieve formal amendment is not the end of the discussion, however. In certain contexts, informal changes might be implemented. The changes implemented by the federal Liberal government in the senatorial selection process, as described in the preceding section, might be one example. Another example pertains to establishing new eligibility criteria for Supreme Court justices. As noted above, the Court's opinion in the Supreme Court Act reference determined that statutory changes to the eligibility criteria fell under the "composition of the Supreme Court" under s. 41 and thus required recourse to the unanimity procedure. Adding a bilingualism requirement to the act is now an unlikely prospect, and it is something that few would have considered Parliament unable to accomplish unilaterally before the reference. Yet the prime minister is not prohibited from simply exercising his discretion – as Justin Trudeau has announced – to appoint bilingual justices to the Court to the exclusion of unilingual ones. Indeed, a long enough record of bilingual appointments and selecting unilingual candidates for the Court could soon be regarded as contrary to conventional practice.

It is clear that the Court's recent jurisprudence makes informal amendment considerably more difficult, particularly if attempts are made to implement changes by statute.[75] Nevertheless, Warren Newman argues that, even in the context of statutes, informal changes to the constitution are permissible so long as they are compatible with, or enhance, the existing constitutional text.[76] In this sense, then, there may remain much flexibility for Parliament to enact amendments under s. 44, or provinces under s. 45, than is apparent following the Court's two 2014 references. Newman points to the *Official Languages Act*, the *Multiculturalism Act*, and the *Clarity Act* as examples of quasi-constitutional, or "organic," legislative amendments to the constitution.[77] Similarly, there might be several "residual aspects" of the Crown, which Parliament or a provincial legislature might change using the unilateral procedures, that do not fundamentally alter the office of the Queen, governor general, or

75 Dennis Baker and Mark D. Jarvis, "The End of Informal Constitutional Change in Canada?," in *Constitutional Amendment in Canada*, ed. Emmett Macfarlane (Toronto: University of Toronto Press, 2016).

76 Warren J. Newman, "Constitutional Amendment by Legislation," in *Constitutional Amendment in Canada*, ed. Emmett Macfarlane (Toronto: University of Toronto Press, 2016).

77 *Ibid*.

lieutenant governor, but that are nonetheless important, such as certain aspects of first ministers' appointing powers.[78]

Finally, another context is one in which formal amendment becomes a necessity following a precipitating event beyond the control of elected actors. One example of this might be judicial decisions. A court challenge heard in 2015 to the Canadian *Succession to the Throne Act, 2013*, which was passed by Parliament following agreement among Commonwealth countries that a first-born could become monarch regardless of gender,[79] was predicated on the argument that provinces should have been consulted.[80] The rules of succession may implicate the office of the Queen and therefore require a formal amendment under s. 41(a) of the unanimity procedure. If the challenge had been successful, Canada could have been compelled to enact a formal amendment or risk, one day, having a different person succeed to the throne than the rest of the Commonwealth. To remain with the example of the Crown, a more dramatic exogenous shock would occur if the United Kingdom decided to abolish the monarchy altogether, something that would compel certain textual changes to the Canadian constitution under the same procedure.

This brief outline of possible ways forward to confront what Richard Albert has called the "constructive unamendability" of the constitution is not intended to be comprehensive.[81] After 150 years, the challenges and complexity of constitutional change in Canada are, perhaps, at their most daunting. The amending formula, its interpretation by the Court, and the politics of federalism conspire to act as a constitutional straitjacket. Yet it is important to remember that to the extent that this straitjacket threatens a constitutional stasis, it is neither absolute nor inevitable; it simply remains to be seen whether the political will, leadership, and creativity exist to escape its confines.

---

78 Philippe Lagassé and Patrick Baud, "The Crown and Constitutional Amendment after the Senate Reform and Supreme Court References," in *Constitutional Amendment in Canada*, ed. Emmett Macfarlane (Toronto: University of Toronto Press, 2016).

79 It should probably have recognized the distinction as one relating to sex or gender rather than just gender, but this language is consistent with legislation passed in the other Commonwealth realms.

80 Carmel Kilkenny, "Quebec Challenge to Britain's Line of Succession," *Radio Canada International*, 15 June 2015, http://www.rcinet.ca/en/2015/06/15/quebec-challenge-to-britains-line-of-succession/.

81 Richard Albert, "Constructive Unamendability in Canada and the United States," *Supreme Court Law Review* (2d) 67 (2014) 181.

3 Section 96: Striking a Balance between Legal Centralism and Legal Pluralism

PAUL DALY*

Introduction: Judicial Exegesis

The subject of this paper is s. 96 of the *Constitution Act, 1867*, but its objectives go beyond this provision to satisfy the broader ambitions of this collection.

First, although my focus is on judicial doctrine, it is not limited to the field of constitutional (or even public) law; it also captures private law and civil procedure. Drawing lessons from these fields illuminates important aspects of the s. 96 jurisprudence. More generally, it could be said that my approach eschews the typical divide between public and private law.

Second, my analysis of s. 96, by establishing what David Milward describes as "legal space" for interpretive and institutional pluralism, supports the legitimacy of the approaches developed by some of my fellow contributors. In particular, Asha Kaushal argues in favour of a federalism that would enhance the autonomy of minority communities, and Milward makes a forthright case for Aboriginal self-government (a rallying cry to which Kaushal also responds), while Howard Kislowicz disapproves of Ontario legislation that restricts individuals' ability to arbitrate differences by reference to religious standards.[1] My account of s. 96, an account that draws on sources from public and private law, can be seen as opening up some of the possibilities discussed in these contributions. And in many ways,

* Senior Lecturer in Public Law, University of Cambridge, and Derek Bowett Fellow in Law, Queens' College, Cambridge. Particular thanks go to Mary Liston and Emmett Macfarlane for comments and to Melissa Miraula for research assistance.

1 See Asha Kaushal, chap 7 in this volume; David Milward, chap 9; and Howard Kislowicz, chap 6.

my account builds, from a contemporary perspective, on Harry Arthurs's groundbreaking historical work on legal pluralism.[2] At the same time, legal space does not mean a legal black hole; as I suggest, courts retain an important role, not just in policing the boundaries of interpretive and institutional pluralism but also in ensuring that what goes on inside the legal space is consistent with fundamental legal values.

Section 96 seems innocuous – an "uninstructed reading of the section itself" reveals little[3] – providing simply that judges of the superior courts (and the now-defunct district and county courts) are to be appointed by the federal executive.[4] Quite what the drafters hoped to achieve remains obscure. The conventional explanation is that they wished to "secure the impartiality and the independence of the Provincial Judiciary,"[5] but it is difficult to see how this would be compromised by provincial rather than federal appointment of superior court judges.[6]

Other justifications have also been offered over the years.[7] Federal appointment was considered to be merit-based, meaning that judges would be those who "could best be relied upon to administer justice according to law."[8] Less loftily, s. 96 might simply have been a means of ensuring that the federal government contributed financially to the running of the courts[9] or a recognition of the fact that

---

2 Harry Arthurs, *Without the Law: Administrative Justice and Legal Pluralism in Nineteenth Century England* (Toronto: University of Toronto Press, 1985) [Arthurs, *Without the Law*].

3 John Willis, "Section 96 of the British North America Act," *Canadian Bar Review* 18 (1940) 517, 518 [Willis, "Section 96"].

4 "The Governor General shall appoint the Judges of the Superior, District, and County Courts in each Province, except those of the Courts of Probate in Nova Scotia and New Brunswick." By constitutional convention, the governor general acts on the advice of the federal executive.

5 *O. Martineau and Sons Limited v City of Montreal*, [1932] AC 113, 121, Lord Blanesburgh [*O. Martineau*].

6 Peter W. Hogg, "Is Judicial Review of Administrative Action Guaranteed by the British North America Act?," *Canadian Bar Review* 59 (1976) 716, 716 [Hogg, "Administrative Action"].

7 See, generally, Gilles Pépin, *Les tribunaux administratifs et la Constitution: Étude des articles 96 à 101 de l'A.A.N.B.* (Montreal: Les Presses de l'Université de Montréal, 1969), 78–81.

8 *Kazakewich v Kazakewich* (1937), 1 DLR 548 (Alta CA), 573, McGillivray JA.

9 *Re Small Debts Recovery Act* (1917), 37 DLR 170 (Alta SC), 176, Harvey CJ; *Renvoi concernant la constitutionnalité de la loi concernant la juridiction de la Cour de magistrat*, [1965] BR 1, 21, Choquette JA.

the superior courts had a role to play in applying federal *and* provincial legislation,[10] providing a "strong constitutional base for national unity, through a unitary judicial system."[11]

Given that s. 96 and related provisions "n'ont guère retenu l'attention des représentants du peuple,"[12] it is hardly surprising that the objectives of the Fathers of Confederation have never provided clear guidance to those charged with interpreting s. 96. One thing can be said with certainty, however: what was considered to be a provision of "merely trifling importance"[13] has since been embellished with a "judicially-nourished luxuriance"[14] and become an imposing feature of Canada's constitutional landscape. Indeed, s. 96 has been described as a "cardinal provision,"[15] one of the "principal pillars in the temple of justice" that legislatures may not undermine.[16]

Doctrinally, the importance of s. 96 has acted as a brake on provincial legislation creating new decision-making bodies or conferring new powers on existing bodies. While the provinces have broad authority under s. 92(14) with respect to the "administration of justice" and the "organization of provincial courts," a moment's reflection on the seemingly innocuous s. 96 reveals an important potential problem: what if a legislature purports to create or increase the powers of a body that is similar in nature to a superior court, but whose members are not appointed in conformity with s. 96? Without tracing the tortuous history of the judicial treatment of this question,[17] Canadian courts have consistently held that the "broader import" of s. 96 "is to guarantee the core jurisdiction of

10 *Valin v Langlois* (1879), 3 SCR 1, 46, Fournier J; *Toronto Corporation v York Corporation*, [1937] OR 177 (Ont CA), 181, Rowell CJ. See also T.A. Cromwell, "Aspects of Constitutional Judicial Review in Canada," *South Carolina Law Review* 46 (1994–95) 1027, 1028–9.

11 *Re Residential Tenancies Act, 1979*, [1981] 1 SCR 714, 728, Dickson J [*Re Residential*]. See also *Renvoi sur l'article 98 de la Loi constitutionnelle de 1867 (Dans l'affaire du)*, 2014 QCCA 2365, para 49.

12 Pépin, *supra* note 6, 81.

13 John Willis, "Administrative Law and the British North America Act," *Harvard Law Review* 53 (1939–40) 251, 266.

14 Bora Laskin, "Municipal Tax Assessment and Section 96 of the British North America Act: The Olympia Bowling Alleys Case," *Canadian Bar Review* 33 (1955) 993, 993.

15 *O. Martineau*, *supra* note 4, 120 (PC), Lord Blanesburgh.

16 *Toronto Corporation v York Corporation*, [1938] AC 415, 426 (PC), Lord Atkin.

17 The leading text remains Pépin, *supra* note 6, while Willis, "Section 96," *supra* note 3, 517 is also clear and comprehensive.

provincial superior courts"[18] against incursions by the provinces: "The doctrine which the courts have developed is that a province is not permitted to evade s. 96 by investing a tribunal with jurisdiction of a kind which ought properly to be exercised by a superior, district or county court, and by calling that body an inferior court or an administrative tribunal."[19] For a long time, it was thought that s. 96 fettered only the ability of provincial legislatures to pass laws for the administration of justice, but it is now clear that it applies to Parliament as well.[20]

A remarkable recent example of the transformation of an appointing provision to a cornerstone of the Canadian constitutional order is the majority decision of the Supreme Court of Canada in *Trial Lawyers Association of British Columbia v British Columbia (Attorney General)*.[21] At issue were hearing fees prescribed by the province of British Columbia so that litigants would defray some of the costs of trial. The first three days were free, but the fees rapidly escalated thereafter. A ten-day trial would cost $3,600. McLachlin CJ took the view that these elevated hearing fees were unconstitutional.

Plainly, a province has the competence by virtue of its authority over the administration of justice to provide for such fees. How, then, was McLachlin CJ able to conclude nonetheless that the British Columbia regime was unconstitutional? The answer is to be found in the ongoing judicial exegesis of s. 96.[22]

The provincial competence to prescribe fees "does not operate in isolation"; rather, its "ambit must be determined, not only by reference to its bare wording, but with respect to other powers conferred by the Constitution," here s. 96.[23] Indeed, the provincial competence was narrowed down not just by other *express* terms of the constitution but also by elements *necessarily implicit* in the constitution's structure.[24]

---

18 *Trial Lawyers Association of British Columbia v British Columbia (Attorney General)*, 2014 SCC 59, para 29, [2014] 3 SCR 31, McLachlin CJC [*Trial Lawyers Association*]. See also *Alliance des professeurs catholiques de Montréal v Quebec Labour Relations Board*, [1953] 2 SCR 140, 155, Rinfret CJ.

19 Hogg, "Administrative Action," *supra* note 6, 717.

20 *MacMillan Bloedel Ltd. v Simpson*, [1995] 4 SCR 725 [*MacMillan*].

21 *Trial Lawyers Association*, *supra* note 18.

22 See also Benjamin J. Oliphant, "Taking Purposes Seriously: The Purposive Scope and Textual Bounds of Interpretation under the Canadian Charter of Rights and Freedoms," *University of Toronto Law Journal* 65 (2015) 239.

23 *Trial Lawyers Association*, *supra* note 18, para 25.

24 *Ibid*, para 26, citing *British Columbia v Imperial Tobacco Canada Ltd.*, 2005 SCC 49, para 66, [2005] 2 SCR 473, Major J; and *Reference re Senate Reform*, 2014 SCC 32, para 26, [2014] 1 SCR 704.

In particular, it was necessary to take into account the "special and inalienable status" that had been conferred "on what have come to be called the 'section 96' courts."[25] These have a "core jurisdiction"[26] that cannot be abolished or removed by either level of government,[27] a jurisdiction underpinned by the unwritten constitutional principle of the rule of law.[28]

Accordingly, "[a]s access to justice is fundamental to the rule of law, and the rule of law is fostered by the continued existence of the s. 96 courts, it is only natural that s. 96 provide some degree of constitutional protection for access to justice."[29] Hearing fees become constitutionally suspect when they are set so high as to "cause undue hardship to the litigant who seeks the adjudication of the superior court":

> The historic task of the superior courts is to resolve disputes between individuals and decide questions of private and public law. Measures that prevent people from coming to the courts to have those issues resolved are at odds with this basic judicial function. The resolution of these disputes and resulting determination of issues of private and public law, viewed in the institutional context of the Canadian justice system, are central to what the superior courts do. Indeed, it is their very book of business. To prevent this business being done strikes at the core of the jurisdiction of the superior courts protected by section 96 of the *Constitution Act, 1867*. As a result, hearing fees that deny people access to the courts infringe the core jurisdiction of the superior courts.[30]

In the absence of sufficient judicial discretion to waive hearing fees, the British Columbia regime was unconstitutional – this even though "[t]here is no express right of general access to superior courts for civil disputes in the text of the Constitution."[31] And so a humble appointing provision was successfully invoked to strike down regulations established by virtue of clear provincial authority. The remarkable *Trial*

25 *MacMillan, supra* note 20, para 52.
26 *Ibid*, para 29.
27 *Ibid*, para 30.
28 *Reference re Secession of Quebec*, [1998] 2 SCR 217, paras 70–8.
29 *Trial Lawyers Association, supra* note 18, para 39.
30 *Ibid*, para 32.
31 *Ibid*, para 92, Rothstein J, dissenting.

Lawyers Association decision is ample proof of the dramatic increase in the scope of s. 96 and its effect on the administration of justice in Canada.

Section 96's Twenty-First-Century "Core"

Yet these judicial references to a protected "core" that is beyond the reach of the legislative and executive branches have to be reconciled with the realities of modern litigation. Earlier cases set up tribunals presided over by judges as an ideal-type of superior court jurisdiction, with their "powers of examination, inspection and discovery of documents, power to hear witnesses on oath, to give costs, and the rest."[32] In particular, a "litigant's 'day in court', *in the sense of a trial*, may have traditionally been regarded as the essence of procedural justice and its deprivation the mark of procedural injustice."[33] To this one might add Pickup CJ's observation that the "twin pillars" of the Canadian constitution are parliamentary sovereignty and "the supremacy of a common law administered in the ordinary Courts independent of the Executive."[34]

Today, however, few litigants are likely to have their rights and entitlements determined by a traditional trial in front of a judge in an oak-panelled courtroom.[35] Rather, the key decisions that shape the lives of litigants and individuals will most likely be taken by administrative decision makers, arbitrators, or a motions judge who does not hear live testimony.

Indeed, the Supreme Court of Canada's decision in *Hryniak v Mauldin*[36] offers an important contrast to the veneration of the core of superior court jurisdiction in *Trial Lawyers Association*. This case concerned the use of the summary judgment procedure in Ontario, a procedure that has equivalents in the other common law provinces. Ontario's *Rules of Civil Procedure* permit judges to resolve claims by weighing evidence, evaluating credibility, or drawing inferences from the evidence without

32 Willis, "Section 96," *supra* note 3, 542. See, generally, *Québec (Procureur général) c. Slanec*, [1933] 2 DLR 279 (Quebec CA).

33 *Irving Ungerman Ltd. v Galanis* (1991), 4 OR (3d) 545, 550, Morden ACJO (emphasis added).

34 *Re Scott*, [1954] OR 676, 554, 4 DLR 546.

35 See, e.g., BC Justice Review Task Force, *Effective and Affordable Civil Justice: Report of the Civil Justice Reform Working Group to the Justice Review Task Force* (November 2006), 92; John H. Langbein, "The Disappearance of Civil Trial in the United States," *Yale Law Journal* 122 (2012) 522.

36 2014 SCC 7, [2014] 1 SCR 87 [*Hryniak*].

a trial or *viva voce* evidence, where "satisfied that there is no genuine issue requiring a trial" (or on consent of the parties), unless it would be "in the interest of justice for such powers to be exercised only at a trial."[37]

Karakatsanis J began her analysis by noting that "a culture shift is required in order to create an environment promoting timely and affordable access to the civil justice system," which "entails simplifying pre-trial procedures and moving the emphasis away from the conventional trial in favour of proportional procedures tailored to the needs of the particular case."[38] Trials will not always be required and are not to be set up as an ideal-type against which "a fair and just adjudication" shall be measured.[39] As Karakatsanis J counselled in a notable passage, "[t]he interest of justice cannot be limited to the advantageous features of a conventional trial, and must account for proportionality, timeliness and affordability."[40]

Moreover, judges are no longer passive observers of counsel and witnesses, but must "actively manage the legal process"[41] to achieve more efficient dispute resolution, recognizing all the while that "new models of adjudication can be fair and just."[42] Far from remaining a neutral arbiter perched above the fray as counsel cite jurisprudence and question witnesses, the modern judge must become a proactive case manager as parties try to settle their differences as swiftly and efficiently as possible; indeed, Quebec's new *Code of Civil Procedure* notes that the judicial mission "includes ensuring proper case management" and "further includes, both in first instance and in appeal, facilitating conciliation."[43] Counsel, too, must "act in a way that facilitates rather than frustrates access to justice,"[44] an idea also formally enshrined in Quebec's *Code*.[45]

---

37 RRO 1990, Reg 194, r 20.04.

38 *Hryniak, supra* note 36, para 2.

39 *Ibid*, para 50.

40 *Ibid*, para 56.

41 *Ibid*, para 32.

42 *Ibid*, para 2.

43 Compilation of Québec Laws and Regulations c C-25.01, s 9 [*Quebec Code*].

44 *Hryniak, supra* note 36, para 32.

45 *Quebec Code, supra* note 43, s 18:

> The parties to a proceeding must observe the principle of proportionality and ensure that their actions, their pleadings, including their choice of an oral or a written defence, and the means of proof they use are proportionate, in terms of the cost and time involved, to the nature and complexity of the matter and the purpose of the application.

A particularly striking application of the *Hryniak* principles is found in British Columbia's *Civil Dispute Resolution Tribunal Act*, which permits the tribunal to require that "before a person makes a request for tribunal resolution, the person must attempt to resolve the dispute using online dispute resolution services provided by the tribunal."[46] Moreover, the tribunal "may use electronic communication tools in conducting all or part of a tribunal proceeding" and even "require ... parties or other persons" to use those tools in relation to matters within the tribunal's jurisdiction.[47] Some legal disputes over land and cases in which less than $25,000 is at stake will thus be resolved without the parties ever seeing the inside of a courthouse or looking a decision maker in the eye.[48]

That is not all. Consistent with "the principle of primacy of private ordering" in the Canadian legal system,[49] individuals may give up their right to access a court altogether: "Parties to an arbitration agreement have the freedom to identify those disputes that will be resolved through arbitration, choose the person who will resolve their dispute, and set out the procedure they will follow during the arbitration process or alternatively have the arbitrator determine the rules of procedure they will follow."[50] Adhesion clauses in consumer contracts often, subject to judicially or legislatively imposed limitations,[51] require individuals to submit to arbitration or alternative dispute resolution processes in the case of a dispute. Moreover, even though provincial legislatures have created statutory rights of appeal from arbitration decisions, these rights of appeal are often restrictively drawn, and judges must accordingly be "careful" not to open the courthouse door too wide.[52]

---

46 SBC 2012, c 25, s 5.

47 SBC 2012, c 25, s 19. See also s 39(1): "In resolving a dispute, the tribunal may conduct a hearing in writing, by telephone, videoconferencing or email, or through use of other electronic communication tools, or by any combination of those means."

48 See the contributions of Asha Kaushal (chap 7) and David Milward (chap 9) for even more expansive approaches.

49 *BG Checo International Ltd. v British Columbia Hydro and Power Authority*, [1993] 1 SCR 12, 27, La Forest J.

50 *0927613 B.C. Ltd. v 0941187 B.C. Ltd.*, 2015 BCCA 457, para 61. See also the contribution of Howard Kislowicz (chap 6) on the traditional position that parties can provide for arbitrators to determine their rights and obligations by reference to religious standards.

51 See, e.g., *Tilden Rent-A-Car Co. v Clendenning* (1978), 18 OR (2d) 601, 1978 CanLII 1446 (ON CA); *Seidel v TELUS Communications Inc.*, 2011 SCC 15, [2011] 1 SCR 531.

52 *Sattva Capital Corp. v Creston Moly Corp.*, 2014 SCC 53, para 54, [2014] 2 SCR 633, Rothstein J [*Sattva*].

For all the importance of the core of superior court jurisdiction, then, the core may be smaller than one would instinctively think. At the same time, there is only a contrast between *Trial Lawyers Association* and *Hryniak*, not a contradiction: "A norm which would strive to provide access to the courts for everyone would better reflect the underlying attitude and it might be better expressed by stating that everyone has a right to access to the courts, but not necessarily to a trial."[53] *Trial Lawyers Association* guarantees access to a judge, but not necessarily to trial-type procedures; *Hryniak* confirms that access to justice need not mean access to a trial, and the principle of private ordering indicates that access to justice need not even mean direct – or perhaps any – access to the judicial system.

Institutional and Interpretive Pluralism in the Canadian Legal System

These light tones of contrast are the product of a judicially created constitutional climate of institutional pluralism. By this, I mean simply that Canadian courts recognize that pure trial-type procedures are not always necessary to the administration of justice. Institutional pluralism is nothing new in the common law tradition, where diverse forms of dispute resolution procedure have long existed.[54] The question is how it can be compatible with the central role given to the superior courts by the *Constitution Act, 1867*: "Section 96 may be given a reasonable application in relation to the provincial need to be able to create new regulatory and social welfare jurisdictions but it cannot be read out of the constitution."[55] Yet the development of a constitutional climate favourable to legislative and administrative experimentation, a climate shaped in part by the judicial exegesis of s. 96, began some time ago.

Even the Privy Council – so often a convenient scapegoat of Canadian commentators on constitutional affairs[56] – appreciated the desirability of reading s. 96 so as to permit provincial innovation in dispute resolution,

53 W.A. Bogart, "Summary Judgment: A Comparative and Critical Analysis," *Osgoode Hall Law Journal* 19 (1981) 552, 598.

54 See, generally, Arthurs, *Without the Law*, *supra* note 2.

55 Gerald E. LeDain, "Sir Lyman Duff and the Constitution," *Osgoode Hall Law Journal* 12 (1974) 261, 332.

56 See, e.g., W.P.M. Kennedy, "The British North America Act: Past and Future," *Canadian Bar Review* 15 (1937) 428, 429; F.R. Scott, "The Privy Council and Minority Rights," *Queen's Quarterly* 37 (1930) 677; Raphael Tuck, "Canada and the Judicial Committee of the Privy Council," *University of Toronto Law Journal* 4 (1941–42) 33.

thereby opening up a space for institutional pluralism. When presented with the occasion to opine on the compatibility of administrative tribunals with s. 96 in *Labour Relations Board of Saskatchewan v John East Iron Works*,[57] their Lordships were unequivocal in their advice: the board's functions represented a "striking departure from the traditional conception of a court"[58] and were designed instead to give effect to the "new conception of industrial relations,"[59] something that could be achieved only by technocrats familiar with the domain and qualified to "bring an experience and knowledge acquired extra-judicially to the solution of their problems."[60] Accordingly, the "subject-matter" of the board's industrial relations jurisdiction was "such as profoundly to distinguish" it from a s. 96 court.[61] Finally, any "alleged judicial function" had to be considered "in relation to its other duties."[62] The upshot was to give legislatures greater scope to address "problems of a modern nature requiring governmental intervention of a continuous and specialized character."[63]

Several decades later, Dickson J exhaustively reviewed the s. 96 jurisprudence and formulated a three-stage test for determining the limits of institutional pluralism in Canadian constitutional law.[64] First, the court must ask "whether the power or jurisdiction" conferred on the body in question "conforms to the power or jurisdiction" of the s. 96 courts "at the time of Confederation."[65] Second, the court must determine whether the "nature of the question" to be decided is "judicial" in the particular "institutional setting" – whether, in other words, it is required to apply "a recognized body of rules in a manner consistent with fairness and impartiality" or rather to make a policy determination "involving competing views of the collective good of the community as a whole."[66] Third, the court must assess the "tribunal's function as a whole in order to appraise the impugned function in its entire

57 [1949] AC 134 (PC).

58 *Ibid*, para 149.

59 *Ibid*, para 150.

60 *Ibid*, para 151.

61 *Ibid*.

62 *Ibid*.

63 Morris C. Shumiatcher, "Section 96 of the British North America Act Re-examined," *Canadian Bar Review* 27 (1949) 131, 131.

64 *Re Residential*, *supra* note 11. Private dispute resolution procedures agreed to by the parties are not subject to this test.

65 *Ibid*, para 734.

66 *Ibid*, paras 734–5.

institutional context,"[67] an assessment weighted towards a conclusion of validity, for a finding of unconstitutionality will issue only where the "adjudicative function is a sole or central function of the tribunal."[68]

Although this institutionally sensitive test did not save the Residential Tenancy Commission,[69] it gives significant scope to legislatures to design institutions that, viewed in the round, do not encroach too far on the territory of the s. 96 courts:

> [T]he recent course of decision, especially in the Supreme Court of Canada, indicates that a pragmatic approach has taken over, and that provincial administrative agencies will be judged not only by what they do (even if it is analogous to jurisdiction exercised by a superior court at confederation or later) but as well by how they do it (that is, by a procedure unlike that of a court in the strict sense) and by the purpose to be served (for example, the administration of a social insurance scheme as in workmen's compensation, rather than the determination of individual liability).[70]

In addition, Canadian courts have given a "somewhat narrow definition" of the protections of the *Canadian Charter of Rights and Freedoms*[71] that might fetter the implementation of regulatory policy by administrative decision makers.[72] For instance, search and seizure powers that are rigorously scrutinized when police officers apply them against individuals are subject to much more relaxed oversight when employed to enforce regulatory requirements;[73] and the courts have been very

---

67 *Ibid*, para 735.

68 *Ibid*, para 736. See also *Tomko v Labour Relations Board (Nova Scotia) et al*, [1977] 1 SCR 112.

69 See also *Séminaire de Chicoutimi v La Cité de Chicoutimi*, [1973] SCR 681 (Quebec Provincial Court) [*Chicoutimi*]; *Attorney General (Que.) et al v Farrah*, [1978] 2 SCR 638 (Quebec Transport Tribunal).

70 Bora Laskin, *The British Tradition in Canadian Law* (London: Stevens and Sons, 1969), 112.

71 Being Schedule B to the *Canada Act 1982* (UK), 1982, c 11.

72 *R v Wigglesworth*, [1987] 2 SCR 541, 558, Wilson J (referring to s 11 of the *Charter*).

73 These protections are set out in s 8 of the *Charter*. See, generally, *Thomson Newspapers Ltd. v Canada (Director of Investigation and Research, Restrictive Trade Practices Commission)*, [1990] 1 SCR 425 and, in particular, La Forest J, 507: "there can only be a relatively low expectation of privacy in respect of premises or documents that are used or produced in the course of activities which, though lawful, are subject to state regulation as a matter of course. In a society in which the need for effective regulation of certain spheres of private activity is recognized and acted upon, state inspection of premises and documents is a routine and expected feature of participation in such activity."

reluctant to characterize regulatory penalties "primarily intended to maintain compliance or to regulate conduct within a limited sphere of activity"[74] as penal provisions attracting the full range of procedural protections associated with criminal offences.[75]

To this must be added the principle that, on procedural matters, administrative tribunals are "masters in their own house."[76] Such procedural flexibility is a central part of Quebec's *Act Respecting Administrative Justice,* which requires the administration to conduct itself "according to simple and flexible rules devoid of formalism, with respect, prudence and promptness."[77] Were administrative hearings to adopt the trappings of courts, the efficiency gains sought to be achieved by the legislature would be compromised. Canadian courts have, in addition, adopted a deferential posture in respect of administrators' procedural policy choices. While the courts retain the final word on whether administrative procedures comply with the duty of fairness,[78] they must "take into account and respect the choices of procedure made by the agency itself":[79] "The determination of the scope and content of a duty to act fairly is circumstance-specific, and may well depend on factors within the expertise and knowledge of the tribunal, including the nature of the statutory scheme and the expectations and practices of the [relevant] constituencies."[80]

Indeed, "a degree of deference to an administrator's procedural choice may be particularly important when the procedural model of the agency under review differs significantly from the judicial model with which courts are most familiar."[81] It is fair to say, then, that the s. 96 jurisprudence has permitted legislatures to carve out spaces to be occupied by alternative decision-making structures to the superior courts. Furthermore, the "[c]onsiderable deference"[82] envisaged by Canadian

74 *Guindon v Canada,* 2015 SCC 41, para 45, [2015] 3 SCR 3.

75 These protections are set out in s 11 of the *Charter*. See, generally, *Martineau v M.N.R.,* 2004 SCC 31, [2004] 3 SCR 737.

76 *Prassad v Canada (Minister of Employment and Immigration),* [1989] 1 SCR 560, 568–9, Sopinka J.

77 Compilation of Québec Laws and Regulations c J-3, s 4(1).

78 See, generally, *Knight v Indian Head School Division No. 19,* [1990] 1 SCR 653.

79 *Baker v Canada (Minister of Citizenship and Immigration),* [1999] 2 SCR 817, para 27, L'Heureux-Dubé J.

80 *Council of Canadians with Disabilities v VIA Rail Canada Inc.,* 2007 SCC 15, para 231, [2007] 1 SCR 650, Abella J [*VIA Rail*].

81 *Re: Sound v Fitness Industry Council of Canada,* 2014 FCA 48, para 42, [2015] 2 FCR 170, Evans JA.

82 *VIA Rail, supra* note 80, para 231, Abella J.

administrative law jurisprudence allows those responsible for operating these novel decision-making structures additional scope to design their procedures to render decisions "fairly, justly and in an orderly and timely way."[83]

In combination, these developments have created a climate of institutional pluralism in which legislatures are free to depart from the core of s. 96 and to experiment with alternative forms of decision-making structure. The Administrative Tribunal of Quebec, sitting in *de novo* review of decisions made by government departments and other bodies, somewhat like a Québécois *Conseil d'État*, is one example. Ontario's new "tribunal clusters," designed "to ensure that adjudicative tribunals are accountable, transparent and efficient in their operations while remaining independent in their decision-making,"[84] are another. And British Columbia's Civil Dispute Resolution Tribunal, with its heavy emphasis on the use of technology to resolve litigation, is perhaps Canada's most striking example to date. An approach to the interpretation of s. 96 that is sensitive to institutional pluralism and the desirability of legislative creativity in institutional design has permitted the development of these innovative bodies.

Moreover, although it has occasionally been insisted that the resolution of "pure question[s] of law" is a matter for the superior courts alone,[85] a "duty" that they cannot "abdicate" to administrative tribunals,[86] Canadian courts' policy of deference on interpretive matters is now well established:[87] "the courts do not have a monopoly on deciding all questions of law."[88] On matters within the "specialized jurisdiction" of an administrative tribunal,[89] courts must "give due consideration to the

83 *Maritime Broadcasting System Limited v Canadian Media Guild*, 2014 FCA 59, para 63, 373 DLR (4th) 167, Stratas JA. See, generally, Roderick A. Macdonald, "A Theory of Procedural Fairness," *Windsor Yearbook of Access to Justice* 1 (1981) 3.

84 *Adjudicative Tribunals Accountability, Governance and Appointments Act*, SO 2009, c 33, Sched 5, s 1. See, generally, Lorne Sossin and Jamie Baxter, "Ontario's Administrative Tribunal Clusters: A Glass Half-Full or Half-Empty for Administrative Justice?," *Oxford University Commonwealth Law Journal* 12 (2012) 157.

85 *R v Ontario Labour Relations Board, ex parte Ontario Food Terminal Board* (1963), 38 DLR (2d) 530 (Ont CA), 532, Laidlaw JA.

86 *Canada (Attorney General) v Mossop*, [1993] 1 SCR 554, 557, La Forest J.

87 See, generally, John M. Evans, "Triumph of Reasonableness: But How Much Does It Really Matter?," *Canadian Journal of Administrative Law and Practice* 27 (2014) 101.

88 Thomas A. Cromwell, *Appellate Review: Policy and Pragmatism*, Isaac Pitblado Lectures on "Appellate Courts: Policy, Law and Practice" (Winnipeg: Law Society of Manitoba, 2006), V-12.

89 *CUPE v NB Liquor Corporation*, [1979] 2 SCR 227, 236, Dickson J [*CUPE*].

determinations of decision makers,"[90] intervening only where a decision maker's interpretation "cannot be rationally supported by the relevant legislation."[91] There is "a margin of appreciation within the range of acceptable and rational solutions."[92] Indeed, the decision maker "holds the interpretative upper hand: under reasonableness review, we defer to *any* reasonable interpretation adopted by an administrative decision maker, even if other reasonable interpretations may exist."[93] The effect is to carve out an interpretive "space" for administrative decision makers,[94] one in which they are free to adopt their own interpretation – which may be different than the interpretation a court would have preferred – by having regard to policy or other considerations.[95]

This interpretive space has also recently been afforded to arbitrators' interpretations of contractual provisions. In *Sattva Capital Corp. v Creston Moly Corp.*,[96] Rothstein J expressly borrowed from the Supreme Court of Canada's administrative law jurisprudence to justify a deferential approach on questions of mixed fact and law. Both involve review of non-judicial decision makers by generalist courts that are relatively less expert: "where parties choose their own decision maker, it may be presumed that such decision makers are chosen either based on their expertise in the area which is the subject of dispute or are otherwise qualified in a manner that is acceptable to the parties."[97] Rothstein J upheld as reasonable the arbitrator's interpretation of a clause concerning the date at which the payment of a finder's fee ought to be calculated. The implications for different areas of Canadian law explored by other contributors to this volume are quite clear: carving out spaces for community self-determination by minority groups (including First Nations) would be consistent with the Canadian courts' preference for interpretive and institutional pluralism.

---

90 *Dunsmuir v New Brunswick*, 2008 SCC, para 49, [2008] 1 SCR 190, Bastarache and LeBel JJ [*Dunsmuir*].

91 *CUPE*, *supra* note 89, 237, Dickson J.

92 *Dunsmuir*, *supra* note 90, para 47, Bastarache and LeBel JJ.

93 *McLean v British Columbia (Securities Commission)*, 2013 SCC 76, para 40, [2013] 3 SCR 895, Moldaver J (emphasis in original).

94 Peter Strauss, "'Deference' Is Too Confusing – Let's Call Them '*Chevron* Space' and '*Skidmore* Weight,'" *Columbia Law Review* 112 (2012) 1143.

95 See, generally, Paul Daly, *A Theory of Deference in Administrative Law: Basis, Application and Scope* (Cambridge: Cambridge University Press, 2012).

96 *Sattva*, *supra* note 52.

97 *Ibid*, 105.

Over the years – and, as I will intimate in the next section, occasionally still today – the core of superior court jurisdiction has been invoked to defeat novel attempts to create innovative decision-making institutions or to cabin the interpretive space of non-judicial decision makers,[98] but the constitutional climate that permits institutional and interpretive pluralism to flourish is now relatively stable.

A Section 96 for the Twenty-First Century

Alternative methods of dispute resolution – alternative, that is, to the ideal-type of adversarial trials in wood-panelled courtrooms – "emerge, survive and subside as they serve the needs of the group or fail to respond to changes within it."[99] Yet it is necessary also to "seek to give effect to the Constitution as we understand it," "however worthy the policy objectives."[100] The question, then, is how to preserve the s. 96 courts as central pillars of the Canadian legal order, their "prime importance in the constitutional pattern,"[101] while also preserving space for institutional and interpretive pluralism by maintaining a favourable constitutional climate for legislative experimentation.

The contrast between *Trial Lawyers Association* and *Hryniak* suggests an answer: that the s. 96 courts – and lawyers more generally – should stand up for the values "fundamental to the legal order as a whole,"[102] while also appreciating the limitations of traditional lawyerly analysis, thereby establishing the "parameters of legal tolerance"[103] in a way that is respectful of the desirability of legislative and administrative flexibility in meeting new challenges.

Canadian courts' treatment of privative clauses, which purport to oust judicial review of administrative decisions, is instructive. If such provisions were taken literally, they could do grievous violence to the rule of law by sheltering entire areas of administrative decision making from judicial control. But there are various lawyerly ways of dodging

---

98 Pépin, *supra* note 7 and Willis, "Section 96," *supra* note 3, 517 provide early accounts. See also David Mullan, "The Uncertain Constitutional Position of Canada's Administrative Appeal Tribunals," *Ottawa Law Review* 14 (1982) 239.

99 Arthurs, *Without the Law*, *supra* note 2, 202.

100 *Re Residential*, *supra* note 11, 750, Dickson J.

101 *AG Can v Law Society of BC*, [1982] 2 SCR 307, 327, Estey J.

102 Peter W. Hogg, "Judicial Review: How Much Do We Need?," *McGill Law Journal* 20 (1974) 157, 175.

103 J.N. Lyon, "Comment," *Canadian Bar Review* 49 (1971) 365, 379.

these clauses: one can say that a privative clause is designed only to protect decisions within a decision maker's jurisdiction, not decisions tainted by legal error;[104] or that such provisions unconstitutionally deprive superior courts of one of their core competencies, that of performing judicial review of administrative action.[105] Such judicial manoeuvring, however, would run counter to a clearly expressed legislative intent to protect administrative decision makers from judicial oversight.[106] Accordingly, Canadian courts have consistently treated privative clauses as indicating that a relatively greater degree of deference should be accorded by courts to the decision maker under review.[107] They have taken statutes seriously, without compromising the core function of judicial review or fundamental legal values.[108]

Striking an appropriate balance may occasionally mean making hard choices and, in particular, not yielding too easily to the clarion call of policy considerations. For instance, administrative tribunals may be tempted to take a generous view of their power to reconsider their own decisions. Although the scope of reconsideration is limited at common law by a desire to preserve the finality of administrative action,[109] tribunals often have statutory powers that exceed the narrow confines of the common law.[110] It has been suggested by several members of the British Columbia Court of Appeal that an administrative tribunal may, in effect, perform judicial reviews of its own decisions;[111] that is, a party who is displeased with a decision can challenge it on

---

104 See, most famously, *Anisminic v Foreign Compensation Commission*, [1969] 2 AC 147; *Metropolitan Life Insurance Co. v International Union of Operating Engineers*, [1970] SCR 425.

105 *Crevier v AG (Québec)*, [1981] 2 SCR 220.

106 See, generally, David Dyzenhaus, "Disobeying Parliament: Privative Clauses and the Rule of Law," in *The Least Examined Branch: The Role of Legislatures in the Constitutional State*, ed. Richard W. Baumann and Tsvi Kahana (Cambridge: Cambridge University Press, 2006), 499.

107 See, e.g., *United Brotherhood of Carpenters and Joiners of America, Local 579 v Bradco Construction*, [1993] 2 SCR 316, 333.

108 See, generally, Paul Daly, *A Theory of Deference in Administrative Law* (Cambridge: Cambridge University Press, 2012), 289–93.

109 See, generally, *Chandler v Alberta Association of Architects*, [1989] 2 SCR 848.

110 See, e.g., *An Act Respecting Administrative Justice, Compilation of Québec Laws and Regulations*, c J-3, s 154 (Administrative Tribunal of Quebec).

111 *Lysohirka v British Columbia (Workers' Compensation Board)*, 2012 BCCA 457, para 32, Garson JA; *Fraser Health Authority v Workers' Compensation Appeal Tribunal*, 2014 BCCA 499, paras 62–3, Newbury JA, dissenting [*Fraser*].

reconsideration within the administrative process rather than seek judicial review in a superior court of record. This is said to be justified by considerations of access to justice:[112] why force parties down the longer and more expensive route of judicial review when an internal avenue can be created?[113]

However valid these policy objectives, however, they would have the unfortunate result of denuding one of the well-established core functions of the superior courts. Conducting a judicial review of a judicial review gives rise to serious problems. One is constitutional in nature: judicial functions cannot be hived off from the superior courts and vested in statutory bodies.[114] Another is analytical: the question will no longer be the legality and fairness of the original decision – which is the question a court must ask itself on judicial review – but whether the *reconsideration* decision was lawful and fair. This inserts a layer of opacity between the reviewing court and the decision affecting a person's "rights, privileges or interests."[115] The constitutional and analytical problems are interrelated, for the resultant opacity undermines a reviewing court's ability to perform its constitutionally guaranteed role of ensuring that the decision maker stayed within the boundaries of legality. In any event, duplicating a core function of the superior courts in the administrative process hinders access to justice by adding an additional layer of internal decision making, after which judicial review will be available anyway.

While the s. 96 cases, including *Trial Lawyers Association*, insist upon maintenance of some purely judicial core, they also envisage à la *Hryniak* a penumbral area of judicial oversight or involvement in which institutional and interpretive pluralism are respected. What must be guarded against is dogmatic insistence on lawyerly modes of analysis. For instance, it has been suggested that where the application by a s. 96 court of the principles of statutory interpretation indicates that there is one "right" answer to a legal question, a judge should insist upon it – indeed, that "[t]he rule of law requires nothing less."[116] But as has been pointed out, "In debates over the relationship of the courts to the administration,

112 See, generally, Access to Justice Committee, *Reaching Equal Justice Committee: An Invitation to Envision and Act* (Ottawa: Canadian Bar Association, 2013).

113 *Fraser, supra* note 111, para 66, Newbury JA, dissenting.

114 *Chicoutimi, supra* note 69; *MacMillan, supra* note 20.

115 *Cardinal v Director of Kent Institution*, [1985] 2 SCR 643, para 14.

116 *Qin v Canada (Citizenship and Immigration)*, 2013 FCA 263, para 33, Evans JA.

the Rule of Law remains the rallying-cry for those who favour judicial intervention."[117] As I have argued in the context of judicial review of administrative interpretations of law, s. 96 courts should adopt an oversight role, checking decisions for "flaws or fallacies that undermine the integrity of the legal system,"[118] but should not insist that administrative decision makers adopt the methodology of judges and lawyers: "The technical principles of statutory interpretation should play no role in this analysis."[119] In addition, the notion of a core of superior court jurisdiction should not be expanded so far as to imperil Canadian courts' well-established respect for institutional pluralism. Developing "a category of core … inherent powers which can never be transferred" adds "uncertainty to the law" and compromises the flexibility of legislators and administrators.[120] A restrained judicial approach is required instead.

Appropriately restrained judicial oversight of or involvement in alternative forms of dispute resolution procedure preserves the core of the jurisdiction of the superior courts without imposing a strait-jacket on legislators and administrators who wish to take innovative approaches to meet novel challenges.[121] In this regard, it is also interesting to note the Federal Court's insistence that where the parties to "public law applications" settle matters on consent, they must furnish "a cogent reason, other than their consent, for setting aside a decision of a tribunal"[122] – a requirement that ensures judicial oversight of public administration, while respecting the ability of the parties to come to a mutually satisfactory arrangement without invoking the full gamut of judicial review jurisdiction.[123]

---

117 Harry Arthurs, "Rethinking Administrative Law: A Slightly Dicey Business," *Osgoode Hall Law Journal* 17 (1979) 1, 4.

118 Paul Daly, "Unreasonable Interpretations of Law," *Supreme Court Law Review* (2d) 66 (2014) 233, 261.

119 *Ibid*, 266.

120 *MacMillan*, *supra* note 20, para 92, McLachlin J, dissenting.

121 See also *MacMillan*, *supra* note 20, para 83, McLachlin J: "Administrative tribunals deal with the factual minutiae of multitudinous disputes; the superior courts ensure that the law is followed and fair process maintained."

122 *Johnson v Canada (Minister of Citizenship and Immigration)*, 2005 FC 1262, para 14, Dawson J.

123 See, similarly, the procedures employed by the Competition Tribunal in respect of consent orders, which are subject to rigorous oversight in a participatory process (*Competition Tribunal Rules*, SOR/94-290, ss 76–96) and may not simply be rubber-stamped by the tribunal. See, generally, *Canada (Director of Investigation and Research) v Palm Dairies Limited* (1986), 12 CPR (3d) 540 (Competition Tribunal).

Conclusion

So far, the s. 96 jurisprudence has memorialized a delicate compromise between "legal centralism" and "legal pluralism,"[124] but preserving it in decades to come will require paying continued attention to the need to strike a balance between the jurisdiction of the s. 96 courts and the legislative and administrative flexibility necessary to resolve pressing social issues. The establishment of innovative administrative tribunals – even online dispute resolution forums – is a significant achievement that ought to be celebrated, as also should be the recognition that non-lawyers have an important role to play in the interpretation and application of regulatory schemes.[125] Maintaining the current constitutional climate into the future will permit further progress to be made in resolving pressing issues without eliminating superior court jurisdiction, one of the fundamental pillars of the Canadian constitutional order.

124 See, generally, Arthurs, *Without the Law*, *supra* note 2.

125 See, generally, Roderick A. Macdonald, "On the Administration of Statutes," *Queen's Law Journal* 12 (1987) 488.

4 Canada's "Constitution outside the Courts": Provincial Non-enforcement of Constitutionally Suspect Federal Criminal Laws as Case Study

WADE K. WRIGHT*

Introduction

The conventional view in the Canadian legal scholarship for a number of decades has been that the courts do and should have the exclusive – or at least primary – word about the constitution's meaning.[1] The political (legislative and executive) branches, on this view, are largely the targets of constitutional interpretation and application, not independent producers of it. They lack the inclination and ability to interpret and apply the constitution, well or at all, and are interested in it only to the extent that they will want to know what the courts are likely to let them get away with.

The concerns underlying the conventional view of the ability and inclination of the political branches to interpret the constitution should be taken seriously. However, the conventional view sweeps too broadly.

Descriptively, the conventional view is hard to square with the way that Canada's constitution operates in practice. The courts play a significant

---

* Assistant professor, Faculty of Law, Western University. I acknowledge the generous financial assistance of the Social Sciences and Humanities Research Council of Canada. For their helpful comments on earlier drafts of this article, thanks are offered to Palma Paciocco, to two anonymous reviewers, and to Paul Daly and the other organizers of and participants in the "Canada at 150" conference at Yale University. The standard disclaimer applies.

1 S. Choudhry and R. Howse, "Constitutional Theory and the Quebec Secession Reference," *Canadian Journal of Law and Jurisprudence* 13 (2000) 143, 151, 153; D. Baker, *Not Quite Supreme: The Courts and Coordinate Constitutional Interpretation* (Montreal and Kingston: McGill-Queen's University Press, 2010), 39 [Baker, *Not Quite Supreme*]; and W.K. Wright, "Courts as Facilitators of Intergovernmental Dialogue: Cooperative Federalism and Judicial Review," *Supreme Court Law Review* (2d) 72 (2016) 365, 372 [Wright, "Courts as Facilitators"].

role in interpreting and applying the constitution, to be sure, but so too do the political branches.[2] The political branches regularly make decisions about constitutionality while formulating, implementing, and enforcing policy that will usually carry the day, at least temporarily, and may do so in the long term as well if a decision is not later challenged in the courts.[3]

Normatively, the conventional view also obscures an appreciation of the "constitution outside the courts."[4] In doing so, it inhibits the exploration of openings available to the political branches to function as complementary safeguards of potentially more robust, fulsome constitutional standards.[5]

There has recently been an increase in legal scholarship that explores the role that the political branches do and should play in interpreting and applying the constitution, or "extrajudicial constitutionalism." For example, some legal scholars (including me) have defended a "dialogic" model of the *Canadian Charter of Rights and Freedoms* that understands the political and judicial branches to co-determine its meaning but treats judicial decisions as authoritative;[6] others have gone further, championing a "coordinate" model that does not require the political branches to accord judicial decisions this authoritative status.[7] However, the legal scholarship in Canada remains "focused largely on how courts work with constitutions,"[8] and the constitution outside the

2 Mary Liston's contribution to this volume also makes the point that constitutional law is much broader than what the courts say it is; see chap 1. See also Paul Daly, chap 3, which provides an interesting account of the constitutional nature of administrative law and civil procedure.

3 B. Slattery, "A Theory of the *Charter*," *Osgoode Hall Law Journal* 25 (1987) 701, 714 [Slattery, "A Theory"].

4 M. Tushnet, "The Constitution outside the Courts," *Valparaiso University Law Review* 26 (1992) 437.

5 For more on this point, see, e.g., Vanessa A. MacDonnell, "The Constitution as Framework for Governance," *University of Toronto Law Journal* 63 (2013) 624; and Vanessa A. MacDonnell, "The Civil Servant's Role in the Implementation of Constitutional Rights," *International Journal of Constitutional Law* 13 (2015) 383.

6 For my contribution, see P.W. Hogg, A.A. Bushell Thornton, and W.K. Wright, "*Charter* Dialogue Revisited – Or Much Ado about Metaphors," *Osgoode Hall Law Journal* 45 (2007) 1 [Hogg, Thornton, and Wright, "Charter Dialogue Revisited"].

7 G. Huscroft, "Constitutionalism from the Top Down," *Osgoode Hall Law Journal* 45 (2007) 91, 101; see also G. Huscroft, "'Thank God We're Here': Judicial Exclusivity in *Charter* Interpretation and Its Consequences," *Supreme Court Law Review* 2d 25 (2004) 241.

8 R.W. Baumann and T. Kahana, "New Ways of Looking at Old Institutions," in *The Least Examined Branch: The Role of Legislatures in the Constitutional State*, ed. R.W. Bauman and T. Kahana (Cambridge: Cambridge University Press, 2006), 1; see also Vanessa A. MacDonnell, "A Theory of Quasi-constitutional Legislation," *Osgoode Hall Law Journal* 53 (2016) 508, 511: ("[c]onstitutional scholarship continues to focus disproportionately on courts").

courts is often overlooked altogether, or discussed only briefly.[9] In addition, in the work that does exist, there is often a tendency to discuss the constitution inside and outside the courts in either-or terms, neglecting an account of when and how the political branches do or might complement the work of the courts.

This paper builds on the work about Canada's constitution outside the courts, with a focus on the *Charter*. It does so by considering one of the many opportunities that is available for the political branches to play an active role in interpreting and applying the *Charter*: provincial non-enforcement of constitutionally suspect federal criminal laws. This opportunity arises because the prosecution of the bulk of the criminal offences in the federal *Criminal Code*[10] falls to the provincial attorneys general, not the federal attorney general. The paper argues that the provincial attorneys general have not only the power but also the duty to refuse to enforce federal criminal laws that they consider to be constitutionally suspect on *Charter* grounds.[11] This duty – called "provincial non-enforcement" throughout this paper, for ease of reference – presents a rich but underappreciated opportunity for the provinces (and the federal system more generally) to play a role in safeguarding the *Charter*.

In making this argument, this paper – in keeping with the spirit of this collection – challenges several conventional views about Canada's constitution. First, its discussion of provincial non-enforcement highlights the role that the political branches (and, through them, societal actors) do and could play in interpreting and enforcing the constitution (here, the *Charter*). This challenges the conventional view, noted earlier, that the courts are the exclusive, or even the primary,

---

9 Political scientists in Canada have devoted more attention to the constitution outside the courts than legal scholars; see, e.g., J. Hiebert, *Charter Conflicts: What Is Parliament's Role?* (Montreal: McGill-Queen's University Press, 2002); Baker, *Not Quite Supreme, supra* note 1; J. Kelly and M. Hennigar, "The Canadian Charter of Rights and the Minister of Justice: Weak-Form Review within a Constitutional Charter of Rights," *International Journal of Constitutional Law* 10 (2012) 36; and J. Hiebert and J. Kelly, *Parliamentary Bills of Rights: The Experiences of New Zealand and United Kingdom* (Cambridge: Cambridge University Press, 2015).

10 RSC 1985, c C-46.

11 There is a rich literature in the United States exploring the constitution outside the courts, including the specific issue of executive (e.g., presidential) non-enforcement on constitutional grounds: for a list of references on the latter, see N. Devins and S. Prakash, "The Indefensible Duty to Defend," *Columbia Law Review* 112 (2012) 507, 521–2.

purveyors of constitutional meaning. Second, the paper complicates two competing visions of Canadian federalism. The first (increasingly beleaguered) vision focuses on the protection of exclusive, independent allocations of federal and provincial jurisdiction; the other (now more popular) vision eschews this emphasis on exclusivity and independence, focusing on coordinating the overlapping, interdependent allocations of jurisdiction thought to typify Canadian federalism in the service of "cooperative federalism."[12] The account offered here of provincial non-enforcement reveals an arrangement where jurisdiction is not clearly demarcated,[13] but fluid and contested – where the provinces operate not as outsiders to federal policies, but as insiders tasked with implementing and enforcing them, and use this power uncooperatively to oppose federal goals in the service of *Charter* rights.[14]

Several key points should be noted at the outset. First, my argument is not that provincial non-enforcement should be the first option for a province concerned about the constitutionality of a provincially enforced federal criminal law. Repeal or amendment by the federal government will always be preferable to provincial non-enforcement, which would leave a constitutionally suspect law on the statute books, perhaps being enforced in other provinces. The provinces should identify, and urge the federal government to address, constitutional defects before such a law is enacted – and, after enactment, push for repeal or amendment. Provincial non-enforcement should occur only if these efforts are or will be unsuccessful.

Second, my argument for provincial non-enforcement should not be taken as an argument against judicial review. I am sceptical that the provinces have an obligation to seek judicial input before engaging in non-enforcement. But judicial input, once sought, should

---

12 For an account of these two visions, see Wright, "Courts as Facilitators," *supra* note 1.

13 I am far from the first to make the point that federal and provincial jurisdiction is not now clearly demarcated, legally or in practice. But the particular federal dynamic highlighted here – provincial administration and enforcement of federal policies – is largely overlooked in the scholarship. An exploration of this dynamic contributes to the picture of jurisdictional overlap and interdependence that has been painted by others.

14 The discussion here resonates with ideas explored, from the US perspective, in J. Bulman-Pozen and H. Gerken, "Uncooperative Federalism, *Yale Law Review* 118 (2009) 1256 [Bulman-Pozen and Gerken, "Uncooperative Federalism"].

be respected.[15] I see provincial non-enforcement as a complementary constitutional safeguard.[16]

Finally, the duty of non-enforcement I describe and defend would arise where a provincial attorney general concludes that a federal criminal law is constitutionally suspect. I use the term *constitutionally suspect* to refer to a federal criminal law that a provincial attorney general believes is unconstitutional under his or her best interpretation of the *Charter*. This definition might seem unsatisfying because it leaves various questions of implementation unanswered, some of which I identify below.[17] Yet the question whether there is a duty of provincial non-enforcement, while related, is distinct from and prior to the question of its exercise.[18] In the interest of space, therefore, the question of its exercise is left for another day.

The paper is organized in four parts. The first part sets the stage for a discussion of the duty of provincial non-enforcement, using as a backdrop the recent calls for Ontario to refuse to enforce the federal government's new sex-work law. Ontario is the focus of the discussion in the paper, but the thrust of the argument for a duty of provincial non-enforcement applies equally in the other provinces. The second part makes the case for the duty of provincial non-enforcement. The third part identifies and answers some of the key criticisms that might be directed at it. Finally, the last part outlines some of the key questions that would need to be addressed in implementing it.

---

15 I have defended this view elsewhere: see Hogg, Thornton, and Wright, "Charter Dialogue Revisited," *supra* note 6, 30–8. But a province would still have a *power* of non-enforcement on *policy* grounds; what it would not have is a *duty* of non-enforcement on *constitutional* grounds: see note 113.

16 An argument that provincial non-enforcement provides an adequate substitute for judicial review for constitutionality seems unlikely to find favour with the courts. In *R v Appulonappa* [2015] 3 SCR 754 [*Appulonappa*], the Supreme Court recently held that ministerial discretion could not be relied upon to save a constitutionally overbroad law, suggesting that the executive's power (or even its duty) to enforce criminal laws in a manner that is consistent with the *Charter* does not, in itself, dispense with the need for judicial review.

17 See "Looking Forward" below.

18 There is an interesting parallel here with debates about judicial review. Legal scholars in Canada have debated for generations how the courts do and should interpret and apply the constitution but, despite this, have not generally asked whether judicial review should exist at all. If a clear standard is expected for the exercise of provincial non-enforcement before the existence of it is accepted, why is the same not expected of judicial review?

Setting the Stage: The New Federal Sex-Work Law

The potential role that the provinces, and the federal system, could play in helping to safeguard the *Charter* was revealed in the wake of the Supreme Court's decision in *Canada v Bedford* (2013).[19] In *Bedford*, the Court held, unanimously, that three provisions in the federal *Criminal Code* that prohibited various aspects of adult prostitution unjustifiably violated sex workers' right to security of the person, contrary to s. 7 of the *Charter*. The Court highlighted the ways in which the provisions prevented sex workers from taking steps to reduce the risks they face. The federal government responded with a new law that amended the *Criminal Code* by, among other things, criminalizing the purchase and advertisement of "sexual services."[20] In doing so, the federal government dismissed the claim, voiced by various (but not all) sex-worker advocacy groups and legal experts, among others, that the new law was also constitutionally suspect because it would recreate, and compound, the harms of the old law.[21]

An interesting thing then happened. The attempt to have these constitutional concerns addressed shifted focus from the federal government to the provinces. In Ontario, this shift manifested in several calls to (then) premier Kathleen Wynne and (then) attorney general Madeleine Meilleur to refer the new law to the Ontario Court of Appeal for a decision on its constitutionality and to refuse to enforce it pending the Court's decision.[22] In response, the premier voiced "grave concerns"

---

19 [2013] 3 SCR 1101.

20 *The Protection of Communities and Exploited Persons Act*, SC 2014, c 25.

21 See, e.g., Letter from Members of the Legal Community to Prime Minister Stephen Harper re Bill C-36, 7 July 2014, https://d3n8a8pro7vhmx.cloudfront.net/pivotlegal/pages/666/attachments/original/1404836275/Harper_07_07_2014.pdf?1404836275; Canadian Bar Association, "The CBA Warns of Possible Constitutional Shortcomings in Bill C-36," 29 October 2014, https://www.cba.org/News-Media/Press-Releases/2014/CBA-warns-of-possible-constitutional-shortcomings; and Canadian Press, "Bill C-36, Tories' Anti-prostitution Law, Still Unconstitutional: Sex Workers, Advocates," 6 November 2014, http://www.huffingtonpost.ca/2014/11/06/bill-c-36-prostitution-law-unconstitutional_n_6116498.html.

22 Antonella Artuso, "Sex Workers Urge Premiers Not to Enforce New Prostitution Law," *Toronto Sun*, 17 December 2014, http://www.torontosun.com/2014/12/17/sex-workers-says-bill-c-36-leaves-them-vulnerable; and Letter from Members of the Legal Community to Ontario Premier and Attorney General re: *Protection of Communities and Exploited Persons Act*, 17 December 2014, http://www.aidslaw.ca/site/letter-from-legal-profession-to-ontario-premier-and-attorney-general/?lang=en.

about the new law and asked the attorney general to provide a legal opinion addressing its constitutional validity and the "options" available if its "constitutionality is in question."[23] However, she seemed to have doubts about whether it was open to the province to refuse to enforce the new law, even if the attorney general returned with an opinion that its constitutionality was indeed in question. She insisted that the province must enforce only "*duly enacted* legislation" and must take steps to uphold "the constitution and the *Charter*," implying that non-enforcement might be an option. But she also said that the "Attorney General of Ontario is *bound* to enforce the *Criminal Code*."[24] In the end, these doubts did not need to be resolved, because the attorney general returned with an opinion finding "no clear unconstitutionality in the law" and noting that twenty-six outstanding prosecutions under it would continue.[25]

The Ontario example can be used to illustrate some basic points about provincial non-enforcement, helping to frame my argument for a duty of provincial non-enforcement in the next part. First, consider why the issue arises at all. Why did we have calls to a provincial government to refuse to enforce a federal criminal law? After all, generally speaking, it falls to federal officials to enforce federal laws and to provincial officials to enforce provincial laws.[26] The answer is that criminal law is an important exception. Since Confederation, the enforcement of the bulk of the *Criminal Code*, a federal law, has fallen to the provinces.[27] The calls for provincial non-enforcement in the Ontario example reflect this state of affairs, revealing a context where federal and provincial jurisdiction is not clearly demarcated.

Second, consider next who is called upon in the Ontario example: the provincial premier and the provincial attorney general. The inclusion of the provincial attorney general reflects the fact that, legally, in Ontario, it is the attorney general who "superintends all matters connected with the administration of justice," a role that extends to the conduct of criminal and regulatory prosecutions, including under the federal *Criminal Code*.[28] The attorney general

23 Statement of Ontario Premier Kathleen Wynne, 7 December 2014.

24 *Ibid* (emphasis added).

25 Allison Jones, "Ontario Review Finds Ottawa's Sex-Work Law Constitutional, Wynne says," *Globe and Mail*, 1 April 2015.

26 See, e.g., *R v Hauser* [1979] 1 SCR 984, 993 [*Hauser*].

27 The provincial role is codified in the federal *Criminal Code*; see s 2.

28 *Ministry of the Attorney General Act*, RSO 1990, c M17, s 5 [*MAGO*].

has broad "prosecutorial discretion" in carrying out this function. In exercising this prosecutorial discretion, the attorney general is expected to "act independently of political pressures from government" – something that is considered "so fundamental to the integrity and efficiency of the criminal justice system that it is constitutionally entrenched."[29]

Finally, consider the question how a non-enforcement decision is implemented. The actual conduct of criminal prosecutions generally falls not to the attorney general personally, but to provincial Crown attorneys.[30] The calls for provincial non-enforcement in Ontario did not specify how non-enforcement decisions could and should be communicated to the province's Crown attorneys. It now seems well accepted that the provincial attorney general has the legal authority to issue "Crown policies" or "guidelines" that help guide or structure (but do not preclude altogether) the individualized determinations that prosecutorial discretion is commonly thought and expected to entail. Such policies or guidelines are now common. Here the assumption seemed to be that the attorney general had the legal authority to do more – to issue a policy or guideline (or directive) ordering the province's Crown attorneys to refrain from enforcing the law at all. I argue in the next part for a duty of provincial non-enforcement. I take for granted that the attorney general has the legal tools to implement this duty and leave questions about its implementation to future work.[31]

---

29 *Miazga v Kvello Estate* [2009] 3 SCR 339, para 46.

30 See *Crown Attorneys Act*, RSO 1990, c C49. An additional complication, left for another day, is the role of the police, who generally decide whether to lay the initial charge.

31 In *Carter v Canada* [2016] 1 SCR 13, the minority (but not the majority) of the Court rejected Quebec's request for an exemption from the extension sought by the federal government of the suspended declaration of invalidity issued in *Carter v Canada* [2015] 1 SCR 335, which had been issued in relation to the federal prohibition on assisting death in the *Criminal Code*. The minority suggested that the Quebec exemption was unnecessary because Quebec's minister of justice had already issued a directive to the province's director of criminal and penal prosecutions not to prosecute under the federal prohibition any physician who respected the Quebec law (para 10). The minority expressed no reservations about the minister's authority to issue the provincial non-enforcement directive. The majority granted Quebec's request for an extension without expressing an opinion about the permissibility of the directive.

The Case for Provincial Non-enforcement

There is surprisingly little commentary that considers whether provincial attorneys general have the duty, or even the power, to refuse to enforce constitutionally suspect federal criminal laws. Some, like John Whyte, Mark Carter, and Dennis Baker, have suggested that the provinces have a general power to refuse to enforce federal criminal laws that extends beyond constitutional concerns;[32] others, like Lorne Sossin and the late Justice Marc Rosenberg, have suggested that there is no such power.[33] However, there has been little commentary about the situation where questions arise about the constitutionality of a federal criminal law. In 1989, then Ontario attorney general Ian Scott suggested that the provinces must prosecute even a constitutionally suspect federal law, but he conceded that he had "not yet formed a clear view based on principle about this issue."[34] Premier Wynne's response, noted earlier, can be read to support this view.

This part argues that the attorney general has a duty – and not a mere power – to refuse to enforce constitutionally suspect federal criminal laws. The argument for such a duty turns on two claims, addressed in turn below.

The Attorney General's Duty to Respect the Charter

The first claim that underlies the argument for provincial non-enforcement is that the provincial attorney general has a legal duty to ensure that all provincial laws and decisions are lawful. At its most basic, this duty imposes an obligation on the attorney general to ensure that all provincial government action respects the law.[35] Significantly,

---

32 J. Whyte, "The Administration of Criminal Justice and the Provinces," *Criminal Reports* (3d) 38 (1984) 184; M. Carter, "Recognizing Original (Non-delegated) Provincial Jurisdiction to Prosecute Criminal Offences," *Ottawa Law Review* 38 (2006–07) 163, 166 [Carter, "Provincial Jurisdiction"]; and D. Baker, "The Provincial Power to (Not) Prosecute *Criminal Code* Offences," *Ottawa Law Review* 48 (2017) 419 [Baker, "Provincial Power"].

33 L. Sossin, "Federal-Provincial Dispute over Ontario Pension Plan Has to Stop," *Globe and Mail*, 10 August 2015; and M. Rosenberg, "The Attorney General and the Prosecution Function in the Twenty-First Century," *Queen's Law Review* 43 (2009) 813, 822.

34 I. Scott, "Law, Policy and the Role of the Attorney General," *University of Toronto Law Journal* 39 (1989) 109 [Scott, "Law, Policy"].

35 I. Scott, "The Role of the Attorney General and the *Charter of Rights*," *Criminal Law Quarterly* 29 (1986–87) 187, 189.

this includes the *Charter*, which is part of the constitution of Canada, "the supreme *law* of Canada."[36]

The attorney general performs a number of important functions, including "advis[ing] the Government upon all matters of law connected with legislative enactments" and "all matters of a legislative nature," "conduct[ing] and regulat[ing] all litigation for and against the Crown," and, as noted, conducting criminal prosecutions.[37] The attorney general's positive duty to ensure that the *Charter* is respected is triggered in performing all these functions – including, importantly, the conduct of criminal prosecutions.[38]

This positive duty is codified in the attorney general's constitutive statute.[39] However, this codification is simply an instantiation of a broader constitutional duty that is imposed on all public decision makers to respect the *Charter*. This broader duty is implicit in s. 32(1) of the *Charter*, which provides that the *Charter* applies to "the Parliament and government of Canada" and "to the legislature and government of each province" in respect of all matters within their jurisdiction. It is consistent with the underlying constitutional principle of the rule of law, which "requires that all government action must comply with the law, including the Constitution."[40] It also finds support in various Supreme Court cases.[41]

The conventional view, described and criticized earlier, might lead to a difference of opinion at this point. For advocates of the conventional view, the claim that the statutory duty placed on the attorney general to ensure that all government action complies with the law (including the *Charter*) is merely an instantiation of a broader constitutional duty might provoke scepticism because it is hard to square with the assumption that the *Charter* operates by imposing limits (and not duties) on the political branches, limits that are interpreted and applied exclusively (or at least primarily) by judicial interlocutors. This paper works from the position, defended elsewhere, that all public decision makers have a duty to respect, and thus interpret and

---

36 *Constitution Act, 1982*, s 52 (emphasis added).

37 *MAGO, supra* note 28, s 5.

38 See, e.g., *R v Anderson* [2014] 2 SCR 167, para 45 [*Anderson*].

39 *MAGO, supra* note 28, s 5: "The Attorney General … shall see that the administration of public affairs is in accordance with the law."

40 *Reference re Secession of Quebec* [1998] 2 SCR 217, paras 71–2 [*Secession Reference*].

41 See, e.g., *NS v Martin* [2003] 2 SCR 504, para 28.

apply, the *Charter*[42] – a duty that the attorneys general have a special obligation to ensure is satisfied. The harder, more interesting issue, in my view, is what this duty entails in any given context, especially where constitutional views diverge. This is the issue I consider next.

The Attorney General's Duty and Provincial Non-enforcement

The second claim underlying my argument for a duty of provincial non-enforcement is that the provincial attorney general's duty to ensure that the *Charter* is respected is and would be breached by the decision to enforce a federal criminal law that is constitutionally suspect. This second claim implicates a structural question of relative interpretative power; it is distinct from, and prior to, the claim that a federal or provincial view best reflects the *Charter* in any individual case. The contrary argument – that the provincial attorney general should enforce constitutionally suspect federal criminal laws – is, at root, an argument that the provincial attorney general should defer to the constitutional views of the federal government and, thus, that its word should be determinative. I criticize this argument in this part.

It is important to acknowledge, before going any further, that there is an ongoing debate about the source and nature of provincial jurisdiction to prosecute criminal offences in the federal *Criminal Code* – a debate that has implications for discussions of provincial non-enforcement. In a series of decisions released in the late 1970s and early 1980s, the Supreme Court held that the prosecution of federal criminal offences fell within the federal legislative power in s. 91(27) of the *Constitution Act, 1867* over "The Criminal Law" and "Procedure in Criminal Matters."[43] In doing so, the Court rejected the claim, accepted by (then) Dickson J, in dissent, that the prosecution of s. 91(27) federal criminal law offences falls exclusively within the provincial legislative power in s. 92(14) over "The Administration of Justice in the Province."

These decisions make it clear that the federal government has the power to define *and* enforce *Criminal Code* offences. But provincial enforcement remains the norm, and questions linger about the source

---

42 Hogg, Thornton, and Wright, "Charter Dialogue Revisited," *supra* note 6, 32–8; see also Slattery, "A Theory," *supra* note 3.

43 *Hauser*, *supra* note 26; *AG (Can) v Can Nat Transportation* [1983] 2 SCR 206; and *R v Wetmore* [1983] 2 SCR 284. See also *R v Aziz* [1981] 1 SCR 188.

of this provincial authority.[44] The decisions can be read to support the claim that federal jurisdiction is exclusive and thus that the provincial attorney general's authority to prosecute *Criminal Code* offences rests solely on the statutory delegation in s. 2 of the *Criminal Code*.[45] However, they can also be read to support the claim that federal jurisdiction is concurrent and thus that the provinces share original, non-delegated jurisdiction to prosecute *Criminal Code* offences. The better view is the second. This view is shared by most commentators,[46] and it is easier to reconcile with the Court's recent decisions, which tend to embrace overlapping claims to jurisdiction.[47] My discussion of provincial non-enforcement thus proceeds from the premise that provincial jurisdiction has a constitutional, and not merely a statutory, foundation.

THE INCONCLUSIVENESS OF TEXT, HISTORY, AND PRECEDENT

What support is there for the claim that the provincial attorney general's duty to respect the *Charter* extends to the non-enforcement of constitutionally suspect federal criminal laws? This section will argue that text, history, and precedent are, at best, inconclusive. The remaining sections of this part will then describe the support that exists for this claim.

Consider first the text of the constitution. The text of the *Constitution Act, 1867* – in particular, the text of s. 91(27) and s. 92(14) – was invoked by the Supreme Court in the decisions, described in the previous section, that found that there is federal jurisdiction over criminal prosecutions.[48] The Court's textual arguments have been addressed in detail in other scholarship. The conclusion of many scholars – with which I agree – is that the text of the constitution is

---

44 See, e.g., P. Stenning, *Appearing for the Crown* (Cowansville, QC: Brown, 1986), ch. 10 [Stenning, *Crown*].

45 Section 2 provides that "'Attorney General' means the Attorney General … of a province in which … proceedings [under the Code] are taken," with certain exceptions.

46 See, e.g., Stenning, *Crown, supra* note 44; and P.W. Hogg, *Constitutional Law of Canada* (Toronto: Carswell, 2007), sec. 19.6 [Hogg, *Constitutional Law*]. See also *R v Fok*, 2001 ABQB 150 (Alta QB).

47 See, further, Wright, "Courts as Facilitators," *supra* note 1.

48 The Court also discussed ss 129 and 135, transitional provisions relating to law and executive power post-Confederation, which are relevant to prosecutorial authority.

capable of sustaining a federal and/or a provincial claim to prosecutorial jurisdiction.[49] It is similarly unhelpful on the specific issue of provincial non-enforcement of federal criminal laws.

History is also inconclusive. The prosecution of the federal *Criminal Code* has fallen largely to the provinces since Confederation, and *attorney general* was defined, by s. 2 of the *Criminal Code*, as the "Attorney General ... of the province" from 1892 until 1969, when the term was amended to refer to the federal attorney general in certain situations, precipitating the Supreme Court decisions described earlier. This history might be taken to support provincial jurisdiction over criminal prosecutions, on a theory that it reflects expectations of provincial jurisdiction dating back to Confederation. But there is an enduring debate about whether this history reflected a "practical accommodation" or (perceived) constitutional limitation – and, indeed, about whether history is a valuable source of constitutional meaning.[50] Even if we assume its value, history is not any more helpful than the text on the issue of provincial non-enforcement.[51] The provinces have occasionally explicitly refused to enforce federal criminal laws.[52] Provincial non-enforcement may also be more common than it seems since non-enforcement decisions may not be formalized or publicized and thus may manifest as case-specific exercises of prosecutorial discretion.[53] Yet the comments, noted earlier, of Ian Scott, a former Ontario attorney

49 E.P. Apps and R.K. Wilkins, "The Prosecution of Criminal Offences," *University of Toronto Faculty of Law Review* 43 (1985) 145, 156; Stenning, *Crown, supra* note 44, 165; and Hogg, *Constitutional Law, supra* note 46, sec. 19.6.

50 For discussion, see, e.g., Stenning, *Crown, supra* note 44; and K. Swinton, *The Supreme Court and Canadian Federalism* (Toronto: Carswell, 1990), chap 4, esp. 96–8 [Swinton, *Canadian Federalism*].

51 Compare Baker, "Provincial Power," *supra* note 32.

52 For example, in the late 1970s, following several unsuccessful prosecutions of Dr Henry Morgentaler, Quebec's then attorney general announced that the province would no longer pursue prosecutions under the abortion provisions of the *Criminal Code*. A more in-depth historical examination might yield interesting insights into how the criminal law power was understood during Confederation and in the years after it; it might also yield additional examples of, and insights into, provincial non-enforcement. However, such an examination is, unfortunately, beyond the scope of this paper, and while I do not question its value, I am doubtful that it would change my argument in *this* paper.

53 Baker, "Provincial Power," *supra* note 32, 440 ("many provisions of the *Criminal Code* ... are not enforced by the provinces as a matter of routine policy").

general, and Kathleen Wynne, its former premier, betray a reticence about provincial non-enforcement, even in constitutional cases.[54]

Finally, consider precedent, which is also inconclusive. Provincial non-enforcement might seem to fall offside decisions – like the Manitoba Court of Appeal's decision in R *v Catagas* (1977)[55] – that condemn assertions of a Crown (executive) power to "suspend" the operation of a law entirely for a time or to "dispense" with it in favour of a specific person or group. These controversial powers of "suspension" and "dispensation" were abolished by the English *Bill of Rights* of 1689. However, important differences exist. Provincial non-enforcement is a duty that flows from the provincial attorney general's general duty to uphold the constitution, while Crown suspension and dispensation were powers exercised for any reason. The federal context is also important. Provincial non-enforcement does not involve a provincial official subverting a provincial law, but rather a provincial official refusing to enforce a federal law – a law that can still be enforced federally.[56] The rule of law concerns that underlie cases like *Catagas* cannot be dismissed out of hand and will be addressed later. For now, the key point is that there would seem to be no case that deals directly and decisively with provincial non-enforcement of federal criminal law.

THE ARGUMENT FROM FEDERAL STRUCTURE

Text, history, and precedent are inconclusive at best on the issue of provincial non-enforcement. But the previous paragraph, about precedent, hints at the first argument that, in my view, weighs in favour of provincial non-enforcement – a structural argument that invokes the federal system established by and underlying Canada's constitution. Structural arguments draw implications from the structures of government created by and underlying the constitution and then apply them

---

54 It is interesting to note, though, that, in the wake of the Supreme Court's decision in *Bedford*, Ontario, along with New Brunswick, refused to proceed with prosecutions under the old law, even though the Court had suspended its declaration of invalidity for a year. Quebec also issued a non-enforcement directive in the wake of the *Carter* decision, even though the Court had suspended, and then extended, its declaration of invalidity declaring the federal prohibition on assisted dying unconstitutional; see, further, *supra* note 31.

55 (1977) 81 DLR (3d) 396 (MBCA).

56 Carter, "Provincial Jurisdiction," *supra* note 32, 182; and Baker, "Provincial Power," *supra* note 32.

to the constitutional issue at hand. The Supreme Court has repeatedly affirmed that a federal system of government was established by and underlies Canada's constitution and has invoked structural arguments that draw implications from this "underlying principle of federalism" – admittedly, not always without controversy.[57]

The federal system underlying Canada's constitution supports my claim that there is a duty of provincial non-enforcement. How? The federal system contemplates two independent, constitutionally protected orders of government – federal and provincial.[58] These two orders of government are "coordinate," not "subordinate," and so it generally falls to federal officials (and, through them, the federal electorate) to determine when and how to wield federal legislative and executive power and to provincial officials (and, through them, their provincial electorates) to determine when and how to wield their province's legislative and executive power.[59] Provincial non-enforcement by the provincial attorney general of constitutionally suspect federal criminal laws respects the institutional lines of authority and accountability that flow from this federal system, whereas provincial enforcement circumvents them, implicating the provincial attorney general, and the province, in potential unconstitutionality by the federal government.

To help see why, consider the ongoing debate about whether and when an attorney general's power and duty to act independently in the prosecutorial context extends beyond case-specific prosecutorial decisions. Some have argued that the attorneys general have a broad scope to assert and act upon independent constitutional views that are not shared by the relevant government and legislature – for example, by conceding unconstitutionality during litigation.[60] Others, though, have insisted that the

57 See, e.g., *Secession Reference, supra* note 40, paras 49–60; *Reference re Supreme Court Act*, ss 5 and 6 [2014] 1 SCR 433 [*Supreme Court Reference*]; and *Reference re Senate Reform* [2014] 1 SCR 704 [*Senate Reference*].

58 This is distinct from the question whether federalism, properly understood, also entails exclusive allocations of federal and (perhaps especially) provincial *jurisdiction*.

59 See, e.g., *Liquidators of the Maritime Bank v Receiver General of New Brunswick* [1892] AC 437, 441–2 (PC); and *Reference re Securities Act* [2011] 3 SCR 837, para 71. There are exceptions, such as judicial appointments: see *Hauser, supra* note 26, 933.

60 See, e.g., J. Ll. J. Edwards, "The Role of the Attorney General and the Charter of Rights," in R.J. Sharpe, ed., *Charter Litigation* (Toronto: Butterworths, 1987); Scott, "Law, Policy," *supra*, note 34; and K. Roach, "Not Just the Government's Lawyer," *Queen's Law Review* 31 (2005–06) 598 [Roach, "Government's Lawyer"].

attorneys general have a limited scope to assert and act upon independent constitutional views, due either to the convention of Cabinet collective responsibility (which requires that laws and policies pursued by the Cabinet be respected)[61] or to their "constitutional duty" to their legislature (which requires that laws and policies approved by it be respected).[62]

These arguments, in favour of a limited scope to assert and act upon independent constitutional views, might seem to weigh against provincial non-enforcement. But this would neglect the federal context of the duty. The provincial attorneys general would be refusing to enforce a constitutionally suspect law pursued by the *federal* government and enacted by the *federal* Parliament – not the *provincial* governments they serve as attorneys general or the *provincial* legislatures to which they are accountable. The provincial attorneys general are the chief legal officers of an independent, coordinate branch of government – not servants of the federal government or the federal Parliament, obliged to respect federal constitutional views.

The argument that a provincial attorney general should enforce constitutionally suspect federal criminal laws is, in essence, an argument that he or she should defer to federal constitutional views – that the provincial attorney general's duty to uphold the *Charter* in the prosecutorial context is a duty to uphold the *Charter* as interpreted and applied by the federal government. But neither the constitution nor any provincial statute requires the provincial attorney general to defer to federal constitutional views.[63] And such an argument sits uncomfortably with

---

61 Hogg, *Constitutional Law, supra* note 46, sec. 36.5(d) (accepting that if an attorney general's advice that a law or policy raises constitutional issues is ignored, it would be difficult for him or her "to remain in cabinet, *where of course he would be under an obligation to support the policy*") (emphasis added).

62 G. Huscroft, "Reconciling Duty and Discretion: The Attorney General in the Charter Era," *Queen's Law Review* 34 (2008–09) 773.

63 It might be argued that the federal power to define the criminal law in s 91(27) includes, by implication, a duty on the provinces to defer to federal constitutional views on the basis that provincial non-enforcement would give the provinces the power to "destroy" the federal power. This argument might have some force if the provinces were held to hold an exclusive power to enforce s 91(27) offences. But, as noted, s 91(27) has been held to confer a federal enforcement power: see *supra* note 43. Since the federal government could enforce provincially unenforced laws, this argument is unconvincing. It is also a nice question whether a province can statutorily delegate the power or duty to determine constitutionality to a federal decision maker. At a minimum, I think that such a delegation, if permissible, must be made explicit – which it has not been in this context.

Canada's federal structure, and the coordinate governments it contemplates, leaving the provincial attorney general beholden to federal constitutional views and subverting provincial lines of accountability.[64]

THE ARGUMENT FROM FEDERAL PURPOSE

Another argument that can be offered for provincial non-enforcement is that it would further two of the important purposes that the federal system is (or at least could be) understood to promote in Canada.[65]

The first is the safeguarding of individual rights. The idea that a federal system can help safeguard individual rights, or "liberty," by checking government overreach has a long, distinguished history in the United States, where it has been accepted by many courts and scholars.[66] In Canada, however, there has been less of a tendency to ascribe federalism such a purpose – at least more recently. And yet, in some (mostly older) cases, judges have occasionally flirted with the idea that the division of powers ought to be interpreted as promoting individual rights – especially in cases concerned with the division of powers in relation to criminal law.[67] And there was once a robust debate in the legal scholarship about whether this idea was defensible on the historical record or, at least, normatively.[68] This debate has been reignited by more recent scholarship, which suggests that the preservation of liberty was, indeed, a key concern of the "Founders"[69] – a concern that animated how they allocated the division of powers in relation to criminal justice, hoping that "a tyrannical federal criminal law might be mitigated by provincial non- or under-enforcement."[70] Whatever their

---

64 Provincial officials will likely not have the same ability to fix the law or hold federal officials to account, and a province's voters may lack the same clout federally.

65 While this sort of purposive argument is much more common in *Charter* cases, the courts have acknowledged that federalism serves certain purposes and that constitutional issues that engage federalism issues should be approached with those federal purposes in mind; see, e.g., *Canadian Western Bank v Alta* [2007] 2 SCR 3, paras 22–4.

66 B. Friedman, "Valuing Federalism," *Minnesota Law Review* 82 (1997) 317, 402–5.

67 For a discussion of the cases, see Swinton, *Canadian Federalism, supra* note 50, 180–94. For a recent example, see *R v Demers* [2004] 2 SCR 489, paras 78–93, per LeBel J, dissenting [*Demers*].

68 For discussion, see, e.g., *Demers, supra* note 67, paras 80–2 (discussing the opposing views of F.R. Scott, on the one hand, and Bora Laskin and Paul Weiler on the other).

69 J. Ajzenstat, *The Canadian Founding: John Locke and Parliament* (Montreal and Kingston: McGill-Queen's University Press, 2007).

70 Baker, "Provincial Power," *supra* note 32, 8.

accuracy historically, these claims at least help remind us that one of the useful purposes that Canada's federal system generally – and the allocation of criminal justice jurisdiction specifically – *could be* understood to promote is the safeguarding of individual rights.[71]

Provincial non-enforcement would help advance this individual rights–protecting purpose. Most obviously, it would do so by preventing the enforcement of a provision of the *Criminal Code* that the provincial attorney general believes to be inconsistent with the individual rights and freedoms protected by the *Charter*. This would let the province serve as a vehicle for the articulation of an alternative, possibly broader, understanding of these rights and freedoms. In addition, provincial non-enforcement would allow the provinces to become a rallying point for those who believe that their *Charter*-protected rights and freedoms are being, or will be, violated by the provision – as it did in Ontario for those opposed to the new federal sex-work law. Finally, provincial non-enforcement – actual or threatened – might also force the federal government to repeal or amend the provision to address the *Charter* concerns raised provincially. More subtly, even if the provision is not repealed or amended, provincial non-enforcement – actual or threatened – may impact the constitutional arguments offered by the federal government to support the provision by taking certain, particularly questionable, arguments off the table or altering the emphasis placed on them. To be sure, the federal government may feel strongly enough to reject the provincial attorney general's position, to trigger a judicial reference to the Supreme Court to try to vindicate its own constitutional views, and/or to decide to enforce the provision itself. However, political and resource constraints would likely preclude it from doing so in at least some cases, forcing it to choose between leaving the law unenforced in the province and accommodating the constitutional concerns raised; and a judicial reference, if pursued, would (at least help) address such constitutional concerns.

The previous paragraph points to another, second and related, federal purpose that would be advanced by provincial non-enforcement: democratic participation. The Supreme Court has acknowledged in various cases that the promotion of democratic participation is a purpose underlying Canada's federal system. In *Canadian Western Bank v Alberta* (2007), for example, the Court suggested that one of the "fundamental objectives of federalism" in Canada was and still is "to promote

71 Compare Swinton, *Canadian Federalism, supra* note 50, chap 6; Swinton is more sceptical of this idea.

democratic participation by reserving meaningful powers to the local or regional level."[72]

Provincial non-enforcement would help advance this democratic-participation purpose as well. Provincial non-enforcement increases the opportunities available for popular participation in constitutional decision making, providing an additional vehicle for individuals and groups to vindicate their *Charter* rights. And since the provincial attorney general is accountable to his or her provincial legislature, which is, of course, democratically elected, provincial non-enforcement is (at least) less prone to the democratic objection often directed at judicial review. In addition, provincial non-enforcement – actual or threatened – might trigger a broader *Charter* debate, inside and outside the province, and among and between governments and the public, opening up a space for additional participants and perspectives.[73] Finally, provincial non-enforcement, and the public debate it triggers, might force the federal government to consider *Charter* issues that it may have ignored or overlooked, "facilitat[ing] more detailed public scrutiny and oversight."[74]

The idea that the political process might actually help protect *Charter* rights might seem misguided, or at least naive, particularly where the rights of democratic outsiders (like politically unpopular minorities) are at stake. It bears repeating that the proposal here is not to do away with judicial review, which, in my view, has an important role to play in helping to protect *Charter* rights that are not adequately protected in the political process. And yet, the role that provincial non-enforcement might play in safeguarding the *Charter* should not be neglected. Democratic outsiders may find it easier to convince one or more provincial attorneys general who are more sympathetic to them of the risk that a federal criminal law poses to their *Charter* rights than a less sympathetic federal government, and the adoption of their constitutional views in these provinces may enhance the persuasiveness of their message elsewhere.[75]

---

72 *Supra* note 65, para 22.

73 For further exploration of this point, but in the context of Australian federalism, see S. Stephenson, "Federalism and Rights Deliberation," *Melbourne University Law Review* 38 (2014) 709.

74 *Ibid*, 750–1.

75 For a general discussion of this point, but in the context of American federalism, see H. Gerken, "Dissenting by Deciding," *Stanford Law Review* 57 (2005) 1745. For a call for new thinking about federalism and jurisdiction in response to present realities, one that resonates with some of the themes explored here, see also chap 7 by Asha Kaushal in this volume.

THE COMPARATIVE INSTITUTIONAL COMPETENCE ARGUMENT

Another argument for provincial non-enforcement – and the last that I will mention in this article – is comparative institutional competence. The provincial attorneys general are just as well placed as the federal attorney general to determine whether a criminal law is constitutionally suspect.[76] Indeed, there may actually be reason to prefer the constitutional views of the provincial attorneys general in the criminal law context.

The federal government may enact a constitutionally suspect federal criminal law for several reasons.[77] The first is a lack of knowledge: the federal government may simply fail to anticipate a potential constitutional problem, perhaps because it fails to foresee how the law might or will be applied. The second is reasonable disagreement; the federal government may have formed an honest but mistaken belief that the law is not constitutionally suspect due to good faith disagreement about constitutional meaning or application.[78] Finally, the federal government may pursue a constitutionally suspect law intentionally, making a calculated decision that the electoral, ideological, and other benefits of pursuing the law outweigh the risks of potential constitutional invalidation.

If the provincial attorneys general were more likely to fall prey to these constitutional shortcomings than the federal government, this might be an argument against provincial non-enforcement. But there is no good reason to believe that this is the case. The federal minister of justice (who is also the federal attorney general) has a statutory duty to review every proposed federal government bill to determine whether it is "inconsistent" with the *Charter* and to report any inconsistencies to the House of Commons.[79] All proposed government bills are now vetted for potential unconstitutionality by the federal Department of Justice. While a similar statutory requirement to report inconsistencies does not

---

76 It is the federal attorney general/minister of justice who plays the primary role in vetting proposed federal legislation for potential unconstitutionality: see note 79 below. The federal attorney general also usually prosecutes non–*Criminal Code* federal criminal laws.

77 W.K. Wright, "The Political Safeguards of Canadian Federalism," *National Journal of Constitutional Law* 36 (2016) 1, 14–15.

78 For a recent discussion of the role of "good faith" and "honest and reasonable belief" in constitutional vetting by the executive branch, see *Schmidt v Canada (Attorney General)*, 2016 FC 269 [*Schmidt*].

79 *Department of Justice Act*, RSC 1985, c J-2, s 4.1.

generally exist provincially, provincial attorneys general also "engage in similar pre-enactment scrutiny because of their statutory obligations to ensure that the government is conducted in accordance with law."[80] There is simply no evidence to suggest that the federal constitutional review process is somehow superior to the provincial review process.[81]

In fact, there may be good reason to prefer the constitutional views of the provincial attorneys general. The role that the provincial attorneys general play in enforcing the *Criminal Code* may give them an advantage in flagging potential *Charter* issues because a history of actual enforcement may bring these issues into clearer focus. And provincial attorneys general may be more inclined and better equipped to flag potential *Charter* issues than their federal counterpart. Since the law is not a provincial law but rather a federal law, they may be less concerned about the potential for friction and fallout, not only politically but also interpersonally, and thus have more institutional leeway to assert and act upon their constitutional views. Provincial non-enforcement would permit the provincial attorneys general to bring these valuable comparative institutional advantages to bear.

Potential Objections to Provincial Non-enforcement

The previous part makes the case, briefly, for provincial non-enforcement of constitutionally suspect federal criminal laws. This part describes, and briefly responds to, potential objections to the idea.

The Federalism Objections

There are at least two federalism-based objections that might be directed at provincial non-enforcement. The first is that provincial non-enforcement would interfere impermissibly with the federal power over "criminal law" granted by s. 91(27) and thus be unconstitutional. The objection here would probably be something to the effect that provincial non-enforcement would confer a power to "destroy"[82] or nullify, or

---

80 Roach, "Government's Lawyer," *supra* note 60, 601–2.

81 Indeed, see J. Bond, "Failure to Report: The Manifestly Unconstitutional Nature of the *Human Smugglers Act*," *Osgoode Hall Law Journal* 51 (2013–14) 377 (discussing the shortcomings of the *federal* review process).

82 See *McCulloch v Maryland* 17 US (4 Wheat.) 316, 431 (USSC) (the "power to tax involves the power to destroy" – to "defeat and render useless the power to create").

at least interfere impermissibly with, the power that s. 91(27) grants the federal government to determine the substance of the criminal law. The implication would be that the provinces lack the constitutional power, both legislative and executive, to pursue a general non-enforcement policy in this context.[83]

However, such an objection would, in my view, be unfounded. This argument might have some force if the federal government lacked the constitutional authority to enforce its own criminal laws.[84] But, as noted, the Supreme Court has clearly held that the federal government does, in fact, have the constitutional authority to do so.[85] An argument that provincial non-enforcement might "destroy" Parliament's power to define the criminal law seems hard to take seriously when the federal government could counteract provincial non-enforcement by simply enforcing the law itself.[86]

In addition, a provincial attorney general could make it clear that provincial non-enforcement is aimed at regulating the discretion of provincial officials, with an eye to ensuring that they are not made party to potential *Charter* violations – a matter that falls within provincial jurisdiction.[87] This would help stave off an argument that provincial

---

83 To put this in traditional division-of-powers terms, the argument might be that the provinces lack this power either under the pith and substance doctrine because it relates in pith and substance to a matter that falls under the federal criminal law power (s 91(27)) or under the inter-jurisdictional immunity doctrine because its application would impair the "core" of this federal criminal law power. Note one unusual feature of this argument – that it would seem to require the provinces to act to enforce federal law. We do not usually think of the division of powers operating to impose positive duties on governments to act.

84 But see Baker, "Provincial Power," *supra* note 32, which argues for a general provincial power (but not a duty) to refuse to enforce federal criminal laws, notwithstanding this argument. See also Carter, "Provincial Jurisdiction," *supra* note 32, 177–8, arguing that such a power exists as a matter of positive law.

85 See the text accompanying *supra* note 43.

86 Take the inter-jurisdictional immunity argument referred to *supra* note 83. The argument that provincial non-enforcement would invade the core of federal jurisdiction over criminal law would presumably link the federal government's power to define the criminal law to its enforcement. But even if this core existed, it would not be impaired here since the federal government has the ability to enforce its criminal laws itself. Accordingly, there would, in my view, be no good claim for inter-jurisdictional immunity.

87 The Court's decision in *Re Same-Sex Marriage* [2004] 3 SCR 698 may seem to sit uncomfortably with this claim. There, the Court found invalid a declaratory provision in federal legislation recognizing same-sex marriage that sought to

non-enforcement intrudes improperly on the federal power to determine what constitutes a crime.[88]

Finally, any attempt to invoke an invalidity argument to challenge provincial non-enforcement in the courts would have to contend with thorny questions surrounding the reviewability of prosecutorial discretion in this context. The courts are generally very reluctant to interfere with exercises of prosecutorial discretion.[89] True, an exception has been carved out where breaches of "constitutional obligations" under the *Charter* are involved. This exception may extend to other aspects of the constitution, opening up exercises of prosecutorial discretion that may violate the division of powers to judicial review.[90] But even if this is so, thorny questions still remain. For example, if provincial non-enforcement decisions are communicated in a Crown policy or guideline, any attempt to invoke the invalidity argument would have to contend with the Court's recent suggestion that "Crown policies and guidelines do not have the force of law, and cannot themselves be subjected to *Charter* scrutiny in the abstract"[91] – a claim that presumably extends, as Paul Daly rightly notes, to "general constitutional scrutiny."[92]

The second federalism objection that might be directed at provincial non-enforcement is a federal paramountcy objection.[93] The federal paramountcy doctrine applies where overlapping and otherwise valid federal and provincial laws conflict, rendering the provincial law inoperative to

affirm the "freedom of officials of religious groups to refuse to perform" same-sex marriages, on the basis that who may or must perform marriages falls within provincial jurisdiction. However, the case is distinguishable. Provincial non-enforcement would speak to enforcement of a federal criminal law *provincially*; it would not regulate or preclude its enforcement *federally*.

88 This would go to a possible argument under the pith and substance doctrine.

89 *Anderson*, *supra* note 38, paras 46–50.

90 *Ibid*, para 45.

91 *Ibid*, para 56.

92 P. Daly, "Prosecutorial Discretion and Assisted Suicide, Again," *Administrative Law Matters* (blog), accessed 1 November 2015, http://www.administrativelawmatters.com.

93 This sort of federal paramountcy objection would be unusual in at least two respects. First, if accepted, it would seem to contemplate a positive duty on the provinces to enforce federal law – which, as noted earlier, is unusual because we do not usually think of the division of powers imposing positive duties to act; see *supra* note 83. Second, as noted at the conclusion of this paragraph, it also seems to assume that a provincial non-enforcement decision is a provincial "law" that the doctrine can render inoperative – which is not obvious.

the extent of the conflict. A conflict exists where dual compliance is impossible or the provincial law frustrates the purpose of the federal law. The objection to provincial non-enforcement might be that it would frustrate the purpose of the federal criminal law, effectively nullifying the particular criminal prohibition. But, here again, such an objection would be unfounded. As with the invalidity objection, the claim that provincial non-enforcement would frustrate the purpose of the criminal prohibition seems difficult to take seriously. Where the federal government has the ability to enforce the prohibition itself, any frustration of federal purpose that arises could just as easily be chalked up to federal enforcement choices as to provincial non-enforcement. In addition, provincial non-enforcement may actually be consistent with the federal purpose in some cases.[94] Finally, any attempt to invoke a federal paramountcy objection would have to contend with similar questions about the reviewability of prosecutorial discretion. Difficult questions would arise here about whether a provincial non-enforcement decision constituted a provincial "law" that could be rendered inoperative under the doctrine of federal paramountcy.

The Rule of Law Objections

There are also several rule of law–related objections that may be directed at provincial non-enforcement.[95] One is that provincial non-enforcement would be prone to abuse. The concern here is that the provincial attorneys general might unilaterally choose the federal criminal laws to enforce – choices that might vary arbitrarily over time and by attorney general and reflect "political" rather than genuine *Charter* considerations, thereby ushering in a rule of man or woman, not a rule of law.

---

94 Take, e.g., s 117 of the federal *Immigration and Refugee Protection Act*, which was discussed recently by the Supreme Court in *Appulonappa*, *supra* note 16. The provision required the attorney general of Canada's consent to prosecute. The Court pointed to excerpts from the parliamentary debates, which suggested that this consent requirement was inserted to allow for selective enforcement, to prevent the prohibition from being applied too broadly. The Court rejected the attempt to invoke ministerial discretion to avoid *Charter* issues.

95 The meaning of the rule of law is hotly contested. The rule of law–related objections that I address are usually associated with even "thin" understandings of the rule of law. For an excellent discussion of leading accounts of the rule of law, see M. Liston, "Governments in Miniature: The Rule of Law in the Administrative State," in *Administrative Law in Context*, ed. C.M. Flood and L. Sossin, 2nd ed. (Toronto: Emond, 2013).

This is a concern that should be taken seriously. The constitutional views of the provincial attorney general might be clouded in some cases by political considerations, or even mistaken. Yet similar claims are, of course, made about judicial review.[96] It might be thought that, on the whole, provincial non-enforcement is more likely to reflect constitutional views that are tainted by politics, or mistaken, than judicial review. But if this is not the case, this claim no more weighs against provincial non-enforcement than judicial review. And even if it is the case, the extent to which judicial review has the advantage here might be less pronounced than we might imagine given the good faith disagreements that exist about what the *Charter* permits or requires and the seeming inevitability of mistakes.

Moreover, judicial review remains an option. It is open to the federal government to countermand provincial non-enforcement decisions by initiating a judicial reference defending the law. It is far from obvious that the provinces have a duty to enforce federal criminal laws – even those the courts find to pass constitutional muster.[97] But a judicial decision finding a provincial attorney general's constitutional concerns unwarranted would make such concerns harder to sustain. Judicial review (actual or anticipated) might thus be expected to restrain the abuse of provincial non-enforcement.

In addition, the provincial attorneys general, unlike judges, are answerable, formally and informally, to their Cabinet colleagues, their legislatures, and ultimately their provincial constituents. This, and the very real possibility that the federal government will challenge provincial non-enforcement decisions, might have a strong disciplining effect. Because of the potential for litigation and other forms of pushback, provincially and federally, provincial non-enforcement might come at the expense of other items on the agenda of the provincial attorney general or the government. As a result, non-enforcement decisions are unlikely to be taken lightly. Indeed, the bigger concern may well be constitutional avoidance, not abuse.

Finally, to the extent that a risk of abuse exists, transparency could help mitigate it. If provincial attorneys general were required to articulate

96 For discussion of such claims, see, e.g., W. Wright, "Beyond Umpire and Arbiter: Courts as Facilitators of Intergovernmental Dialogue in Division of Powers Cases" (JSD diss., Columbia Law School, Columbia University, 2014), 324–7, http://dx.doi.org/10.7916/D87D2S7R.

97 See the earlier section "The Federalism Objections," especially note 84.

publicly the constitutional concerns justifying provincial non-enforcement decisions, the chances that they would refuse to enforce laws they oppose for political rather than constitutional reasons would be reduced because the reasons provided would be open to public scrutiny and critique.[98]

A second rule of law–related objection that might be directed at provincial non-enforcement is that the discrepancy that would result between the law on the books and the law as enforced would lead to uncertainty and confusion about the rules that individuals are expected to observe, thus hindering their ability to govern their affairs accordingly.[99] In some cases, individuals might be overly cautious, observing the law on the books, even though it was not being enforced provincially, while in other cases, they may be insufficiently cautious, underestimating its enforcement.

This is also an objection that should not be taken lightly. It would be preferable, as I noted at the outset, if the federal government addressed any constitutional concerns raised by a provincial attorney general legislatively, either pre- or post-enactment. But where this does not occur, provincial non-enforcement remains a valuable safeguard. The advanced-notice concerns that result from the incongruence between the law as enacted and the law as enforced are perhaps, to some extent at least, baked into our legal system. Due to resource constraints, evolving senses of what is important, and the various layers of discretion involved in the criminal justice system, some *Criminal Code* provisions are enforced less often than others, and some not at all, to varying degrees over time.[100] In addition, it bears noting that this sort of incongruence can also result from judicial review in *Charter* and other cases – for example, where a law struck down by the courts is not repealed, and so is left on the statute books, but is not being enforced. Finally, this is another concern that transparency could help address. The provincial attorneys general could help mitigate advanced-notice concerns by publicizing their non-enforcement decisions.[101]

---

98 Thought would need to be given to how this sort of transparency would be ensured. One possibility, of course, is a statutory obligation; another is a Cabinet policy.

99 For articulations of this concern, see, e.g., *R v Nur*, [2015] 1 SCR 773, para 91.

100 Baker, "Provincial Power," *supra* note 32, 440.

101 Enforcement policies already shape the meaning and significance of the law, but such policies are often opaque and thus resistant to accountability. If greater transparency and accountability resulted from this proposal, this would arguably be a welcome thing.

A third rule of law–related objection that might be directed at provincial non-enforcement is a provincial equality objection. The objection here would be that provincial non-enforcement is problematic on rule of law grounds because the enforcement of the *Criminal Code* – which is a federal, and thus, at least notionally, a national statute – would vary by province, raising rule of law–related concerns about the equal application of the law.

And yet, the enforcement of the *Criminal Code* already varies considerably by province due to "differing provincial government policies."[102] This sort of differential application may be an inevitable by-product of a division of responsibility federally and provincially between criminal law definition (federal) and enforcement (provincial).[103] Indeed, the Supreme Court has suggested that the "differential application of federal law can be a legitimate means of forwarding the values of a federal system" and is thus to be "constitutionally fostered," recognizing "that different approaches to the administration of the criminal law are appropriate in different territorially based communities."[104] In any event, if differential application seems or becomes undesirable, the federal government has an option at its disposal: it could elect to enforce the law itself, thereby "provid[ing] a more uniform application of the law."[105]

The Federal Comity Objection

The need for federal comity is another objection that might be directed at provincial non-enforcement. Here the objection might be that provincial non-enforcement is undesirable because it would demonstrate insufficient regard by the provincial attorneys general for the constitutional views of their federal counterpart, fostering intergovernmental friction.[106]

---

102 L. Sterling and H. Mackay, "The Independence of the Attorney General in the Civil Sphere," *Queen's Law Review* 34 (2009) 891, 907; see also Baker, "Provincial Power," *supra* note 32, 441–2.

103 Variations almost certainly exist intra-provincially as well, on a more local level.

104 *R v S (S)* [1990] 2 SCR 254, 289–90 (cited with approval in *R v Regan*, [2002] 1 SCR 297, para 71, per LeBel J, for the majority). I read the reference to administration in this passage to include enforcement, at least on the institutional level contemplated here.

105 Baker, "Provincial Power," *supra* note 32, 442.

106 See, for evidence of this view, Scott, "Law, Policy," *supra* note 34, 123–4.

A concern for federal comity is, in my view, an unconvincing objection to provincial non-enforcement. It is true, as I have discussed elsewhere, that intergovernmental cooperation plays a valuable role in a federal system.[107] It is also true that intergovernmental cooperation has a strong supporter in the Supreme Court; in recent federalism decisions, it has regularly cast the courts as "facilitators" of "cooperative federalism."[108] Yet the Court has stopped short of insisting that intergovernmental cooperation is required, as opposed to simply desirable.[109] In addition, an overemphasis on intergovernmental cooperation risks obscuring the real and often underappreciated benefits that can result in some cases from "uncooperative federalism."[110]

Provincial non-enforcement is a good case in point. Provincial non-enforcement presents a rich but underappreciated opportunity for the provinces to play a valuable role in safeguarding *Charter*-protected rights and freedoms. True, federal and provincial disagreement and conflict might be the result, at least for a time. But the clash of constitutional views that provincial non-enforcement might generate would trigger a worthwhile debate about constitutional meaning, within and between the federal and provincial governments and possibly society

---

107 Wright, "Courts as Facilitators," *supra* note 1, 451–2.

108 See, e.g., *Canadian Western Bank*, *supra* note 65, paras 22–4, 37, 42; *Chatterjee v Ontario (Attorney General)*, [2009] 1 SCR 624, para 32; *NIL/TU,O Child and Family Services Society v BCGSEU*, [2010] 2 SCR 696, paras 42–4; *Reference Re Assisted Human Reproduction Act*, [2010] SCR 457, para 139; *Quebec (Attorney General) v Canadian Owners and Pilots Association*, [2010] 2 SCR 536, paras 44–5; *Quebec (AG) v Canada (AG)*, [2015] 1 SCR 693, paras 15–21, 148–56, 189, 197; *Saskatchewan (Attorney General) v Lemare Lake Logging Ltd.*, [2015] 3 SCR 419, paras 21–3, 78, 118; *Alberta (Attorney General) v Moloney*, [2015] 3 SCR 327, paras 15, 27, 104, 112, 127; *Rogers Communications v Châteauguay (City)*, 2016 SCC 23, paras 38–9, 85, 110. See also Wright, "Courts as Facilitators," *supra* note 1, 373–89; and the interesting discussion of "cooperative federalism" from the Quebec perspective in chap 5 by Noura Karazivan in this volume.

109 Wright, "Courts as Facilitators," *supra* note 1, 381–2. An exception is where the constitution's formal amendment provisions are triggered, engaging provincial interests in the process: see, e.g., *Senate Reference*, *supra* note 57; and *Supreme Court Reference*, *supra* note 57. However, if the relevant amendment procedures are not triggered, due to inaction or the particular type of change contemplated, intergovernmental cooperation is not required.

110 Wright, "Courts as Facilitators," *supra* note 1, 452. See also Bulman-Pozen and Gerken, "Uncooperative Federalism," *supra* note 14 (discussing the virtues of "uncooperative federalism" in the US context).

as a whole. It might also expose constitutional shortcomings, perhaps obviating the need for judicial review.

The Judicial Review Objection

Another objection that might be directed at provincial non-enforcement – and the last I will mention in this paper – is that it is unnecessary, even undesirable, because judicial review is available to catch the *Charter* breaches that would be caught by provincial non-enforcement. This objection to provincial non-enforcement was advanced by Ian Scott, Ontario's former attorney general, who argued that "in *Charter* questions, ... it is desirable that the critical determinations be made ... by judges."[111]

Those accustomed to viewing the courts as the exclusive, or at least the primary, interpreter and applier of the constitution are likely to find this argument against provincial non-enforcement attractive – even decisive. But for those, like me, who understand the political and judicial branches to play a shared, complementary role in interpreting and applying – and thus safeguarding – the *Charter*, this objection to provincial non-enforcement comes up short. It reflects a view of the institutional role of the courts and political branches that is descriptively inaccurate and normatively unattractive – descriptively inaccurate because it underestimates the significant role that political actors already play, in practice, as *Charter* decision makers and normatively unattractive because it underestimates the value of, and need for, multiple, complementary, and interactive *Charter* safeguards. Provincial non-enforcement recognizes the important role that political actors do, can, and should play – outside, but in concert with, the courts – in interpreting and applying, and thus safeguarding, the *Charter*.

The argument advanced is not as radical as it might seem. It is not aimed at taking the *Charter* away from the courts – or even at taking the decisive, authoritative word about its interpretation away from the courts.[112] Provincial attorneys general who have concerns about the constitutionality of a federal criminal law would remain free to look to the courts for redress or guidance. In addition, while there is no duty

111 Scott, "Law, Policy," *supra* note 34, 124.

112 See *supra* note 15 and accompanying text.

to seek judicial input before provincial non-enforcement occurs, judicial views, once sought, should still, in my view, be respected.[113] The argument advanced is, rather, for provincial non-enforcement as one of several complementary *Charter* safeguards.[114]

In any event, even if judicial review is thought to be the preferred route to resolve a provincial attorney general's concerns about the constitutionality of a federal criminal law, there is still an argument for provincial non-enforcement. Judicial review might not always be a practical option.[115] Even where it is an option, judicial challenges to a law can take considerable time to resolve – and even where a law is invalidated on *Charter* grounds, the declaration of invalidity is often suspended for several months to allow the government time to respond. The problem is that, in the interim, a (potentially) constitutionally suspect law is left on the books, perhaps being enforced.[116] Provincial non-enforcement responds to these problems, providing a proactive mechanism to avoid the potential constitutional harm from the outset or to check it faster than the courts.[117]

Looking Forward

At least two sets of questions arise from this discussion of provincial non-enforcement that deserve further thought. First, further thought needs to be given to how this duty of provincial non-enforcement would be implemented. For example, how would the provincial attorneys general determine whether a law is constitutionally suspect, triggering the duty of provincial non-enforcement? Would it be sufficient if, say, the law were merely possibly unconstitutional, or would some

---

113 For a previous discussion of why I think this is generally desirable (with a few key exceptions), see Hogg, Thornton, and Wright, "Charter Dialogue Revisited," *supra* note 6, 30–8. I do not deny that political and social actors are free to disagree with judicial decisions under the *Charter*; the issue is whether, when, how, and how much they are free to act upon those views.

114 But, since the provinces arguably have no duty to enforce even constitutional federal laws, the non-enforcement option would remain: see *supra* note 84.

115 Criminal trials, e.g., are costly, time-consuming, and unpredictable, and, as a result, most criminal defendants plead guilty rather than exercise their rights to a trial – let alone mount *Charter* challenges, which are also costly, time-consuming, and unpredictable.

116 For an exploration of this point, see R. Leckey, *Bills of Rights in the Common Law* (Cambridge: Cambridge University Press, 2015).

117 This occurred, e.g., in Ontario and New Brunswick following the *Bedford* case; see *supra* note 47.

stricter standard be applied?[118] Would the proper focus be on gauging only the likely response of the courts? If not, how would what the *Charter* permits or requires be determined? In addition, what would be the mechanics of a duty of provincial non-enforcement? Would a formal, written policy or guideline be required, or would something more informal be sufficient? Would non-enforcement decisions need to be made public, and, if so, how? Would reasons for the decision be required? Would a system of intra-provincial precedent be established, and, if so, what would it entail? Would Cabinet – or perhaps legislative – approval be required, either before or after the fact? What internal decision-making procedures might be established to help ensure accountability and prevent abuse? These and other questions about the implementation of the duty of provincial non-enforcement deserve further thought. The answer provided might help considerably to answer or mitigate some of the concerns that provincial non-enforcement might raise.

Second, further thought needs to be given to what provincial non-enforcement has to teach us about extrajudicial constitutionalism – or the constitution outside the courts. Clear instances of provincial non-enforcement are hard to find, on constitutional and other grounds (but, since non-enforcement decisions may not be formalized or publicized, and thus may manifest as ordinary exercises of prosecutorial discretion, they may be more common than it seems). If provincial non-enforcement is as rare as it seems, one important question is why. The answer may yield valuable insight into the willingness, or ability, of extrajudicial actors in Canada to articulate and defend (at least openly) the "counter-interpretations"[119] that are an essential prerequisite of provincial non-enforcement and to interpret, apply, and safeguard the constitution.[120] It might also yield important insight into the sorts of changes that might be required to facilitate them.

---

118 For a recent judicial exploration of this issue, see *Schmidt, supra* note 78.

119 On the relationship between "counter-interpretations" and a robust constitution outside the courts, see, e.g., J. Braver, "Counter-interpretation, Constitutional Design, and the Right to Family Life," *UK Constitutional Law Association* (blog), 6 January 2014, accessed 1 November 2015, http://ukconstitutionallaw.org/blog/.

120 The willingness – or is it the ability? – of extrajudicial (and, in particular, political) actors to respond to the constitutional understandings of the courts has been hotly contested in the literature about "Charter dialogue" in Canada; compare, e.g., Hogg, Thornton, and Wright, "Charter Dialogue Revisited," *supra* note 6 with E. Macfarlane, "Dialogue or Compliance? Measuring Legislatures' Policy Responses to Court Rulings on Rights," *International Political Science Review* 34 (2012) 39.

Conclusion

This paper makes the case for a duty of provincial non-enforcement. It argues that the provinces (and, in particular, the provincial attorneys general) have not only the power but also the duty to refuse to enforce federal criminal laws that are constitutionally suspect. Its discussion of provincial non-enforcement highlights the potential of legal scholarship that explores the role that political actors do, could, and should play in interpreting and applying the *Charter*. It also reaffirms the (recently underappreciated) relationship between federalism and rights protection, showing how provincial non-enforcement could be used to safeguard *Charter* rights.

A general objective of the collection in which this paper is included is that it aims to look at Canada's constitution with "fresh eyes," challenging conventional views about its past and present, with an eye to its future. With that broader objective in mind, while making the case for a duty of provincial non-enforcement, this article has also challenged several conventional views that have animated Canadian constitutional law.

First, and most obviously, the paper's discussion of provincial non-enforcement highlights the role that non-judicial actors and institutions do, could, and should play in interpreting and applying an aspect of the constitution (here, the *Charter*), challenging conventional accounts that focus disproportionately on the contribution of the courts. Provincial non-enforcement engages the political branches – particularly the provincial attorneys general – in safeguarding *Charter* rights, preventing the enforcement of a federal criminal law that a provincial attorney general believes to be constitutionally suspect, and allowing for the articulation, provincially, of an alternative, possibly broader understanding of the *Charter*. Provincial non-enforcement also provides another opportunity for social (not just political) actors to vindicate *Charter* rights, thereby creating a space for the provinces to serve as a rallying point for those who might lack the democratic power federally to ensure that their *Charter* rights are respected. By engaging this broader range of actors and mechanisms, the account that is provided sits uncomfortably with the conventional view that the courts have the exclusive, or at least the primary, word about the *Charter*.

Second, and perhaps less obviously, the paper complicates two competing visions of Canadian federalism, both described earlier in the introduction. The first (increasingly beleaguered) "classical" vision focuses on the protection of exclusive, distinct allocations of federal and provincial jurisdiction, conceptualizing them as "watertight compartments."[121] The second (now more popular) vision eschews this emphasis on exclusivity and distinctness; it builds on a "modern paradigm" that embraces overlapping, interdependent allocations of federal and provincial jurisdiction and focuses on coordinating these allocations of jurisdiction in the service of a "cooperative federalism."[122]

This paper's account of provincial non-enforcement complicates both visions, offering a fresh take on a long-standing feature of Canada's federal system: provincial enforcement of federal criminal law. Jurisdiction here is fluid and contested, not demarcated clearly or coordinated cooperatively. The provinces do not operate as outsiders to federal policies, reigning over an exclusive, distinct zone of jurisdiction, as the classical view suggests, but as insiders, tasked with implementing and enforcing federal policies. They do not use this power cooperatively, as the "cooperative" view suggests, but uncooperatively, to oppose federal policies with an eye to safeguarding the *Charter*.

121 *A-G Can v A-G Ont* [1937] AC 325, 354 per Lord Atkin (PC, Can).

122 See, further, Wright, "Courts as Facilitators," *supra* note 1; see also chap 5 by Noura Karazivan in this volume.

5 Cooperative Federalism in Canada and Quebec's Changing Attitudes

NOURA KARAZIVAN*

Introduction

This chapter seeks to analyse cooperative federalism from the point of view of the relationship between Quebec and the Canadian constitution. Cooperative federalism transfers a focus on *boundaries* to a focus on *effectiveness* and is often seen as a renewed version of classical or dualist federalism. While the principle is not a newcomer to Canadian law, it has been the subject of a great deal of recent attention[1] as it was called on to play what many commentators hoped would be a leading

* Associate professor, Faculty of Law, University of Montreal. I thank Howard Kislowicz and Mike Pal for comments on an earlier version of this chapter, as well as the organizers and participants in the "Canada at 150" conference held in December 2015 at Yale University.

1 See Warren J. Newman, "The Promise and Limits of Cooperative Federalism as a Constitutional Principle," *Supreme Court Law Review* 76 (2016) 67; Jean-François Gaudreault-DesBiens and Johanne Poirier, "From Dualism to Cooperative Federalism and Back? Evolving and Competing Conceptions of Canadian Federalism," in *Oxford Handbook of the Canadian Constitution*, ed. Peter Oliver, Patrick Macklem, and Nathalie Desrosiers (Oxford: Oxford University Press, 2017), 391; Ian Peach, "The Supreme Court of Canada Long-Gun Registry Decision: The Constitutional Question behind an Intergovernmental Failure," *Constitutional Forum constitutionnel* 24 (2015) 1; Eugenie Brouillet, "Canadian Federalism and the Principle of Subsidiarity: Should We Open Pandora's Box?," *Supreme Court Law Review* 54 (2011) 601; Bruce Ryder, "Equal Autonomy in Canada's Federalism: The Continuing Search for Balance in the Interpretation of the Division of Powers," *Supreme Court Law Review* 54 (2011) 566; Wade K. Wright, "Facilitating Intergovernmental Dialogue: Judicial Review of the Division of Powers in the Supreme Court of Canada," *Supreme Court Law Review* 51 (2010) 635 [Wright, "Facilitating Intergovernmental Dialogue"]; Marie-France Chartier and Peter Oliver, "La juge Charron et le fédéralisme coopératif," in *Principles*

role in two recent division of powers cases that opposed Quebec and Ottawa: securities regulation[2] and the long-gun registry.[3] Each conflict led to a Supreme Court of Canada decision that both clarified the potential role of cooperative federalism in Canadian law and evidenced its weaknesses.

The first part of this chapter will briefly address the scepticism that cooperative federalism inspires in Quebec, at least from a traditional point of view. More than fifty years ago, Justice Jean Beetz, former dean of the Faculty of Law at the Université de Montréal, explained the roots of this scepticism in his famous paper on Quebec's changing attitudes towards the 1867 constitution.[4] Drawing on his insights, this part will also discuss how this scepticism has been fuelled by perceived threats from more functionalist approaches to federalism, including those that value efficiency over formal respect of "territorial" division of powers lines.

The second part will draw a portrait of cooperative federalism in Canada by looking at both *judicial* cooperative federalism and *executive* cooperative federalism. These two categories reflect the two main functions performed by the principle of cooperative federalism: on the one hand, cooperative federalism has been used as a means of relaxing the centralizing potential of classical constitutional law doctrines, such as the doctrines of paramountcy and inter-jurisdictional immunity, and favouring the doctrines of pith and substance and double aspect. Because this take on cooperative federalism is mainly fuelled by courts, and does not rest on any evidence of cooperation among governments or legislators, I call this category *judicial* cooperative federalism.

---

and Pragmatism: Essays in Honour of Louise Charron, ed. Graham Mayeda and Peter Oliver (Markham, ON: Lexis-Nexis Canada, 2014), 189; Hugo Cyr, "Autonomy, Subsidiarity, Solidarity: Foundations of Cooperative Federalism," *Constitutional Forum constitutionnel* 23 (2014) 20; Paul Daly, "L'abolition du registre des armes d'épaule: le rôle potentiel des principes non écrits," *Constitutional Forum constitutionnel* 23 (2014) 41; Jean-François Gaudreault-DesBiens, "Cooperative Federalism in Search of a Normative Justification: Considering the Principle of Federal Loyalty," *Constitutional Forum constitutionnel* 23 (2014) 1.

2 *Reference Re Securities Act*, 2011 SCC 66, [2011] 3 SCR 837 [*Securities Reference*].

3 *Quebec (AG) v Canada (AG)*, 2015 SCC 14, [2015] 1 SCR 693 [*Quebec v Canada (long-gun registry)*].

4 J. Beetz, "Les Attitudes changeantes du Québec à l'endroit de la Constitution de 1867," in *The Future of Canadian Federalism*, ed. P.-A. Crépeau and C.B. Macpherson (Toronto: University of Toronto Press, 1967, 113 [Beetz, "Les Attitudes changeantes du Québec"].

On the other hand, this concept has been used as a justification for judicial restraint when courts have been presented with an intergovernmental agreement or partnership that contemplates an interlocking or integrated exercise of the respective heads of power. I refer to this category as *executive* cooperative federalism.

The third part of this chapter will return to Quebec's attitudes towards cooperative federalism by looking at the two recent Quebec-Canada cases referred to above and by illustrating how attitudes towards cooperative federalism may change, considering the stakes. In the end, I conclude that even though both *judicial* and *executive* cooperative federalism have permeated the legal discourse, the limits of cooperative federalism are still real. Paradoxically, those limits also serve to neutralize any remaining scepticism towards cooperative federalism on the part of Quebec.

This contribution by no means intends to devise an exhaustive inventory of cooperative federalism's definitions, forms, or roles, nor does it seek to reduce cooperative federalism to the courts' rendition of it. Of course, a large part of intergovernmental relations takes part "outside the courts," as both Wade Wright and Asha Kaushal point out in their respective papers in the present volume. The primary focus, here, on judicial reception of cooperative federalism, seeks to evince its limited, often instrumentalized, and almost rhetorical role and invite critical reflection on what lies ahead for cooperative federalism.

Quebec and Cooperative Federalism

According to Jean Beetz, the very first attitude that Quebeckers held about the federal constitution was a passive one: the 1867 constitution was viewed as a shield protecting the French-speaking, Roman Catholic "Quebec minority" from the rest of Canada. This shield was to be provided by the interpretation that courts would make of the division of powers provisions in the *Constitution Act, 1867*. Being in charge of Canadian appeals until 1949, the Privy Council would play that role by narrowing down potentially invasive federal heads of jurisdiction such as the trade and commerce power[5] and the peace, order, and good government provision[6] and by expanding provincial heads of power such as property and

5 S 91(2) *Constitution Act*, 1867. See, e.g., *Citizens Insurance Co. of Canada c Parsons* (1881), 7 AC 96 (PC).

6 S 91, *in limine, Constitution Act, 1867*. See, e.g., *In re Board of Commerce Act* [1922] 1 AC 191 (PC) and *Toronto Electric Commissioners v Snider* (1925) AC 396 (PC).

civil rights, going as far as to render s. 92(13) akin to a residuary provision.[7] It also famously developed the "watertight compartments"[8] metaphor, deriving it from the need to maintain the exclusivity of legislative powers distributed by ss. 91 and 92, *Constitution Act, 1867*.

This approach has been much commented upon.[9] It has also, indirectly, fostered the blooming of a method of interpretation that Beetz calls analytical or qualitative jurisprudence.[10] According to this method, qualifying a law to render a decision on its *vires* implies an enquiry into the matter it covers (What is it that the law does?), coupled with a conceptual definition of the heads of power involved, respect for Privy Council precedents, and recourse to exegetic analysis – all of which exude an appearance of "great objectivity."[11] But more importantly, this analytical strategy implies a rejection of functional arguments that would tie competence to efficiency. Of course, federalism involves a search for economies of scale,[12] and it is not rare to see efficiency concerns aligned with division of powers issues in Canada. But efficiency is not the only value fostered by federalism: so are autonomy, diversity, and proximity. To strike the (right) balance among these values, Beetz argues, provincial autonomists will be generally suspicious of any type of argument that has its roots in a discourse of efficiency and functionalism[13] and will prefer exclusivity-driven arguments, precisely because those exclusive boundaries act as a shield against the perception of growing federal interference in provincial autonomy.

---

7 See Beetz, "Les Attitudes changeantes du Québec," *supra* note 4, 119.

8 *Attorney-General for Canada v Attorney General for Ontario* (1937) AC 326 (PC) [*Labour conventions case*].

9 See, generally, William Francis O'Connor, *Report Pursuant to the Resolution of the Senate to the Honourable Speaker by the Parliamentary Counsel Relating to the Enactment of the* British North America Act, 1867, *any Lack of Consonance between Its Terms and Judicial Construction of Them and Cognate Matters* (Ottawa: King's Printer, 1939); Alan C. Cairns, "The Judicial Committee and Its Critics," in *Essential Readings in Canadian Politics*, ed. Christian Leuprecht and Peter H. Russell (North York, ON: University of Toronto Press, 2011), 201.

10 Beetz, *"Les Attitudes changeantes du Québec," supra* note 4, 120.

11 On the appearance of objectivity, see Andrée Lajoie et al, who comment on the (sometimes) "strategic" use of the analytical process just described: A. Lajoie et al, "Jean Beetz: sur la société démocratique," *in Mélanges Jean Beetz* (Montreal, Thémis, 1995), 509, 537.

12 A. Breton and A. Scott, *The Economic Constitution of Federal States* (Toronto: University of Toronto Press, 1978), 5–6.

13 Beetz, "Les Attitudes changeantes du Québec," *supra* note 4, 120.

Because it was perceived that a more diffuse or informal approach to division of powers would increase centralization, there was, and still is, a certain scepticism regarding concurrent heads of jurisdiction and the validation of both provincial and federal laws governing a single matter. Cooperative federalism, which tends to recognize the validity of laws emanating from both federal and provincial legislatures, is seen in this light as implying a new concession to the federal government, what Beetz calls "yet another centralization."[14] Cooperative federalism is also, and more tragically, viewed as "the implicit admission of federalism's weaknesses."[15]

Beetz thus openly questions those "Canadian jurists" who consider quantitative criteria sufficient to determine the validity of laws or who rely on the "intuition" of the judge in interpreting the constitution.[16] Doing so, in his opinion, would diminish the very concept of law: a product of reason, which can be "*completely* systematized."[17] But it would also threaten Quebec's "collective identity."[18] Thus, where those "Canadian jurists," such as Bora Laskin, saw cooperative federalism as a trigger for the

14 *Ibid*, 137 (my translation).

15 *Ibid*.

16 *Ibid*, 121. I offer a more detailed account of the functional approach in "Le fédéralisme coopératif entre territorialité et fonctionnalité: le cas des valeurs mobilières," *Revue générale de droit* 46 (2016) 419, 431–6 [Karazivan, "Le fédéralisme coopératif entre territorialité et fonctionnalité"].

17 J. Beetz, "Allocution," *in Mélanges Jean Beetz* (Montreal: Thémis, 1995), 42 (my translation; emphasis added). It is not difficult to find, in the work of former dean and Supreme Court chief justice Bora Laskin, support for a more functional approach to division of powers, which Beetz so strongly opposed. According to Laskin, writing in 1955, the qualification of a law for the purpose of division of powers analysis is "a choice depending on court's view of the purpose of the legislation and the ambit of various heads of powers"; see B. Laskin, "Tests for the Validity of Legislation: What's the Matter?," *University of Toronto Law Journal* 11 (1955) 114 at 121. Laskin also believed that the economic, social, and political impact of legislative policy ought to influence its constitutional validity. In his view, legal decisions are judicial choices; precedents are useful, but heads of jurisdiction evolve over time, so decision making should not be static; matters reflect the "capacities for legislative action" that can be expanded or restricted by courts (*Ibid* at 127). See also, on his judicial philosophy, Katherine Swinton, *The Supreme Court and Canadian Federalism: The Laskin-Dickson Years* (Toronto: Carswell, 1990), 226.

18 Beetz, "Les Attitudes changeantes du Québec," *supra* note 4, 121.

Supreme Court of Canada's "adjustment" of the division of powers boundaries,[19] Beetz considered erasing those lines a major threat to provincial autonomy.

Beetz was writing in 1967; the events surrounding the patriation of the constitution in 1981–82 (well captured by Macfarlane's contribution in the present volume) exacerbated rather than eased this attitude by generating what Leclair describes as a perception of treason in Quebec.[20] Needless to say, the following Meech and Charlottetown episodes further eroded the "bond of trust between Quebec and the rest of Canada."[21] This is probably one reason why Quebec jurists have adhered to, and maintained, a "legalist view of the division of powers"[22] and hence, at least in theory, why some are dubitative towards cooperative federalism.[23]

A Portrait of Cooperative Federalism

Now that we have outlined the reason behind Quebeckers' scepticism towards the idea of cooperative federalism, it is time to look at how this principle came into being and what it actually achieves in practice.

---

19 See B. Laskin, "Reflections on the Canadian Constitution after the First Century," *Canadian Bar Review* 45 (1967) 395, 396–8: "The assumption [that the constitutional division of powers must remain untouched] is, however, unacceptable to an evolving society. … The responsibility of the courts, and especially of the Supreme Court of Canada, as an agency of adjustment is, of course, a heavy one."

20 J. Leclair, "Constitutional Principles in the *Secession Reference*," in *Oxford Handbook of the Canadian Constitution*, ed. Peter Oliver, Patrick Macklem, and Nathalie Desrosiers (Oxford: Oxford University Press, 2017), 1009 at 1016.

21 *Ibid*, 1017. On the point of failed reconciliation, see also Guy Laforest, *Trudeau et la fin d'un rêve canadien* (Sillery, QC: Septentrion, 1992), 150–1.

22 N. Karazivan and J.-F. Gaudreault-DesBiens, "On Polyphony and Paradoxes in the Regulation of Securities within the Canadian Federation," *Canadian Business Law Journal* 49 (2010) 1, 3 [Karazivan and Gaudreault-DesBiens, "On Polyphony and Paradoxes"]. See also, on the "fetishism of formal law," J.-F. Gaudreault-DesBiens, "The Fetishism of Formal Law and the Fate of Constitutional Patriotism in Communities of Comfort: A Canadian Perspective," in *Ties That Bind: Accommodating Diversity in Canada and the European Union*, ed. J.E. Fossum et al (Brussels: Peter Lang, 2009), 301.

23 See, e.g., E. Brouillet, "Le fédéralisme et la Cour suprême du Canada: quelques réflexions sur le principe d'exclusivité des pouvoirs," *Revue québécoise de droit constitutionnel* 3 (2010), 8.

A Short History of Cooperative Federalism[24]

It is not uncommon for the rise of cooperative federalism to be described as coinciding with the end of dualism or with the triumph of "efficacy over formalism."[25] In fact, the Supreme Court of Canada itself puts forward this narrative in the *Reference Re Securities Act*, as I will briefly describe here.[26]

According to the Court, in its first stage, federalism was conceptualized by the Privy Council as a way to conceive legislative powers as mostly, but not always, "watertight compartments."[27] This approach tended towards a dualist view of the division of powers and favoured exclusivity. As was noted in the first part of this chapter, the Privy Council introduced a restrictive interpretation of the federal heads of power, especially the power over trade and commerce, and a wide interpretation of provincial powers over property and civil rights.

The second stage, which started after appeals to the Privy Council were abolished in 1949, was described by the Court as favouring a "more flexible"[28] view of the division of powers by permitting a certain amount of overlap between federal and provincial heads of power and by encouraging intergovernmental arrangements. The Court provided a few examples of what it called the now "dominant approach."[29]

---

24 This section draws partially from Karazivan, "Le fédéralisme coopératif entre territorialité et fonctionnalité," *supra* note 16, 436–40.

25 *Quebec (Attorney General) v Canadian Owners and Pilots Association*, [2010] 2 SCR 536, para 44 [*COPA*].

26 See *Securities Reference*, *supra* note 2, paras 53–62. For a discussion of the distinct logics and structural differences between dualist and cooperative federalism, see J. Poirier, "Souveraineté parlementaire et armes à feu: le fédéralisme coopératif dans la ligne de mire?," *Revue de droit de l'Université de Sherbrooke* 45 (2015) 47, 54–7 [Poirier, "Souveraineté parlementaire et armes à feu"].

27 *Labour conventions case*, *supra* note 8.

28 *Securities Reference*, *supra* note 2, para 57.

29 The Court mentions, for instance, *OPSEU v Ontario (Attorney General)*, [1987] 2 SCR 2 (where provincial legislation regarding eligibility of provincial public servants to run in federal elections was validated as legislation relating to the constitution of the province and not as legislation relating to federal electoral law) and *PEI Potato Marketing Board v HB Willis Inc.*, [1952] 2 SCR 392 (where a cooperative federal-provincial regime, which included a federal delegation to a provincial board of the power to commercialize potatoes interprovincially, was validated).

Finally, in recent years, the Court dispelled any remaining doubts as to its position by endorsing cooperative schemes and by rejecting "rigid formalism in favour of accommodating intergovernmental efforts."[30] The Court recalls that, in those cases, the "constitutional creativity and cooperative flexibility"[31] of Canadian federalism were praised.

Respectfully, in spite of the appeal that such a transformative theory of federalism may have, cooperative federalism is not a shift in Canadian constitutional law, nor is it fair to describe it as a departure from Privy Council precedents. Cooperative federalism has always coexisted with dualist federalism. In fact, according to Justice Dickson, cooperative federalism is as old as the *Constitution Act, 1867* itself.[32] The Privy Council was not opposed to it – quite the contrary. For instance, when the Supreme Court endorsed, in 1952, an integrated scheme for the commercialization of potatoes[33] and confirmed the constitutional validity of delegation from the federal legislature to a provincial board, it was by referring to Privy Council advice that the Court endorsed Parliament's legislative efforts. According to Rinfret CJC, Parliament

> was following the advice of the Judicial Committee in the several judgments which it rendered on similar Acts and, more particularly, on the *Reference concerning the Natural Products Marketing Act,* adopted by Parliament in 1934 (S. of C. 24 and 25 George V, c. 57), (1937) that the proper way to carry out legislation of that character in Canada, in view of the distribution of legislative powers under the British North America Act, was for Parliament and the Legislatures to act by co-operation.[34]

As early as 1914, Viscount Haldane stated that the demarcation among heads of power was not airtight: "[t]he language of [ss. 91 and 92] and of the various heads which they contain obviously cannot be

30 *Ibid,* para 58.

31 *Ibid,* citing Abella J in *Fédération des producteurs de volailles du Québec v Pelland,* 2005 SCC 20, [2005] 1 SCR 292 [*Pelland*], para 15.

32 *R v Wetmore,* [1983] 2 SCR 284, 307, Dickson J: "The balance struck between sections 91(27) and 92(14) of the *Constitution Act* is a reflection of the faith the framers of the Constitution placed in a cooperative, federalist approach to addressing an issue both of national dimension and of local concern."

33 *PEI Potato Marketing Board v Willis, supra* note 29.

34 *Ibid,* 396–7.

construed as having been intended to embody the exact disjunctions of a perfect logical scheme."[35] There is thus little doubt that Viscount Haldane's statement implies that he "endorsed cooperative federalism."[36] But the Privy Council was also, and at the same time, endorsing the principle of exclusivity and the idea of watertight compartments. How can these two positions be reconciled? According to Leclair, by doing so, the Privy Council was in fact "*imposing* on the federal government an obligation to cooperate with provinces."[37] Exclusivity and watertight compartments put the provinces and the federal government in a constitutional "impasse,"[38] which had only cooperation as a potential way out.

At this point, it is necessary to introduce the distinction, alluded to above, between cooperative federalism as a judicial device and executive cooperative federalism.

Judicial Cooperative Federalism

Federalism assumes the existence of an impartial judiciary tasked with resolving disputes between the central governing authority and the federated entities.[39] A good deal of this task involves recourse to constitutional doctrines. In division of powers cases, a judge will first seek to determine the pith and substance of a statute and assign it to a head of power (doctrine of pith and substance). If the statute falls under a head of power assigned to the adopting level of government, the law is valid. In the case of a provincial law, the next step is often to examine its applicability (doctrine of inter-jurisdictional immunity) and the risk of operational conflict with a valid federal statute (doctrine of paramountcy). Therefore, at one point or another, courts will have to make

---

35 *John Deere Plow Co. v Wharton*, 338, per Viscount Haldane, as cited in *Multiple Access v McCutcheon*, [1982] 2 SCR 161, 180 [*Multiple Access*]. See also, for another endorsement of cooperative federalism, *In Re Board of Commerce Act, 1919, and the Combines and Fair Prices Act*, [1922] 1 AC 191 (PC).

36 As per Laskin CJ in *Re: Anti-Inflation Act*, [1976] 2 SCR 373, 422.

37 J. Leclair, "Please, Draw Me a Field of Jurisdiction," *Supreme Court Law Review* 51 (2010) 555, 578–9.

38 F. Chevrette and H. Marx, *Droit constitutionnel* (Montreal: Presses de l'Université de Montréal, 1982), 234–5.

39 K.C. Wheare, *Federal Government* (Oxford: Oxford University Press, 1950), 58–9 [Wheare, *Federal Government*].

use of these doctrines in responding to a challenge relating to the validity, applicability, or operational compatibility of a statute.

What is the role of cooperative federalism within this judicial framework? It is in the *attenuation* of rigid interpretative doctrines that cooperative federalism is called upon to play a role. In fact, once relaxed, these doctrines open up the possibility of a more porous demarcation of the federal and provincial heads of power. In other words, it is "by allowing for overlapping powers through the application of [these interpretative doctrines] that co-operative federalism is able to meet [the] needs [of an increasingly complex society] and, in this sense, to enable the goals of federalism to be realized."[40] As LeBel and Binnie JJ put it for the majority in *Canadian Western Bank*,

> Canadian federalism is not simply a matter of legalisms. The Constitution, though a legal document, serves as a framework for life and for political action within a federal state, in which the courts have rightly observed the importance of co-operation among government actors to ensure that federalism operates flexibly.[41]

The following section examines three of the ways in which the Supreme Court of Canada has made use of cooperative federalism in the application of these constitutional doctrines.

A FLEXIBLE PITH AND SUBSTANCE DOCTRINE

In the determination of the pith and substance of an impugned law, cooperative federalism played a distinct (although not determinative) role in two recent cases. The *Reference Re Assisted Human Reproduction Act* provides the first example of an analysis, influenced by cooperative federalism, of the validity of several provisions of a federal act. Among others, the challenge concerned s. 10 of the *Assisted Human Reproduction Act*, which sought to regulate treatments for infertility and recourse to assisted reproduction. For McLachlin CJC, as she then was, joined by three other justices, the pith and substance of s. 10 came within the scope of the federal criminal law power and was, *a priori*, valid. According to McLachlin CJC, s. 10 ought to be construed in light of s. 68 of the act, which favours cooperation and "pragmatic lawmaking."[42] She

40 *Quebec v Canada (long-gun registry)*, *supra* note 3, para 148 (LeBel J).

41 *Canadian Western Bank v Alberta*, [2007] SCR 3, para 42 [*Canadian Western Bank*].

42 *Reference Re Assisted Human Reproduction Act*, [2010] SCR 457, para 139.

encouraged this legislative strategy, which would allow provincial law to apply where it was equivalent to federal legislation, and federal law to apply only in the absence of such provincial legislation, while maintaining the validity of both laws, in these terms:

> The complexity of modern legislation will often render it impossible for one level of government to fulfill its constitutional mandate without trespassing on the jurisdiction of the other level. The Court's endorsement of a flexible, cooperative approach to federalism suggests that this kind of pragmatic lawmaking should be encouraged.[43]

In this case, it is ironic that pragmatic law-making was referred to, and encouraged, when there was no indication that the provincial governments had ever agreed to this "cooperative" approach. Quebec strongly opposed what it perceived was federal trespassing on provincial jurisdiction in health matters. It should be noted that the reports preceding the *Canadian Assisted Reproduction Act* did consider the interaction with provincial governmental authority, but not in a way that respected provincial powers.[44] Perhaps cooperative federalism can allow both provincial and federal governments to legislate following the pragmatic law-making model, but if they do not agree to do so, it is unclear how recourse to the principle of cooperative federalism can be helpful.

Cooperative federalism was also at play in the characterization of the municipal notice of reserve, which was impugned in *Rogers Communications v. Châteauguay (City)*.[45] In that case, the majority, led by McLachlin CJ, as she then was, held that, in pith and substance, the municipal notice, which had prevented the radio-communications antenna from being installed in a certain location, related to radio-communications, a matter within exclusive federal jurisdiction. Hence, it was *ultra vires* the province. Cooperative federalism, the majority found, was irrelevant here; flexibility "had its limits," and those limits had been met in that

43 *Ibid* (references omitted).

44 On the Baird Commission's recommendations to the provinces, see Guy Tremblay, "La compétence fédérale et le projet de loi sur la procréation assistée," *Les Cahiers de droit* 44 (2003) 519, 535. Another report, also tabled before the act came into force, accepted the inclusion of an "equivalent agreements" provision as a necessary tool of cooperative federalism (*Assisted Human Reproduction: Building Families*, Standing committee on health. Bonnie Brown, December 2001, 23). This provision (s 68) was included in the final act.

45 *Rogers Communications Ltd v Châteauguay (City)*, [2016] 1 SCR 467, 2016 SCC 23.

the municipal notice, in pith and substance, had sought to choose the location of the radio-communications infrastructure.

Gascon J, dissenting, held that it was a case of double aspect – that is, the order pertained to a subject that, "in one aspect and for one purpose"[46] (the health and well-being of residents) was provincial and, in another aspect and for another purpose (the siting of antennas), fell within federal jurisdiction. He made this point by referring explicitly to the spirit of cooperation animating modern conceptions of federalism. The net outcome, for the municipality, was the same: Gascon J found that the order did not apply to the federally regulated company since it impaired the core of the competence over radio-communications. But cooperative federalism was influential in the way in which the municipal notice had been characterized.

A DWINDLING DOCTRINE OF INTER-JURISDICTIONAL IMMUNITY

The doctrine of exclusivity, or inter-jurisdictional immunity, relates to the applicability of (most often[47]) provincial legislation to federally controlled entities (such as works, undertakings, enterprises, etc.).[48] No doubt this doctrine is the clearest expression of dual federalism, in the sense that it immunizes federally regulated works or undertakings or companies from provincial intrusion. In *Canadian Western Bank*, a case that raised the question of the applicability of provincial consumer protection laws to federally regulated banks, the Court narrowed down the scope of this doctrine by stating that, from then on, the doctrine of inter-jurisdictional immunity would be available only in cases where a provincial statute struck at the core of a federal head of power peremptorily identified by the courts.[49] The court also substituted the easily met standard of "affect" for the higher standard

46 The double aspect doctrine was formulated in *Hodge v. The Queen* (1883), 9 App. Cas. 117, 130.

47 In two recent cases, the arguments on inapplicability of *federal* law to a *provincial* health care entity were brushed aside by the Supreme Court, mainly because no core was recognized to the health care power; see *Canada (Attorney General) v PHS Community Services Society*, 2011 SCC 44, para 68 and *Carter v Canada (Attorney General)*, 2015 SCC 15, para 53.

48 R. Elliot, "Interjurisdictional Immunity after *Canadian Western Bank* and *Lafarge Canada Inc.*: The Supreme Court Muddies the Doctrinal Waters – Again," *Supreme Court Law Review* 43 (2008) 433 [Elliot, "Interjurisdictional Immunity"].

49 *Canadian Western Bank, supra* note 41, paras 77–8.

of "impair."[50] In practice, it means that it will be harder for a federal undertaking or company to make the claim that it ought to be immune from provincial legislation.

More importantly, it is said to be by virtue of cooperative federalism that this doctrine came to be weakened. It may be ironic that *Canada Western Bank* is so often associated with the necessity of recognizing cooperative federalism when the reality is that no provincial or federal legislators cooperated. The attorney general of Canada intervened in favour of the bank's immunity from provincial insurance legislation. Some say that recourse to the principle of cooperative federalism in this case should be viewed as an invitation to cooperate in the future.[51] Whether this invitation can be a prelude for inter-parliamentary or inter-governmental cooperation remains to be seen: it is rather banks that will have to "cooperate" with legislators from both levels of jurisdiction to comply with both sets of laws.

Cooperative federalism has not eradicated this doctrine completely: a few years after *Canadian Western Bank,* the majority of the Supreme Court found a provincial law inapplicable to federally regulated aerodromes.[52] On the other hand, the Court rejected the doctrine in a case where the provincial law did not impair the federal core, invoking the need, in an era of cooperative federalism, for the intrusion to be significant.[53]

All in all, the role of cooperative federalism in this context, following the new analytical framework proposed by the Supreme Court, is to narrow down the scope of the doctrine of inter-jurisdictional immunity – whether or not there is evidence of cooperation between federal and provincial legislatures. More often than not, when division of power cases reach the courts, cooperation among federal partners is nowhere to be found.

A RESTRAINED DOCTRINE OF PARAMOUNTCY

The doctrine of paramountcy comes into play when two statutes, one provincial and one federal, are simultaneously valid, but where both

50 *COPA, supra* note 25, para 45.

51 According to Wade K. Wright, the Supreme Court seemed to assume that intergovernmental dialogue would follow from a decision to accommodate overlap in jurisdiction; see W.K. Wright, "Facilitating Intergovernmental Dialogue," *supra* note 1, para 44.

52 *COPA, supra* note 25.

53 *Marine Services International Ltd. v Ryan Estate,* [2013] 3 SCR 53, paras 56 and 60.

laws cannot be complied with, either because of an operational conflict or because of a conflict of purpose; this means that a provincial enactment frustrates the purpose of a federal enactment.[54] Cooperative federalism is invoked to restrain the scope of this doctrine. A restrained doctrine of paramountcy simply means elevating the threshold for determining the presence of a conflict and making it more difficult to declare provincial legislation inoperable.[55]

Here again, there is often no sign of cooperation between provincial and federal actors; still, it is partly on behalf of cooperative federalism that the attenuation of the paramountcy doctrine is justified. The connection, it seems, lies in the potentially explosive combination of a flexible approach to division of powers matters with a strong doctrine of federal paramountcy, which would lead to the weakening of provincial heads of power. For this reason, the Supreme Court has reiterated that it is necessary to balance the diversity of regional experimentation, on the one hand, with the need to maintain national unity on the other.[56] Hence, the Court will favour, when possible, the cohabitation of parallel legislative schemes (as long as one doesn't say yes and the other no).

Two recent Supreme Court of Canada decisions considered the doctrine of federal paramountcy in light of cooperative federalism.[57] In *Lemare Lake*, the majority of the Court went so far as to say that to be consistent with cooperative federalism, the objective of federal legislation, for the purpose of paramountcy, must be defined as narrowly as possible to reduce a potential conflict of purpose, thus raising the question of the usefulness of the two-pronged test:

> This means that the purpose of federal legislation should not be artificially broadened beyond its intended scope. To improperly broaden the intended purpose of a federal enactment is inconsistent with the principle of cooperative federalism. At some point in the future, it may be argued that the two branches of the paramountcy test are no longer analytically necessary or useful, but that is a question for another day.[58]

---

54 E.g., a conflict of purpose is the basis for Court intervention in *Québec (AG) v Canada (Human Resources and Social Development)*, 2011 SCC 60, [2011] 3 SCR 635.

55 See *Multiple Access, supra* note 35, 190.

56 *Securities Reference, supra* note 2, para 60; *Canadian Western Bank, supra* note 41, para 24.

57 *Saskatchewan (Attorney General) v Lemare Lake Logging Ltd.*, [2015] 3 SCR 419 [*Lemare Lake*]; *Alberta (Attorney General) v Moloney*, [2015] 3 SCR 327 [*Moloney*].

58 *Lemare Lake, supra* note 57, para 23.

Cooperative federalism was used, in this case, to narrowly define the purpose of the federal law in a way that the dissenting judge severely criticized:

> My colleagues, following the clarion call of co-operative federalism, stress the need to take a "restrained approach" in frustration of purpose analysis. But while co-operative federalism is undoubtedly an important principle, a yearning for a harmonious interpretation of both federal and provincial legislation cannot lead this Court to disregard obvious purposes that are pursued in federal legislation and that are, by this Court's jurisprudence, paramount.[59]

In *Moloney*, the majority and dissenting judges offered contrasting views of how cooperative federalism would play out in the application of the first and second branches of the paramountcy test,[60] but they all agreed that there was a conflict that rendered the provincial law inoperative.

To sum up, cooperative federalism in division of powers cases delivers less than it promises: it amounts to little more than courts' rhetorical endorsement of cooperation (or, more accurately, of the idea of cooperation). It seldom reorients the qualification of impugned statutes at the stage of the pith and substance doctrine. With inter-jurisdictional immunities and paramountcy, recourse to cooperative federalism produces mixed results. To be sure, cooperative federalism has allowed the Supreme Court to devise a more *flexible* application of the three constitutional doctrines explored above, but not necessarily producing more *cooperative* results – or predictable ones.

Executive Cooperative Federalism

According to Peter Hogg, "the essence of cooperative federalism is a network of relationships between the executives of the central and regional governments."[61] This facet of cooperative federalism, sometimes called "executive federalism,"[62] depends on the presence of

---

59 *Ibid*, para 78 (per Côté J, dissenting).

60 See esp. paras 15, 27, 104, and 127.

61 P.W. Hogg, *Constitutional Law of Canada*, student ed. (Toronto: Carswell, 2011), 5–46.

62 *Ibid*, para 17. See also, generally, Alain-G. Gagnon, "Executive Federalism and the Exercise of Democracy," in *The Case for Multinational Federalism: Beyond the All-Encompassing Nation*, ed. Alain-G. Gagnon (London: Routledge, 2010), 67.

actual – and not merely rhetorical – cooperation between federal and provincial players. It should be remembered that the classical definition of federalism supposes a division of powers between two coordinated, but not subordinate, entities.[63] In this sense, cooperation can be seen as favouring the harmonious exercise of the *respective* heads of power of each legislature, as a way of ensuring that each legislature "properly discharges its responsibility to the public in a coordinated fashion."[64] Cooperation is not an end per se, but an instrument at the service of greater coordination among the federated entities. The result of cooperation and its various occurrences have been described as instances of "power-sharing."[65] A "venerable chain of judicial precedents"[66] has validated recourse to intergovernmental agreements, which transfer powers from a legislature to an administrative agency and seek to overcome the practical incapacity of each level of jurisdiction to achieve by itself, in certain matters, satisfying results.

However, there are at least two blind spots in the field of executive cooperative federalism: the first relates to the evidence sufficient to serve as indicia of this cooperation, and the second goes to the normative force of executive cooperative federalism. Here again, we turn to courts: of course, cooperation can go unnoticed and unchallenged, but when the conditions pertaining to the cooperation fail, frustrated parties turn to the courts to obtain judicial enforcement of cooperation. Hence, those decisions become primordial to enhance our understanding of cooperative federalism's potential and limitations.

The first element to consider is the evidence of cooperation. Determining that a relationship is indeed cooperative in nature can be an ambiguous task. In Quebec, for example, there is an online database of all federal-provincial and interprovincial agreements to which Quebec is or has been a party since 1922.[67] However, intergovernmental agreements are not the only way to create partnerships – nor are they sufficient proof of such partnerships. According to Johanne Poirier, an agreement can be established by an exchange of letters or through

63 Wheare, *Federal Government, supra* note 39.

64 *Securities Reference, supra* note 2, para 9.

65 *Ibid*, para 48.

66 Pelland, *supra* note 31, para 52.

67 Secrétariat aux relations canadiennes du Québec, "Relations canadiennes," accessed 14 March 2016, http://www.saic.gouv.qc.ca/affaires-intergouvernementales/ententes-intergouvernementales/index.asp.

notices signed by the representatives of the concerned governments. In essence, identifying something as an intergovernmental agreement will depend on an "array of indicators," which will include its title and the manner in which it was created.[68]

These indicators were analysed by both the majority and the dissenting judges in *Quebec (Attorney General) v Canada (Attorney General)*, the long-gun registry case, which will be discussed in more depth below. In this case, the majority of the Supreme Court of Canada found the indicators, which included declarations and the *Accord financier Canada-Québec relatif à l'administration de la Loi sur les armes à feu*, insufficient to support the existence of a partnership. The fact that there was no interlocking legislative scheme was, it seems, fatal to the claim. Indeed, the majority noted that the Canadian Firearms Registry "flows directly from federal legislation and is not dependent on any provincial statutes,"[69] and it refused to speculate as to the effects that a truly interlocking scheme could have had on their reasons.

In this finding, the five justices agreed with the unanimous panel of five judges at the Quebec Court of Appeal, who found little evidence of cooperation.[70] For their part, the four dissenting justices recognized the existence of a partnership, in the spirit of cooperative federalism,[71] that was more than a simple financial arrangement. Agreeing with the trial judge, they found that Quebec's implication in the implementation of the federal statute and, in particular, the role played by the provincial police were sufficient indicators to support the existence of a partnership.

There is also, it seems, a need for an administrative body responsible for the exercise of delegated authority. In *Quebec (Attorney General) v Moses*,[72] the Supreme Court was asked to interpret the James Bay and Northern Quebec Agreement, an agreement among the federal, Quebec, and Cree governments that provided an environmental assessment scheme for the exploitation of natural resources.[73] In this case, the majority and dissenting justices could not seem to agree on

---

68 J. Poirier, "Une source paradoxale du droit constitutionnel canadien: les ententes intergouvernementales," *Revue québécoise de droit constitutionnel* 1 (2009) 12n47 (my translation).

69 *Quebec v Canada (long-gun registry)*, *supra* note 3, para 4.

70 *Canada (Attorney General) v Quebec (Attorney General)*, 2013 QCCA 1138 (CanLII).

71 *Quebec v Canada (long-gun registry)*, *supra* note 3, paras 134, 149.

72 2010 SCC 17, [2010] 1 SCR 557.

73 *Ibid*, paras 9, 63.

the existence of a cooperative scheme or on the status to give to the agreement. For LeBel and Deschamps JJ, dissenting, the agreement was an intergovernmental partnership and an example of cooperative federalism. Also, the agreement, as a treaty, fell within the scope of s. 35 of the *Constitution Act, 1982*, which gave it constitutional status.[74]

According to the majority, the dissenting judges "refer to the treaty as a manifestation of cooperative federalism, but with respect, as they interpret it, the Treaty turns out to be a vehicle for provincial paramountcy."[75] The majority found that the agreement could not exclude federal assessment of a project that fell within the scope of fisheries.[76] An example of cooperative federalism would have been if Quebec and Canada had agreed to harmonize their assessment procedures, which they had not, partly because no joint body had been established, as required by the federal law.[77] We can deduce from this that, for the majority, an intergovernmental agreement, on its own, is insufficient to be considered an exercise in cooperative federalism. There ought to be, in addition, a joint body, or the delegation of powers to a body, as well as an agreement to harmonize legislation.[78]

The majority opinion was endorsed in *Nil/TU,O Child and Family Services Society v BC Government and Service Employees' Union*, where the Supreme Court recognized the existence of a cooperative scheme stemming from an agreement among provincial, federal, and First Nations governments and a delegation of powers to an agency.[79] These examples show that, at a minimum, for the Supreme Court to conclude that a practice of executive cooperative federalism has been established, it should be satisfied that there is an intergovernmental agreement, coupled with an interlocking legislative scheme, and delegation of powers to an administrative agency responsible for carrying out the provincial statute, the federal statute, or both. Of course, such delegation should remain within the limits of parliamentary sovereignty – that is, it should not constitute an abdication of legislative authority. Examples of successful cooperative federalism structures include the extensive

---

74 *Ibid*, para 84.
75 *Ibid*, para 13.
76 *Ibid*.
77 *Ibid*, para 29.
78 *Ibid*.
79 2010 SCC 45, [2010] 2 SCR 696, paras 42, 43.

delegation systems that permit the commercialization, across Canada, of potatoes,[80] eggs,[81] milk,[82] and poultry.[83]

Once a practice of cooperative federalism is established, the second question is what normative force it should be invested with (if any). When challenged by a third party, intergovernmental agreements, coupled with an interlocking legislative scheme and overseen by administrative bodies, will incite the courts to show greater *judicial restraint* – what Jean-François Gaudreault-DesBiens calls "benevolent tolerance."[84] Such was the case in *Pelland*, where the Court found that the purpose of the provincial law was to control agricultural production and that, in the context of an integrated scheme, it could incidentally affect extra-provincial trade, an area that is otherwise *ultra vires* the province.[85] In *Grisnich*, the importance of integrated schemes in overcoming the fact that neither legislative branch was entirely competent in a given area, like the commercialization of agricultural products, was invoked to justify this deference.[86] And in the *Reference re Agricultural Products Marketing*, Pigeon J praised the accomplishment that followed forty years of "sincere cooperative effort" and pressed that "it would really be unfortunate if this was all brought to nought."[87]

However, deference or judicial restraint stops when one of the "cooperating" parties repudiates the partnership or wants to restrict its scope. In such case, the courts will show less restraint and will call upon parliamentary sovereignty[88] or the exclusive jurisdiction over a given head of power.[89] It also stops when the courts reach the conclusion that some

80 *PEI Potato Marketing Board v Willis*, *supra* note 29.

81 *Reference Re Agricultural Marketing*, [1978] 2 SCR 1198.

82 *British Columbia (Milk Board) v Grisnich*, [1995] 2 SCR 895.

83 *Pelland*, *supra* note 31.

84 Jean-François Gaudreault-DesBiens, "The 'Principle of Federalism' and the Legacy of the Patriation and Quebec Veto References," *Supreme Court Law Review* 54 (2017) 96–7.

85 *Pelland*, *supra* note 31, para 23.

86 *British Columbia (Milk Board) v Grisnich*, *supra* note 82.

87 [1978] 2 SCR 1198 at 1296.

88 See *Reference Re Assistance Plan (BC)*, [1991] 2 SCR 525, 548: "It is conceded that the government could not bind Parliament from exercising its powers to legislate amendments to the *Plan*. To assert the contrary would be to negate the sovereignty of Parliament."

89 See *Quebec (AG) v Moses*, where the Court found that federal legislative authority could not be limited by the James Bay and Northern Quebec Agreement.

parts of the interlocking legislative scheme outstep the division of powers. In such case, the courts will invalidate that part and sever it from the otherwise valid legislative scheme.[90] Or the courts may find that there was actually *no* cooperation to begin with, as in the long-gun registry case. All in all, as Johanne Poirier points out, up to now, "judicial reengineering of federalism has been limited to comforting cooperation, and not sanctioning non-cooperation among federal partners."[91] In the face of non-cooperation, she adds, courts tend to resort to a "more dualist conception of the Canadian federation."

Two Case Studies from a Quebec Point of View

The previous section draws a portrait of cooperative federalism in the Canadian constitutional landscape, but as is the case with most paintings, the work cannot be appreciated until one takes a step back and looks at the broader picture. In Quebec, attitudes towards cooperative federalism, like attitudes towards federalism altogether, have been changing. Let us briefly return to Jean Beetz's article, cited above. If the first stage identified by Beetz was one of passive hiding behind the shield of the constitution, the second stage is one of proactive government activity in the commercial field; it is, simply put, Quebec taking active control of its economy and occupying the fields that the constitution has allocated to it. Signalling this shifting attitude, Beetz wrote that Quebec's control over the economy, including over securities regulation, was what mattered most at the time of his writing (1967), much more than the control over "civil rights" in the province.[92]

The first case study, the *Securities Reference*, involves a perceived threat to that provincial control over securities, a threat that was fought hard by, among others, Quebec and Alberta. Quebec, particularly, opposed arguments based on efficiency and functionalism, and it advocated a

90 E.g., *Re Agricultural Products Marketing Act*, where s 2(2)a(a) of the federal act was found *ultra vires* the federal Parliament because it delegated to the provincial board the authority to impose levies related to the intra-provincial market. Parliament could not delegate this power to a provincial agency because it is a power within provincial jurisdiction.

91 J. Poirier, "Souveraineté parlementaire et armes à feu," *supra* note 26, 52 (my translation).

92 J. Beetz, "Les Attitudes changeantes du Québec," *supra* note 4, 126–7.

strict division of powers analysis. Its arguments amounted to a rejection of allegations that cooperation and economic efficiency would be sufficient to transfer the regulation of securities to the federal Parliament. The attorney general of Canada, on the other hand, argued that cooperative federalism was fostered by the progressive opting-in features of the proposed law.

But if scepticism characterized Quebec's initial attitude towards cooperative federalism, and certainly its stance in the *Securities Reference*, it is paradoxically Quebec that attempted to take cooperative federalism to another normative level. In the long-gun registry case, our second example, Quebec went so far as to argue for recognition that cooperative federalism might force the federal government to act in a certain way and provide access to data it threatened to destroy. The attorney general of Canada replied that cooperative federalism was not a principle that could bind Parliament, reduce its legislative authority, force Canada to act in a collaborative way, or do away, even slightly, with ss. 91 and 92 of the *Constitution Act, 1867*.[93]

Cooperative federalism is thus being instrumentalized by both parties in federal disputes; it is not surprising, in this context, that courts are retreating behind old boundaries (ss. 91 and 92) and old principles (parliamentary sovereignty), as the next section will demonstrate, thus seriously weakening the role of cooperative federalism.

The Securities Reference*: Quebec's Scepticism towards Cooperative Federalism*

Provinces in Canada have regulated securities for over a century, but Canada remains one of the only federations in the world to lack a single (national or federal) securities regulator. For over fifty years, the federal government has attempted to find ways to regulate the field, and those attempts culminated in the first *Securities Reference*, in which the Supreme Court of Canada analysed the validity of the *Draft Securities Act*. This proposed law would have regulated all aspects of securities, including registration of issuers and protection of investors, matters that were clearly within provincial jurisdiction. The Court unanimously

93 *Factum of the Respondent Attorney General of Canada*, paras 71, 98, and 99, https://www.scc-csc.ca/WebDocuments-DocumentsWeb/35448/FM030_Respondent_Attorney-General-of-Canada-et-al.pdf.

found – rightly so, in my view[94] – that the proposed federal legislation was *ultra vires* the federal power over trade and commerce because it regulated each and every aspect of securities, rather than individual aspects, such as systemic risk or data collection, which, the Court found, would have been within federal jurisdiction. Moreover, the Court was not convinced that the provinces were constitutionally unable to legislate with relation to the general aspects of securities regulation since they had been doing precisely that for more than one hundred years. Finally, because the *Draft Securities Act* provided for gradual opting in, the Court was not convinced that the failure of one province to enter the scheme would jeopardize the operation of the whole scheme.[95]

The attorney general of Canada argued that "while securities trading may once have been mainly a local matter, it has evolved to become a matter of transcendent national concern that brings it within the s. 91(2) general trade and commerce power."[96] The attorney general stressed the fact that the gradual, voluntary opting-in scheme reflected cooperative federalism, which sought to achieve the desired result (a national securities regulator) "through cooperation rather than coercion."[97] The attorney general of Quebec reminded the Court that provinces were already cooperating by putting in place the passport system. He also made the point that the cost of having thirteen regulators ought to be irrelevant when considering the validity of the proposed legislation, as were general arguments based on the alleged greater efficiency of the proposed federal legislation.[98]

The Court seemed to agree with this last argument because it stressed the fact that for a head of power to be "transferred" to the federal Parliament, there ought to be a strong factual foundation, empirical evidence, and not "mere conjecture."[99] Here the Court found the factual matrix

---

94 Karazivan and Gaudreault-DesBiens, "On Polyphony and Paradoxes," *supra* note 22.

95 The Court applied the five indicia for finding jurisdiction over trade and commerce; see *Securities Reference*, *supra* note 2, para 108.

96 *Ibid*, para 114.

97 *Factum of the Attorney General of Canada*, http://www.scc-csc.ca/WebDocuments-DocumentsWeb/33718/FM010_Attorney-General-of-Canada.pdf, para 5; see also paras 69, 120, and 132.

98 *Factum of the Attorney General of Quebec*, http://www.scc-csc.ca/WebDocuments-DocumentsWeb/33718/FM095_Intervenant_Procureur-général-du-Québec.pdf.

99 *Securities Reference*, *supra* note 2, para 116. The Court did not display the same relative ease with which it had found, in *General Motors*, that competition, to be regulated effectively, had to be regulated federally. The Court's laconic analysis on that point was criticized; see, e.g., Karazivan and Gaudreault-DesBiens, "On Polyphony and Paradoxes," *supra* note 22.

insufficient. The analysis of the pith and substance of the proposed law led the Court to conclude that the proposed law was not qualitatively different from provincial laws and, ultimately, to invalidate it. However, it also found that had the law focused mainly on systemic risks and data collection, it could have been *intra vires* the federal Parliament since it would have been, in pith and substance, a law on the preservation and stability of capital markets, an objective that could not be achieved by provinces acting alone or in cooperation.

All in all, the fact that several provinces, including Alberta and Quebec, opposed the federal scheme may have triggered the invitation the Court made to the parties in the very last paragraphs of its reasons. The Court noted, in its concluding remarks, a "growing practice" of "seeking cooperative solutions" instead of following a territorial, "either/or" dichotomy.[100] In this sense, both the federal and the provincial levels of government have jurisdiction over some aspects of the regulation of securities, and "each can work in collaboration with the other to carry out its responsibilities."[101]

Two ideas flow from these remarks: first, that a takeover of provincial jurisdiction is not true cooperation, especially if some provinces object to it, and even if opting-out provisions are included in the proposed legislation; second, that if and when parties decide to cooperate, division of powers frontiers ought to be respected.

In the new version of the scheme, those lines seem to have been respected: the federal Parliament will enact the draft *Capital Markets Stability Act*, aiming at the protection of systemic risks, data collection, and the regulation of economic crime, which will be applicable throughout Canada; and the five participating provinces and one territory (at the time of writing) will enact a combined provincial/territorial *Capital Markets Act* aimed at the regulation of all matters of securities regulation within their territorial or provincial jurisdiction. Both federal legislators and participating provincial/territorial legislators will delegate to a single, hybrid entity (called the Capital Markets Regulatory Authority) the task of making regulations and administering the laws.

Quebec, predictably, disagrees that this cooperative scheme complies with the division of powers. It is of the opinion that the federal government is using cooperative federalism as "a pretext to push aside

100 *Securities Reference, supra* note 2, para 132.
101 *Ibid*, para 131.

the division of powers"[102] in the area of securities. To protect its own legislative autonomy, it has launched a new round of constitutional and administrative challenges. The attorney general of Quebec, in its factum for the Court of Appeal, endorses Quebec's Beetz-style dubitative attitude towards cooperative federalism and holds on to dualist federalism: by opting for dualist federalism, as opposed to cooperative or administrative federalism, Quebec argues that the Fathers of Confederation "wished to guarantee that provinces would enjoy the autonomy necessary for the development of their society, within their own spheres of competence, and, in particular, they wished to protect Quebec's capacity to exercise its powers in a way that preserves its language and culture."[103]

The Court of Appeal partially sided with Quebec in finding that the delegation scheme established among the five participating provinces, federal government, and one territory infringed on parliamentary sovereignty.[104] While the Supreme Court of Canada's opinion is pending, we may observe that its invitation to cooperate in the 2011 reference bore fruit – the question now is whether that fruit is forbidden. What is clear, however, is that Quebec is firmly convinced that it is. Even though the current scheme involves an intergovernmental protocol, an interlocking legislative framework, and delegation from the participating provincial legislatures and the federal legislature to an administrative agency, Quebec argues that it is still beyond Parliament's jurisdiction and must be struck down. Cooperative federalism, it seeks to convince the Supreme Court judges, is unhelpful here, "regardless of the positive

102 *Quebecers: Our Way of Being Canadians/Policy on Québec Affirmation and Canadian Relations* (Quebec City: Secretariat of Canadian Intergovernmental Affairs, 2018), 116 [*Policy on Québec Affirmation*], http://www.sqrc.gouv.qc.ca/documents/relations-canadiennes/politique-affirmation-en.pdf.

103 *Factum of the Attorney General of Quebec*, para 90 (my translation).

104 *Reference of the Government of Quebec in Virtue of Order in Council 642-2015 Concerning the Constitutionality of the Implementation of Pan-Canadian Securities Regulation*, 2017 QCCA 756 (CanLII). The Court also found that the federal statute could be mostly classified as falling within federal jurisdiction over trade and commerce. One voting mechanism provision had to be severed from the remainder of the law for it to be *intra vires* Parliament. Further discussion of this case is provided in N. Karazivan, "Cooperative Federalism v. Parliamentary Sovereignty: Revisiting the Role of Courts, Parliaments and Governments," in *Canadian Federalism and Its Future: Actors and Institutions*, ed. Alain-G. Gagnon, Johanne Poirier, Eugénie Brouillet, and Guy Laforest (2018).

rhetoric surrounding the phenomenon of cooperation within the Canadian federation."[105]

The Long-Gun Registry: Quebec Embracing Cooperative Federalism[106]

Quebec ironically contributed to this positive rhetoric by its position in the long-gun registry case. The Canadian *Firearms Act* established a regime (the Canadian Firearms Regime) to regulate the possession of three defined types of firearms: long guns, restricted firearms, and prohibited firearms. It also created two registries: one that kept track of licences to possess, and one that accounted for the registration of, these three types of firearms. The registration data was collected under the supervision of one registrar for all Canada, whereas the licensing information was collected through the collaboration of the thirteen chief firearms officers (one for each province and territory). The Canadian Firearms Registration System compiled the data coming from these two registries, and both federal and provincial authorities had access to it.

When the federal government announced its intention to abolish the long-gun *registration* requirement and destroy the data related to the long-gun registry, Quebec announced its intention to start its own long-gun registry and sought to obtain the transfer of the data pertaining to Quebec. The government of Canada refused, and a trial judge in Quebec held that Canada's destruction of the data violated cooperative federalism and that s. 29 of the *Ending the Long-gun Registry Act* (ELRA), the provision ordering the destruction of all long-gun registration data, was *ultra vires* the federal Parliament. Canada was ordered to transfer the data to Quebec. The Quebec Court of Appeal overturned the trial judgment, unanimously holding that Quebec had no right to the data and that the trial judge had erroneously identified a partnership in the operation of the Canadian Firearms Regime. Quebec turned to the Supreme Court of Canada and asked whether the principle of cooperative federalism constrained Parliament's power to order the destruction

105 *Factum of the Respondent Attorney General of Quebec*, para 52, http://www.scc-csc.ca/WebDocuments-DocumentsWeb/37613/FM035_Respondent_Attorney-General-of-Québec.pdf.

106 This section draws from a case summary co-authored with Han-Ru Zhou, "Cooperative Federalism Cannot Limit the Scope of Legislative Authority," 2016 *Public Law International Survey* 1, 133–5.

of the data, whether Quebec had a right to obtain a copy of the long-gun registry data, and whether s. 29 of the ELRA was *ultra vires* the federal government's powers over criminal law. Quebec offered a surprisingly vibrant plea in favour of cooperative federalism:

> *Canadian federalism is flexible and not formalist. It encourages cooperation among the two levels of government,* who are not subordinated to one another, and seeks to reconcile the legitimate diversity of regional experimentation with the need for national unity.[107]

The Supreme Court reformulated Quebec's position and took it one step further. In essence, it wrote, Quebec was "asking us to recognize that the principle of cooperative federalism prevents Canada and the provinces from acting or legislating in a way that would hinder cooperation between both orders of government."

The Supreme Court split 5–4. As mentioned above, the majority of the Court was not convinced that the Canadian Firearms Regime was a truly interlocking, cooperative regime. Intergovernmental agreements or funding arrangements were not, in themselves, evidence of cooperative federalism. In the view of the majority, the regime derived entirely from federal legislation and depended on no provincial legislation. Moreover, as Parliament was sovereign, it had all the liberty to change its mind – that is, repeal the legislative provision creating the regime and arrange for the destruction of the data collected through it.

The judges were of the opinion that where the federal government acted within its jurisdiction, no principle of cooperative federalism could alter the division of powers or impose limits on *how* this legislative power ought to be exercised. In other words, cooperative federalism imposed no duty to facilitate cooperation, even when the very purpose of federal legislation was to make it more difficult for provinces to adopt the legislation. The provision being *intra vires* the federal Parliament in this case, there could be no right to obtain the data.

The dissenting judges, including all three judges from Quebec, believed that there was, in fact, cooperation in the establishment, administration, and enforcement of the regime. But this finding, in itself, did not lead the dissenting judges to answer affirmatively the first question because, like the majority of the Court, they adhered to

107 *Ibid*, para 56 (emphasis added).

the division of powers' analytical framework and rigid constitutional boundaries. Nor did the finding of cooperation lead the dissenting judges to conclude that Quebec had a right to the data: the province did not have such a right. Because the cooperative arrangements were political, so too ought to be the remedy.

The finding of cooperation, however, came into play in the analysis of the question whether s. 29 of the federal legislation (the provision ordering the destruction of the long-gun registry data) was *ultra vires* the federal Parliament. When applying the test for invalidating a provision based on the ancillary effects doctrine, the dissenting judges assessed the seriousness of the impact that abolishing the long-gun registry and destroying its data had on Quebec. Indeed, the dissenting justices noted that when putting an end to a partnership, the legislature could cause a greater encroachment than the one being remedied.[108]

This is where Quebec's arguments became relevant. Quebec pleaded that it would suffer harm from the refusal to transfer the data since it would be practically impossible to retrace the chain of ownership of over a million firearms after registration ceased to be mandatory.[109] Quebec had, for a number of years, relied on the federal firearms control program, all the while facilitating its application within the province.[110] Quebec, in other words, did not deem it necessary to create its own registry since the federal registry provided access to data and permitted the integration of its own licensing information. It then suffered from the consequences of this reliance, which were put in these terms:

> By depriving provinces of existing data, and imposing on them a human, administrative and financial burden for the reconstitution of those data, Parliament attempts to dissuade the implementation of a provincial long-gun registry.
>
> As the implementation of such registry would necessarily take time, the interveners would, in the meantime, be unable to exercise their functions and this would impact upon Quebec's constitutional responsibilities in the field of arms control within its territory.[111]

---

108 *Quebec v Canada (long-gun registry), supra* note 3, para 159.

109 *Ibid*, para 181.

110 *Ibid*, para 180.

111 *Factum of the Attorney General of Quebec*, 10 June 2016, paras 109–10, http://www.saic.gouv.qc.ca/affaires-intergouvernementales/institutions-constitution/dossiers-judiciaires/documents/memoire-renvoi-constitution.pdf (my translation).

For the majority, however, even though the effect of s. 29 was to make it "prohibitively expensive and complicated for [Quebec] to create its own long-gun registry,"[112] financial repercussions were not a consideration when analysing the constitutional validity of the legislation. Once the power to legislate was recognized, cooperative federalism *could not* limit the exercise of a valid head of power.

Again, two ideas derive from the majority opinion in this case: first, that both financial, administrative burdens and efficiency-driven arguments are irrelevant in division of powers cases; second, that if you respect the division of powers, you do not need to be nice. The dissenting judges disagreed with the latter point: they believed that the provision had been adopted with the sole intent of harming the provincial legislature and that this intent to harm was contrary to the spirit of cooperative federalism.[113]

Conclusion

This chapter has described the roles of cooperative federalism, as both a judicial tool in division of power cases and an executive practice in intergovernmental relations. It has also underlined the specific attitude of Quebec towards cooperative federalism. Two sets of conclusions are thus relevant. First, if we return to the Court's three-step narrative described above, it seems that what it has attempted to do is align the rise of cooperative federalism with the demise of dual federalism and the formalism often associated with it. The narrative is that the development of less stringent division of powers doctrines reflects cooperative federalism and promotes the triumph of "efficacy over formalism."[114]

But as the earlier parts of this chapter demonstrate, recent cases on *judicial* cooperative federalism neither call for the end of dualism nor rely on a finding of cooperation between federal and provincial actors. More important, efficiency-driven arguments do not seem to win any popularity contest. In assessing the role of *judicial* cooperative federalism in division of powers cases, courts navigate between a less formalistic way of adjudicating these cases and the limits set out by the written constitution. Dualism is thus, at the same time, the impulse behind cooperative federalism and the brake that slows its expansion.

---

112 *Ibid*, para 34. This was the argument put forth by the attorney general of Quebec.
113 *Ibid*, para 189.
114 *COPA*, *supra* note 25, para 44.

The same can be said of *executive* cooperative federalism. Where parts of a scheme are contrary to the division of powers, they will be struck down, even though the parties do not mind the encroachment.[115] Conversely, when seized with a matter in which cooperation has stopped, or arguably never existed, the courts tend to retreat behind parliamentary sovereignty as a limit on the full expression of cooperative federalism. It is only when faced with an integrated cooperative regime, backed by interlocking legislation, which none of the involved parties contest, that true cooperative federalism will be given some weight.

The limits on cooperative federalism thus come from two sources: the (written, exclusive, dual, and formal) division of powers, on the one hand, and the (sacrosanct) principle of parliamentary sovereignty on the other. The Supreme Court has frequently stated that, by virtue of the primacy of written constitutionalism, cooperation cannot, in any case, modify the division of powers or displace the constitutional boundaries set out in ss. 91 and 92 of the *Constitution Act, 1867*.[116] This is an important caveat as it echoes the fears described earlier and Quebec's scepticism towards the principle.[117] The Court gave a similar warning in the long-gun registry decision by emphasizing that one should also recognize the limits of the principle of cooperative federalism, which is that of the primacy of the written constitution, *especially when cooperation fails*.[118]

The second set of conclusions relates to the position of Quebec. In this context, the fears expressed by Justice Beetz seem to have been largely unfounded, perhaps justifying the shift in Quebec's attitude

115 *Reference Re Agricultural Marketing, supra* note 81.

116 *Securities Reference, supra* note 2: "While flexibility and cooperation are important to federalism, they cannot override or modify the separation of powers. The *Secession Reference* affirmed federalism as an underlying constitutional principle that demands respect for the constitutional division of powers and the maintenance of a constitutional balance between federal and provincial powers. … [N]otwithstanding the Court's promotion of cooperative and flexible federalism, the constitutional boundaries that underlie the division of powers must be respected. The 'dominant tide' of flexible federalism, however strong its pull may be, cannot sweep designated powers out to sea, nor erode the constitutional balance inherent in the Canadian federal state" (paras 61–2). See also *Rogers Communications Ltd v Châteauguay (City), supra* note 45, para 39.

117 See "Quebec and Cooperative Federalism" earlier in this chapter.

118 See *Quebec v Canada (long-gun registry), supra* note 3, para 18, citing W.R. Lederman, "Some Forms and Limitations of Co-operative Federalism," in *Continuing Canadian Constitutional Dilemmas* (Toronto: Butterworths, 1981), 314, 315.

towards cooperative federalism. It is less dubitative, more assertive, but only when cooperative federalism can serve provincial autonomy. This attitude can be described not as an open endorsement of the benefits of cooperation, but rather as a careful, piecemeal approach to cooperation.

In the case of securities regulation, Quebec invoked cooperative federalism to demonstrate how provinces (without the federal government) could achieve desirable ends. But it was, and still is, highly suspicious of the federal government's use of the argument of cooperation, alleging that, in the case of the Securities Reference, it was a pretext to take over Quebec's exclusive jurisdiction over securities. In the long-gun registry case, which was issued between the first and second round of the securities constitutional challenge, Quebec argued in favour of cooperative federalism and praised its virtues. It also argued that administrative burdens and financial costs were relevant to division of powers adjudication, while it had said the exact opposite in the Securities Reference.

This ambiguity can be attenuated when one accounts for the distinction between concurrent powers and exclusive powers. Cooperation is more welcome, from Quebec's point of view, in areas of shared jurisdiction.[119] Criminal law is a federal power, but the administration of justice is provincial; hence, a form of cooperation is inevitable. But Quebec perceives that most, if not all, aspects of securities regulation fall within its exclusive jurisdiction.

The same ambiguity can also be perceived in the relationship Quebec entertains with federalism in general. A hybrid position is evident in Quebec's most recent affirmation policy, in which it praises cooperative arrangements as "the flexible way of conducting Canadian relations,"[120] while reiterating that formal division of powers, and, we might add, the enforcement of dualist federalism, represents the "strongest guarantee"[121] that its national identity will endure and thrive. Pierre Trudeau reached a similar conclusion in 1961: Quebeckers have defence mechanisms, which are triggered by every attempt by the federal elites to remove a power enjoyed by the provincial elites. Scrupulous respect for the established rules of federalism, he wrote,

119 *Policy on Québec Affirmation, supra* note 102, 117.
120 *Ibid*, 115.
121 *Ibid*, 107.

would render these defence mechanisms superfluous and create a positive climate for addressing the issue of provincial autonomy. But to survive, he added, Canadian federalism must also be geared towards collaboration.[122]

Cooperative federalism is malleable. Now the next challenge for the Supreme Court of Canada is to find a way to distinguish different forms of cooperative federalism, circumscribe its roles, and avoid instrumentalization.

122 Pierre Elliott Trudeau, "The Practice and Theory of Federalism," in *Social Purpose for Canada*, ed. Michael Oliver (Toronto: University of Toronto Press, 1961), 371–93 esp. p 385.

6 Religious and Political Communities in the Canadian Judicial Imagination: Two Tensions, Two Questions

HOWARD KISLOWICZ*

Introduction

Should a Sikh student be allowed to wear his kirpan in a public high school? Should town councils be allowed to begin their meetings with a prayer? Should a religious exemption be available for driver's licence photos when those photos are used in a digital database designed to combat identity fraud? Should a province be required to fund all denominational schools equally?

The Supreme Court of Canada (SCC) has addressed each of these difficult questions.[1] Each case, in its own way, raises issues regarding the relationships between Canada's religious and political communities. This theme recurs in Canadian jurisprudence, in part, because of two underlying and related tensions. First, courts understand particular religious communities as constitutive of the Confederation: but for the Catholic-Protestant compromise, there would have been no union. On the other hand, courts emphasize that Canada has no established religion, which makes for an awkward fit with the constitutionalized privileges of Protestant and Catholic groups. Second, the constitutional

---

* Assistant professor, Faculty of Law, University of Calgary. Thanks very much to Geneva McSheffery for her excellent research assistance. Thanks also to the other contributors to this volume for their insights on an earlier draft and to the helpful suggestions of the editors and anonymous peer reviewers. Special thanks to Dr. Naomi Lear and Gabriel Kislowicz.

1 *Multani v Commission scolaire Marguerite-Bourgeoys*, [2006] 1 SCR 256; *Mouvement laïque québécois v Saguenay (City)*, 2015 SCC 16; *Alberta v Hutterian Brethren of Wilson Colony*, [2009] 2 SCR 567; *Adler v Ontario*, [1996] 3 SCR 609; *Reference re Bill 30*, [1987] 1 SCR 1148.

protection of religious freedom can be read as emerging from an individualistic liberal tradition, but many religious practices are necessarily communal, and some religious perspectives are thoroughly collectivist.

The individual/collective dichotomy can, roughly, be understood to track Asha Kaushal's distinction between rights and jurisdiction in chapter 7 of this volume. While all rights are concerned with an agent's capacity to be self-governing to some degree, collective rights claimants are more likely to argue for autonomy on a group level, which implies at least some measure of a group setting its own norms.[2] Courts have, perhaps for reasons of both their liberal theoretical perspective and their reluctance to cede the state's jurisdiction, been inconsistent in their receptiveness to rights claims involving collective religious practices.

Looking beyond the 150th anniversary of Confederation, the most pressing questions emerging from these tensions are, first, how will the state relate to religious minority communities who were not part of the constitutional compact, whose world views may differ from those of the majority? Second, when confronted with questions surrounding the cultural identity of public institutions, what course will the law chart? In her contribution to this volume (see chapter 8), Vrinda Narain addresses these questions from a different vantage point. Her critical approach to multiculturalism, nurtured by the theory of intersectionality, has great potential to help us think carefully about the agency of women in religious communities, while being wary of essentializing religious or cultural communities.

In this chapter, I focus more squarely on religious communities as collectives and components of Canada's political communities. This is not to say, however, that it should be for the state to define the community or that any community can be understood monolithically. To the extent that I support religious communities' collective identities and aspirations, it is on the basis of bottom-up conceptions of such identities, in which members of the communities in some way express their will to be treated as a group, such as by instituting claims in the name of the community or its institutions.

Like Kaushal's contribution, this chapter is motivated in part by Canada's changing religious demographics, but also the changing

2 Cases involving Aboriginal rights raise some of the clearest examples of collective rights claims in the Canadian experience. As David Milward shows in chap 9, these claims can be thought of as implicating the value of group-level self-determination.

relationship between the Canadian state and religion more generally. Accordingly, on the basis of key moments in Canadian constitutional jurisprudence, this chapter considers two central tensions of Canadian courts' engagement with religious communities: the no religious establishment/Catholic-Protestant origin story and the individual/collective religious freedom jurisprudence. It then uses these tensions to analyse courts' responses to the state's treatment of minority communities and the courts' emerging articulation of a non-religious identity for Canada.

Two Tensions

Tension 1: No Religious Establishment/Catholic-Protestant Origin Story

The tension between legal narratives about Canada as (1) a state with no established religion[3] and (2) a state constituted by the coming together of Catholic and Protestant Christian groups can be seen in the text of the constitution itself. On the one hand, the *Canadian Charter of Rights and Freedoms* guarantees religious freedom and prohibits discrimination on the basis of religion.[4] On the other, the *Constitution Act, 1867* protects the rights and privileges of denominational schools as they existed at the time of the union, making specific reference to "the Queen's Protestant and Roman Catholic Subjects."[5]

In twice coming to the conclusion that *Charter* equality protections could not invalidate unequal school-funding practices in Ontario (where Catholic schools are publicly funded but no other religious

---

3 Before Confederation, the *Constitutional Act of 1791* established the Church of England as the official church. The equality of religious denominations was recognized by legislation in 1854: see Janet Epp Buckingham, *Fighting over God: A Legal and Political History of Religious Freedom in Canada* (Montreal and Kingston: McGill-Queen's University Press, 2014), 177.

4 *Constitution Act, 1982,* being Schedule B to the *Canada Act 1982* (UK), 1982, c 11, ss 2(a), 15.

5 *Constitution Act, 1867* (UK), 30 & 31 Vict, c 3, s 93, reprinted in RSC 1985, App II, No 5. Quebec and Newfoundland and Labrador have passed constitutional amendments to deconfessionalize their school boards. See also *Saskatchewan Act,* SC 1905, c 42, s 17; *Alberta Act,* SC 1905, s 17; J Kent Donlevy, "Re-visiting Denominational Cause and Denominational Breach in Canada's Constitutionally Protected Catholic Schools," *Journal of Education and Law* 15, no. 2 (2005) 85.

schools are),[6] the SCC explained that the educational protections for Catholics and Protestants were crucial to reaching an agreement on Confederation. Justice Wilson wrote, "s. 93 was part of a solemn pact resulting from the bargaining which made Confederation possible."[7] Justice Estey treated the protection of denominational schooling rights as "part of the pattern of the sharing of sovereign power between the two plenary authorities created at Confederation."[8]

Framing the narrative of Confederation this way implies that the country was Roman Catholic and Protestant in its constituent parts; in addition to being composed of geographic units, Canada was composed of religious units, and of only two worth mentioning in 1867.[9] The Court understands denominational schooling rights as a response to the problem that the religious units, which "functioned as central social and cultural institutions,"[10] did not always match the geographic units and that the distribution of religious populations might change over time.[11] This meant that schooling rights were allocated only on religious lines, even though language might now be understood to be a more common marker of shared culture. In 1916, the Privy Council emphasized the religious, rather than linguistic, character of the constitutional right when it denied a Catholic school board's attempt to resist legislation regulating the use of French in its schools.[12] The Privy Council held that no such privilege had been reserved either by the constitution or by past legislation.

More to the point, members of religious communities that were neither Catholic nor Protestant had to either be assimilated into one of

---

6 *Reference re Bill 30*, *supra* note 1; *Adler v Ontario*, *supra* note 1.

7 *Reference re Bill 30*, *supra* note 1 (Wilson J), 1173; see also *Brophy v Manitoba (Attorney General)*, [1895] AC 202 (PC).

8 *Reference re Bill 30*, *supra* note 1 (Estey J), 1153.

9 In the Privy Council's words, the 1867 Act "protects the rights which at the Union belonged to the Roman Catholic population as a class, as well as those belonging to the Protestant population as a class … who substantially made up the whole population of the Province at the time of the Union"; see *Hirsch v Protestant Board of School Commissioners of Montreal*, [1928] 1 DLR 1041 (PC), 1052. As Kaushal points out in chap 7, this understanding has never been completely true to Canada's demographics given the presence of Aboriginal populations. It has, moreover, become increasingly untrue over time.

10 Buckingham, *supra* note 4, 175.

11 See *Brophy v Manitoba (Attorney General)*, *supra* note 7, 266.

12 *Ottawa Roman Catholic Separate School Board (Trustees of) v Mackell*, [1916] 32 DLR 1 (PC).

those categories or be left outside the denominational schooling system. In 1903, the Quebec Superior Court held that a Jewish parent could not compel the local Protestant School Commissioners to accept his son because the parent did not own "real estate inscribed on the Protestant panel for the purposes of the City school tax."[13] In response, Quebec's legislature passed an act providing that "persons professing the Jewish religion shall, for school purposes, be treated in the same manner as Protestants."[14] In the 1920s, responding to a reference question on that act's constitutionality, the Privy Council held it unconstitutional for Quebec's legislature to allow Jewish people "to be appointed to the Protestant Board of School Commissioners in the City of Quebec or Montreal or to any Protestant Board of Examiners or to take part with Protestants in the establishment of a dissentient school outside those cities." Nor could it "confer the right of attendance at dissentient schools outside the cities of Quebec and Montreal upon persons of religious faith different from that of the dissentient minority."[15]

In the 1950s, a similar issue arose when Paul Emile Perron, a Jehovah's Witness, sought an order compelling a Protestant school to admit his children. Quebec's Superior Court held that Mr. Perron was not a Protestant and his claim could, therefore, not succeed.[16] On appeal, however, the Quebec Court of Queen's Bench held that "to be considered a Protestant it is sufficient to be a Christian and to repudiate the authority of the Pope."[17] The Court opined:

> Our legislation has always reflected the characteristic which the idea of justice, tolerance and freedom of conscience *with respect to the two nationalities imprinted upon it, not as such in themselves, but by reason of their different religious faith.*[18]

In this passage, the Court raises the universalist themes of "justice, tolerance and freedom of conscience" only to immediately restrict them to

---

13 *Pinsler v Protestant Board of School Commissioners of Montreal*, as summarized in *Hirsch v Montreal Protestant School Board of School Commissioners*, *supra* note 9.

14 *Hirsch*, *supra* note 9.

15 *Ibid*, 1054–5.

16 *Perron v School Trustees of the Municipality of Rouyn and Attorney-General of Quebec* (1955), 1 DLR (2d) 414 (QCQB), 416.

17 *Ibid*, 417.

18 *Ibid*, 418–19 (emphasis added); see also John Ciaccia, "*Perron v School Trustees of the School Municipality of Rouyn*," *McGill Law Journal* 2 (1956) 42.

the "two nationalities," distinguished from each other by "their different religious faith." The narrative of Canada's formation by two religious peoples was so deeply engrained in the Court's imagination that it did not even identify the tension between universalism and particularism.[19] Further, whereas in *Hirsch* the difference between Jews and Protestants was too great to ignore, the Court's ruling in *Perron* erased the differences between Jehovah's Witnesses and other non-Catholic Christians.[20] While this may be taken to demonstrate a more universalist approach in that a Jehovah's Witness was successful in obtaining the remedy sought, it may equally be seen as a misrecognition of Jehovah's Witnesses by homogenizing all minority Christian communities in Quebec.

Around the same time, the SCC made several decisions defending the rights of religious minorities on the basis of more universalist principles. In *Saumur*, the Court assessed a municipal by-law that prohibited the distribution in the streets of "any book, pamphlet, booklet, circular, tract what ever without having previously obtained for so doing the written permission of the Chief of Police."[21] The Court ultimately held that the by-law should be read down to the extent it prohibited Mr. Saumur, a Jehovah's Witness, from distributing religious texts on the streets.[22] Justice Rand's opinion in *Saumur* has received scholarly attention[23] for articulating a theory of an implied bill of rights.[24] He held that "freedom of speech, religion and the inviolability of the person, are original freedoms which are at once the necessary attributes and

19 See Benjamin L. Berger, "Children of Two Logics: A Way into Canadian Constitutional Culture," *International Journal of Constitutional Law* 11, no. 2 (2013) 319.

20 For the complicated history of Jewish schools in Montreal, see David Fraser, *Honorary Protestants: The Jewish School Question in Montreal, 1867–1997* (Toronto: University of Toronto Press, 2015), 38: "The central question that would arise within the context of the Jewish School Question [in Montreal] is exactly how a group, defined religiously and culturally as separate from the denominational structures that controlled public education, could in fact, and in law, find any place at all, let alone a place that would allow them to become equal British subjects and Canadians."

21 *Saumur v City of Quebec*, [1953] 2 SCR 299, 320.

22 *Ibid*, 322 (Kerwin J).

23 See, e.g., David J. Mullan, "Underlying Constitutional Principles: The Legacy of Justice Rand," *Manitoba Law Journal* 34 (2010) 73.

24 Rand and Abbott JJ articulated a similar theory around freedom of expression in *Switzman v Elbling and AG of Quebec*, [1957] SCR 285, 305, 326–7; the majority opinion of Kerwin CJ disposed of this case more simply, holding that this was a matter of criminal law and therefore within federal jurisdiction.

modes of self-expression of human beings and the primary conditions of their community life within a legal order."[25] The legal order established by the *Constitution Act, 1867* rests "ultimately on public opinion reached by discussion and the interplay of ideas. If that discussion is placed under license, its basic condition is destroyed."[26] In other words, a system of government "similar in principle" to the United Kingdom's implies the guarantee of certain political freedoms, including the freedoms of speech and religion.[27]

Other judgments[28] forming the majority view preferred to rest their decisions more squarely on a pre-Confederation statute, still in force in Quebec, which provided that

> the free exercise and enjoyment of Religious Profession and Worship without discrimination or preference so as the same be not made an excuse for acts of licentiousness or justification of practices inconsistent with the peace and safety of the Province is by the constitution and laws of this Province allowed to all Her Majesty's subjects within the same.[29]

In this regard, Justice Kellock rejected the argument that Jehovah's Witnesses did not qualify as a "religious denomination" and that the religious freedom protected by the statute was limited to worship activities.[30] In a similarly universalist tone, Justice Estey held that the "right of the free exercise and enjoyment of religious profession and worship, is a personal, sacred right."[31] Justice Locke also emphasized the inequality of treatment received by Jehovah's Witnesses at the hands of the chief of police.[32] On the basis of the 1852 statute Justice Kerwin

---

25 *Saumur v City of Quebec, supra* note 21, 329 (Rand J). In a memorable passage, 332, Justice Rand cites a passage from the biblical book of Jeremiah to demonstrate that "public ways, in some circumstances the only practical means available for any appeal to the community generally, have from the most ancient times been the avenues for such communications."

26 *Ibid*, 330 (Rand J).

27 Justice Rand also held that the regulation of religion was a matter of national dimension and thus appropriate for federal rather than provincial legislation, *Ibid*, 329 (Rand J).

28 *Ibid*, 341–2 (Kellock J).

29 *Statute of 1852 of Old Province of Canada*, 14–15 Vict c 175, as cited in *Ibid*, 321.

30 *Ibid*, 341–3 (Kellock J).

31 *Ibid*, 359 (Estey J).

32 *Ibid*, 369 (Locke J).

agreed that Jehovah's Witnesses could not be prevented from proselytizing, although he also emphasized the absence of a bill of rights in Canada.[33] In these respects, *Saumur* shows a tendency of at least some judges towards a more universal guarantee of religious freedom.[34] Nevertheless, even on Justice Rand's strong civil libertarian view, the particularistic history of Canada's protection of religious freedom was unavoidable. Justice Rand held that religious freedom had been legislatively "recognized as a principle of fundamental character" since 1760, all the while acknowledging that such was guaranteed only to the "Christian religion," which stood "in the first rank of social, political and juristic importance."[35]

Some two years after *Saumur*, the SCC again addressed discrimination against Jehovah's Witnesses in Quebec, using even stronger universalist language. In *Chaput v Romain*, a Jehovah's Witness minister brought suit against police officers who "broke up an admittedly orderly religious meeting … seized a Bible, some hymn books and a number of booklets on religious subjects, and ordered those present to disperse."[36] The Court unanimously required the officers to pay damages of $2,000.[37] Justice Taschereau invoked many of the liberal themes that have more recently come to be associated with religious freedom under the *Charter*, including the non-establishment of religion, the equality of all religious groups, the individual's freedom of conscience, and the dangers of an oppressive majority for minority groups.[38] In a concurring opinion, Justice Locke identified the same pre-Confederation statute relied upon in *Saumur* as the source of these notions.[39]

The cases discussed in this section demonstrate the coexistence of two distinct themes in Canada's jurisprudence as regards the relationship

---

33 *Ibid*, 323–4 (Kerwin J).

34 But see Fred Kaufman, "The Saumur Case," *McGill Law Journal* 1 (1952) 223, 229: "On the question of religion … the [Saumur] court was deadlocked, but, since the case at bar had already been decided on other points, the matter did not assume as much importance as it might easily have done had the court's alignment on the issues of 'pith and substance' and 'undue interference' varied even slightly."

35 *Saumur v City of Quebec*, *supra* note 21, 326–7 (Rand J); see also Norman Chambers, "Civil Liberties after the Saumur Case," *University of Toronto Faculty Law Review* 12 (1954) 12.

36 *Chaput v Romain*, [1955] SCR 834, 834.

37 Approximately $18,900 in 2018: "Inflation Calculator," http://www.bankofcanada.ca/rates/related/inflation-calculator/.

38 *Chaput v Romain*, *supra* note 36, 840.

39 *Ibid*, 864 (Locke J).

between the state and religious communities. In some cases, even predating the *Charter*, Canada is imagined as a state in which religious freedom and freedom from religious discrimination are fundamental aspects of the system of government. The courts are concerned that all are treated equally regardless of their religious affiliations. In other cases, the state is imagined as emerging from the joining together of Catholics and Protestants, with other communities left out or uncomfortably homogenized into those categories. When the two values are brought expressly into conversation before the courts, the universalist guarantees of the *Charter* cannot displace the privileges constitutionally bestowed on particular religious groups.[40]

Tension 2: Individual/Collective Religious Freedom

A second tension in the judicial consideration of claims made by religious communities is internal to the notion of religious freedom: is religious freedom best understood as an individual right, a group right, or some combination of the two? Canada's constitution guarantees "freedom of conscience and religion" to "everyone."[41] The placement of conscience as the first aspect of the guarantee and the use of a singular pronoun might be taken as textual support that the constitutional right inheres in the individual. This said, many religious practices and world views have a significant, and sometimes fundamental, collective element; to speak of them in individual terms is to misapprehend their significance.[42] In addition, for many, religious practices and beliefs are significant as an aspect of identity or self-understanding.[43] These identities can be understood in relational terms:[44] a person may identify as belonging to a religious tradition through their relationships with

---

40 Benjamin Oliphant, "School Prayer in Alberta," 12 November 2015, *Policy Options*, http://policyoptions.irpp.org/2015/11/12/school-prayer-in-alberta-the-irresistible-charter-force-hits-an-immovable-constitutional-object/.

41 *Constitution Act, 1982, supra* note 4, s 2(a).

42 The collectivist world view and lifestyle of the Hutterian Brethren, described most recently in *Alberta v Hutterian Brethren of Wilson Colony, supra* note 1, discussed below, provides a most compelling example.

43 Richard Moon, "Freedom of Religion under the Charter of Rights: The Limits of State Neutrality," *University of British Columbia Law Review* 45 (2012) 497.

44 On identity as a dialogic concept, see Charles Taylor, "The Politics of Recognition," in *Multiculturalism*, ed. Amy Gutmann (Princeton, NJ: Princeton University Press, 1992).

family or fellow community members. To describe religion in purely individual terms risks misrecognizing this aspect of religious identity.

More recent forms of this debate focus on whether collectives, such as religious institutions or private corporations, can themselves claim a right to religious freedom.[45] As noted above, in terms of Kaushal's distinction between rights and jurisdiction,[46] when a claimant is an institution or a group and the right is collective, the right takes on a jurisdictional flavour as some decision-making body claims norm-setting authority over its members. Consider, for example, the right of Aboriginal title discussed in David Milward's contribution (chapter 9). When the right is held by the group, it can create a "legal space" where the group makes rules regarding use of the land. Because the right is held collectively, there will need to be some decision-making process through which the group's interests and agency are represented. Although called an Aboriginal "right," the norm-setting aspect of title has aspects of jurisdictional control.

Canadian judicial decisions reveal elements of both individual and collective conceptions of religious freedom, although some argue that the Canadian legal tradition skews towards individualistic understandings. Benjamin Berger, for example, argues that Canadian law's understanding of religion emerges from a liberal world view, which results in a view of religion as a private, individual matter, valuable because a person chooses it.[47]

The SCC's definition of religion, articulated in *Amselem*, is a good starting point to examine the individual/collective tension. Justice Iacobucci, for the majority, held,

> Defined broadly, religion typically involves a particular and comprehensive system of faith and worship. Religion also tends to involve the belief in a divine, superhuman or controlling power. In essence, religion is about freely and deeply held personal convictions or beliefs connected to an individual's spiritual faith and integrally linked to one's self-definition

---

45 Paul Horwitz, "Defending (Religious) Institutionalism," *Virginia Law Review* 99 (2013) 1049; Richard Schragger and Micah Schwartzman, "Against Religious Institutionalism," *Virginia Law Review* 99 (2013) 917; *Burwell v Hobby Lobby*, [2014] 573 US; Kathryn Chan, "Identifying the Institutional Religious Freedom Claimant," *Canadian Bar Review* 95, no. 3 (2017).

46 See chap 7.

47 Benjamin L. Berger, "Law's Religion: Rendering Culture," *Osgoode Hall Law Journal* 45 (2007) 277.

and spiritual fulfilment, the practices of which allow individuals to foster a connection with the divine or with the subject or object of that spiritual faith.[48]

This approach to religion is individualistic, emphasizing *personal* beliefs and choices. Although it engages with identity, it never discusses community or relationships. This begets a test for religious freedom primarily concerned with sincerely held *subjective* beliefs.[49] In a later decision, a community of Hutterian Brethren argued that a photo requirement on driver's licences interfered with both their religious practice of not making graven images and their religious practice of living as a self-sustaining collective.[50] The SCC's individualistic approach manifested in its holding that "[c]ommunity impact does not ... transform the essential claim – that of the individual claimants for photo-free licences – into an assertion of a group right."[51] While the majority of the SCC allowed for the consideration of community impact in assessing the proportionality of the rights infringement, it maintained that the religious freedom right is one that inheres in the individual rather than the group.[52]

More recently, however, the SCC's approach to religious freedom has shown some change in the inclusion of collective aspects of religious practice within the religious freedom right.[53] In 2015's *Loyola*, the majority of the SCC referred to "the socially embedded nature of religious belief, and the deep linkages between this belief and its manifestation through communal institutions and traditions."[54] A concurring minority similarly held that the "communal character of religion means that protecting the religious freedom of individuals requires protecting the religious freedom of religious organizations."[55] The minority judgment set out a special test for recognizing the religious freedom rights of institutional (rather than

48 *Syndicat Northcrest v Amselem*, 2004 SCC 47, para 39.

49 *Ibid*, paras 53–6.

50 *Alberta v Hutterian Brethren of Wilson Colony, supra* note 1.

51 *Ibid*, para 31.

52 See Howard Kislowicz, "Religious Freedom and Canada's Commitments to Multiculturalism," *National Journal of Constitutional Law* 31 (2012) 1.

53 Buckingham, *supra* note 4, 176.

54 *Loyola High School v Quebec (Attorney General)*, 2015 SCC 12, para 60.

55 *Ibid*, para 91. McLachlin CJC was a co-author of this opinion and had previously authored the majority in *Alberta v Hutterian Brethren of Wilson Colony, supra* note 1.

individual) actors,[56] which the majority held to be unnecessary for the resolution of the case.[57]

The tension between individualist and collectivist approaches to religion is sometimes displayed in disputes where both parties raise a religious claim, whether based on religious freedom or religious equality, as has happened in some employment litigation where the employer is a religious institution. The SCC confronted such a situation in *Caldwell v Stuart*.[58] The question was whether a Catholic school[59] had violated British Columbia's *Human Rights Code* by dismissing a Catholic teacher who had married "a divorced person in a ceremony outside the Church." The Court described the case as "a conflict between two legally established rights, that of the individual to freedom from discrimination in employment, and that of a religious group to carry on its activities in the operation of its denominational school according to its religious beliefs and practices."[60] The Court sided with collective religious interests, reasoning that for the school to achieve its purpose, teachers could legally be required "to observe and comply with the religious standards ... so that students see in practice the application of the principles of the Church ... and thereby receive what is called a Catholic education."[61]

The Court also found legislative support for this position. Under certain circumstances, British Columbia's *Human Rights Code* explicitly allows a religious organization to preferentially hire members of its faith community.[62] The Court understood this provision to protect free association and "to preserve for the Catholic members of this and other groups the right to the continuance of denominational schools."[63]

Ontario's Court of Appeal came to a similar conclusion when it assessed the constitutionality of Ontario legislation that prohibited

---

56 *Loyola High School v Quebec (Attorney General), supra* note 54, paras 99–101.

57 *Ibid*, paras 33–4.

58 *Caldwell et al v Stuart et al*, [1984] 2 SCR 603.

59 This case did not raise issues under s 93 of the *Constitution Act, 1867* as "the rights of denominational schools in British Columbia were very limited at the time of Confederation" (*Ibid*, 629). It also did not raise religious freedom issues under the *Charter* as the school was neither a government actor nor implementing a government program.

60 *Ibid*, 606.

61 *Ibid*, 618–19.

62 *Human Rights Code*, RSBC 1996, c 210, s 41 (at the time of the case, substantially the same provision was found at s 22 of the *Code*).

63 *Caldwell et al v Stuart et al, supra* note 58, 625–6, 628.

Roman Catholic school boards from preferentially hiring Roman Catholic teachers if prospective teachers agreed "to respect the philosophy" of the school.[64] The Court held that Catholic schools had constitutional rights to take into account the religion of teachers for the purposes of hiring and dismissal.[65] In the Court's view, the constitutional guarantee in s. 93 "is based on the conclusion that there is a link between the transmission of religious values and education."[66] The religious interest here – the group's control over the inter-generational preservation of its faith and heritage – could be understood only as collective in nature. The individual rights of non-Catholic teachers who wished to have access to employment at Catholic schools, whether understood as rights of equality or rights of religious freedom, came second.[67]

In sum, there is strong support in the case law for the claim that Canadian courts' understanding of religion stems from an individualistic world view, which can misapprehend or neglect communal aspects of religious faith and practice. There are, nevertheless, instances both recent and more distant where courts have recognized the collective aspects of religious life and, at times, even granted them priority over individuals' interests in religious freedom and non-discrimination. The pendular appearance of the jurisprudence reflects a tension at the heart of religious freedom. Courts want to protect individuals' interests in choosing their own faith and practice but also at times recognize that individuals have choices mostly because communities of faith (and non-faith) offer them.

---

64 *Daly v Attorney General of Ontario*, [1999] 44 OR (3d) 349 (CA), 352. A legally significant difference from *Caldwell*, and of interest in the context of the current discussion, is that Catholic schools in Ontario have constitutional protections under s 93 of the *Constitution Act, 1867*, while Catholic schools do not have the same protections in British Columbia. The Ontario schools, therefore, were able to rely on their constitutional rights to invalidate provincial legislation, whereas the litigation in *Caldwell* proceeded between private parties and came down, legally, to the application of human rights legislation in a private context.

65 *Ibid*, 359.

66 *Ibid*, 361.

67 But see *Ontario Human Rights Commission v Christian Horizons*, 2010 ONSC 2105, where the Court held that a religious organization could not discriminate against an employee on the basis of her having entered into a same-sex relationship because, as a support worker in a community living environment, adherence to a lifestyle and morality agreement was not shown to be a bona fide occupational requirement.

Two Questions

One hundred fifty years after Confederation, the two tensions discussed above will continue to have a bearing on two important questions for religious communities. First, how will the judiciary contribute to the relationships between the state and religious minority communities? Second, if the judiciary increasingly emphasizes that Canada is a religiously disestablished state, how will the courts participate in the articulation of Canadian identity and values?

Question 1: How to Relate to Minority Communities

State institutions and rules are generally designed with the needs of the majority in mind.[68] Canadian jurisdictions mark Christmas and Easter as statutory holidays, but no non-Christian religious holidays.[69] This is an example, however banal in appearance, of how the needs of some Christian observers are taken into account by existing institutions, while the needs of other religious groups are not. Similarly, methods of identification tend to be developed along dominant expectations of propriety and privacy. That most people in Canada do not have a religious objection to having their photo taken may help explain why provinces invest in facial recognition technologies rather than other identification technologies.[70] Likewise, that the practice of carrying a kirpan is not widespread in Canada[71] might help explain why it seemed

68 Martha Minow, *Making All the Difference: Inclusion, Exclusion, and American Law* (Ithaca, NY: Cornell University Press, 1990), 43.

69 See, e.g., the definitions of *holiday* found in federal, provincial, and territorial interpretation statutes: *Interpretation Act*, RSC 1985, c I-21; s 35(1); *Interpretation Act*, RSA 2000, c I-8, 28(1)(x)(ii); *Interpretation Act*, RSBC 1996, c 238, s 29; *The Interpretation Act*, CCSM c I80, s 22(1); *Interpretation Act*, RSNB 1973, c I-13, s 38; *Interpretation Act*, RSNL 1990, c I-19, s 28(1); *Interpretation Act*, RSNWT 1988, c I-8, s 28(1); *Interpretation Act*, RSNS 1989, c 235, s 7(1)(j); *Interpretation Act*, RSNWT (Nu) 1988, c I-8, s 11. Similar designations of Christmas and Easter as holidays can also be found in employment standards, retail days of business, liquor control, and other public service statutes in each province.

70 *Alberta v Hutterian Brethren of Wilson Colony*, *supra* note 1.

71 According to the 2011 National Household Survey conducted by Statistics Canada, the Sikh population of Canada is roughly 454,000 (out of a total population of 34.3 million), and not all Sikhs engage in the kirpan practice; see Statistics Canada, "Religion, Immigrant Status and Period of Immigration, Age Groups and Sex of the Population in Private Households," in *National Household Survey*,

obvious to members of Quebec's National Assembly that knives in the cafeteria present no safety risk, but the kirpan presents too grave a risk to be allowed in the legislative chamber.[72]

Minority religious groups have faced particular challenges in seeking accommodation when their practices were perceived as conflicting with dominant or official values.[73] Muslim communities have recently been at the centre of legislative attention in this regard. The *Zero Tolerance for Barbaric Cultural Practices Act*[74] of 2015 presents perhaps the most vivid language in this respect. The act focuses principally on polygamy and forced marriages. It also alters the criminal defence of provocation such that an accused may rely on the defence only where the provoking act was an indictable offence. The act's sponsor described this latter as a response to so-called "honour killings."[75] The use of the language of barbarism led some to argue that the act was designed to build political support at the expense of marginalized and racialized communities, and Muslim communities in particular.[76] The controversy here is less about religious freedom than it is about asserting a Canadian identity in opposition to a caricaturized Other, not explicitly labelled, but understood by many to mean Muslim people of colour.

---

data tables (Ottawa: Statistics Canada, 2011), http://www12.statcan.gc.ca/nhs-enm/2011/dp-pd/dt-td/Rp-eng.cfm?LANG=E&APATH=3&DETAIL=0&DIM=0&FL=A&FREE=0&GC=0&GID=0&GK=0&GRP=0&PID=105399&PRID=0&PTYPE=105277&S=0&SHOWALL=0&SUB=0&Temporal=2013&THEME=95&VID=0&VNAMEE=&VNAMEF=.

72 "Kirpan Banned at Que. National Assembly," *CBC News*, 9 February 2011, http://www.cbc.ca/news/canada/montreal/kirpan-banned-at-que-national-assembly-1.1113333h. The decision to ban the kirpan came after members of the World Sikh Organization, invited to testify in a parliamentary hearing regarding Bill 94, arrived carrying their kirpans. See Quebec, National Assembly, *Journal des débats de l'Assemblée nationale*, 39th Leg, 1st Sess, Vol 41, No 170 (9 February 2011) (Mme Louise Beaudouin), http://www.assnat.qc.ca/fr/travaux-parlementaires/assemblee-nationale/39-1/journal-debats/20110209/30891.html.

73 Benjamin L. Berger, *Law's Religion: Religious Difference and the Claims of Constitutionalism* (Toronto: University of Toronto Press, 2015), chap 3.

74 *Zero Tolerance for Barbaric Cultural Practices Act*, SC 2015, c 29. See Vrinda Narain's treatment of this act, as well as the *Charter of Quebec Values*, in chap 8.

75 Ashley Csanady, "Barbaric Cultural Practices' Bill to Criminalize Forced Marriage, Tackle 'Honour Killings' Passes Final Vote," *National Post*, 17 June 2015, http://news.nationalpost.com/news/canada/barbaric-cultural-practices-bill-to-criminalize-forced-marriage-tackle-honour-killings-set-for-final-vote.

76 See, e.g., "BILL S-7: 'Zero Tolerance for Barbaric Cultural Practices Act,'" *South Asian Legal Clinic of Ontario*, http://www.salc.on.ca/sw00nb4.html.

Muslim veiling practices have also sometimes been understood as conflicting with the dominant value of sexual equality and have been directly targeted by state institutions. In the 2015 federal election, for example, the question whether a person could wear a niqab at a citizenship swearing-in ceremony became a central campaign issue. The incumbent Conservative prime minister took the position that niqabs in such ceremonies were "contrary to [Canadians'] own values, ... unacceptable to Canadians, unacceptable to Canadian women."[77] Both the Liberal and New Democratic Party leaders took an opposing view.[78]

In a similar vein, in the 2013 Quebec provincial election campaign, the incumbent Parti Québécois made the development of a "Charter of Quebec Values" a central plank in its campaign platform. Among other things, the legislation would have prohibited those fulfilling public duties from wearing "headgear, clothing, jewelry or other adornments which, by their conspicuous nature, overtly indicate a religious affiliation."[79] Commentators have noted that although the bill would have affected several forms of religious attire, "the niqab and hijab were very much at the center of contemplation."[80] The Parti Québécois was defeated in 2013.

The subsequent Liberal government introduced a softer bill that offered a general rule of providing and receiving public services with an uncovered face, but also envisaged a process of accommodation.[81] When the bill was passed in October 2017, Quebec's Liberal minister of

77 Aaron Wherry, "Justin Trudeau and the Niqab," *Maclean's*, 10 March 2015, http://www.macleans.ca/politics/justin-trudeau-and-the-niqab/; see also Benjamin L. Berger, "Belonging to Law: Religious Difference, Secularism, and the Conditions of Civic Inclusion," *Social and Legal Studies* 24, no. 1 (2014) 47, 54–5.

78 Wherry, *supra* note 77; Andy Blatchford, "Mulcair Digs In on Niqab Stance, Despite the Fact It Could Cost the NDP Votes in Quebec," *National Post*, 25 September 2015, http://news.nationalpost.com/news/canada/mulcair-digs-in-on-niqab-stance-despite-the-fact-it-could-cost-the-ndp-votes-in-quebec.

79 Bill n°60, *Charter affirming the values of State secularism and religious neutrality and of equality between women and men, and providing a framework for accommodation requests*, 1st Sess, 40th Leg, Quebec, 2013 (introduced by Bernard Drainville, minister responsible for democratic institutions and active citizenship).

80 Berger, *supra* note 77, 54; Dia Dabby, "Constitutional (Mis)adventures: Revisiting Quebec's Proposed Charter of Values," *Supreme Court Law Review* (2d) 71 (2015) 353.

81 Bill n°62, *An Act to foster adherence to State religious neutrality and, in particular, to provide a framework for religious accommodation requests in certain bodies*, 1st Sess, 41st Leg, Quebec, 2015 (introduced by Mme Stéphanie Vallée, minister of justice).

justice initially said that a woman wearing a niqab or a burka would be required to unveil while using public transit.[82] The minister later said that a person would have to remove a face covering only for reasons of identification, communication, or security.[83] Although the government has defended the law, saying that it applies to all face coverings, the circumstances demonstrate that the legislature is still concerned with regulating women's veiling practices. At the time of writing, a court challenge had just been initiated.[84]

In Ontario, Muslims found themselves at the centre of a public debate over religious family arbitration. When a Muslim lawyer announced his intention to create the Islamic Institute of Civil Justice as an arbitration forum for family disputes, public concern (or perhaps "moral panic"[85]) led to a government-commissioned review of religious family arbitration.[86] The resulting report recommended the continued availability of religious family arbitration, subject to additional safeguards.[87] The Liberal government rejected this proposal, declared instead that there would be "one law for all Ontarians,"[88] and

---

82 *CBC News*, "What You Need to Know about Quebec's Religious Neutrality Legislation," http://www.cbc.ca/news/canada/montreal/burqa-niqab-national-assembly-quebec-liberal-government-stephanie-vallee-1.4357463.

83 *CBC News*, "Breaking Down Bill 62: What You Can and Can't Do while Wearing a Niqab in Quebec," http://www.cbc.ca/news/canada/montreal/bill-62-examples-ministry-release-1.4369347.

84 *CBC News*, "Quebec's Face-Covering Law Heads for Constitutional Challenge," http://www.cbc.ca/news/canada/montreal/quebec-niqab-bill-62-legal-challenge-face-covering-1.4390962.

85 Natasha Bakht, "Were Muslim Barbarians Really Knocking on the Gates of Ontario: The Religious Arbitration Controversy – Another Perspective," *Ottawa Law Review* 40th Anniversary Edition (2006) 67.

86 Much has been written about this debate, and it is beyond the scope of this chapter to give a full account. See, e.g., Anna Korteweg and Jennifer A Selby, eds., *Debating Sharia: Islam, Gender Politics, and Family Law Arbitration* (Toronto: University of Toronto Press, 2012); Sherene Razack, "The 'Sharia Law' Debate in Ontario: The Modernity/Premodernity Distinction in Legal Efforts to Protect Women from Culture," *Feminist Legal Studies* 15 (2007) 3; Audrey Macklin, "Multiculturalism Meets Privatisation: The Case of Faith-Based Arbitration," *International Journal of Law in Context* 9, no. 3 (2013) 343.

87 Marion Boyd, *Dispute Resolution in Family Law: Protecting Choice, Promoting Inclusion* (Toronto: Ministry of the Attorney General, 2004).

88 Ontario Ministry of the Attorney General, "McGuinty Government Declares One Law for All Ontarians," news release, 15 November 2005, http://news.ontario.ca/archive/en/2005/11/15/McGuinty-Government-Declares-One-Law-For-All-Ontarians.html.

amended the *Arbitration Act* to require that family arbitrators apply either the "substantive law of Ontario" or one of "another Canadian jurisdiction."[89] As Paul Daly notes in chapter 3, this stance is opposed to normative pluralism, which would generally support the proliferation of rule-making forums like arbitral tribunals.[90] Here I underscore the more limited point that non-Muslim individuals had been making use of religious arbitrators for many years to resolve their family law disputes. Such practices, however, did not give rise to the same level of alarm as did the prospect of sharia law, nor has any prior government suggested that the use of religious arbitrators and norms in the resolution of family disputes was inconsistent with Canadian law.

How will Canadian courts respond when a particular religious group is singled out by legislatures, like Jehovah's Witnesses in 1950s Quebec? Muslim practices have been the subject of two recent appellate decisions in Canada. In *R v NS*, the SCC addressed whether a complainant in a sexual assault prosecution could wear a niqab while testifying.[91] The majority reasons of Chief Justice McLachlin allowed for the possibility that a witness might testify with a face covering. They ultimately suggest, however, that where a complainant's credibility is at issue, as it almost always is in a sexual assault prosecution, the witness will have to remove her niqab to testify.[92]

In one sense, the majority opinion is sensitive to N.S.'s claim, reminding lower courts that the inconsistency in religious practice is not necessarily indicative of insincerity[93] and requiring judges to "consider the broader societal harms of requiring a witness to remove the niqab in order to testify."[94] The universalist theme of Canadian religious freedom appears in the Court's apparent commitment to the principle that all religious practices should be subject to the same constitutional analysis. However, dominant conceptions of what makes a trial fair and the importance of seeing a witness's face ultimately controlled the outcome of the decision, and this despite a strong consensus in

89 *Arbitration Act, 1991*, SO 1991, c 17, s 32(4).

90 Anver M. Emon, "Islamic Law and the Canadian Mosaic: Politics, Jurisprudence, and Multicultural Accommodation," *Canadian Bar Review* 87, no. 2 (2009) 391.

91 *R v NS*, 2012 SCC 72.

92 *Ibid*, para 38; chap 8 by Narain comes to similar conclusions on the case. See also Faisal Bhabha, "*R. v N.S.*: What Is Fair in a Trial? The Supreme Court of Canada's Divided Opinion on the Niqab in the Courtroom," *Alberta Law Review* 50 (2013) 871.

93 *R v NS*, *supra* note 91, para 13.

94 *Ibid*, para 37.

the social sciences that seeing a person's face does nothing to aid in determinations of credibility.[95] The judgment is not explicitly driven by the Catholic-Protestant origin story of Canada, but members of those communities do not face the same challenges in Canadian courts as niqabi women, whose religious needs are not built into trial processes. Trial fairness here takes its substance from long-standing practices of Anglo-Canadian courts, themselves influenced by the cultural milieux in which they developed.

More recently, the Federal Court heard an application brought by Zunera Ishaq, a niqabi woman who challenged a Citizenship and Immigration Canada policy manual stating that citizenship candidates "will need to remove their face covering during the taking of the oath."[96] In a decision upheld on appeal, Justice Boswell held that the policy was inconsistent with the *Citizenship Regulations*, which require citizenship judges to allow "*the greatest possible freedom* in the religious solemnization or the solemn affirmation"[97] of the citizenship oath. Ultimately, Ms. Ishaq was able to swear her citizenship oath in her niqab.[98] The judicial reasoning that led to this conclusion was abbreviated because the Court chose not to answer the constitutional question of religious freedom, which would have required a more searching analysis than the "greatest possible freedom" requirement of the *Citizenship Regulations*. Nevertheless, the Court's decision in *Ishaq* might be read as consistent with a more universalist vision of religious freedom, applying regardless of the particular religion of the claimant.

Other religious communities have found themselves at the centre of controversy when their practices put them at odds with the equality claims of LGBTQI individuals and groups. In one case, even when the

---

95 Natasha Bakht, "What's in a Face? Demeanour Evidence in the Sexual Assault Context," in *Sexual Assault in Canada: Law, Legal Practice, and Women's Activism*, ed. Elizabeth A. Sheehy (Ottawa: University of Ottawa Press, 2012), 591; Natasha Bakht, "Objection, Your Honour! Accommodating Niqab-Wearing Women in Courtrooms," in *Legal Practice and Cultural Diversity*, ed. Ralph Grillo et al (Farnham, UK: Ashgate, 2009), 115; Lynn Smith J, "The Ring of Truth, the Clang of Lies: Assessing Credibility in the Courtroom," *University of New Brunswick Law Journal* 63 (2012) 10.

96 *Ishaq v Canada (Citizenship and Immigration)*, 2015 FC 156 (aff'd 2015 FCA 194), para 3.

97 SOR/93-246, s 17(1)(b); *Ibid*, para 53 (emphasis added).

98 *CBC News*, "Zunera Ishaq, Who Challenged Ban on Niqab, Takes Citizenship Oath Wearing It," 5 October 2015, http://www.cbc.ca/news/politics/zunera-ishaq-niqab-ban-citizenship-oath-1.3257762.

99 *Hall (Litigation guardian of) v Powers* (2002), 59 OR (3d) 423, para 28.

religious community held denominational schooling rights under s. 93 of the *Constitution Act, 1867*, the equality right was held to prevail. When a Catholic school board sought to prevent student Mark Hall from bringing a male date to his high school prom, Justice MacKinnon of the Superior Court of Justice found in favour of the student's "freedom of expression and equality rights."[99] Justice MacKinnon held that while it was not for the Court to determine "what the Catholic faith should require on the issue of homosexuality," it was the Court's role to determine whether "Catholic teachings and Board policy in fact proscribe 'homosexual behaviour' and a 'homosexual lifestyle.'"[100] The Court concluded that, given the "diversity of opinion within the Catholic community on pastoral care regarding homosexuality," allowing Mr. Hall to attend the prom with his boyfriend did not prejudice the Catholic school board's denominational schooling rights.[101]

The Court's approach to denominational rights here is significantly different from the jurisprudence on religious freedom, which asks what an individual sincerely believes rather than what the religious teachings "in fact" require. This reflects, perhaps, the difficulty in assessing the religious claims of a public institution rather than those of individuals or even private institutions.

The clash between equality rights for LGBTQI individuals and the religious freedom rights of a religious community is currently at play in the controversy surrounding a law school proposed by Trinity Western University (TWU). The proposal is contentious principally because TWU's community covenant, which students and faculty must sign, allows for sexual intimacy only between married, opposite-sex couples.[102] Litigation has ensued surrounding some provincial law societies' decisions to deny accreditation to the proposed law school.[103] So far, three appellate

---

100 *Ibid*, para 31.

101 *Ibid*, paras 44–5.

102 See Elaine Craig, "The Case for the Federation of Law Societies Rejecting Trinity Western University's Proposed Law Degree Program," *Canadian Journal of Women and the Law* 25 (2013) 148; Dwight Newman, "On the Trinity Western University Controversy: An Argument for a Christian Law School in Canada," *Constitutional Forum constitutionnel* 22, no. 3 (2013); Elaine Craig, "TWU Law: A Reply to Proponents of Approval," *Dalhousie Law Journal* 37 (2014) 621.

103 In December 2013, the Federation of Law Societies of Canada accredited the school's program, and British Columbia's minister of advanced education approved it as well. The law societies of Alberta, Saskatchewan, New Brunswick, Prince Edward Island, and Yukon approved the school's program. The Law Society

decisions have been rendered with conflicting results: the Nova Scotia and British Columbia Courts of Appeal found in favour of TWU (although for different reasons), and the Court of Appeal for Ontario found in favour of the Law Society of Upper Canada.[104] The Ontario court accepted the argument that the law society could deny accreditation to TWU's proposed law school in service of maintaining equality of opportunity with respect to membership in the provincial bar. The British Columbia court, on the other hand, held that the refusal of accreditation had a "severe impact" on religious freedom rights, while granting accreditation would have had "minimal impact ... on the access of LGBTQ persons to law school and the legal profession."[105]

The TWU litigation illustrates some challenges faced by religious communities not party to the constitutional compact. Courts analyse the case as a contest between two universally held rights. The outcome of this balancing exercise is hard to predict, as seen in the conflicting decisions of the various appellate courts. In contrast, when "founding" religious groups have asserted rights to institutional autonomy, as in *Caldwell* and *Daly*, the courts have usually held that the claims of individuals cannot override the claims of the institution, which acts in the name of the community.[106] The question moving forward is whether

---

of Upper Canada (Ontario) and the Nova Scotia Barristers' Society refused to accredit the school. The Law Society of British Columbia initially approved the program, but later reversed that decision. See Trinity Western University School of Law, "Timeline," http://twu.ca/academics/school-of-law/timeline.html. See also *Loke v British Columbia (Minister of Advanced Education)*, 2015 BCSC 413 (petitioner sought judicial review of the initial decision to approve the law school; application was found to be moot once decision was reversed).

104 *Trinity Western University v Nova Scotia Barristers' Society*, 2016 NSCA 59; *Trinity Western University v The Law Society of British Columbia*, 2016 BCCA 423; *Trinity Western University v The Law Society of Upper Canada*, 2016 ONCA 518. Only the British Columbia and Ontario decisions were appealed. The SCC's decision was rendered on 15 June 2018, upholding the decision of the Law Society of British Columbia not to approve the school.

105 *Trinity Western University v The Law Society of British Columbia*, *supra* note 104, para 191. See also *Trinity Western University v British Columbia College of Teachers*, 2001 SCC 31. Nova Scotia ruled on administrative law grounds and did not offer its views on the *Charter* aspect of the dispute; see *Trinity Western University v Nova Scotia Barristers' Society*, *supra* note 104.

106 Some have also argued that judges are more likely to at least be familiar with the background norms of dominant religious and cultural groups, making their claims easier to understand by courts. Some religious minorities have successfully

and how courts might level the playing field so that the claims of all religious communities are treated similarly. Will they extend rights of collective autonomy to more groups, constrain the autonomy of the founding groups, or retain the current unequal approach?[107]

There is little that courts can do about the constitutional privileges bestowed on Catholic and Protestant groups (although perhaps *Hall* is an example of how a court may achieve consistent results across public schools). But courts can work harder to appreciate the perspectives of minority groups and the importance they attach to communal autonomy. As I have argued elsewhere, courts are most successful at understanding religious freedom claims when they adopt the values and techniques associated with cross-cultural communication.[108] When judges analyse religious practices, they should be guided by the values of respect and self-awareness. Maintaining respect means recognizing that religious norms emerge from culturally specific contexts and making the effort to understand the background justifications that underlie those norms. To do this effectively, judges must maintain the self-awareness that their own views are shaped by the cultural context from which they came.

In the TWU litigation, the SCC ought to approach TWU's community covenant with respect by reading it within its particular cultural and religious context. Judges must also maintain an awareness that their own views on sexual morality are culturally situated, rather than being somehow above or without culture.[109] They must also remain aware that the privileges that the constitution bestows on Catholics and Protestants in some circumstances reflect a commitment to the importance of community autonomy, which can help inform religious freedom analyses for the claims of other groups. This does not necessarily mean that TWU's religious freedom claim, or other similar claims, should succeed. Taking this approach, however, will strengthen the Court's analysis by making plain exactly what is at stake for all parties in practical, religious, and dignitary terms.

---

negotiated this cultural gap by framing their practices around shared values. For example, counsel described the Sikh practice of wearing a kirpan as a symbol of resisting oppression and sexual equality. See Valerie Stoker, "Zero Tolerance? Sikh Swords, School Safety, and Secularism in Québec," *Journal of the American Academy of Religion* 75, no. 4 (2007) 814.

107 *Waldman v Canada*, HCROR, 67th Sess, Annex, Comm No 694/1996 (1996).

108 Howard Kislowicz, "Faithful Translations? Cross-cultural Communication in Canadian Religious Freedom Litigation," *Osgoode Hall Law Journal* 52, no. 1 (2014) 141.

109 See Benjamin L. Berger, "The Cultural Limits of Legal Tolerance," *Canadian Journal of Law and Jurisprudence* 21 (2008) 245, 246–7.

There are reasons to be hopeful about courts' abilities in this regard. In *Multani*, for example, instead of seeing the kirpan simply as a weapon, the SCC was able to maintain its self-awareness by comparing the kirpan to other potentially dangerous objects, "such as scissors, compasses, baseball bats and table knives in the cafeteria," routinely allowed in schools.[110] There are also, however, reasons to be sceptical of courts' cross-cultural communication skills. The majority of the Quebec Court of Appeal in *Multani*, for instance, remarked that "[s]tripped of its symbolic religious significance, the kirpan has all of the physical characteristics of an edged weapon."[111] By stripping the kirpan of its cultural context, reducing it to a single meaning, and not considering the similarly dangerous objects allowed in schools, the Court of Appeal failed to live up to the values of respect and self-awareness. Arguably, similar failures can be seen in the SCC's decisions in *Hutterian Brethren* and *NS*.

Question 2: How to Articulate a Non-religious Identity

A second question that looms in considering the 150th anniversary of Confederation is whether and how courts will contribute to constructing a narrative of the state not tethered to a religious tradition. The text of the constitution does not necessarily point in this direction; there is no explicit provision requiring a "general separation of church and state."[112] Further, in addition to the specific protections for Catholics and Protestants found in the *Constitution Act, 1867*, the preamble to the *Canadian Charter of Rights and Freedoms* provides that "Canada is founded upon principles that recognize the *supremacy of God* and the rule of law."[113]

---

110 *Multani*, *supra* note 1, paras 46, 58.

111 *Commission Scolaire Marguerite-Bourgeoys v Singh Multani*, 241 DLR (4th) 336, para 89.

112 Richard S. Kay, "The Canadian Constitution and the Dangers of Establishment," *DePaul Law Review* 42 (1992), 361, 362.

113 *Constitution Act, 1867*, *supra* note 3 (emphasis added); Lorne Sossin, "The Supremacy of God, Human Dignity and the Charter of Rights and Freedoms," *University of New Brunswick Law Journal* 52 (2003) 227; Jonathon W. Penney and Robert J. Danay, "The Embarrassing Preamble: Understanding the Supremacy of God and the Charter," *University of British Columbia Law Review* 39 (2006) 287; Buckingham, *supra* note 3, 20; George Egerton, "Trudeau, God, and the Canadian Constitution: Religion, Human Rights, and Government Authority in the Making of the 1982 Constitution," in *Rethinking Church, State and Modernity: Canada between Europe and the United States*, ed. David Lyon and Marguerite Van Die (Toronto: University of Toronto Press, 2000), 102, 106.

Since early *Charter* jurisprudence, however, the SCC has interpreted the guarantee of religious freedom as prohibiting governments from legislating in service of a religious purpose. This line of legal thought originated in the consideration of federal Sunday closing legislation. The SCC held,

> In an earlier time, when people believed in the collective responsibility of the community toward some deity, the enforcement of religious conformity may have been a legitimate object of government, but since the *Charter*, it is no longer legitimate. ... The state shall not use the criminal sanctions at its disposal to achieve a religious purpose.[114]

If it is no longer legitimate for the state to express a particular religious identity, how might courts contribute to reimagining a state previously understood as constituted by Catholics and Protestants? In its recent decision in *Saguenay*, the SCC gave some indication of the role it will play in this regard.[115] The *Saguenay* case addressed a challenge by a citizen to his municipal council's practice of opening its meetings with a prayer that incorporated the sign of the cross and the words "[i]n the name of the Father, the Son and the Holy Spirit."[116] The complaint originated at Quebec's Human Rights Tribunal, and the SCC affirmed the tribunal's decision that the practice was a violation of religious freedom and equality. In coming to this conclusion, Justice Gascon held for the majority that the state's duty of religious neutrality "results from an evolving interpretation of freedom of conscience and religion."[117] Justice Gascon tells a story of Canada in which there has been a growing distance between state and religious authorities. The state now acts "as an essentially neutral intermediary in relations between the various denominations and between those denominations

114 *R v Big M Drug Mart*, [1985] 1 SCR 295, 351. At 353, the SCC also held that legislation that has as its purpose the compulsion of religious observance cannot be saved by the "reasonable limits" clause of the *Charter*. This marked a strong departure from *Robertson and Rosetanni v R*, [1963] 41 DLR (2d) 485 (SCC), where the same law was upheld in the context of a challenge under the *Canadian Bill of Rights*, SC 1960, c 44.

115 *Saguenay, supra* note 1.

116 *Ibid*, para 6.

117 *Ibid*, para 71.

118 Gascon J adopts this narrative from the minority judgment of LeBel J in *Congrégation des témoins de Jéhovah de St-Jérôme-Lafontaine v Lafontaine (Village)*, 2004 SCC 48, para 67; *Saguenay, supra* note 1, para 71.

and civil society."[118] The state, in fulfilling this role, must "neither favour nor hinder any particular belief ... [or] non-belief."[119]

The image of the state here is quite different than that expressed in most of the case law on denominational schooling rights. Rather than a state constituted by two religious groups, whose institutions bear the imprints of those groups, the state is understood as a facilitator of social interaction. This posture of neutrality arguably has fairly clear implications for a municipal council that opens its meetings with a prayer.[120] Denominationally specific prayers are certainly not neutral. Non-denominational prayers also raise thorny challenges as governments will need to make determinations about what content is sufficiently non-denominational and who may offer the prayers.[121] In this context, the special protections given to Catholic and Protestant schools appear increasingly anachronistic. As Kaushal argues in chapter 7 of this volume, Canada is deeply different demographically than it was when these terms were agreed upon; the case law suggests that the intellectual trajectory has changed significantly as well.

But if the duty of state religious neutrality requires that state institutions abstain from particular practices and that laws with religious purposes are constitutionally invalid, on what normative bases can legislative projects proceed? As seen above, there are questions that require an answer from the state where neutrality is not an option. Law societies must decide whether to accredit TWU's law school. The result of such decisions is that either accreditation is denied on the basis of a religious practice or accreditation is granted, and aspiring LGBTQI law students are not offered the same array of opportunities as everyone else.

Some positive articulation of Canadian values is required to help define the range of constitutionally permissible decisions. *Saguenay*'s answer is the value of inclusive neutrality. But as when dealing with religious minorities, courts can fulfil the promise of inclusive neutrality only when they are willing to fully consider the culturally contingent, and therefore non-neutral, assumptions underlying practices generally seen as commonplace. From this perspective, *Saguenay* was an easy

---

119 *Saguenay*, *supra* note 1, para 72.

120 On the other hand, the SCC in *Saguenay* suggested that the court's jurisdiction may not extend to legislatures because of the doctrine of parliamentary privilege, *Ibid*, para 142.

121 Christopher C. Lund, "Legislative Prayer and the Secret Costs of Religious Endorsements," *Minnesota Law Review* 94 (2009) 972, 978–9.

case as the prayer had clear Christian connotations. Cases like *NS* are more difficult because the cultural contingency of legal processes is harder for courts to see. To this end, an increasing emphasis on judicial diversity – understood in terms of religion, culture, gender, sexuality, race, socio-economic background, etc. – might provide some assistance in the interrogation of culturally infused assumptions.

Conclusion

In the *Secession Reference*, the SCC held that the protection of denominational schooling rights in the *Constitution Act, 1867* was an example of the underlying constitutional principle of protecting minority populations.[122] This position embodies the two tensions highlighted above. It connects the particularist protections afforded to Catholics and Protestants with the universalist value of protecting minorities from tyrannical majorities. It also leaves open whether the collective rights embodied in denominational schooling protections, which give a limited kind of jurisdiction to religious communities, are the appropriate model for minority protection or whether an individualist model is more consistent with contemporary constitutional law. In a federal state with a complicated religious history, and a far-from-perfect record of accommodating and welcoming religious minorities, these tensions are not likely to disappear completely. Instead, they are likely to ebb and flow as our legal institutions respond to changing religious demographics and debates over the relationship between the civic and religious communities. We are best served if we address these tensions explicitly.

---

122 *Reference re Secession of Quebec*, [1998] 2 SCR 217, paras 79–80.

7 Collective Diversity and Jurisdictional Accommodations in Constitutional Perspective*

ASHA KAUSHAL

Introduction

In 1867, three colonies agreed to confederate. They became four provinces. Their political identities loosely tracked their territorial boundaries. The new constitutional federation was underwritten by a narrative of two founding nations – first, Upper Canada and Lower Canada; later, French Canada and English Canada – which survive in the popular imagination as representative of the sociopolitical reality of 1867. The Aboriginal peoples were notably absent from the constitutional conferences of 1864. It is often remarked that there is no singular constitutional moment in Canadian history, that the constitutional framework is an ongoing process of becoming. To this end, several more colonies would join the national project over the next decades. By the turn of the century, Canada had grown to seven provinces and two territories.

In 2017, Canada contains ten provinces, three territories, and twenty-two self-governing Aboriginal nations. It is made up of national minorities, municipalities, separate communities, and various other collectivities. Some of these are constitutional creatures; others are not. The narrative of two founding nations remains firmly lodged in the constitutional consciousness, although it is increasingly contested in the popular one. Provinces have assumed more functions in areas of concurrent jurisdiction, municipalities have created urban autonomy regimes, and identity groups have fought for constitutional exemptions. It is increasingly obvious that, from the French fact in Canada to the creation of Nunavut to the political backlash against the niqab,

* This chapter won first prize in the Baxter Family Competition on Federalism in 2018.

heterogeneity is part of the Canadian constitutional landscape. A key part of the constitutional process of becoming, in other words, has turned out to be a negotiation with diversity.

This chapter is a meditation on historical and emergent constitutional concepts of jurisdiction in the Canadian context of diversity. It explores the shifting composition of the Canadian population against the background of current constitutional values. This exploration reconsiders the constitutional accommodation of diversity in jurisdictional terms. The chapter is divided into two main parts. The first part examines the contemporary sociopolitical landscape and the nature and kind of legal conflicts generated from it. I begin by arguing that the composition of the people over whom the constitution has authority is changing. The first section describes the statistical terms of this demographic and social shift. I predict that this shift will expose new sites of tension in constitutional theory and adjudication. The old fault lines were French versus English Canada, in identitarian terms; or Quebec versus other provinces, in juridical terms. Now Quebec hosts its own set of tensions among French Québécois, English Quebeckers, Aboriginal peoples, and newcomers. These tensions can be extrapolated, albeit with slightly different cleavages, to the country at large, which is beset by new categories of conflicts. At first glance, this presents a problem of mis-mapping, in which old constitutional forms are transposed onto a new constitutional population.

Constitutional power, however, has two iterations: rights and jurisdictions.[1] In the second part of this chapter, I suggest that we should shift our focus to jurisdictions. I argue that there are multiple, proliferating forms of jurisdiction in constitutional law. By returning to the terms of legal authority – how it is parcelled out and to whom – we can locate the constitutional values of jurisdictional allocations *and* analyse the potential of new jurisdictional forms and allocations. In Canadian constitutionalism, the prototypical understanding of jurisdiction is a division of powers between the federal and provincial governments. The judicial interpretation of constitutional federalism sorts cases according to the relevant head of power. Already it is possible to see that the constitution parcels out jurisdiction territorially to the provinces and the federal government but also functionally, based on subject matter, and that some of these subjects are concurrent. The second part analyses constitutional jurisdiction in three settings: federalism,

1 Heidi Libesman, "Book Review: Indigenous Difference and the Constitution of Canada by Patrick Macklem," *Osgoode Hall Law Journal* 40, no. 2 (2002) 200.

linguistic minorities, and Aboriginal peoples. By comparing and contrasting traditional territorial jurisdiction to other functional, flexible, and personal forms of jurisdiction, its potential is made clear.

First, though, what exactly does jurisdiction mean in this chapter? Jurisdiction is the "signature canon in law."[2] It tells us where law can speak and shows us where law is authoritative. In a general sense, jurisdiction denotes the "scope" or "reach" of a thing or activity. It is through jurisdiction that "a life before the law is instituted, a place is subjected to rule and occupation, and an event is articulated as juridical."[3] Reliance on the idea of jurisdiction as "legal authority over" illuminates both constitutional allocations of power and contemporary conflicts over constitutional power. This takes the old fault lines of federalism – the primary model for distributing jurisdiction in Canada – and extends them outwards for a new constitutional population. This mode of thinking about parcels of legal authority illuminates the constitutional potential outside of rights for resolving issues of diversity. In short, the potential of jurisdiction is to take constitutional law beyond the rights paradigm to deal with issues of difference.

Governing the New Constitutional Population

The Constituency of the Constitution

Canada has a population of over thirty-five million people. The Canadian population in 2017 is dramatically different from the Canadian population in 1791 or 1867 or even 1982.[4] All these people are covered by the constitution to varying extents. The breadth and depth of this coverage is found in a combination of the original constitution and

---

2 John Brigham, "Seeing Jurisdiction: Some Jurisprudential Issues Arising from Law Being '... All Over,'" *Law and Policy* 31 (2009) 381. See also Mariana Valverde, "Jurisdiction and Scale: Legal 'Technicalities' as Resources for Theory," *Social and Legal Studies* 139.

3 Shaunnagh Dorsett and Shaun McVeigh, "Questions of Jurisdiction," in *Jurisprudence of Jurisdiction*, ed. Shaun McVeigh (New York: Routledge-Cavendish, 2007), 3.

4 *Constitutional Act 1791*, 31 Geo III, c 31 (UK), reprinted in RSC 1985, App II, No 3 (dividing Quebec into the provinces of Lower Canada and Upper Canada); *Constitution Act, 1867* (UK), 30 & 31 Vict, c 3, reprinted in RSC 1985, App II, No. 5 (bringing together three colonies into a federal structure); *Canadian Charter of Rights and Freedoms, Part 1 of the Constitution Act, 1982, being Schedule B to the Canada Act 1982* (UK), c 11.

ongoing contestations. There have been multiple moments of public consultation and contestation about the constitutional text. Although only some of them have been entrenched, each articulation is a dialogue about constitutional identity and values. Nonetheless, the historical pull of the original constitutional text is undeniable. The original constitutional solutions – first, jurisdiction and then rights – were designed for a particular, albeit evolving, population based in the provinces, and they have strong roots. In this section, I provide a brief historical overview of the constitutional population and the corollary constitutional compromises and resolutions. I use jurisdiction as a means to consider how the constitutional population was conceived and categorized. I then turn to the new constitutional population to set the stage for considering alternative jurisdictional compromises and resolutions.

The diversity of the Canadian population is not new, but the nature of that diversity has changed over time. In the very beginning, constitutionally speaking, there were almost 3.5 million people in Canada.[5] Most but not all of them had been born in Canada or had come from France or England.[6] Almost all of them were either Roman Catholic or Protestant. There were Aboriginal peoples, although their numbers had been decimated by the violence of European contact. These identities were included in the constitutional text through a combination of constitutional federalism and exceptional rights regimes. The 1867 text specifically enumerated and thus accommodated the French fact to the extent that it coincided with the province of Quebec, in addition to linguistic and religious minorities in constitutional educational regimes. The constitutional questions then rolled out as questions about the relative powers of the federal government and the provinces as well as the coexistence of French and English ethnic and linguistic populations.[7]

Canada is a settler society, which means it is a country of immigration. This has several implications, most notably that its nation-building project is closely tied to immigration and thus diversity. This diversity has morphed over time from historically Irish, Greek, and Ukrainian arrivals to contemporary Asian and South Asian arrivals. As the Canadian

---

5 Statistics Canada, *Censuses of Canada, 1665 to 1871*, vol. 4 of Statistics of Canada, Cat. no. 98-187-X (Ottawa: Statistics Canada, 2000).

6 Statistics Canada, *Canada Year Book 1867*, https://www66.statcan.gc.ca/eng/1867/186700160016_The Census.pdf.

7 Alan Cairns, *Citizens Plus: Aboriginal Peoples and the Canadian State* (Vancouver: UBC Press, 2000).

population grew, reaching twenty million people in 1967, the harbingers of change were already on the horizon.[8] From a diversity standpoint, two decisive events marked the one-hundred-year anniversary of Confederation. First, it was the year of the first report of the Royal Commission on Bilingualism and Biculturalism (B&B Commission) – the report that ultimately led to the adoption of multiculturalism.[9] Strains of public discord objected to the bicultural framework of the commission. Ultimately, the B&B Commission recognized the voices of these "other Canadians," who had argued that they did not fit neatly into the categories of French Canada and English Canada. It used the term *Third Force* to refer to this group of Canadians.

Second, 1967 was the year that Canadian immigration laws abandoned national origin as an admission criterion.[10] Immigration law switched over to the points system, which prioritized human capital over nationality. This would greatly change the composition of immigrant flows to Canada. Together, then, these events changed the people coming to Canada and the terms of their welcome once here. At the time, though, the composition of the Canadian population remained overwhelmingly European in origin.[11] The glimmer of new articulations of identity was visible but not yet manifest.

There is one more piece to develop in this historical overview: the details of the policy of multiculturalism. Multiculturalism is a set of ideas about groups that end up living together in a state because of immigration.[12] It is a territorial construct; the very idea of multiculturalism contains within it the idea of a shared national space.[13] As a set of ideas about identities and groups that live together within a territory, multiculturalism has almost no legal content. The first reason for that is the nature of its inclusion in the *Charter*. Multiculturalism appears in s. 27 of the *Charter* as an interpretative principle of construction,

8 Statistics Canada, *Censuses of Canada, supra* note 5.

9 Royal Commission on Bilingualism and Biculturalism, *Report*, vol. 1 (Ottawa: Queen's Printer, 1967).

10 Peter S. Li, "Cultural Diversity in Canada: The Social Construction of Racial Differences" (Ottawa: Department of Justice, 2000).

11 *Ibid.*

12 Catherine Dauvergne, *The New Politics of Immigration and the End of Settler Societies* (New York: Cambridge University Press, 2016).

13 Ghassan Hage writes of multiculturalism as a "nationalist practice" that loses meaning without a national territory in which to be applied; see Ghassan Hage, *White Nation* (New York: Routledge, 2000), 28–32.

which means it effectively either piggybacks on or conflicts with specific rights such as freedom of religion.[14] The second reason is the historical backdrop to multiculturalism, which is framed by the battle for identity and sovereignty between French and English Canada. One expression of that limiting backdrop is visible in the judicial interpretation of exceptional national minority rights, which are insulated from both s. 15 and s. 27: "the natural nexus between section 27's cultural protections and linguistic, educational and religious rights is artificially severed."[15] These historical turns have rendered multiculturalism somewhat insubstantial in the face of identity claims.

The last of the constitutional dialogues, the Charlottetown Accord, ended in failure in 1992.[16] Despite the relative recency of those negotiations, they did not address the nature of the diversity that is making contemporary headlines. In Canada, the population is aging, and birth rates are falling. In 2006, natural increase, the historical pattern of population growth in Canada, reversed, and migratory increase came to account for two-thirds of Canadian population growth.[17] Statistics Canada projects that, by 2030, immigration will be the only growth factor for the Canadian population.[18] Thus, immigration has become integral to sustaining the Canadian population even as it presents new challenges for that population.

Alongside – or inside – these numbers, immigration flows have shifted away from European countries towards Asian countries (China, India, and the Philippines). These recent immigrants are building new forms of difference into society: visible minorities, multilingual speakers, non-Christian religions, and myriad cultures. Statistics Canada projects that, by 2031, one in three Canadians will be a visible minority and visible minorities will outnumber non-visible minorities in Canada's major cities.[19] Tracking

---

14 *See Roach v Canada (Minister of Multiculturalism and Culture)*, [1994] 2 FC 406 (FCA) (striking out the s 27 claim on the basis that it was not a substantive provision capable of being violated); see also *Grant v Canada (Attorney General)*, [1995] 1 FC 158 (TD) (finding that s 27 provided no independent *Charter* right).

15 Vern W. DaRe, "Beyond General Pronouncements: A Judicial Approach to Section 27 of the Charter [forthcoming?]," *Alberta Law Review* 33 (1995) 551, 2.

16 Charlottetown Accord, *Draft Legal Text, October 9, 1992* (Ottawa: Queen's Printer, 1992).

17 Statistics Canada, *Canadian Demographics at a Glance*, Cat. no. 91-003-X (Ottawa: Statistics Canada, 2008).

18 *Ibid.*

19 I recognize that *visible minority* is a controversial term. I use it here to denote "observable difference," in keeping with official government terminology. See *Employment Equity Act*, SC 1995, c 44.

these projections, one in seven Canadians will have a non-Christian religious denomination, and half of those Canadians will be Muslim. One in three Canadians will speak neither English nor French as their mother tongue.[20]

As the composition of immigration has shifted, so too have the contours of settlement and integration. It is already possible to see the effects of these changing demographics.[21] These include larger numbers of visible minority immigrants on the ground, some of whom settle in enclaves; pressures in the public sphere surrounding integration and tolerance; and tensions in the legal sphere between equality and religious freedoms. What does this demographic transformation, with its multiplying vectors of diversity, portend for constitutional federalism? It demands a rethinking of the coincidence of territory and nation that underwrites the model of federalism as federal and provincial heads of power. The idea of "landedness," in the words of Alan Cairns, is no longer descriptively accurate.[22] Even for the original nations or communities of the constitution – its multiple *demoi* – landedness no longer captures a bounded political nation or even its political imagination. Aboriginal peoples are scattered across rural and urban settings; Quebec is host to French Quebeckers as well as English Quebeckers, Aboriginal peoples, and newcomers. Perhaps most important, those categories fracture further along religious, linguistic, and cultural lines. In the sections that follow, I examine the territorial heft of jurisdiction in three constitutional regimes: federalism, national linguistic minorities, and Aboriginal self-government arrangements.

Jurisdiction in the Constitution

In the Canadian constitutional system, there are two pathways for collective difference, and these pathways mirror the two iterations of constitutional power: rights and jurisdictions. There are some jurisdictions embedded in the constitutional text – namely, the federal and provincial division of legislative powers, linguistic and religious minority rights, and, to some extent, Aboriginal rights. In this section, I place these

20 Statistics Canada, *Canadian Demographics at a Glance*, *supra* note 17.
21 See also Joe Friesen, "The Changing Face of Canada: Booming Minority Populations by 2031," *Globe and Mail*, 9 March 2010.
22 Cairns, *supra* note 7.

existing jurisdictional forms into conversation with new collectivities of difference to locate the opportunities and obstacles for accommodation.

The Federal Jurisdictional Paradigm

Federalism is a means of political and legal organization that combines the search for unity with respect for autonomy.[23] It is a response to internal diversity. Such forms of diversity are internal to the state to the extent that they are already present at the time of federation. This is to be distinguished from external diversity, including from immigration, which is conceived as being outside the state. As a response to internal diversity, federalism produces a sticky, institutional version of autonomy that is rooted in history and territory. It is ostensibly oriented towards diversity – this is the whole point of the federal form – but it is closed to identities and communities that are not part of the original territorial division. This is not to say that federalism is static; it is possible to be sympathetic to the claim that federalism "amplifies the polity's capacity for politics," while acknowledging its distinctive historical and territorial drag.[24]

In the constitution, the concept of federalism appears only once, in the preamble reference to the colonies' "desire to be federally united into one Dominion."[25] It united three British colonies into a federation made up of four provinces, and then legislative powers were divided among them.[26] The division of powers articulated in ss. 91 and 92, which allocates jurisdiction to the federal government and the provincial governments, is the primary textual expression of the principle of federalism in Canada. The two levels of government are coordinate, each sovereign within its sphere of action.[27] The federal and provincial

23 Pierre Pescatore, preface to *Courts and Free Markets: Perspectives from the United States and Europe*, ed. Terrance Sandalow and Eric Stein (New York: Clarendon Press, 1982).

24 Cristina M. Rodriguez, "Federalism and National Consensus" (unpublished manuscript, 2010); Heather Gerken, "The Supreme Court 2009 Term – Foreword: Federalism All the Way Down," *Harvard Law Review* 124 (2010) 4.

25 Marc Chevrier, "The Idea of Federalism among the Founding Fathers of the United States and Canada," in *Contemporary Canadian Federalism*, ed. Alain-G. Gagnon (Toronto: University of Toronto Press, 2009), 11.

26 It united Canada, Nova Scotia, and New Brunswick into Canada, creating the provinces of Ontario, Quebec, Nova Scotia, and New Brunswick.

27 *Hodge v The Queen* (1883) 9 App Cas 117. This is complicated by tolerance of overlap as well as two concurrent powers – agriculture and immigration.

governments are the only levels of government that have constitutionally protected jurisdiction.[28]

There are, however, other collectivities marked by constitutional jurisdiction. These collectivities are French- and English-language speakers, Protestant and Catholic parents, Quebec, New Brunswick, and Indigenous peoples. The inclusion of these collectivities (and not others) may be traced to historical federalist compromises as well as the particular evolution of federalism in the Canadian context. The drawing of provincial boundaries made some collectivities into majorities and others into minorities. For example, francophone Quebeckers and scholars have viewed Quebec as "an essential bulwark of the French fact in North America."[29] But it was never the case that all members of a collective – whether French-speaking Quebeckers or English-speaking provinces, Catholics or Protestants, or Aboriginal peoples – were neatly contained within a province without others. Indeed, federalism has a more complex set of tools at its disposal: divorce was made federal so that Protestants in Quebec would not be subject to restrictions imposed by that province's Roman Catholic majority.[30]

For constitutional lawyers, it is axiomatic that federalism articulates constitutional values.[31] For several of them, federalism is instrumental – not a value in itself, but rather a means to realize other political values.[32] The nature of those values is a matter of some dispute. They tend to be some combination of the diffusion of power and the prevention of tyranny, the promotion of diversity and experimentation, and the efficiency of local governance and the enhancement of democracy.[33] Underwriting these values and objectives, or at least orbiting around them, is the value of identity. In many ways, at its core, federalism is about autonomy in the service of identity. In this sense, federalism is the original constitutional

28 Jeremy Webber, *The Constitution of Canada: A Contextual Analysis* (Oxford: Hart Publishing, 2015), 134. Arguably, Aboriginal governments have some measure of constitutional jurisdiction; see "The Jurisdiction of Aboriginal Self-Government" below.

29 *Ibid*, 47.

30 *Ibid*, 32.

31 Robert C. Post, "Justice Brennan and Federalism," *Constitutional Commentary* 7 (1990) 227.

32 Richard Simeon and Katherine Swinton, "Rethinking Federalism in a Changing World," in *Rethinking Federalism*, ed. Karen Knop et al (Vancouver: UBC Press, 1995), 7.

33 Erwin Chemerinsky, "The Values of Federalism," *Florida Law Review* 47 (1995) 499; Post, *supra* note 31; Malcolm Feeley and Edward Rubin, *Federalism: Political Identity and Tragic Compromise* (Ann Arbor: University of Michigan Press, 2011).

form of identity politics, closely linked to ideas about the relationship between identities and the state.

The identities within the ambit of federalism are collective in nature. Felix Frankfurter articulated the now-familiar communitarian notion that individual identity is formed in conjunction with the communities and states in which individuals live as one of the key normative values of federalism.[34] In the Canadian context, Richard Simeon and Ian Robinson have remarked that, to understand Canadian federalism, one must pay attention to collective identities.[35] Patrick Monahan has written that "the rights of collectivities lie at the very core of federal theory."[36] This identity frequently has several dimensions, but, in the context of federalism, its primary or dominant projection must be political identity.[37] So, for example, Quebec is the federal construct of political identity, but its conceivable other identities are linguistic (francophone), cultural (Canadien), religious (French-Catholic), and even civic (province of Quebec).

However, once federalism is on the terrain of collective identity, the queue of new and competing identities comes into view. Societal diversity is often categorized according to its nature as multicultural or multinational or both.[38] The nature of accommodation will differ depending on the categorization.[39] Multicultural diversity is immigrant- and ethnic group–based, and it is matched with multiculturalism. Multinational diversity is national minority–based, and it is matched with federalism. Despite significant focus on multinational federalism, there has been little attention paid to its multicultural counterpart. As discussed above, the policy of multiculturalism is hollow accommodation. It is concerned with representations of culture, not identities and rights.

34 Felix Frankfurter, quoted in Post, *supra* note 31, 233.

35 Richard Simeon and Ian Robinson, "The Dynamics of Canadian Federalism," in *Canadian Politics*, ed. James Bickerton and Alain-G. Gagnon (Toronto: University of Toronto Press, 2009), 155.

36 Patrick Monahan, "At Doctrine's Twilight: The Structure of Canadian Federalism," *University of Toronto Law Journal* 34 (1984) 47, 83.

37 Feeley and Rubin, *supra* note 33, chap 1.

38 Will Kymlicka, *Multicultural Citizenship* (Oxford: Oxford University Press, 1995); Will Kymlicka, *Finding Our Way: Rethinking Ethnocultural Relations in Canada* (Oxford: Oxford University Press, 1998).

39 Jean-François Caron and Guy Laforest, "Canada and Multinational Federalism: From the Spirit of 1982 to Stephen Harper's Open Federalism," *Nationalism and Ethnic Politics* 15 (2009) 27, 28.

It amounts to a welcome mat, not more. Federalism may be only for national minorities, but what kinds of logic and values underwrite its approach to diversity? The question is not only whether new and multiple bases of identity in modern society can find some representation but also whether, as Jane Jenson queries, federalism institutionalizes the territorial distribution of power to the detriment and even harm of other groups.[40]

Federalism is simply a "formalised transaction of a moment in the history of a particular community."[41] It secures a particular mode of autonomy – the territorial province – but it precludes or at least abbreviates other modes of autonomy.[42] This matters because it is not only that diversity runs across provincial borders but also that the provinces are rife with internal differences. This is particularly challenging in the context of immigration and collective heterogeneity for new sociological identities that "cannot be handled by federalism."[43] Immigration challenges the federal constitutional order by challenging its "assumptions of both space and time": the practices of privileging territorial diversity and historic communities.[44] The strength of federalism is to match collective identities with pockets of territorial autonomy. Its weakness, however, is precisely in channelling the same form again and again.

The organizing principle of federalism is territorial, and this is a key part of its heft and its presentation.[45] Malcolm Feeley and Edward Rubin have described the grip of the geographical framework for federalism along two axes: first, geographical divisions are mutually exclusive in a way that functional divisions are not; and second, geographic entities reiterate the structure of the state.[46] This means that "we are compelled by the nature of physical space to define [geographic] regions as separate from each other."[47] And while these two qualities might seem

---

40 Simeon and Swinton, *supra* note 32, 8.

41 Monahan, *supra* note 36, quoting Davis, n144.

42 Jane Jenson, "Citizenship Claims: Routes to Representation in a Federal System," in *Rethinking Federalism*, ed. Karen Knop et al (Vancouver: UBC Press, 1995); see "They [collective actors] dispute the definition of constitutional politics as being 'about' federalism," 111.

43 Alan Cairns, "Constitutional Government and the Two Faces of Ethnicity: Federalism Is Not Enough," in *Rethinking Federalism*, ed. Karen Knop et al (Vancouver: UBC Press, 1995), 19.

44 *Ibid*, 30.

45 Preston King, *Federalism and Federation* (Baltimore: Johns Hopkins Press, 1982).

46 Feeley and Rubin, *supra* note 33, 13.

47 *Ibid*.

to make territorial federalism rigid and centric, they actually permit divisions in service of creating more bases and possibilities for political identity.[48] These are the logics of federalism – to modulate political identity so that loyalties can be multiple and overlapping.

Territory has two faces in federalism. On the one hand, territory is the basis for autonomy, permitting diversity and dividing the state into sub-state units. On the other hand, this division is in service of the state maintaining its territorial integrity and ultimately its existence.[49] Indeed, constitutional federalism relies on territory as the constant over time. Following Feeley and Rubin, territory's qualities of being authoritative and exclusive provide the basis for binding future generations and for justifying the division as it was done. It is territory that provides some resolution of the paradox of constituent power, enabling the constitution to carry forward without mass dislocation. This is partly because territory – and, specifically, divisions of territory – forges a narrative of Canadian identity. The result is that territory that is part of the framework of constitutional federalism is conceptually and qualitatively different from other territories. A province is categorically distinct from Chinatown or Brampton. The basis for that distinction is territorial jurisdiction and the division of powers.

At this point, I want to offer some tentative thoughts about the limits of the federal framework and the potential for jurisdiction. By homing in on the purposive nature of federalism, the potential value of the federal form is crystallized. Feeley and Rubin suggest,

> The point of granting partial independence, and thus the point of federalism, is to allow normative disagreement among the subordinate units so that different units can subscribe to different value systems.[50]

In other words, federalism can provide what rights cannot: a resolution of incommensurable values and subjective disagreements. It provides a sphere within which governments and people may decide how to order provincial priorities. These include deeply normative social issues such as funding fertility treatments and safe injection sites.[51] In contrast,

---

48 *Ibid*, 14.

49 David Storey, *Territories: The Claiming of Space* (New York: Routledge, 2012).

50 Malcolm Feeley and Edward Rubin, *Judicial Policy Making and the Modern State* (Cambridge: Cambridge University Press, 2000), 174.

51 *Globe and Mail*, "Ontario Government Sets Age Limit at 43 for IVF Coverage," 1 October 2015; *Canada (Attorney General) v PHS Community Services Society*, [2011] 3 SCR 134.

rights, in their simplified form, provide individual protection from state interference. They do not allow collectives to order any part of their affairs but rather provide for individual members to express themselves or practise their religion or to be free from discrimination. Many years ago, Alan Cairns argued that "federalism is not enough," claiming that it precluded the inclusion of minorities within minorities.[52] He suggested that constitutional practitioners needed to link federalism and rights in a category called "charter federalism." He acknowledged that these two forms did not create an "ethnically level playing field" but were a "commendable attempt at fairness."[53] What rights or a charter lack is the ability to put power in the hands of minorities. However, this non-equivalence between federal and non-federal and territorial and non-territorial collective identities is not inevitable. Jurisdiction is a means to put them on the same plane in terms of offering the same goods.

It is possible to extrapolate this by suggesting that federalism in Canada builds in forms of functional jurisdiction and that these open the door to new modes of value variance and autonomy. The notion of jurisdiction as both territorial and functional expands the horizons of jurisdiction in the constitutional context. The territorial piece is self-explanatory – the constitution apportions jurisdiction to territorial units called provinces – but the nature of this apportionment is partly functional because it does not assign *everything* to the provinces. It is not a wholesale grant of legal authority. Rather, it assigns specific heads of jurisdiction, particular subject matters to each level. The nature of functions is that they are "socially constructed in their entirety," and the "functional divisions depend on the way they are defined."[54] This means that they bump up against each other and require judicial intervention to settle and categorize. Indeed, this is how the provincial jurisdiction over property and civil rights has come to subsume so much: because it is functional and permissive of interpretation and definition, in line with philosophical positions and policy choices.

From here, it becomes possible to imagine parcelling out other kinds of functional jurisdiction to other kinds of (possibly non-territorial) collectivities. This is not to make the case for wholesale self-governance by religious and cultural collectivities. Rather, I am suggesting that pockets of jurisdiction that exist alongside state norms may go some distance

52 Cairns, *supra* note 43.

53 *Ibid*, 33.

54 Feeley and Rubin, *supra* note 33.

towards integrating new, non-constitutional collectivities. Indeed, it is important to note that the logic of most, if not all, these collectivities is concerned to secure a mix of inclusion and autonomy. It is a more robust and complex inclusion. It contrasts to the self-determination logic of a collectivity such as Quebec, which points away from inclusion in the larger state and towards political autonomy on the basis of difference.[55] It is essential to remember that the collectivities that make it into federalism are part of the distribution of state power. They are not neutral territorial containers but political and juridical actors. The reconsideration of federal jurisdictional allocations along functional lines reveals jurisdiction as a negotiable instrument with other possible permutations.

Other Jurisdictional Paradigms

NATIONAL MINORITIES AS EXCEPTIONAL JURISDICTIONAL REGIMES

This section focuses on the extension of jurisdictional allocations to collectivities that are not provinces and thus not captured by federalism but are nonetheless constitutional. There are two historical sets of collective rights in the constitutional text that fall into two overlapping categories: language rights and education rights. Section 23 provides for minority-language education rights in French and English, while s. 29 guarantees special educational rights previously granted to "denominational, separate or dissentient schools," specifically the Protestants in Quebec and the Roman Catholics in Ontario.[56] In this section, I focus on the two language groups directly protected by the *Charter*.[57] French- and English-speaking citizens enjoy the right, even where they are in the minority, to use their languages in some courts and legislatures, to have legislation enacted in their languages, to receive federal government services in those languages, and to have their children educated in their mother tongue.[58] It is this last right – to education in a particular language – that is the focus of several Supreme Court cases. It is

55 Webber, *supra* note 28.

56 *Canadian Charter of Rights and Freedoms*, Part Const Act 1982 Sched B Can Act 1982 UK 1982 C 11 [*Canadian Charter of Rights and Freedoms*]. Note that other provinces have included such protections in their acts of accession to Confederation.

57 Denise G. Réaume and Leslie Green, "Education and Linguistic Security in the Charter," *McGill Law Journal* 34 (1989) 777.

58 *Canadian Charter of Rights and Freedoms*, *supra* note 56.

also this provision that is the most interesting for jurisdictional analysis and collective difference because it enumerates a constitutional minority and bestows it with a certain measure of self-rule "where numbers warrant."

Section 23 of the *Charter* is designed to preserve and promote the two official languages of Canada by ensuring that each flourishes in provinces where it is not spoken by the majority of the population. It grants minority-language educational rights to minority-language parents throughout Canada according to a sliding scale where there is a sufficient minority population. In *Mahe v Alberta,* a francophone father sued the province of Alberta for refusing to establish an independent francophone school board pursuant to s. 23.[59] The Court determined that francophones in Alberta were entitled to be represented on the school board.

The judgment is notable in three respects: it establishes the minority-language rights regime as an exception; it confirms language as a collective and social good; and it establishes a uniquely calibrated approach to the group exercising the right. First, the Court confirmed that language rights in s. 23 were "a novel form of legal right," both in genesis and in form.[60] Section 23 "confers upon a group a right which places a positive obligation on government to alter or develop major institutional structures."[61] The form is unusual because most rights are not differentiated by group identity, nor are they subject to a numbers constraint.[62] The Court then carved out s. 23 as an exceptional "comprehensive code" for minority-language education rights, thus insulating it from the application of ss. 15 and 27. Section 23 was, "if anything, an exception to the provisions of ss. 15 and 27 in that it accords these groups, the English and the French, special status in comparison to all other linguistic groups in Canada."[63]

The conflation of ss. 15 and 27 ignored the fact that s. 15 is a substantive right, while s. 27 is an interpretative provision that speaks to the value of group culture, making it rationally applicable to a discussion about language as a group attribute that is coterminous with culture. In constructing the language provisions as a comprehensive code separate

59 *R v Mahe,* [1990] 1 SCR 342.
60 *Ibid,* para 37.
61 *Ibid.*
62 Réaume and Green, *supra* note 57.
63 *R v Mahe, supra* note 59.

from other *Charter* obligations, the Court insulated them from review, restricted them to the two recognized groups, and reinforced the nation as a composite of French and English.

Second, Chief Justice Dickson focused on the role of schools as community centres "where the promotion and preservation of minority language culture can occur," as locations where the language community can meet and express its culture.[64] He confirmed that the purpose of s. 23 was to preserve and promote the official languages of Canada and their respective cultures:

> My reference to cultures is significant: it is based on the fact that any broad guarantee of language rights, especially in the context of education, cannot be separated from a concern for the culture associated with the language. Language is more than a mere means of communication, it is part and parcel of the identity and culture of the people speaking it. It is the means by which individuals understand themselves and the world around them.[65]

This dual approach highlights the universality of language as an aspect of collective identity and culture, yet particularizes its protection by referring to the unique political compromise.[66] This is a jurisdictional technique, holding the universal and particular in equipoise and then finding resolution through politics. Even though s. 23 is legal, contained in the constitutional text, it is also political and historical, immune from the constitution's other rights requirements.

Third, the Court broadly interpreted the criterion for "where numbers warrant," opting for a sliding scale approach that correlated the level of rights and services appropriate to the number of students involved. In cases where the numbers stipulate, minority-language parents acquire a right to management and control over the educational facilities in which their children are taught. Section 23 speaks of "wherever in the province" the "numbers warrant." This means that the calculation of the relevant numbers is not restricted to existing school boundaries. The numbers test should be applied on a local basis throughout the province.[67] This is a significant territorial delimitation. The *degree* of

---

64 *Ibid.*

65 *Ibid*, para 362.

66 On language rights as political compromise, see *Société des Acadiens v Association of Parents*, [1986] 1 SCR 549.

67 *Reference re Bill 30, An Act to Amend the Education Act (Ont)*, 1 SCR 1148 (1987).

management and control ranges from an independent school board to guaranteed representation on a shared school board. The purpose is to give the group control over those aspects of education that pertain to or affect their language and culture.[68] The result is that these parents are entitled to a certain level of self-rule over their children's schools.

This case shows how group rights are still held collectively, even when individuals have standing to enforce them.[69] The right to minority-language education is legally enforceable by individuals, but it operates only when a critical mass of minority students makes such an institution viable, and it entails a collective territorial right by a minority linguistic community to manage and control the facilities.[70] This group right constitutes the group by drawing its ambit loosely around school boundaries *and* by defining the nature and content of its right according to a sliding scale. But this constitution is fluid: the majority-minority characterization is evasive, appearing and disappearing depending upon where one stands and how many others stand there, too. Where the boundaries are drawn determines whether the group is a minority. Despite its references to minority-language rights and provincial accommodation, s. 23 is distinctly nationalist in orientation.

The combined effect of the national scope of the right and the mobility rights of individuals is the erosion of the provincial jurisdictional threshold. Provincial jurisdiction over education is delimited by the exceptionality of s. 23, in which jurisdiction attaches to the family, not the province. Minority-language rights travel across provincial borders with the family.[71] This is the jurisdictional threshold in motion, only crystallizing when the family relocates to a province where the language of instruction is discontinuous with their children's former education, thus triggering law's application. It is also a jurisdictional threshold imbued with national and bilingual commitments, embodying the principle of subsidiarity, and transposing these commitments to the community level. Put differently, it is possible to imagine a bilingual nation state in which provinces or regions speak different languages;

68 *R v Mahe*, *supra* note 59.

69 Sujit Choudhry, "Group Rights in Comparative Constitutional Law: Culture, Economics or Political Power?," in *Oxford Handbook of Comparative Constitutional Law*, ed. Michel Rosenfeld and Andras Sajo (Oxford: Oxford University Press, 2012), 1099.

70 Allen Buchanan, "Liberalism and Group Rights," in *In Harm's Way: Essays in Honor of Joel Feinberg*, ed. Allen Buchanan and Jules Coleman (Cambridge: Cambridge University Press, 1994), 1.

71 *Solski (Tutor of) v Quebec (Attorney General)*, [2005] 1 SCR 201, 2005 SCC 14.

it is more difficult to conjure this scheme of spatial language pockets and moving minority/majority designations. And yet this kind of flexible jurisdictional form should reveal the complex potential of jurisdiction to manage the intersecting pieces of collective identities.

THE JURISDICTION OF ABORIGINAL SELF-GOVERNMENT

The protection of Aboriginal and treaty rights is contained in s. 35 of the *Constitution Act, 1982* and reaffirmed in s. 25 of the *Charter*.[72] The precise nature and content of these rights is a matter of ongoing contestation. The law of Aboriginal rights functions as a kind of conceptual umbrella under which the rights shift and evolve.[73] In *Delgamuukw*, which considered the title claim of the Gitksan and Wet'suwet'en peoples in British Columbia, the Supreme Court created two categories of rights: Aboriginal rights, which are free-standing rights such as the right to hunt or fish; and Aboriginal title, which is a beneficial interest in the land.[74] In this section, I briefly explain the relationships among Aboriginal rights, title, and self-government from the perspective of jurisdiction.

The juridical understanding of Aboriginal title conceives of it as a proprietary interest, a specialized interest in land, which should be incorporated into property law. In contrast, Aboriginal peoples have understood title as a means to autonomy, including self-determination and self-government.[75] Aboriginal title to land and other Aboriginal and treaty rights are communal in nature, vested in the collective.[76] Jeremy Webber explains that this does not mean that Aboriginal peoples internally hold their land in undivided co-ownership.[77] Rather, it represents a jurisdictional allocation from other governments. Those governments are indicating that the allocation of those land rights is a matter for the Aboriginal nation in question; they are recognizing a sphere of territorial jurisdiction.[78]

72 *Canadian Charter of Rights and Freedoms, supra* note 56; *Constitution Act, 1982*, Sched B Can Act 1982 UK 1982 C11 [*Constitution Act, 1982*].

73 Webber, *supra* note 28, 228.

74 *Ibid*, 239.

75 *Ibid*.

76 Kent McNeil, "The Jurisdiction of Inherent Right Aboriginal Governments," research paper for the National Centre for First Nations Governance, 11 October 2007, 16.

77 Webber, *supra* note 28, 235.

78 Jeremy Webber, "The Public Law Dimension of Indigenous Property Rights," in *The Proposed Nordic Saami Convention: National and International Dimensions*, ed. Nigel Bankes and Timo Koivurova (Oxford: Hart Publishing, 2013).

> Even the notion that the Aboriginal dimensions of the constitution are fundamentally about rights, about claims against the state, is misleading. They are more about federalism: about the recognition of a sphere in which Aboriginal law and institutions of governance are predominant.[79]

Yet, or perhaps because, Aboriginal title implicates self-government, the status of self-government as an Aboriginal right in constitutional law remains an open question.[80] Approaches to carving out jurisdictional space for Aboriginal peoples occur against the backdrop of the constitutional division of powers. As an organizing principle of the constitution, the division of powers leans towards legislative jurisdiction as already allocated.[81] In light of these difficulties, the courts have proved reluctant to recognize and delineate Aboriginal self-government. The political negotiation track has been more fruitful.

There are currently twenty-two self-government agreements involving thirty-six Aboriginal communities.[82] Eighteen of these are part of a comprehensive land claims agreement. At present, Indigenous and Northern Affairs Canada counts ninety self-government negotiating tables in Canada. These negotiations are sometimes wholesale, comprehensive self-government agreements and other times sectoral transfers of authority or arrangements to particular fields or subject areas.[83] The agreements include powers that are defined in a manner unlike other constitutional powers. These include laws that are not defined on the basis of territory but rather on the basis of citizenship.[84] Those laws could apply to members who are not living on a First Nation's land base – for example, to those living in an urban area. The scope and subject matter of negotiations ranges from full discussion about government structures, internal constitutions, membership, marriage, Aboriginal languages, education, health, social services, and policing to partial jurisdiction over spheres such as divorce, some administration of justice issues, and gaming and fisheries co-management to no

---

79 Webber, *supra* note 28, 228.

80 *Ibid.*

81 John M. Olynyk, "Approaches to Sorting out Jurisdiction in a Self-Government Context," *University of Toronto Faculty of Law Review* 53 (1995) 235, 269.

82 Indigenous and Northern Affairs Canada, "Fact Sheet: Aboriginal Self-Government," 2 April 2015, https://www.aadnc-aandc.gc.ca/eng/1100100016293/1100100016294.

83 Jill Wherrett, "Aboriginal Self-Government" (Ottawa: Library of Parliament, Parliamentary Research Branch, 1999).

84 Olynkyk, *supra* note 81.

jurisdiction over national defence or foreign relations. I examine three examples of self-government arrangements, below, to illuminate the different forms of jurisdiction in play.

The Champagne and Aishihik First Nations Self-Government Agreement came into effect in 1995.[85] The agreement gives the Champagne and Aishihik First Nations four categories of law-making powers: exclusive powers (primarily for internal matters of administration), powers applying over settlement land (territorial jurisdiction over matters related to the local or private administration of land), powers applying to citizens (personal jurisdiction related to subject matters throughout the entire Yukon, depending on citizenship in a First Nation), and emergency powers.[86] This last type of jurisdiction, which is delimited first by citizenship in a First Nation and then further delimited by the territory of the Yukon, has no parallel in the constitutional text. This kind of personal jurisdiction makes the application of law dependent upon the identity of the individual. The intersection between the Champagne and Aishihik agreement and the Yukon territory, both creatures of federal jurisdiction, not constitutional jurisdiction, means that they could have concurrent powers.[87]

Perhaps the most recognizable Aboriginal jurisdiction to date is Nunavut, created from the Tungavik Federation of Nunavut land claims agreement in 1999.[88] In Nunavut, self-government aspirations are expressed through a public government; political rights are guaranteed to a self-government. This marks the creation of a new player in the territorial jurisdictional field that closely resembles constitutional forms of jurisdiction. Nunavut has jurisdictional powers and institutions similar to the Northwest Territories government. It is often held out as an exemplar, in part because it mimics the federal form. It is a territorial jurisdiction and government with authority over and representation of all the people living on its territory. Yet it is also embedded in a larger federal system, and this delimits its jurisdiction. Territories are not co-sovereigns in the same way as the provinces; they exercise

---

85 Champagne and Aishihik First Nations Self-Government Agreement among the Champagne and Aishihik First Nations and the Government of Canada and the Government of the Yukon, 29 May 1993, enacted as *First Nations (Yukon) Self-Government Act*, SY 1993, c 5 and *Yukon First Nations Self-Government Act*, SC 1994, c 34.

86 Olynkyk, *supra* note 81.

87 *Ibid.*

88 The federal government, the Northwest Territories, and Tungavik Federation of Nunavut signed a political accord in 1992.

delegated federal powers, and this places Nunavut outside the constitution. While remarkable, it is also likely inimitable: its physical location meant that its creation did not threaten existing jurisdictional arrangements in quite the same way as contemporary urban claims might do – there was both territory and jurisdiction available.

The Nisga'a Final Agreement, in comparison, does not create a federal form akin to Nunavut, but it is the first treaty under which self-government powers are constitutionally protected under s. 35. The Nisga'a Treaty came into effect in 2000. It is territorial: it covers both Nisga'a and non-Nisga'a people. Non-Nisga'a people do not have the right to vote in Nisga'a elections, but there are inbuilt protections for non-Nisga'a residents who live on Nisga'a lands. It creates two orders of government: the Nisga'a Lisims Government (external affairs) and the Nisga'a Village Governments (internal affairs). The Nisga'a Lisims Government has principal authority over its own administration, management of its lands and assets, and Nisga'a citizenship, language, and culture. Under these matters, both Nisga'a and federal or provincial orders of government may pass laws, but, where there is a conflict, the Nisga'a law will prevail.[89]

The opposite holds with regard to other subject matters, including the use of Nisga'a assets off Nisga'a lands, public order, peace and safety, the solemnization of marriages, social services, health services, intoxicants, and emergency preparedness. These jurisdictional allocations are delimited by the application of *Charter* rights to the Nisga'a government. This is another layer in the relationship between the Canadian state and the Nisga'a nation because it gives the federal state jurisdiction over Nisga'a member's *Charter* rights.

In this somewhat abbreviated analysis, it is clear that there are several self-government models, each with its own jurisdictional categories and allotments. Aboriginal nations are differently incorporated into the Canadian constitution and into Canadian law in general. Some are territories – outside the formal constitution but part of its *de facto* division of powers; others are protected under s. 35; still other collective self-government forms are outside the constitution altogether. More than this, Aboriginal jurisdictional forms are variously territorial, personal, and subject-matter-based and sometimes a combination of these.

89 However, the treaty includes important limitations on Nisga'a authority – e.g., the Nisga'a cannot make valid laws about Nisga'a citizenship that deal with immigration or Canadian citizenship.

This kind of jurisdictional variety is productive for moving past the federal form.

Conclusion: The Space between Rights and Jurisdictions

These three jurisdictional iterations layer progressively more complicated ideas of jurisdiction onto the constitutional framework. The first and by far the most predominant setting is constitutional federalism. This is territorial jurisdiction, and it is the original accommodation of diversity. The second setting, national minority regimes, is equally constitutionally entrenched but less fixed in time and space. This is floating jurisdiction loosely tethered to territory but closely tied to the collective. The third setting, Aboriginal self-government, is somewhat indeterminately constitutionally entrenched. It takes various jurisdictional forms, including traditional territorial jurisdiction and other non-territorial forms. The coincidence of territory and identity that underwrites federalism survives and is carried forward in different jurisdictional frameworks, but those frameworks alter the shape and content of that coincidence.

Together, these existing constitutional understandings of jurisdiction adjudicate the fault lines of diversity and autonomy in Canada. As the population shifts to incorporate new kinds of heterogeneity and different concentrations of diversity, these fault lines will shift, and constitutional understandings of jurisdiction will need to move in tandem. In some sense, federalism is the most productive jurisdictional lens because it gets to the root of the measure of legal or political autonomy that is at issue. Whenever rights are granted to a collectivity, there must be some kind of public law dimension to that grant because the state is handing over some measure of authority to the collective to decide how that right will run inside its edges.[90] The most prominent example is rights over land, particularly Aboriginal title, where the recognition of title implicates the law of the collective. Aboriginal communities must have "decision-making authority over how those rights can be exercised."[91] That collective must have some kind of constitutional law to make decisions about that land.[92] One could also envision this with respect to rights over family law matters. Because federalism

90 Webber, *supra* note 78.
91 McNeil, *supra* note 76, 17.
92 Webber, *supra* note 78.

transposes this measure of autonomy onto a located and bounded collective, it rationalizes constitutional jurisdiction. This jurisdiction is theoretically mutually exclusive and territorial, but, as this chapter has noted, in practice it is functionally overlapping.

To meet the collective identity challenges ahead, we need to complicate the federal model. Federalism is a vestige of privilege for the territories and temporalities of the constitutional moment; it does not contain internal mechanisms of inclusion for new or different collectivities. Several contemporary collectivities and their individual members are not seeking federal jurisdictional solutions, but neither are they satisfied with individual rights exemptions on a case-by-case basis. They are seeking something in between – something akin to limited autonomy over personal or particular decisions. The place to draw the line will differ from case to case. Kent McNeil describes how the judicial approach to Aboriginal jurisdiction establishes jurisdiction piece by piece.[93] It forces the nations to start with an empty box and to prove that each matter over which they claim jurisdiction is integral to their distinctive culture. While this is clearly the wrong approach for Aboriginal self-governments, which should receive plenary jurisdiction, it has some merit for identity groups that are not seeking self-government but rather some form of expression or freedom.

There have been some forays into these kinds of original hybrid or creative jurisdictional forms – most notably, Ayelet Shachar's suggestion of inter-jurisdictional accommodation – but they are dated now. We need to take seriously the deep meaning of self-determination as a constitutive human value to understand why distributions of constitutional power ultimately matter.[94] The challenge, then as now, is to create flexible jurisdictional nodes that permit collectivities some measure of decision-making autonomy without ceding the ground of democratic freedom and equality. It is in many ways a very old problem – where to locate the balance between the individual and the collective – but it is in a new context with new expressions of difference. And it will fall to constitutional lawyers to re-conceive jurisdictional forms inside and outside the constitution to make room for diversity.

93 McNeil, *supra* note 76.
94 Libesman, *supra* note 1.

8 Difference and Inclusion: Reframing Reasonable Accommodation

VRINDA NARAIN

Introduction

Multiculturalism is a body of thought in political philosophy about the proper way for a state to respond to cultural and religious diversity.[1] Multiculturalism policy can be characterized as the state's response to diversity – the constitutional, legal, and policy framework by which minority rights are recognized and accommodated. Reasonable accommodation is the framework within which the state accommodates minority difference by balancing competing rights; it is a critical aspect of the implementation of multiculturalism policy. Controversy swirls over multiculturalism and the accommodation of difference as the tension between religious freedom and non-discrimination principles becomes increasingly acute. There is a perceived tension between women's equality rights on the one hand and multiculturalism and religious freedom on the other, whereby minorities seek exemption from rules of general application.[2] Popular discourse reflects anxiety about the "illiberal" practices that Muslim immigrants, in particular, bring to Canada's liberal democracy.[3] Focusing on "cultural" practices such as honour

1 Sarah Song, "Multiculturalism," in *Stanford Encyclopedia of Philosophy*, ed. Edward N. Zalta (Spring 2014), http://plato.stanford.edu/archives/spr2014/entries/multiculturalism/.

2 Leti Volpp, "Feminism versus Multiculturalism," *Columbia Law Review* 10, no. 5 (2001) 1181, 1181 [Volpp, "Feminism versus Multiculturalism"]. See also Vrinda Narain, "Critical Multiculturalism," in *Feminist Constitutionalism: Global Perspectives*, ed. Beverley Baines et al (Cambridge: Cambridge University Press, 2012).

3 Will Kymlicka, "The New Debate on Minority Rights (and Postscript)," in *Multiculturalism and Political Theory*, ed. Anthony Simon Laden and David Owen (Cambridge: Cambridge University Press, 2007), 25, 54–5 [Kymlicka, "Minority Rights"].

killing, veiling, and polygamy, public policy increasingly reflects popular discourse as the "crisis of multiculturalism" is articulated around the need to counter gender inequality within racialized minority groups.[4]

Official multiculturalism focuses on what differences the state should accommodate and the extent to which they should be accommodated.[5] Reasonable accommodation is "itself a tool of governmental intervention to manage diversity-related conflict."[6] Through governmentality regulated by a particular understanding of gender normativities, Muslim women, in particular, are portrayed as unassimilable and as threats to democratic values, to gender equality, to the nation and its "legitimate" citizens. Simultaneously, they are perceived as victims, lacking agency and therefore in need of saving.[7] This representation of Muslim women animates the politics of reasonable accommodation. The premise of reasonable accommodation continues unquestioned, and it remains for "us" to decide which aspects of "their" difference must be accommodated. Consequently, structural racism and systemic discrimination are unchallenged, and practices that are accommodated are seen as exceptions to a relatively unquestioned state multiculturalism, reinforcing its legitimacy of governance.

Will Kymlicka notes that multiculturalism in Canada has moved from a focus on ethnicity and race to a focus on religious difference, and we see the rise in minority justice claims for the accommodation of religious difference.[8] In the first part of this paper, I draw from Sirma Bilge's

---

4 Volpp, "Feminism versus Multiculturalism," *supra* note 2. See also Canada, Citizenship and Immigration Canada, *Discover Canada: The Rights and Responsibilities of Citizenship* (Ottawa: CIC, 2011), 9 [*Discover Canada*]; Bill 60, *Charter Affirming the Values of State Secularism and Religious Neutrality and of Equality between Women and Men, and Providing a Framework for Accommodation Requests*, 1st Sess, 40th Leg, Quebec, 2014 [*Quebec Charter of Values*]; *Zero Tolerance for Barbaric Cultural Practices Act*, SC 2015, c 29 [*BPA*]; Iris M. Young, "Structural Injustice and the Politics of Difference," in *Multiculturalism and Political Theory*, ed. Anthony Simon Laden and David Owen (Cambridge: Cambridge University Press, 2007), 60, 87 [Young, "Structural Injustice"].

5 Young, "Structural Injustice," *supra* note 4, 84–6.

6 Sirma Bilge, "Reading the Racial Subtext of the Québécois Accommodation Controversy: An Analytics of Racialized Governmentality," *Politikon* 40, no. 1 (2013) 157, 158 [Bilge, "Racial Subtext"].

7 Sherene Razack, "The 'Sharia Law Debate' in Ontario: The Modernity/Premodernity Distinction in Legal Efforts to Protect Women from Culture," *Feminist Legal Studies* 15, no. 1 (2007) 3, 7, 10, 15 [Razack, "'Sharia Law Debate'"].

8 Will Kymlicka, "The Three Lives of Multiculturalism," in *Revisiting Multiculturalism in Canada*, ed. Shibao Guo and Lloyd Wong (Toronto: Springer, 2015), 17, 26–7.

insights to discuss how governmentality and state multiculturalism have erased race in the discussions around reasonable accommodation.[9] I then consider key cases and legislative and policy initiatives that illustrate the rhetoric of multiculturalism and, with it, the limits of the reasonable accommodation framework, focusing on the Supreme Court's decision in *R v NS* and the *Zero Tolerance for Barbaric Cultural Practices Act*, among others, to better understand judicial responses and legislative initiatives that regulate racialized minority women. Beyond questioning which differences should be accommodated and which not, I consider the discursive construction of the identity of accommodated subjects, and how they are framed as citizens, to underscore the particular vulnerability of racialized, (often) immigrant minority women.[10]

I end by elaborating new strategies for responding to minority rights claims. I come to this issue by drawing from the insights of critical multiculturalism, critical race feminist theory, and postcolonial feminist theory. My modest aim here is to contribute to the dialogue on the inclusion of racialized women: I argue that it is imperative to formulate a policy of critical multiculturalism and reframe the accommodation of difference to strengthen the commitment to substantive equality and minority rights. This paper is inscribed in the context of the current debates on the limits of religious freedom and the accommodation of group difference in Canada.

Theoretical Framework

Multiculturalism

Official multiculturalism is a method of governmentality that serves "as a collection of cultural categories for ruling or administering, and communities claim their 'representational status' as direct emanations of social ontologies."[11] The fluidity of identities and the reality of multiple allegiances are not adequately acknowledged, and at the heart of such a policy is a notion of culture that is static, leading to what Anne Phillips

9 Bilge, "Racial Subtext," *supra* note 6; Sirma Bilge, "Mapping Québécois Sexual Nationalism in Times of 'Crisis of Reasonable Accommodation,'" *Journal of Intercultural Studies* 33, no. 3 (2012) 303 [Bilge, "Québécois Sexual Nationalism"].

10 Bilge, "Racial Subtext," *supra* note 6, 157.

11 Himani Bannerji, *The Dark Side of the Nation: Essays on Multiculturalism, Nationalism, and Gender* (Toronto: Canadian Scholars' Press, 2000), 6 [Bannerji, *Dark Side of the Nation*].

calls "a falsely homogenizing reification."[12] The refusal to problematize culture has contributed to a reification of stereotypical views of racialized minority groups. It is premised on an understanding of culture that homogenizes and essentializes groups and rejects diversity within them.[13] Members of these groups are seen as being profoundly different in their practices, beliefs, and values, leading critics of multiculturalism to claim that minority groups are inherently opposed to the values of the Canadian liberal democratic state, thereby posing a threat to political stability.[14]

This understanding of cultural difference animating official multiculturalism is premised on dichotomies such as East/West, modernity/tradition, and culture/feminism. It raises troubling issues of representation, agency, and authenticity. It also raises issues of democratic participation and the inclusion of minorities within minorities: the paradox of multicultural vulnerability. While invariably the focus of multiculturalism policies, minority racialized women are excluded from the articulation of group interests and the definition of group identity, both by the state and by community leaders.

A policy based on cultural difference focuses on what aspects of difference are permissible by the state and what are not, such as the kirpan, the niqab, or the get. Public debate on the limits of accommodation displaces structural problems onto issues of culture, tending to ignore structural issues of racism, poverty, unemployment, poor education, and access to justice, while magnifying issues related to religion and culture. Public discourse continues to be preoccupied with stereotypical images of racialized immigrant women and issues of cultural difference. This preoccupation forms the context for the critique that critical multiculturalism aims to provide. Critical multiculturalism moves away from a simplistic focus on culture and instead argues for a multiculturalism that is located at the intersection of inequality, culture, and power. My intervention is premised on the distinction between a multiculturalism policy based on cultural difference and one that is designed as a response to structural inequality. The politics of structural

---

12 Anne Phillips, *Multiculturalism without Culture* (Princeton, NJ: Princeton University Press, 2007), 14.

13 *Ibid*, 162–3.

14 *Ibid*, 3–24; Azizah Y. al-Hibri, "Is Western Patriarchal Feminism Good for Third World/Minority Women?," in *Is Multiculturalism Bad for Women?*, ed. Joshua Cohen, Matthew Howard, and Martha C. Nussbaum (Princeton, NJ: Princeton University Press, 1997), 41, 41.

difference focuses on issues of exclusion and inclusion, examining how norms and standards, rather than perpetuating systemic inequality, can be revised to recognize minority difference.

While it is important to accommodate cultural difference by recognizing distinct cultures and practices that can respond to a dominant nationalism, in responding to minority claims, it is critical to challenge systemic inequality by paying attention to structural inequalities. So doing exposes the structural dimensions of the processes of exploitation, marginalization, and normalization that keep groups in subordinate positions. Moving away from an oppositional understanding of women's substantive equality and minority rights, Iris Young has argued that an effective policy of multiculturalism must focus not just on cultural differences but also on exclusions that result from structural inequalities.[15] Rejecting a reductive binary between recognition and redistribution, as Nancy Fraser argues, it is imperative to reconceptualize the justice of minority claims in which both recognition and redistribution inform the notion of justice.[16] Maleiha Malik articulates such an understanding, which she terms "progressive multiculturalism," that is concerned with the context of minority women who demand not just recognition but full inclusion in social, economic, and political institutions. This understanding of multiculturalism can better respond to the challenge of "cultural racism," focusing on confronting racism and discrimination as barriers to inclusive equality.[17]

Reasonable Accommodation

Reasonable accommodation is one of the ways in which negotiation is framed within the Canadian multiculturalism framework, and it has become a tool of governmentality for the management and governance of religious diversity.[18] The framework of multiculturalism and reasonable accommodation determines the extent to which diversity

---

15 Young, "Structural Injustice," *supra* note 4.

16 Nancy Fraser, "From Redistribution to Recognition? Dilemmas of Justice in a 'Post-Socialist' Age," *New Left Review* 212 (1995) 68; N. Fraser and A. Honneth, *Redistribution or Recognition: A Political-Philosophical Exchange* (London: Verso, 2003).

17 Maleiha Malik, "Progressive Multiculturalism," *International Journal of Minority and Group Rights* 17 (2010) 447, 458 [Malik, "Progressive Multiculturalism"].

18 Lori Beaman, "Introduction: Exploring Reasonable Accommodation," in *Reasonable Accommodation*, ed. Lori Beaman (Vancouver: UBC Press, 2012), 1, 5, 3, 9 [Beaman, "Exploring Reasonable Accommodation"].

is accepted and sets limits on its accommodation.[19] As Martha Minow writes, "constitutional and legal frameworks affect the room available for expressing and maintaining cultural difference, while also arranging how conflicts between mainstream and minority groups will be identified, addressed and resolved. Public policy and legal responses to immigrants are closely tied to a nation's stance towards multiculturalism, neutrality about religion and race, gender equality and universal notions of human rights."[20] It is therefore important to understand how "aspects of law and policy reinforce the substantive beliefs and values of the mainstream and how much cultural diversity is permissible."[21] Which diversities are constructed and accommodated in this contested terrain and in "the struggles over accommodation?"[22]

Bilge argues that reasonable accommodation is commonly seen to be about religion and secularism, not race, effectively resulting in an erasure of race.[23] Although race is embedded in the contested terrain of reasonable accommodation, the debate around it has been "largely cast as raceless."[24] The discourse of accommodation focuses on minorities' religious differences as problems that must be accommodated. Himani Bannerji asserts that it is necessary to question the rhetoric of official multiculturalism and its discursive uses, which obscure power relations, and its "politicized understanding of cultural representation."[25] Reasonable accommodation discourse is embedded in the governmentality of equity and diversity policies rather than demonstrating the political will to engage minorities and challenge institutionalized racism. A multiculturalism policy in which identities are state-imposed based on stereotypical, essentialized perceptions of minority cultures results in a notion of governmentality and state control that "eludes notions of equality."[26]

---

19 *Ibid*, 3.

20 Richard A. Schweder, Martha Minow, and Hazel Rose Markus, "Engaging Cultural Differences," in *Engaging Cultural Differences: The Multicultural Challenge in Liberal Democracies*, ed. Richard A. Schweder, Martha Minow, and Hazel Rose Markus (New York: Russell Sage Foundation, 2002), 1, 12.

21 *Ibid*, 2.

22 Bilge, "Racial Subtext," *supra* note 6, 158.

23 *Ibid*, 159.

24 *Ibid*, 158.

25 Bannerji, *Dark Side of the Nation*, *supra* note 11, 5.

26 Lori G. Beaman, "'It Was All Slightly Unreal': What's Wrong with Tolerance and Accommodation in the Adjudication of Religious Freedom?," *Canadian Journal of Women and the Law* 23 (2011) 442, 447 [Beaman, "What's Wrong with Tolerance"].

The reasonable accommodation framework is an integral part of the state's response to difference, yet the legitimizing function of inequality it sustains has not been adequately interrogated. Invariably, minority practices are measured against unquestioned mainstream norms that set the limits of accommodation; difference becomes the special exception, while mainstream culture is normalized.[27] As will be seen in the jurisprudence and legislative initiatives below, the focus of reasonable accommodation is on the limits of toleration rather than a consideration of minority women's rights. In public discourse, reasonable accommodation has come to be understood as synonymous with the accommodation of religious diversity.[28] While race is erased from the accommodation discourse, whiteness as privilege is also unnamed. The discourse around reasonable accommodation normalizes race privilege and fails to adequately consider inherent power relations and hierarchies in the accommodation of difference. It obfuscates issues of structural inequality, institutionalized racism, and the construction of difference, and it reifies the terms of the debate into an us-versus-them binary.[29] Unless we insert race into the analysis, it will remain little more than a way to sustain the racial status quo. Power hierarchies will remain intact.[30]

Cases and Legislative Initiatives

Cases

In recent years, recognizing Canada's growing diversity, the Supreme Court has underscored the centrality of equality, multiculturalism, and the accommodation of difference in responding to minority claimants seeking exemption from mainstream norms.[31] Constitutional scholar Sujit Choudhry notes that the Supreme Court of Canada has developed a strong religious freedom jurisprudence, setting out the constitutional

27 *Ibid*, 447–51, 449. See, e.g., Catharine MacKinnon, "Difference and Domination: On Sex Discrimination," in *Theorizing Feminisms: A Reader*, ed. Elizabeth Hackett and Sally Haslanger (Oxford: Oxford University Press, 2005).

28 Beaman, "Exploring Reasonable Accommodation," *supra* note 18, 3.

29 Beaman, "What's Wrong with Tolerance," *supra* note 26, 443–5.

30 Bilge, "Racial Subtext," *supra* note 6, 158.

31 Richard Moon, "Liberty, Neutrality, and Inclusion: Religious Freedom under the *Canadian Charter of Rights and Freedoms*," *Brandeis University Law Journal* 41, no. 3 (2002) 2.

doctrine around s. 2(a). The Court adapted the reasonable accommodation framework, an idea originally developed under human rights codes in the employment context, incorporating it into *Charter* adjudication.[32] It has elaborated on the framework of reasonable accommodation in the context of balancing the right to religious freedom with other rights, notably equality rights.[33]

Early Supreme Court decisions taken under s. 2(a) held that "the duty to accommodate was part of the minimal impairment analysis" under s. 1.[34] However, in later decisions, the Court limited the reach of duty to accommodate in its narrow legal sense to individual administrative decisions and did not extend it to laws of general application.[35] Invariably, s. 2(a) challenges also concern s. 15, as indeed s. 15 challenges invoke s. 2(a), where religion is the basis of discrimination. Outside the courtroom, all these claims became seen as reasonable accommodation claims for exemptions from laws and for accommodation in existing institutional structures.[36]

REASONABLE ACCOMMODATION IN JURISPRUDENCE

R v Big M Drug Mart Ltd., which concerned Sunday closing laws, was the first religious freedom case decided by the Supreme Court under the *Charter*.[37] Significantly, the Court invoked multiculturalism to interpret religious freedom: "The power to compel, on religious grounds, the universal observance of the day of rest preferred by one religion is not consistent with the preservation and enhancement of the multicultural heritage of Canadians recognized in s. 27 of the *Charter*." In *Syndicat Northcrest v Amselem*, the Supreme Court specified that the state could not rule on religious dogma and accommodated Mr. Amselem's construction of a succah.[38]

In *Multani v Commission scolaire Marguerite-Bourgeoys*, the Court upheld the right of a Sikh boy to carry a kirpan, invoking

---

32 Sujit Choudhry, "Rights Adjudication in a Plurinational State: The Supreme Court of Canada, Freedom of Religion, and the Politics of Reasonable Accommodation," *Osgoode Hall Law Journal* 50 (2013) 575, 585, 586 [Choudhry, "Rights Adjudication"].

33 *Ibid*.

34 *Ibid*, 586.

35 *Ibid*. See also *Alberta v Hutterian Brethren of Wilson Colony*, 2009 SCC 37, paras 67–9, [2009] 2 SCR 567 [*Hutterian Brethren*].

36 Choudhry, "Rights Adjudication," *supra* note 32.

37 *R v Big M Drug Mart Ltd.*, [1985] 1 SCR 295, 1985 CanLII 69 [*Big M*].

38 *Syndicat Northcrest v Amselem*, 2004 SCC 47, para 50, [2004] 2 SCR 551 [*Amselem*].

multiculturalism to send a powerful message of equality among all religions. Multiculturalism, reasonable accommodation, and religious freedom were highlighted as fundamental organizing principles of Canadian life.[39] In particular, Justice Charron, writing for the majority of the Court, held that the duty to accommodate religious difference to the point of undue burden is "helpful to explain the burden resulting from the minimal impairment test with respect to a particular individual."[40] Note that the Court was divided, however, on the relevance of reasonable accommodation to the s. 1 Oakes analysis. In her dissent, Justice Abella affirmed the relevance of reasonable accommodation to the question whether a school board's decision to prohibit the kirpan was reasonable in the administrative law sense, but she denied its usefulness to the *Oakes* minimal impairment test as the latter concerned not only the individual but also the societal impact of the law.[41]

In *Bruker v Marcovitz*, the Court emphasized that Canada's growing diversity had resulted in the judicial recognition of multiculturalism and respect for difference.[42] As Justice Abella explained, while claims for exemptions and accommodation could not always be privileged and must be balanced with public interest, deciding what aspects of difference could be accommodated must be a contextual, purposive exercise focused on providing the benefit of the protection of the *Charter* on the claimant.[43] Moving away from the understanding of reasonable accommodation articulated in earlier jurisprudence, in *Alberta v Hutterian Brethren of Wilson Colony*, the Court limited religious freedom, signalling a greater deference to secular, government objectives.[44] Indeed, a majority of the Court held the reasonable accommodation analysis inappropriate where laws of general application were concerned. Seizing on Justice Abella's dissent on this point in *Multani*, Chief Justice McLachlin held that "the question the court must answer is whether the *Charter* infringement is justifiable in a free and democratic society, not whether a more advantageous arrangement for a particular claimant could be envisioned."[45]

---

39 *Multani v Commission scolaire Marguerite-Bourgeoys*, 2006 SCC 6, paras 71, 78, [2006] 1 SCR 256 [*Multani*].

40 *Ibid*, para 53.

41 *Ibid*, paras 129, 131–2.

42 *Bruker v Marcovitz* 2007 SCC 54, para 1, [2007] 3 SCR 607 [*Bruker*].

43 *Ibid*, para 2.

44 *Hutterian Brethren, supra* note 35, paras 66–71.

45 *Ibid*, para 69.

More recently, in *R v NS*, concerning the right of a Muslim woman to wear a niqab, a face veil, while testifying, the Supreme Court displayed tensions in its understanding of multiculturalism and the accommodation of religious difference.[46] The issue of the niqab raised questions at the intersection of gender equality, religious freedom, and multiculturalism and tested the limits of the accommodation. Interestingly, however, in *Loyola High School v Quebec (Attorney General)*, where the Court considered a challenge to the constitutionality of the state imposing secular instruction on a religious school, the Court upheld the school's right to religious freedom, despite state policy objectives of spreading the message of tolerance, equal respect, and multiculturalism.[47]

In framing the notion of reasonable accommodation to adjudicate religious freedom cases, the Supreme Court has developed a constitutional analysis premised on minority rights, equality, and multiculturalism, folding these considerations into the s. 1 analysis of proportionality and minimal impairment. Choudhry argues that although *Amselem*, *Congrégation des témoins de Jéhovah de St-Jérôme-Lafontaine v Lafontaine (Village)*,[48] *Bruker*, *Multani*, and *Hutterian Brethren* may not all have been decided or analysed using the framework of reasonable accommodation in its narrow legal sense, it was at the root of these decisions.[49] The Court's decisions on religious freedom and reasonable accommodation are part of the context of the increasingly sharp rhetoric and public debate about reasonable accommodation and the limits of toleration. Choudhry suggests that the Court is acutely aware of this context and how it is impacted by, and impacts, jurisprudence.[50] The Court's decisions were not well received in Quebec. In particular, *Multani* provoked public outcry, resulting in the creation of the Consultation Commission on Accommodation Practices Related to Cultural Differences, commonly known as the Bouchard-Taylor Commission.[51]

Choudhry argues that this awareness of the sensitive political and social context, and the differences between Quebec and the rest of Canada, has led the Supreme Court to craft the idea of state neutrality

46 *R v NS*, 2012 SCC 72, [2012] 3 SCR 726 [*NS*].
47 *Loyola High School v Quebec (Attorney General)*, 2015 SCC 12, [2015] 1 SCR 613.
48 *Congrégation des témoins de Jéhovah de St-Jérôme-Lafontaine v Lafontaine (Village)*, 2004 SCC 48, [2004] 2 SCR 650.
49 Choudhry, "Rights Adjudication," *supra* note 32, 585.
50 *Ibid*, 588.
51 *Ibid*, 586.

as a way of mediating the tension between the two.[52] State neutrality has been used to resist claims for reasonable accommodation in many instances.[53] In *Amselem*, state neutrality was the basis for the refusal of the dissenting judges, including Justices LeBel and Deschamps, to incorporate the notion of reasonable accommodation into their analysis. Justice LeBel's dissent in *Lafontaine*, refusing to accept any claim for state action to support religious practice, was based on a concern to maintain the state's religious neutrality. In *Multani*, arguably, the principle of neutrality formed the basis of Justice Deschamps's reluctance to invoke the *Charter* to resolve an administrative law issue.[54] In *Bruker*, neutrality was arguably the premise of Justice Deschamps's dissent and her refusal to engage in adjudicating a religious matter, the Jewish get.[55] In the majority opinion in *Hutterian Brethren*, the Court relied on the notion of state neutrality to argue against the accommodation of religious practices.

Most recently, in *Saguenay*, Chief Justice McLachlin, for the majority, affirmed the importance of the principle of state neutrality in a decision barring Catholic prayer at municipal council meetings. Interestingly, the Court invoked multiculturalism as a means to justify the neutrality principle: "a neutral public space free from coercion, pressure and judgment on the part of public authorities in matters of spirituality is intended to protect every person's freedom and dignity."[56] Choudhry argues that the politics around reasonable accommodation in Quebec is embedded in the context of Quebec nationalism, nation building, and identity formation.[57] Extending this argument, I suggest that *R v NS* and the *Zero Tolerance for Barbaric Cultural Practices Act* reflect Canadian anxieties about the illiberal practices of immigrant, racialized minorities and the limits of toleration.[58]

R v NS

In *R v NS*, the Supreme Court had to decide whether N.S., a Muslim woman, bringing a criminal complaint of sexual assault, would be

52 *Ibid*, 580.
53 *Ibid*, 592.
54 *Ibid*, 588.
55 *Bruker*, *supra* note 42, paras 102, 122–32; Choudhry, "Rights Adjudication," *supra* note 32, 600.
56 *Mouvement laïque québécois v Saguenay (City)*, 2015 SCC 16, para 74, [2015] 2 SCR 3 [*Saguenay*].
57 Choudhry, "Rights Adjudication," *supra* note 32, 590.
58 Kymlicka, "Minority Rights," *supra* note 3, 54.

allowed to wear her niqab, a face veil, while testifying.[59] The Court identified the two *Charter* rights engaged: the witness's religious freedom and the accused's fair trial rights. My focus here is on those aspects of the Court's decision that relate to religious freedom, multiculturalism, and reasonable accommodation. There were three opinions in *R v NS*: the majority, the concurrence, and the dissent. I consider each of these as they exemplify different approaches to multiculturalism and the accommodation of difference.

Chief Justice McLachlin, writing the majority opinion on behalf of herself, Deschamps, Fish, and Cromwell JJ, attempted to reach a fair balance with regard to religious freedom, gender justice, secularism, and neutrality and how they implicate public policy. Careful to avoid an all-or-nothing judicial response, she considered the positions of the concurrence and the dissent on the wearing of a niqab in court – that the witness must never be permitted to wear a niqab in court and that she must always be permitted to do so – and rejected both absolute positions. This decision is promising for its recognition of the jurisprudential tradition of a broad and generous interpretation of religious freedom and the accommodation of difference, but it also raises certain concerns for future minority claimants.

McLachlin CJ rejected the view that courtrooms are neutral spaces that should never accommodate personal religious beliefs as being "inconsistent with Canadian jurisprudence" and that to "remove religions from the courtroom was not in the Canadian tradition."[60] She asserted that "such a position would limit religious rights where there is no countervailing right and hence no reason to limit them."[61] Significantly, the majority noted the broader societal harms, particularly in the context of sexual assault complaints, if women were forced to remove their niqab to testify, and drew attention to the extent to which sexual assault crimes remained under-reported.[62]

What equality-seeking religious minority claimants can draw from the majority opinion is a mixed message. On the one hand, the assertion of religious difference in the public sphere, the courtroom, was recognized. On the other hand, the majority did not fully consider the impact on the witness's religious freedom if she were forced to testify

59 *NS, supra* note 46.
60 *Ibid*, paras 53, 102, 122–32.
61 *Ibid*, para 51.
62 *Ibid*, para 37.

without her niqab. Despite promising discussions of reasonable accommodation, the chief justice did not strongly endorse a witness's right to religious freedom, deciding that a witness could testify wearing her niqab unless this unjustifiably impinged on the accused's fair trial rights – and only in cases where there was uncontested evidence.[63] Yet in a sexual assault case, it is unlikely that the evidence will be uncontested, effectively meaning that a witness would not be allowed to testify while wearing her niqab.

Despite this qualification of the accommodation of niqabi women, the Court's acknowledgment of the presumptive right to wear the niqab in the courtroom is noteworthy. From the perspective of religious minority claimants, it is important that the majority rejected the argument that accommodating religion in the courtroom would compromise state neutrality and the neutrality of public institutions.[64] Most important, the majority reaffirmed the place of reasonable accommodation of religious difference in Canadian jurisprudence and reiterated that secularism did not mean the rejection of religion without justification.

In contrast, LeBel and Rothstein JJ's concurring opinion can be characterized as a "clash of civilizations approach" to the accommodation of religious difference and multiculturalism.[65] It reflects an uncritical notion of state multiculturalism, secularism, and neutrality, framing the niqab as a threat to gender equality and democracy and reflecting Andreassen and Lettinga's argument that "the nationalizing of gender equality – by inscribing gender equality as an integrated part of a hegemonic national culture that is being threatened by the culturally 'other' – results in exclusionary and racialized understandings of the national community."[66] According to Justice LeBel, the *R v NS* appeal demonstrated "the tension and changes caused by the rapid evolution of contemporary Canadian society and by the growing presence in Canada of new cultures, religions, traditions and social practices."[67]

63 *Ibid*, para 28.
64 *Ibid*, para 51.
65 See Samuel P. Huntington, "The Clash of Civilizations?," *Foreign Affairs* 72, no. 3 (Summer 1993), accessed 6 February 2015, http://online.sfsu.edu/mroozbeh/CLASS/h-607-pdfs/S.Huntington-Clash.pdf.
66 Rikke Andreassen and Doutje Lettinga, "Veiled Debates: Gender and Gender Equality in European National Narratives," in *Politics, Religion and Gender: Framing and Regulating the Veil*, ed. Sieglinde Rosenberger and Birgit Sauer (London: Routledge, 2012), 17, 21, 31 [Andreassen and Lettinga, "Veiled Debates"].
67 *NS, supra* note 46, para 59.

Drawing on a Canadian constitutional nationalism, he positioned it in opposition to multiculturalism. He insisted that the recognition of multiculturalism must be fixed within the framework of Canadian democracy and core Canadian values, which included the neutrality of the state and its public institutions, and he concluded that it was imperative to establish an absolute prohibition of the niqab in the courtroom.[68]

This emphasis on "Canadian values" imposes an "us and them" binary, deploying stereotypes of racialized minority women whose practices and values are inherently un-Canadian. Arguably, this is a departure from Canadian jurisprudence, which emphasizes a reasonable accommodation approach to competing rights and requires minimal impairment and a stringent justification to limit religious freedom. LeBel J's understanding narrows the scope of the religious freedom guarantee by premising it on a notion of neutrality and secularism that leaves little room for the accommodation of difference.

In her dissent, Abella J considered the impact of denying the right to religious freedom on niqabi women, underscoring that a witness who is not permitted to wear her niqab while testifying is prevented from being able to act in accordance with her religious beliefs.[69] Noting the absence of meaningful choice, she questioned the either/or dichotomy presented to women like NS, having to choose between their religious beliefs and participating in the criminal justice system. Justice Abella argued that insisting that the witness remove her niqab while testifying would have a chilling effect, discouraging women from registering complaints, resulting in a lack of confidence on the part of minorities in the justice system.[70] Pursuing a contextual approach to balancing competing rights, she asserted that "[t]he order requiring a witness to remove her *niqab* must also be understood in the context of a complainant alleging sexual assault."[71] She concluded that, in the context of this case, the witness must be permitted to wear the niqab while testifying.

R v NS reveals the divisions within the Court regarding the scope and limits of religious freedom and multiculturalism and the implications for institutional secularism and democratic freedoms. It reaffirms the judicial consensus that, in balancing competing rights, the limits of accommodation will be set by countervailing public interests and

68 *Ibid*, para 72.
69 *Ibid*, para 93.
70 *Ibid*, para 95.
71 *Ibid*.

values as asserted in *Multani, Bruker*, and *Hutterian Brethren*. It remains unclear what the effect of *R v NS* will be for future constitutional challenges. The most immediate impact of this decision has been seen on NS herself as the case was sent back to the preliminary enquiry judge. Applying the test set out by the majority, unsurprisingly, the preliminary judge, in his decision of 24 April 2013, ruled that NS had to remove her niqab while testifying. Ultimately, NS had to choose between upholding her religious beliefs and testifying. She compromised the wearing of her niqab, only for her case to be rejected.[72]

For future claims asserting difference, it appears that the Supreme Court's decision in *R v NS* does not send a strong enough signal to affirm the rights of racialized minority women. Indeed, all three opinions characterize the niqab as a problem that the courts must contend with through a careful balancing of religious freedom, multiculturalism, gender equality, and state neutrality, and that the right of minorities to "integrate" must be contextualized within certain core principles and Canadian values.

As Lori Beaman notes, *R v NS* reveals how concepts like accommodation maintain unequal power relations, moving those who are Other further away from equality. The decisions differ, however, in their approach to balancing equality, religious freedom, and multiculturalism concerns, in their conceptualization of state neutrality and secularism and the premise for the accommodation of difference. The judicial response to religious freedom and reasonable accommodation seems to be premised on a dialectical tension between difference and belonging. As Faisal Bhabha notes, the development of the religious freedom doctrine "is defined and shaped by the normative priority of respecting difference in a multicultural society, coupled with a concomitant duty of belonging to an integrated society."[73]

CANADA (CITIZENSHIP AND IMMIGRATION) V ISHAQ

Multiculturalism is cast uniquely as a minority matter, aimed at addressing short-term issues related to the transition from immigrant to citizen.

---

72 Alyshah Hasham, "Sex-Assault Case That Led to Supreme Court Niqab Ruling Ends Abruptly," *Toronto Star*, 17 July 2014, https://www.thestar.com/news/gta/2014/07/17/sexassault_case_that_led_to_supreme_court_niqab_ruling_ends_abruptly.html.

73 Faisal Bhabha, "From *Saumur* to *L. (S.)*: Tracing the Theory and Concept of Religious Freedom under Canadian Law," *Supreme Court Law Review* (2d) 58 (2012) 109, 131.

Citizenship acquisition is rendered increasingly difficult and available only after successful integration.[74] The *Ishaq* case demonstrates the link between managing religious difference and democratic citizenship.[75] *Ishaq* concerned the refusal of a woman to remove her niqab while taking the citizenship oath since removing her veil was unnecessary for the purpose of identity or security. Ishaq challenged the governmental policy on two grounds: religious freedom under s. 2(a) and equality under s. 15(1). The policy in question was section 6.5 of the manual of the CIC's Operational Bulletin 359, which provides, "[c]andidates wearing face coverings are required to remove their face coverings for the oath taking portion of the ceremony. If they do not, they will not receive their citizenship certificates and will have to attend a different ceremony. If they again do not comply, then their application for citizenship will be ended."[76]

Her refusal was tied to her religious beliefs:

> My religious beliefs would compel me to refuse to take off my veil in the context of a citizenship oath ceremony, and I firmly believe that based on existing policies, I would therefore be denied Canadian citizenship. I feel that the governmental policy regarding veils at citizenship oath ceremonies is a personal attack on me, my identity as a Muslim woman and my religious beliefs.[77]

The minister of citizenship and immigration, Jason Kenney, declared,

> [The citizenship oath] is an act of public witness, you are standing up in front of your fellow citizens making a solemn commitment to be loyal to the country, and I just think it's not possible to do that with your face covered and it also, I think, just undermines the whole approach that we are trying to do through citizenship, which is to make people fully members of our community. I do not know how you can do that from behind a kind of a mask.[78]

74 Elke Winter, "Becoming Canadian: Making Sense of Recent Changes to Citizenship Rules," *IRPP Study* 44 (January 2014), 20.

75 *Canada (Citizenship and Immigration) v Ishaq*, 2015 FCA 156, [2015] 4 RCF [*Ishaq*].

76 *Ibid*, para 5, citing Canada, Citizenship and Immigration Canada, "Operational Bulletin 359" (Ottawa: CIC, 12 December 2011), s 6.5.

77 *Ibid*, para 6.

78 *Ibid*, para 49.

Ishaq claimed that although the policy purported to be about allowing for visual confirmation of the oath-taking ceremony, in fact, based on the minister's comments in the media, the intended target was Muslim women such as herself, who wear a face covering.[79] The Court noted this: "Indeed, the intention that it be mandatory for people to remove face coverings is also evident in public statements about the new directive when it was introduced. The Minister at the time said during an interview with the CBC on December 12, 2011, that the Policy was adopted after one of his colleagues told him about a citizenship ceremony where four women had been wearing niqabs."[80] The Federal Court ruled in favour of Ishaq and permitted her to wear a niqab during the public citizenship swearing-in ceremony. However, the Court did not discuss *Charter* issues, instead adjudicating her claim on formal legal issues. In response, the federal government filed an appeal against the decision, which was withdrawn by the Liberal government in 2015, soon after it was elected.

Legislative Initiatives

THE *ZERO TOLERANCE FOR BARBARIC CULTURAL PRACTICES ACT*

The *Zero Tolerance for Barbaric Cultural Practices Act* (hereinafter the *BPA*) is an intervention aimed at ending violence against women, honour killings, and polygamy in racialized communities, among others. The *BPA*[81] is "An Act to amend the Immigration and Refugee Protection Act, the Civil Marriage Act and the Criminal Code and to make consequential amendments to other Acts." Part 1 amends the *Immigration and Refugee Protection Act* to specify that a permanent resident or foreign national is inadmissible on grounds of practising polygamy in Canada. Part 2 amends the *Civil Marriage Act* to provide for the legal requirements for a free and enlightened consent to marriage and for any previous marriage to be dissolved or declared null before a new marriage is contracted.

Part 3 amends the *Criminal Code* to (a) clarify that it is an offence for an officiant to knowingly solemnize a marriage in contravention of federal law; (b) provide that it is an offence to celebrate, aid, or participate

---

79 *Ibid*, para 22.
80 *Ibid*, para 49.
81 *BPA*, *supra* note 4.

in a marriage rite or ceremony knowing that one of the persons being married is doing so against their will or is under the age of sixteen years; (c) provide that it is an offence to remove a child from Canada with the intention that an act be committed outside Canada that, if it were committed in Canada, would constitute the offence of celebrating, aiding, or participating in a marriage rite or ceremony knowing that the child is doing so against their will or is under the age of sixteen years; (d) provide that a judge may order a person to enter into a recognizance with conditions to keep the peace and be of good behaviour for the purpose of preventing the person from committing an offence relating to the marriage of a person against their will or the marriage of a person under the age of sixteen years or relating to the removal of a child from Canada with the intention of committing an act that, if it were committed in Canada, would be such an offence; and (e) provide that the defence of provocation is restricted to circumstances in which the victim engaged in conduct that would constitute an indictable offence under the *Criminal Code* that is punishable by five years or more in prison. Finally, the enactment also makes consequential amendments to other acts.

Community organizations, like the South Asian Legal Clinic of Ontario, condemned the *Act* for targeting racialized communities by locating violence in these communities. They alleged that the government had made unnecessary changes in the laws without providing any data or factual basis, but rather appealing to the fear of the Other in Canadian society premised on stereotypes about certain communities. Such laws criminalizing entire communities or families would have a chilling effect on women in these communities, preventing them from reporting any violence and precluding their participation in the justice system. Furthermore, they noted, "In that regard, immigrant and racialized women face additional challenges because of their race and/or their precarious immigration status. Contrary to what the government has stated, the proposed legislative changes will not result in greater protection for women victims of domestic violence, but will have the opposite effect."[82] The Canadian Bar Association also criticized the *Act*: "We do say that the title is divisive and misleading, and oversimplifies

82 SALCO, "Perpetuating Myths, Denying Justice: 'Zero Tolerance for Barbaric Cultural Practices Act,'" press release, http://www.salc.on.ca/FINALBILLS7STATEMENT%20updated%20nov%2018.pdf.

factors that contribute to discrimination and violence against women and children."[83]

THE QUEBEC *CHARTER OF VALUES*

Quebec's *Charter of Values*, Bill 60, highlights the preoccupation with cultural difference. It was introduced by the Parti Québécois in 2013 to respond to the simmering controversy in Quebec over the limits of accommodation, but it died on paper in March 2014 with the defeat of the Parti Québécois by the Quebec Liberal Party. Its avowed purpose was to set out a charter affirming the values of state secularism, religious neutrality, and gender equality and to provide a framework for accommodation requests. The bill proposed a prohibition on religious symbols, including crosses over a certain size, the kippa, hijab, and niqab. Significantly, it permitted the display of the cross in the National Assembly, arguing that it was part of Quebec's cultural heritage rather than simply a religious symbol. The bill limited the right of women wearing the niqab to receive or deliver services from a range of public institutions when it would limit communication, hinder identification of the wearer, or present security risks. It provided that requests for accommodation would be considered, giving particular weight to principles of gender equality and state neutrality with respect to religion as well as considerations of cost.

The *Charter of Values* focused on the status of women within minority groups rather than addressing their systemic disadvantage both inside and outside a group.[84] Clearly targeting Muslim women, this legislative initiative was intended to regulate them as symbols of the threat posed to Quebec identity and core values of secularism, religious neutrality, and gender equality.[85]

BILL 62: *AN ACT TO FOSTER ADHERENCE TO STATE RELIGIOUS NEUTRALITY*

Bill 62, *An Act to foster adherence to State religious neutrality and, in particular, to provide a framework for religious accommodation requests*

---

83 "'Barbaric Cultural Practices' Bill Inflammatory, Says Canadian Bar Association," *CBC News*, 5 May 2015, http://www.cbc.ca/news/canada/ottawa/barbaric-cultural-practices-bill-inflammatory-says-canadian-bar-association-1.3061317.

84 Ghada Mahrouse, "'Reasonable Accommodation' in Québec: The Limits of Participation and Dialogue," *Race and Class* 52, no. 1 (2010) 85.

85 *Ibid.*

in certain bodies, was passed into law by the Quebec legislature on 18 October 2017. Continuing the preoccupation with stereotypical notions of cultural difference and the status of women in racialized minority groups, the bill was introduced by the Quebec Liberal Party in June 2015, following a campaign promise.[86] Largely understood as a Liberal response to the Parti Quebecois' *Charter of Values*, the *Act*'s stated purpose is to reinforce state religious neutrality.[87] The act thus requires that all public services, including education, day care, health care, and municipal transportation services, be rendered with one's face uncovered.[88] Although the *Act* requires that public servants "neither favour nor hinder a person because of the person's religious affiliation or non-affiliation,"[89] it also requires that persons receiving public services do so with their faces uncovered.[90] In this respect, the *Act* goes further than the failed *Charter of Values*, which would have required niqab-wearing service users to uncover their faces only when communication, identification, or security was at issue.

The bill passed 66–51, with all but Liberal members voting against it. Notably, the conservative Coalition Avenir Québec and separatist Parti Québécois opposed the bill, stating that it did not go far enough.[91] Indeed, whereas the *Charter of Values* would have prohibited all religious symbols, the bill prohibits only face coverings, compounding the well-founded perception that the act targets Muslims women. Muslim organizations, civil rights groups, and legislators, as well as the premiers of Ontario and Alberta, have come out strongly against Bill 62. Yet the premier of Quebec, Philippe Couillard, has defended the law,

---

86 Graeme Hamilton, "Shades of PQ's Charter of Values as Quebec Liberals Move to Ban Niqabs in Public Service," *National Post*, 10 June 2015, http://nationalpost.com/opinion/graeme-hamilton-shades-of-pqs-charter-of-values-as-quebec-liberals-move-to-ban-niqabs-in-public-service.

87 Bill 62, *Act to Foster Adherence to State Religious Neutrality and, in Particular, to Provide a Framework for Religious Accommodation Requests in Certain Bodies*, 1st Sess, 41st Leg, Quebec, 2017 (assented to 18 October 2017), SQ 2017, c 19.

88 *Ibid*, ss 2, 8.

89 *Ibid*, s 4.

90 *Ibid*, s 10.

91 Philip Authier, "'Public Services Should Be Given and Received with an Open Face': Couillard," *Montreal Gazette*, 20 October 2017, http://montrealgazette.com/news/quebec/despite-controversy-bill-62-on-state-neutrality-sails-into-law-in-a-badly-split-vote.

saying that it is necessary for reasons related to communication, identification, and security.[92]

The *Act* is expected to have significant distributive consequences for niqab-wearing women, denying them access to health care and education as well as to public employment and childcare services. As the Women's Legal Education and Action Fund (LEAF) noted in reaction to the passing of the act, "[w]omen continue to be the primary care givers in many families, and therefore have a disproportionate need for childcare services." The act will thus further entrench the gendered nature of poverty.[93] As Charles Taylor and others stated in an op-ed, this law unnecessarily restricts women from covering their faces even when not required for reasons of security or identification. The legislation thus contradicts its stated goals of religious neutrality and "interculturalism" by hampering a woman's ability to "interact with other citizens."[94]

In June 2018, Quebec Superior Court Justice Marc-André Blanchard criticized Bill 62 and extended the suspension of s. 10, which stipulates face-veil limits. The court was clear that the process of accommodation provided for under Bill 62 stood on shaky constitutional ground. According to Justice Blanchard, "The Court can only be highly dubious as to the constitutional validity of a legal process that requires a citizen to obtain, in advance, a permission from a state representative to go about her daily life."[95] While Bill 62 provides for the possibility of religious accommodation, it places the burden of seeking accommodation on the individual affected. Ad hoc determinations and accommodations are bound to multiply the opportunities for discrimination.

---

92 Monique Scotti, "Bill 62: Could Ottawa Really Do Anything about Quebec's Face-Veil Ban?," *Global News*, 19 October 2017, https://globalnews.ca/news/3813986/bill-62-quebec-trudeau-intervene/.

93 "LEAF Opposes the Québec Government's 'Religious Neutrality' Bill, Bill 62," Women's Legal Education and Action Fund, accessed 26 March 2018, http://www.leaf.ca/leaf-opposes-the-quebec-governments-religious-neutrality-bill-bill-62/.

94 Jocelyn Maclure and Charles Taylor, "Revenir au texte et à l'esprit du projet de loi 62," *La Press*, 20 October 2017, http://plus.lapresse.ca/screens/220acce6-62c2-4173-8db9-9db9a52c5dd4%7C_0.html.

95 Ingrid Peritz, "Superior Court Judge Censures Quebec's Face-Cover Law Bill 62," *Globe and Mail*, 28 June 2018, https://www.theglobeandmail.com/canada/article-superior-court-judge-censures-quebecs-face-cover-law-bill-62/.

DISCOVER CANADA: THE RIGHTS AND RESPONSIBILITIES OF CITIZENSHIP

Another noteworthy example of government initiatives is the Canadian citizenship guide, which underscores the need to integrate new citizens, emphasizing common Canadian values and exhorting new citizens to adapt themselves to these values.[96] The section titled "The Equality of Women and Men" asserts, "In Canada, men and women are equal under the law. Canada's openness and generosity do not extend to barbaric cultural practices that tolerate spousal abuse, 'honour killings,' female genital mutilation, forced marriage or other gender-based violence. Those guilty of these crimes are severely punished under Canada's criminal laws."[97] The premise is that new immigrants need citizenship training to understand the importance of adhering to the "core Canadian" values of gender equality, democracy, and the rule of law.[98] It draws on stereotypical dichotomies between East/West, illiberal/liberal, irrational/rational, and tradition/modernity to suggest that these values will be unfamiliar to immigrants.[99]

Discussion

These legislative initiatives reflect the persistence of colonial and Orientalist discourses, whereby the liberal state justifies its intervention to save "native" women from their barbaric, outdated customs.[100] The debate is framed around the limits of toleration, the notion that "we" are willing to tolerate some cultural differences but not others.[101] Certain norms and cultural practices are accepted as the yardstick against which "other" cultural values must be measured.[102] Displacing structural problems onto issues of culture, the *BPA* and other legislative and policy initiatives are premised on an inflexible understanding of secularism and neutrality and on an essentialized notion of culture. The *BPA* does not respond to structural inequalities, neglecting to provide an increased number

96 *Discover Canada, supra* note 4, 10.

97 *Ibid*, 9.

98 *Ibid*.

99 Phillips, *supra* note 12, 23.

100 See Edward W. Said, *Orientalism* (New York: Vintage, 1979); Gayatri Spivak, "Can the Subaltern Speak?," in *Marxism and the Interpretation of Culture*, ed. Cary Nelson and Lawrence Grossberg (Basingstoke, UK: Macmillan Education, 1988), 271.

101 Mahrouse, "'Reasonable Accommodation,'" *supra* note 84, 86.

102 *Ibid*, 87.

of domestic violence shelters, aid for women survivors of violence and their children, or improved social services for minority women. Rather than forwarding women's equality, agency, and free choice and promoting minority women's inclusion, the *BPA* disempowers them and moves them further away from equality. It reinforces patriarchal structures of authority over minority women, forcing them to turn inwards in response to mainstream hostility. Thus, legislative initiatives like the *BPA* contribute to reinforcing the Otherness of minority, racialized women under the pretext of secularism and gender equality.[103]

As seen in the jurisprudence and legislative initiatives discussed above, the framework of reasonable accommodation does not enable a challenge to the institutional and structural aspects of discrimination, but instead simply allows for claiming an exception. It is critical to pose a challenge to this top-down notion of governmentality, whereby multiculturalism policy is seen as a way to manage and regulate diversity, rather than a bottom-up version, which seeks to build theory and policy based on the realities of daily life experiences, to refocus multiculturalism and reframe reasonable accommodation as a tool to respond to such inequalities and to challenge the limits of this framework.[104]

Scholars like Natasha Bakht argue for a pragmatic engagement with the framework of reasonable accommodation. While acknowledging the limits of this model, Bakht notes that the conceptual framework of reasonable accommodation has allowed for an expansion of the recognition of minority difference. She argues that engaging with this framework would prevent a rollback of, and backlash against, minority rights.[105] While such a framework of resolving conflicts might be an effective short-term strategy yielding certain tangible short-term benefits, it may not be as effective in forwarding substantive equality in the long term.[106]

Beaman emphasizes that the framework of multiculturalism influences what is deemed reasonable, what is to be accommodated, what notion of diversity is central to this framework, and the limits of

103 *Ibid*, 88.

104 Bilge, "Racial Subtext," *supra* note 6, 162.

105 Natasha Bakht, "Veiled Objections: Facing Public Opposition to the Niqab," in *Reasonable Accommodation*, ed. Lori Beaman (Vancouver: UBC Press, 2012), 70.

106 Vrinda Narain, "The Place of the Niqab in the Courtroom," *Vienna Journal on International Constitutional Law* 9, no. 1 (2015) 41, 50; Shelagh Day and Gwen Brodsky, "The Duty to Accommodate: Who Will Benefit?," *Canadian Bar Review* 75 (1996) 433.

acceptable difference.[107] The understanding of multiculturalism defines and shapes the nature of reasonable accommodation, together with the particular notions of state secularism, neutrality, and gender equality that are implicated in this discourse.[108] Certain types of ideal citizens are constructed, while others are cast out.[109]

Two main arguments against minority religious accommodation are gender equality and state secularism and neutrality.[110] Recent debates illustrate how gender equality and secularism have become pivotal to the construction of national identity.[111] Gerard Bouchard asserts that the fundamental organizing values of the Québécois nation are gender equality and secularism, which might be inconsistent with immigrants' values.[112] This understanding manifests itself beyond the Quebec context, as demonstrated by federal legislative initiatives such as the *BPA*, and results in "discursive affirmations of the nation's core values" – underscoring its links with particular gender normativities.[113] It reifies binaries of feminism versus multiculturalism, secularism versus religion, which reinforce racialized governmentality and set the limits of accommodation.[114] Reasonable accommodation becomes a "device for constructing and ascribing political subjectivities and agencies for those who are seen as legitimate and full citizens and others who are peripheral to this in many senses."[115]

Bilge counters dominant readings of reasonable accommodation, moving the focus away from whether minority religious practices should be accommodated to an analysis of the debate on this issue, how the terms of the debate construct racialized immigrant women, how links are drawn between national belonging and proper subjects of citizenship along racialized lines, and the way in which cultural signifiers are used "as a racializing code."[116] Erasing race, the discussion turns to values and

107 Beaman, "Exploring Reasonable Accommodation," *supra* note 18, 4.

108 *Ibid.*

109 Bilge, "Racial Subtext," *supra* note 6, 167.

110 Bilge, "Québécois Sexual Nationalism," *supra* note 9, 310; Malik, "Progressive Multiculturalism," *supra* note 17, 459.

111 Bilge, "Québécois Sexual Nationalism," *supra* note 9, 303; Bilge, "Racial Subtext," *supra* note 6, 175.

112 Gerard Bouchard, "What Is Interculturalism?," *McGill Law Journal* 56, no. 2 (2011) 437, 448, 454.

113 Bilge, "Racial Subtext," *supra* note 6, 175.

114 *Ibid.*

115 Bannerji, *Dark Side of the Nation*, *supra* note 11, 6.

116 Bilge, "Racial Subtext," *supra* note 6, 176.

similarities and, more important, differences, whereby racialized others can be legitimately excluded from the national family.[117] We see this view reflected in *R v NS* and legislative initiatives such as the *BPA*, where "racial significance is attached to cultural signifiers such as the niqab."[118]

The casting out of Muslims has become central to the Canadian national imaginary, in which Muslim women are depicted as threats to secularism, gender equality, and democracy.[119] The state is constructed as upholding gender equality and secularism.[120] Secularism is reconstructed as signifying modernity, in contrast to religious practices that subordinate minority women, yet its impact on their greater regulation, leading to their disempowerment, remains unacknowledged.[121] A dogmatic conception of secularism is used to justify the regulation of minority women in the name of equality and neutrality and is supported by some mainstream feminists as a universal model of women's freedom.[122] Mainstream feminists' support of legislative initiatives such as the *BPA* results in the continued positioning of minority women as the Other. In this liberal understanding of minority difference, gender is essentialized, culture is homogenized, and stereotypical perceptions of racialized women are reaffirmed; they are constructed and reconstructed as oppressed, without agency.

Liberal feminists, such as Susan Okin and Martha Nussbaum, argue that "granting rights to protect minority or traditional cultural practices jeopardizes the struggle for gender equality because minority and traditional culture so often engage in domination of women."[123] They assert that, given a choice, minority racialized women would choose liberal rights traditions over their cultural traditions.[124] Leti Volpp notes that Okin and Nussbaum suggest that minority women ought to shed their culture and

---

117 *Ibid*, 160.

118 *Ibid*, 161.

119 Bilge, "Québécois Sexual Nationalism," *supra* note 9, 305.

120 Andreassen and Lettinga, "Veiled Debates," *supra* note 66, 21.

121 Razack, "'Sharia Law Debate,'" *supra* note 7, 19–22. See, e.g., Volpp, "Feminism versus Multiculturalism," *supra* note 2, 1181.

122 See Susan Moller Okin, "Is Multiculturalism Bad for Women?," *Boston Review*, 1 October 1997, http://bostonreview.net.

123 Martha Minow, "About Women, about Culture: About Them, about Us," in *Engaging Cultural Differences: The Multicultural Challenge in Liberal Democracies*, ed. Richard A. Schweder, Martha Minow, and Hazel Rose Markus (New York: Russell Sage Foundation, 2002), 252, 255.

124 *Ibid*.

assimilate into mainstream culture to realize their equality rights.[125] They are marginalized in any appeals to universal sisterhood, where inclusion in the feminist project requires shedding their "Other(izing)" culture.[126]

This stance of mainstream feminists, in the (mis)understanding that they are forwarding the cause of gender equality and inclusiveness by supporting legislative restrictions, neither empowers minority women nor recognizes their agency. On the contrary, it reinforces state control and a victim narrative that justifies intervention.

Turning to the responsibility of communities themselves, it is important to acknowledge the complex location of minority women along multiple axes of discrimination and the reality of oppressive patriarchal customs, which impact minority women's response to gender discrimination in their own communities as well as to state-gendered, racialized systems of discrimination. The state's response cannot be increased legislative regulation but, rather, must focus on inclusion and the democratic participation of women in racialized communities.[127] It is essential to work within minority cultures, rather than to abandon women to patriarchal structures of authority by accepting conservative (religious) leaders as the true representatives of the group.[128] Community leaders themselves must be called to account for supporting oppressive customs and practices that disadvantage women.[129]

The discursive construction of Muslim women as victims without agency complicates Muslim women's own challenge to gender disadvantage and patriarchy in the Muslim community.[130] Women in racialized minority communities have difficulty pursuing social change for fear of reinforcing a racist agenda.[131] Community leaders discourage them from critically examining inequalities in the community to maintain group solidarity in the face of mainstream hostility.[132] As Sheema Khan, founder and former president of the Council of American Islamic Relations–Canada, now called the National Council of Canadian Muslims, writes, "Some will be critical of the airing of 'dirty laundry' during difficult times for Muslims. Yet meaningful discussions about the

125 Volpp, "Feminism versus Multiculturalism," *supra* note 2, 1201.
126 *Ibid.*
127 Bannerji, *Dark Side of the Nation, supra* note 11, 173.
128 *Ibid*, 64.
129 *Ibid*, 47–52, 55.
130 Razack, "'Sharia Law Debate,'" *supra* note 7, 6, 29.
131 *Ibid*, 6.
132 *Ibid*, 6–7.

treatment of women have been avoided for far too long. To what end? What we don't need is another lecture about the dress and behaviour of the 'ideal' Muslim woman. Instead, we need to hear more about men taking responsibility for their actions, and treating women as equal human beings."[133]

Drawing from the insights of Austin Sarat, I suggest that there is a dialectical tension between difference and conformity that is reflected in the contests over reasonable accommodation.[134] This dialectic is at the core of the debates over the accommodation of difference, where gender equality is positioned at one end and seemingly irreconcilable assertions to difference at the other. The tension between women's rights and multiculturalism is often expressed as a sharp binary, and invariably, minority women are presented with an either-or choice between culture and rights. We need to avoid an all-or-nothing choice for women between cultural autonomy on the one hand and access to education, employment, and political participation on the other.[135] Focusing on the redistribution of social, economic, and political power to excluded groups, multiculturalism must be re-conceptualized as an anti-racist policy that challenges the culturalism faced by minorities.[136]

Critical multiculturalism and reframing reasonable accommodation challenge liberal feminists' reductive analysis of the needs of minority racialized women, while also seeking to build cross-cultural feminist coalitions. Challenging the epistemic privilege of mainstream feminists, it is important to centre marginalized communities of women in our analysis of social justice.[137] Critical race feminist scholars Mari Matsuda and Adrien Wing note that racialized, minority immigrant women have overlapping identities and experience discrimination

---

133 Sheema Khan, "Muslim Men Must Learn to Treat Women as Equals," *Globe and Mail*, 6 January 2016, https://www.theglobeandmail.com/opinion/muslim-men-must-learn-to-treat-women-as-equals/article28034962/.

134 Austin Sarat, "The Micropolitics of Identity-Difference: Recognition and Accommodation in Everyday Life," in *Engaging Cultural Differences: The Multicultural Challenge in Liberal Democracies*, ed. Richard A. Schweder, Martha Minow, and Hazel Rose Markus (New York: Russell Sage Foundation, 2002), 396, 398 [Sarat, "Micropolitics of Identity-Difference"].

135 Malik, "Progressive Multiculturalism," *International supra* note 17, 464.

136 *Ibid*, 458.

137 See Chandra Mohanty, "Under Western Eyes: Feminist Scholarship and Colonial Discourses," *Feminist Review* 30 (1988) 61; Chandra Mohanty, *Feminism without Borders: Decolonizing Theory, Practising Solidarity* (Delhi: Zubaan, 2006), 231.

along multiple axes.[138] Intersectionality enables us to focus on overlapping identities, highlighting the fact that discrimination occurs along multiple systems.[139] An intersectional framing of the lived experience of the discrimination of minority women is essential to formulating an effective response to exclusion and difference that is attentive to the complex power relationships across multiple axes of discrimination.

Reframing multiculturalism and reasonable accommodation through an intersectional mode of analysis enables us to connect theory and practice. It offers the possibility of a counter-hegemonic political project that is linked with struggle. This link with struggle provides the vital aspect of intersectionality. Without it, an intersectional analysis becomes acontextual and simply a rhetorical tool. As Patricia Hill Collins and Kimberlé Crenshaw argue, intersectionality has struggle and a challenge to systemic inequality at its heart. It is important to connect this effort with the everyday struggles of racialized minority women and the important accommodations that go on in everyday life.[140]

As important, intersectional analysis highlights the violence of legal and administrative systems, which are presented as race- and gender-neutral but are, in fact, what Dean Spade calls "the gendered racialization processes that produce the nation-state."[141] Intersectionality highlights the hybridity of cultures and problematizes claims to a pure, cultural authenticity, thus enabling dialogue by mediating tensions across cultural difference. Intersectionality is of particular significance at this moment, when differences between minority and mainstream women are perceived as irreconcilable.[142] Seeing minority groups primarily in terms of an essentialized culture ignores other identities such as class and sexual orientation, and it pays inadequate attention to issues of structural

---

138 Mari J. Matsuda, "When the First Quail Calls: Multiple Consciousness as Jurisprudential Method," *Women's Rights Law Reporter* 14 (1992) 297; Adrien Katherine Wing and Monica Nigh Smith, "Critical Race Feminism Lifts the Veil? Muslim Women, France, and the Headscarf Ban," *UC Davis Law Review* 39, no. 3 (2006) 743, 748.

139 Patricia Hill Collins, *Black Feminist Thought: Knowledge, Consciousness and the Politics of Empowerment* (New York: Routledge, 1990), 229–30; Kimberlé Crenshaw, "Demarginalizing the Intersection of Race and Sex: A Black Feminist Critique of Antidiscrimination Doctrine, Feminist Theory and Antiracist Politics," *University of Chicago Legal Forum* (1989) 139, 22, 140.

140 Sarat, "Micropolitics of Identity-Difference," *supra* note 134, 401.

141 Sumi Cho et al, "Toward a Field of Intersectionality Studies: Theory, Applications, and Praxis," *Signs* 38, no. 4 (2013) 785, 787.

142 Bannerji, *Dark Side of the Nation, supra* note 11, 7.

disadvantage and systemic racism.[143] Any reliance on fixed cultural categories and binary perceptions of religion/secularism and modernity/tradition misunderstands the ontologies of women's existence and thereby does them epistemic violence. This culturalization of politics has permitted liberal democracies to initiate legislation such as the *BPA* and Quebec's Bill 62, leaving unexamined the roots of oppression in terms of economic disempowerment and political disenfranchisement, reinforcing subalternity by neglecting the political economy of marginalization.

Conclusion

Official multiculturalism, linked with reasonable accommodation, is "an aspect of the ideological apparatus of the state."[144] Official multiculturalism's focus on culture has de-radicalized anti-racist politics and has erased race in its epistemological violence.[145] The uncritical conception of culture and diversity and its co-option by the rhetoric of state multiculturalism has dematerialized the understanding of culture, making it a political tool, while rendering the language of diversity a tool of governance rather than a demonstration of the state's commitment to challenging inequalities.[146] Policies of multiculturalism and reasonable accommodation cannot respond to cultural difference without challenging systemic inequalities; otherwise, they are inadequate to fight the roots of oppression, racism, and discrimination.[147]

Difference cannot be characterized simplistically as a cultural category uninflected by relations of power and cannot be constructed as being separate from structural inequality.[148] The discourse of diversity and reasonable accommodation has to be reframed. It is a contested site that minority racialized women can claim and where they can offer counter-hegemonic, interpretive frameworks of reasonable accommodation and multiculturalism that better reflect their lived realities and engage with their struggles against oppression. These frameworks can challenge the dialectic between conformity and difference in state multiculturalism policy.[149]

---

143 *Ibid*.
144 *Ibid*, 131.
145 *Ibid*, 33.
146 *Ibid*, 17.
147 *Ibid*, 133.
148 *Ibid*, 131.
149 *Ibid*, 120.

9 Freeing Inherent Aboriginal Rights from the Past

DAVID MILWARD

Introduction

John Borrows relates that Canadian constitutional rights have, for the most part, benefited from the conception of common law as a living tree. They have been allowed to evolve through dynamic interpretive exercises that are not enslaved to a historical past so that they can keep up with contemporary needs. The one exception, according to Borrows, is Aboriginal rights under s. 35(1) of the *Constitution Act, 1982*. The interpretation of inherent Aboriginal rights has resulted in restrictive legal tests bound to a stereotyped, historical past.[1]

One purpose of this essay is to set out in detail the tests that form the subject of Borrows's criticism. The other purpose is to argue that the status quo, both in terms of legal doctrine and in terms of the social fallout of colonialism, is simply unacceptable. The law must move forward in a more dynamic and progressive direction. It is no longer a question of ignoring Aboriginal peoples as a small minority. The rest of Canada faces significant repercussions if progress is not made. The discussions occur primarily with reference to Aboriginal aspirations for self-determination over criminal justice as a particularly illustrative example. The chapter begins with an overview of inherent Aboriginal-rights jurisprudence.

1 John Borrows, "Constitutional Cases 2011: (Ab)originalism and Canada's Constitution," *Supreme Court Law Review* (2d) 58 (2012) 351.

Inherent Rights Jurisprudence

The first step a court must take in adjudicating an inherent rights claim is to determine how the right is to be characterized. Chief Justice Lamer wrote in *R v Van der Peet*, "[t]o characterize an applicant's claim correctly, a court should consider such factors as the nature of the action done pursuant to an Aboriginal right, the nature of the governmental regulation, statute or action impugned, and the tradition, custom or right relied upon to establish the right."[2] The practice that is claimed as a right must be phrased in specific, as opposed to general, terms[3] and be cognizable to the Canadian common law system.[4]

The Supreme Court has, for example, since then ruled in *R v Pamajewon* that an inherent rights claim to Aboriginal self-government would cast the judicial enquiry at a "level of excessive generality."[5] Claiming a right to a separate justice system would therefore be unacceptable. What may instead be acceptable is claiming rights to individual practices within that justice system. It is also not enough to show that Aboriginal peoples in general engaged in a practice. The practice must be specific to the Aboriginal society claiming the right.[6] The Court has also since emphasized that inherent rights are communal rights. A practice claimed as an inherent right must have the purpose of ensuring the continued existence of an Aboriginal society.[7]

The next step, or test, is that only practices, traditions, and customs that were integral to distinctive Aboriginal societies before contact with Europeans are protected as inherent Aboriginal rights under s. 35(1).[8] For the Métis, a distinctive group of Aboriginal peoples with ancestral ties to both First Nations and European settlers, the temporal threshold is instead when Canada assumed legal control over their territories.[9] It is not enough for a practice to have been significant to an Aboriginal society

---

2 *R v Van der Peet*, [1996] 2 SCR 507, para 53.
3 *Ibid*, paras 52 and 69.
4 *Ibid*, para 46.
5 *R v Pamajewon*, [1996] 2 SCR 821, para 27.
6 *Ibid*, para 69.
7 *R v Sappier; R v Gray*, [2006] 2 SCR 686, para 26. There is perhaps some parallel here with Howard Kislowicz's recognition in chap 6 that the Court's treatment of the *Charter* freedom of religion remains an individual freedom and yet also has collectivist aspects.
8 *Van der Peet*, *supra* note 2, paras 60–1.
9 *R v Powley* [2003] 2 SCR 207.

before contact. It has to have been "integral" to that society before contact, "one of the things that truly made the culture what it was."[10] Practices that developed solely in response to contact with Europeans are excluded.[11]

Chief Justice Lamer adds, "In assessing a claim for the existence of an Aboriginal right, a court must take into account the perspective of the Aboriginal people claiming the right. … It must also be recognized, however, that the perspective must be framed in terms cognizable to the Canadian legal and constitutional structure."[12] Conclusive evidence of the practices is not required to establish a successful claim. The evidence needs to demonstrate only which practices originated before contact.[13] A practice need not be distinct to only one particular Aboriginal society. The enquiry is whether the practice is integral to a "distinctive" as opposed to "distinct" Aboriginal society. *Distinct* means "unique." *Distinctive* means "different in kind or quality; unlike."[14]

The test also requires continuity between a practice before contact and the practice as it manifests today. There need not be an unbroken chain of continuity. The practice may have ceased for a period of time, then resumed, without offending the requirement for continuity. The test will also permit some modification of the practice so that it can be exercised in a contemporary manner.[15]

Inherent Aboriginal rights are not frozen in the form in which they were limited by law when the *Constitution Act, 1982* came into force. In other words, laws and regulations can now be found unconstitutional if they have imposed limitations on the exercise of Aboriginal rights, even if they were in force before 1982. This can include situations where a law or regulation has the effect of not allowing Aboriginal peoples to exercise their rights in their "preferred manner."[16] The Supreme Court has also made itself clear that the *Van der Peet* tests govern Aboriginal claims to rights involving governance.[17] Aboriginal rights are also subject to constitutionally justifiable infringement.

---

10 *Van der Peet*, *supra* note 2, para 55.
11 *Ibid*, para 73.
12 *Ibid*, para 49.
13 *Ibid*, para 62.
14 *Ibid*, para 71. (Lamer CJC quoted the *Oxford Dictionary* for the meaning of *distinctive*.)
15 *Ibid*, para 64.
16 *R v Sparrow*, [1990] 1 SCR 1075, 1091–3.
17 *Mitchell v Canada (Minister of National Revenue – MNR)*, [2001] 1 SCR 911, para 63; *Pamajewon*, *supra* note 5.

Justifiable Infringement

The Supreme Court notes that the words *recognized and affirmed* mean that s. 35 rights are not absolute and are therefore subject to justifiable limitation.[18] The first stage of the limitation test is whether there is a *prima facie* infringement of an Aboriginal right. Chief Justice Dickson stated in *R v Sparrow*,

> To determine whether the fishing rights have been interfered with such as to constitute a prima facie infringement of s. 35(1), certain questions must be asked. First, is the limitation unreasonable? Second, does the regulation impose undue hardship? Third, does the regulation deny to the holders of the right their preferred means of exercising that right?[19]

In *Gladstone*, the Court affirmed that an Aboriginal litigant did not have to satisfy all three of these tests to demonstrate a *prima facie* infringement. A negative finding on one of the tests would be only one factor to be considered.[20]

The next stage is deciding whether there is a valid legislative objective for infringing the Aboriginal right. In *Sparrow*, the Court stated that "the public interest" was too broad and vague to qualify as a valid objective.[21] The objective needs to be more specific. Recognized examples include the conservation of natural resources, preventing the unfettered exercise of Aboriginal rights in a way that is harmful to either Aboriginal or non-Aboriginal peoples,[22] "the reconciliation of aboriginal prior occupation with the assertion of the sovereignty of the Crown,"[23] providing for non-Aboriginal access to a fishery to ensure "regional and economic fairness,"[24] and economic development.[25]

The next stage is determining whether the measures in pursuit of the objective are justified. In *Guerin v The Queen*, the Supreme Court

18 *Sparrow, supra* note 16, 1109.
19 *Ibid*, 1112.
20 *R v Gladstone*, [1996] 2 SCR 723, para 43.
21 *Sparrow, supra* note 16, 1112.
22 *Ibid*, 1113.
23 *Gladstone, supra* note 20, para 72.
24 *Ibid*, para 75.
25 *Delgamuukw*, [1997] 3 SCR 1010, para 165.

found that the Crown owed fiduciary duties to Aboriginal peoples.[26] Chief Justice Dickson incorporated *Guerin*'s fiduciary obligation into the *Sparrow* justification test: "the honour of the Crown is at stake in dealings with Aboriginal peoples. The special trust relationship and the responsibility of the government vis-à-vis Aboriginals must be the first consideration in determining whether the legislation or action in question can be justified."[27] He added,

> Within the analysis of justification, there are further questions to be addressed, depending on the circumstances of the inquiry. These include the questions of whether there has been as little infringement as possible in order to effect the desired result; whether, in a situation of expropriation, fair compensation is available; and, whether the Aboriginal group in question has been consulted with respect to the conservation measures being implemented.[28]

So what does this mean for Aboriginal aspirations for self-determination?

Limitations in Results

Inherent Aboriginal rights are subject to very strict tests. The insistence on casting the rights in specific instead of general terms may be particularly problematic. For example, in *Lax Kw'alaams Indian Band v Canada (AG)*, the Supreme Court recognized only that the Aboriginal group in question had a right to harvest a specific species of fish, the eulachon, and sell its harvested grease as a lighting fuel. Rights to commercially harvest other fish would require separate rights claims.[29] Similar reasoning would likely extend to Aboriginal claims to rights of governance and self-determination.

That reality is particularly concerning when coupled with the inertia of the status quo pertaining to Aboriginal justice. Chris Andersen argues that contemporary Aboriginal justice initiatives in Canada reflect an effort by the Canadian political hegemony to indirectly

---

26 *Guerin v The Queen*, [1984] 2 SCR 335, 365, 375–6.
27 *Sparrow*, *supra* note 16, 1114.
28 *Ibid*, 1119.
29 *Lax Kw'alaams Indian Band v Canada (AG)*, [2011] 3 SCR 535.

regulate Aboriginal crime and contain Aboriginal aspirations for greater control over justice within certain parameters that, in substance, leave the status quo intact. Aboriginal justice initiatives provide a medium that displays a veneer of community empowerment and accommodation of cultural difference. It is, however, the Canadian state that provides the funding and therefore sets the parameters of the justice initiatives. Those parameters are that Aboriginal accused must plead guilty or otherwise accept responsibility and that the justice initiatives will usually cover only the less serious offences, which the standard justice system would itself be willing to deal with by imposing community-based sentences (e.g., probation, conditional sentence) anyway.

The Canadian state thus accommodates Aboriginal justice initiatives only to the extent that its own interests happen to converge with those of Aboriginal communities. Once there is no longer that convergence – for example, when Aboriginal communities want to apply their own approaches to offences that the standard justice system would want to deal with by incarceration – then the accommodation will stop.[30] Such an argument indeed resonates with Professor Narain's position that multiculturalism is simply a state exercise in co-option and containment of minority aspirations that minimizes disruptions to the status quo.[31]

If an Aboriginal community wished to circumvent such an impasse by litigating for constitutional rights to self-determination over justice, it would have to take on the onerous burden of litigating multiple claims to all the individual justice practices that would form part of its justice system.[32] This makes the constitutional pursuit of independent Aboriginal legal orders through litigation too costly and impractical for Aboriginal communities.[33]

---

30 Chris Andersen, "Governing Aboriginal Justice in Canada: Constructing Responsible Individuals and Communities through 'Tradition,'" *Crime, Law and Social Change* 31 (1999) 303.

31 Vrinda Narain, chap 8 in this volume.

32 Michael Coyle, "Loyalty and Distinctiveness: A New Approach to the Crown's Fiduciary Duty towards Aboriginal Peoples," *Alberta Law Review* 40 (2003) 841.

33 For an example of this argument made with respect to Aboriginal claims to separate justice systems, see Michael Cousins, *The Inherent Right of the Haudenosaunee to Criminal Justice Jurisdiction in Canada: A Preliminary Inquiry* (unpublished master's thesis, Simon Fraser University, 2005).

The "central and integral" test may be equally concerning. Russell Lawrence Barsh and Sakej Henderson criticize the test as an arbitrary and fallacious concept that fails to recognize how everything within a culture is interconnected and interdependent. This false dichotomy gives judges a flimsy pretext to excise much of what could merit protection under s. 35(1) as merely "incidental."[34] Some claims to governance rights may fail to meet the pre-contact threshold, while others could be deemed merely incidental instead of central and integral. The jurisprudence on s. 35(1) tips the scales heavily in favour of the Canadian state.

Judicial Deference

Aboriginal-rights jurisprudence imposes significant constraints on the scope of Aboriginal rights and on the capacity of Aboriginal peoples to pursue their own solutions to the social problems that they face. In that respect, my endeavour is similar to Professor Kaushal's in the sense that I desire to reconfigure Aboriginal-rights jurisprudence to establish a jurisdictional space within which Aboriginal communities can use their own laws to address their own problems.[35] I would suggest that the current framework reflects deliberate judicial deference to Canadian legislative bodies in the sphere of Aboriginal-state relations. A significant amount of Canadian commentary on judicial deference focuses on how the Supreme Court employs the *Oakes* tests to justify limitations on *Charter* rights.[36] The type of deference that manifests there is in how legal tests are applied. I would argue, however, that deference manifests in the initial construction of the legal tests surrounding s. 35(1). That is indeed Borrows's point when he argues that Aboriginal-rights interpretation is tied to a static notion of originalism, while *Charter* rights benefit from a more dynamic approach. There is perhaps more than one explanation for judicial deference when it comes to s. 35(1).

34 Russell Lawrence Barsh and Sakej Henderson, "The Supreme Court's *Van der Peet* Trilogy: Naïve Imperialism and Ropes of Sand," *McGill Law Journal* 42 (1997) 993, 1000–1.

35 Asha Kaushal, chap 7 in this volume.

36 Errol Mendes, "Section 1 of the Charter after 30 Years: The Soul or the Dagger at Its Heart?," *Supreme Court Law Review* (2d) 61 (2013) 293; Rosalind Dix, "The Supreme Court of Canada, Charter Dialogue, and Deference," *Osgoode Hall Law Journal* 47 (2009) 235.

Proper Institutional Limitations

There are arguments that judicial deference is not so much a dereliction of obligations with respect to the constitution. Judicial deference instead recognizes appropriate limitations on the reach of judicial review within a constitutional democracy. At least two such justifications have been advanced. One is institutional competency, that judges do not have the training, expertise, or research resources to address highly complex policy issues in the way that legislatures can. Another justification is that of democratic legitimacy. Judges are not elected and therefore are not directly accountable to the public in the same way that elected officials are. To take constitutional oversight too far can intrude on the legitimate mandate that legislators are given by the voting public.[37]

This theme perhaps resonates in the Court's treatment of s. 35(1). Perhaps the Court is not so much unsympathetic to Aboriginal aspirations, but rather questions its own fitness to resolve the issues. Political negotiations are suggested as a better route than litigation. Catherine Bell suggests that the Court has been conscientious of potential backlash against its decisions and therefore pushes such issues "back into the political arena" because "consensual resolution is preferred to the imposition of perceived chaos."[38] Former Supreme Court justice Michel Bastarache stated,

> I think the Court is not the right forum for determining how the native rights will blend in with the rights of other citizens in the country, and with citizenship and all of those other issues, and I wish there was a way that most of these things could be determined through negotiation. I don't really believe that the Court is going to be able to be the final arbitrator in that area.[39]

---

37 Guy Davidov, "The Paradox of Judicial Deference," *National Journal of Constitutional Law* 12, no. 2 (2001) 133; Jeff King, "Rights, Review and Reasons for Restraints," *Sydney Law Review* 23 (2001) 19; Jeffrey Jowell, "Judicial Deference: Servility, Civility or Institutional Capacity?," *Public Law* (2003) 592.

38 Catherine Bell, "New Directions in the Law of Aboriginal Rights," *Canadian Bar Review* 77 (1998) 36, 65–6.

39 Quoted in Cristin Smitz, "SCC Wrong Forum for Native Land Claims: Bastarache," *Lawyers Weekly* 20, no 34 (19 January 2001).

Justice La Forest also stated a preference for negotiation over litigation in *Delgamuukw*.[40] This rationale may have some justification in that the honour of the Crown does require Canadian governments to pursue a just settlement of unresolved claims, and the test of justifiable infringement typically imposes on the Crown duties to consult with Aboriginal peoples before pursuing actions that will adversely affect their rights.

This approach, if it does explain s. 35(1) jurisprudence, suffers from a certain flaw. The prospect of meaningful negotiations is hampered by the reality that the significant restrictions on inherent Aboriginal rights is simply more conducive to sustaining the social status quo than encouraging equitable negotiations. The restrictive tests allow Canadian political leaders to sustain the status quo because Aboriginal peoples are left in a weak negotiating position.[41]

At this point, I wish to add a little more to why I view alternatives outside of altering judicial precedent with some pessimism. For example, both Professor Wright and Professor Liston explore the potential for adjusting the contours of power and policy through constitutional media outside the classical constitutional litigation setting. Professor Wright explores the potential of provincial governments to refuse to implement federal laws that are possibly or likely unconstitutional as a method of checks and balances in its own right.[42] Professor Liston explores how the distinction between legislative and executive functions can, in practice, prove blurry, and that in turn offers the potential for constitutional actors to play give and take and work out solutions that may not be obvious to those viewing constitutional processes through a more classical lens.[43]

I do not wish to downplay the value of Wright's and Liston's contributions to a more enriched understanding of constitutional process, but I submit that their value to my present endeavour is limited, as is the often touted and threadbare idea of political negotiations. To be fair to

40 *Delgamuukw*, *supra* note 25, para 207.

41 Bell, *supra* note 38, 66; Jonathan Rudin, "One Step Forward, Two Steps Back: The Political and Institutional Dynamics behind the Supreme Court of Canada's Decisions in *R. v. Sparrow*, *R. v. Van der peet*, and *Delgamuukw*," *Journal of Law and Social Policy* 13 (1998) 67, 85.

42 Wade K. Wright, chap 4 in this volume.

43 Mary Liston, chap 1 in this volume.

Wright and Liston, they have objectives in mind that do not focus specifically on Aboriginal issues. Chris Andersen has it right when he says that Aboriginal justice accommodation is a policy of minimization and containment. Aboriginal communities have been striving for decades to obtain more extensive justice accommodations. I will elaborate on this point as I go on, but the current state of affairs shows that they have very little to show for it. For example, modern self-government agreements allow Aboriginal parties a very limited responsibility for criminal justice. Aboriginal parties still have to use *Criminal Code* offences and procedure, and are limited to responsibility for summary (less serious) offences.[44]

The current state of affairs is an example of Aboriginal peoples trying to use alternative processes outside the courtroom and hitting arbitrary walls erected by Canadian authorities. What is needed is a constitutional precedent that expands the jurisdictional space for Aboriginal communities, along with other processes. I realize that my hope for such a precedent may continue to go unrealized, but, without it, the alternatives in and of themselves offer little hope.

Social Status Quo

There is an alternative explanation for judicial deference that is, by comparison, more scathing. Guy Davidov argues that judicial deference is a paradox. Although, ostensibly, judicial deference can be justified as a hesitancy to make a definite subjective choice in matters of complex policy considerations, it itself amounts to a subjective value judgment to give preference to the state over a rights claimant.[45] Trevor Allan argues that deference can become an abdication of the responsibility to safeguard human rights in certain cases. It also becomes an exercise in partiality instead of impartiality since it can involve not seeing through a decision on the merits to enforce constitutional rights against the state.[46]

Barry Friedman, in a very extensive case law review of American court decisions, argues that even though American Supreme Court

---

44 *An Act relating to self-government for the Sechelt Indian Band*, SC 1986, c 27; *Tsawwassen First Nation Final Agreement Act*, Bill 40, 3rd Sess, 38th Parl, 2007, ss 133–6.

45 Guy Davidov, *supra* note 37.

46 Trevor Allan, "Human Rights and Judicial Review: A Critique of 'Due Deference,'" *Cambridge Law Journal* 65, no. 3 (2006) 671.

justices are protected by lifelong tenure and are not elected by the public, the Court has, for the most part, tended to render decisions that are agreeable to what it perceives as the popular will of the American people. The Court technically has the power to strike down even popularly supported laws, particularly if, on the merits, there are strong arguments that those laws are unconstitutional. Friedman nonetheless asserts that even though the justices' positions on the Court are protected for life, they apparently feel constrained, even if indirectly, not to go too far against popular opinion. The Court may still strike down the odd law, but is willing to go only so far.[47] He adds this especially relevant remark: "It simply is the case that the judiciary's capacity to give the Constitution meaning, to protect minority rights, always has been limited by popular support for those decisions."[48]

It could certainly be suggested that inherent Aboriginal rights, the rights of a small and inconvenient minority, are deliberately framed to leave the social status quo intact. Mark Ebert argues that the Court's jurisprudence embodies dispositionism, a psychological tendency towards the preferred outcome of limiting inherent rights to a set of stereotypical assumptions about Aboriginal cultures.[49] It is interesting to note that *sovereignty* is a word frequently used in Supreme Court decisions on Aboriginal rights. For Chief Justice Dickson in *Sparrow*, there was "never any doubt that sovereignty and legislative power, and indeed the underlying title, to such lands vested in the Crown."[50] Chief Justice Lamer stated in *Delgamuukw* that s. 35(1)'s purpose was to reconcile the prior presence of Aboriginal peoples with the assertion of Crown sovereignty.[51] Chief Justice McLachlin in *Haida Nation v British Columbia* likewise affirmed sovereignty, but noted that it was subject to the honour of the Crown to negotiate just settlements of unresolved Aboriginal claims through a treaty-making process.[52]

47 Barry Friedman, *The Will of the People: How Public Opinion Has Influenced the Supreme Court and Shaped the Meaning of the Constitution* (New York: Farrar, Straus and Giroux, 2009).

48 *Ibid*, 380–1.

49 Mark Ebert, "Overcoming the Dispositionism of Aboriginal Rights in Canada: Culture in the Mind versus Life in the World," *University of British Columbia Law Review* 48 (2015) 145.

50 *Sparrow*, *supra* note 16, 1003.

51 *Delgamuukw*, *supra* note 25, para 141.

52 *Haida Nation v British Columbia (Minister of Forests)*, [2004] 3 SCR 511, paras 17, 20.

Numerous scholars have argued that s. 35 jurisprudence reflects a deferential stance that deliberately reinforces Canadian sovereignty at the expense of Aboriginal claims to governance rights and minimizes the capacity of Aboriginal rights to upset the status quo.[53] Gordon Christie and D'Arcy Vermette, in particular, have quite vehemently declared that the underlying motivation is not to protect Aboriginal rights, but to expedite the integration of Aboriginal peoples into mainstream Canadian society.[54] Constance MacIntosh, for example, suggests that the inherent rights jurisprudence is ostensibly cast in terms of cultural identification, which serves to obscure the underlying rationale to avoid a disruption of the economic status quo.[55] And it is indeed interesting to note that Aboriginal-rights claims frequently fail when they involve rights to harvest wildlife resources for commercial sale, such as in *Van der Peet*,[56] *Lax Kw'alaams Indian Band*,[57] and *Gladstone*.[58] Now I go on to discuss reasons why deference to the status quo is simply unacceptable.

Historical and Normative Reasons

Bruce Wildsmith argues that, historically, the British, and Canada post-Confederation, understood the treaties as respecting Aboriginal

---

53 Borrows, *Recovering Canada* (Toronto: University of Toronto Press, 2002); Patricia Monture-Angus, *Journeying Forward: Dreaming First Nations' Independence* (Halifax: Fernwood Publishing, 1999); Gordon Christie, "A Colonial Reading of Recent Jurisprudence: *Sparrow, Delgamuukw,* and *Haida Nation,*" *Windsor Yearbook of Access to Justice* 23 (2005); Leena Heinamaki, "Inherent Rights of Aboriginal Peoples in Canada: Reflections of the Debate in National and International Law," *International Community Law Review* 8 (2006) 155; Michael Asch and Patrick Macklem, "Aboriginal Rights and Canadian Sovereignty: An Essay on *R. v. Sparrow*," *Alberta Law Review* 29, no. 2 (1991) 517; D'Arcy Vermette, "Colonialism and the Suppression of Aboriginal Voice," *Ottawa Law Review* 40 (2008–09) 225.

54 Gordon Christie, "Delgamuukw and the Protection of Aboriginal Land Interests," *Ottawa Law Review* 32 (2001) 85; D'Arcy Vermette, "Dizzying Dialogue: Canadian Courts and the Continuing Justification of the Disposition of Aboriginal Peoples," *Windsor Yearbook of Access to Justice* 29 (2011) 55.

55 Constance MacIntosh, "From Judging Culture to Taxing 'Indians': Tracing the Legal Discourse of the 'Indian Mode of Life,'" *Osgoode Hall Law Journal* 47 (2009) 399.

56 *Van der Peet, supra* note 2.

57 *Lax Kw'alaams Indian Band, supra* note 29.

58 *Gladstone, supra* note 20.

peoples' autonomy over their internal affairs.[59] The Supreme Court stated, "The whole emphasis of Treaty 8 was on the preservation of the Indian's traditional way of life."[60] With reference to Treaty 6, the Court stated, "It [British Crown] also allowed them autonomy in their internal affairs, intervening in this area as little as possible."[61] The Court also noted a letter written by the lieutenant governor of Manitoba and the Northwest Territories, Alexander Morris, to the federal government:

> I then fully explained to them the proposals that I had to make, that we did not wish to interfere with their present mode of living, but would assign them reserves and assist them as was being done elsewhere, in commencing to farm, and that what was done would hold gold for those that were away.[62]

In Wildsmith's view, this historical context meant that the treaties recognized Aboriginal autonomy over internal dispute resolution.[63]

Article 6 of the Wabanaki Compact of 1725, reached between the Wabanaki people and Britain, reads,

> If any Controversy or difference at any time hereafter happen to arise between any of the English and Indians for any reall or supposed wrong or injury done on either side no private Revenge shall be taken for the same but proper application shall be made to His Majesty's Government upon the place for Remedy or induse there of in a due course of Justice. We submitting ourselves to be ruled and governed by His Majesty's Laws and desiring to have the benefit of the same.[64]

59 Bruce H. Wildsmith, "Treaty Responsibilities: A Co-relational Model," (1992), *University of British Columbia Law Review*, Special Edition on Aboriginal Justice 324, 330–1.

60 *R v Horseman*, [1990] 3 CNLR 95 (SCC), 117.

61 *R v Sioui*, [1990] 3 CNLR 127 (SCC), 147.

62 *R v Horse*, [1988] 1 SCR 187, 206.

63 Wildsmith, *supra* note 59, 333–5. For a similar argument, see John Borrows, "Tracking Trajectories: Aboriginal Governance as an Aboriginal Right," *University of British Columbia Law Review* 38 (2005) 285.

64 Wabanaki Compact, 1725, art 6 in letter, with enclosures, of Lt Governor Dummer of New England to Duke of Newcastle, Secretary of States, Calendar of State Papers, Colonial Series (America and West Indies) vol. 35 (8 January 1726), UK Public Records Office, Colonial Office Papers, Series 5/898, 173–4v.

The last sentence could come across as submission to the colonial legal regime. However, the clause makes only specific mention of disputes arising between the Aboriginal peoples and the Crown; it makes no mention of a dispute between members of the same Aboriginal nation. Sakej Henderson argues that this means that the British recognized that the Mi'kmaq retained authority over disputes between their own members.[65]

Others argue that such recognition needs to be carried over to contemporary recognition and implementation. John Borrows argues that the depiction of Canada as founded by two legal traditions, common law and civil law, is inaccurate because it fails to recognize Aboriginal legal traditions as a third and equally important legal foundation for the formation of Canada. And giving effect to that recognition also demands that Aboriginal peoples have the freedom to apply their own laws and traditions in addressing their own needs.[66] The Truth and Reconciliation Commission of Canada, in a summary of its final reports, recently called for Canada to develop a Royal Proclamation of Reconciliation in consultation and partnership with Aboriginal peoples. This Royal Proclamation would recognize Aboriginal peoples as "full partners in Confederation," establish a nation-to-nation relationship between Aboriginal peoples and Canada, and involve the "recognition and integration of Aboriginal laws and legal traditions."[67]

And so there are historical and normative reasons to interpret s. 35 rights more generously. There are equally important and compelling social reasons for that as well.

Social Remedy

Demands for Aboriginal self-determination are far more than abstract demands grounded in legal and political principles. Aboriginal peoples are still faced with numerous social problems stemming from colonialism, and, thus, many scholars have stressed that it is vital that

65 Sakej Henderson, "Constitutional Powers and Treaty Rights," *Saskatchewan Law Review* (2000) 723.

66 John Borrows, *Canada's Indigenous Constitution* (Toronto: University of Toronto Press, 2010).

67 Truth and Reconciliation Commission of Canada, *Honouring the Truth, Reconciling for the Future* (Winnipeg: Truth and Reconciliation Commission of Canada, 2015), 252–3.

Aboriginal communities have the capacity to pursue their own solutions to these problems. There is almost no sphere of life in which the demand for Aboriginal self-determination has not been made. For example, it has been argued that self-determination over education is necessary to ensure that Aboriginal students receive adequate education, with culturally appropriate pedagogies and curriculum, and to improve educational outcomes and economic prospects for Aboriginal students.[68] Demands for Aboriginal self-determination over child welfare are made with reference to the problem of Aboriginal over-representation in child welfare apprehensions, in the hope that extended family networks can be used as a resource that will minimize the need for apprehension and familial disruption.[69] Another example is increasing Aboriginal control over wildlife resources for the sake of Aboriginal peoples' own economic improvement, with the idea that Aboriginal alternative regulatory schemes grounded in traditional cultures can allay wildlife conservation concerns.[70]

Kaushal herself notes that delineating Aboriginal jurisdiction will, of necessity, be highly complex. Aboriginal jurisdiction will need to have territorial dimensions to account for communal ties to historical land bases. It will also need to have personal dimensions to address the very intense needs of individual Aboriginal persons. And it will need to have specificity as to subject matters, particularly those associated with the social fallout of colonialism.[71] There is one subject matter example in particular that I will explore in detail, with a view to showing how

68 Blair Stonechild, *The New Buffalo: The Struggle for Aboriginal Post-secondary Education in Canada* (Winnipeg: University of Manitoba Press, 2006).

69 Cindy Blackstock, "Residential Schools: Did They Really Close or Just Morph into Child Welfare?," *Aboriginal Law Journal* 6 (2007) 71; Cindy Blackstock and Nico Trocmé, "Community-Based Child Welfare for Aboriginal Children: Supporting Resilience through Structural Change," *Social Policy Journal of New Zealand* 24 (2005) 12, 28.

70 Carissima Mathen, "A Precarious Chancy Situation: Aboriginal Gaming Rights in Canada," *University of British Columbia Law Review* 46 (2013) 349; Andre Goldenberg, "Surely Uncontroversial: The Problems and Politics of Environmental Conservation as a Justification for the Infringement of Aboriginal Rights in Canada," *Journal of Law and Equality* 1 (2002) 278; Aaron Mills, "Aki Anishinaabek, kaye tahsh Crown," *Aboriginal Law Journal* 9, no. 1 (2010) 107; Michael Ilg, "Culture and Competitive Resource Regulation: A Liberal Economic Alternative to *Sui Generis* Aboriginal Rights," *University of Toronto Law Journal* 62 (2012) 403.

71 Kaushal, *supra* note 35.

Canadian state law is limiting and insufficient to address the problems, thereby revealing, by extension, how constitutional Aboriginal self-determination is necessary to move past those limitations.

Gladue and *Ipeelee*

A key part of the background is the fact of Aboriginal over-incarceration. Statistical estimates as of 2011 are that Aboriginals amount to 27 per cent of provincial and territorial inmates and 20 per cent of federal inmates.[72] Section 718.2(e) of the *Criminal Code* reads, in part,

> A court that imposes a sentence shall also take into consideration the following principles: ...
>
> (e) all available sanctions other than imprisonment that are reasonable in the circumstances should be considered for all offenders, with particular attention to the circumstances of Aboriginal offenders.

In *R v Gladue*, the Supreme Court stated that this provision was enacted in response to alarming evidence that Aboriginal peoples were incarcerated disproportionately to non-Aboriginal people in Canada.[73] Section 718.2(e) is thus a remedial provision, enacted specifically to oblige the judiciary to reduce incarceration of Aboriginal offenders and seek reasonable alternatives for Aboriginal offenders.[74] The sentencing process and the sentence itself may be crafted "in accordance with the Aboriginal perspective."[75] When determining sentence, a judge must take into account the background and systemic factors that bring Aboriginal people into contact with the justice system, such as poverty, substance abuse, and "community fragmentation."[76] A judge must also consider the role of these factors in bringing a particular Aboriginal accused before a court.[77] A judge is obligated to obtain that information with the assistance of

72 Mia Dauvergne, *Adult Correctional Statistics in Canada, 2010–2011* (Ottawa: Statistics Canada, 2012), 11.

73 *R v Gladue*, [1999] 1 SCR 688, paras 58–65.

74 *Ibid*, para 64.

75 *Ibid*, para 74.

76 *Ibid*, para 67.

77 *Ibid*, para 69.

counsel, or through probation officers through a report, or through other means. A judge must also obtain information on community resources and treatment options that may provide alternatives to incarceration.[78]

It may certainly appear that *Gladue* has some potential to address the social problems stemming from colonialism. It must be recognized, however, that there are very significant limitations involved. First, *Gladue*'s applicability has been limited, for the most part, to less serious offences. It must be kept in mind that s. 718.2(e) is part of the larger framework of s. 718 of the *Criminal Code*, which sets out the general goals of sentencing. Included within those goals are concepts like victim restitution and rehabilitation, but also goals like deterrence and retribution. And the objectives of deterrence and retribution can indeed, and do, work at cross-purposes with *Gladue*.

Lower courts following *Gladue* have still demonstrated a clear preference for incarceration sentences to give effect to deterrence and retribution. Andrew Walsh and James Ogloff analysed 691 reported sentencing decisions to determine the effects of s. 718.2(e). They found that Aboriginal status did not have any correlation with receiving either a custodial or a non-custodial sentence. Instead, the strongest correlates were the presence of standard aggravating or mitigating factors recognized by sentencing law before the passing of s. 718.2(e), with the frequent result that aggravating factors rendered an offence too serious for *Gladue* to justify a non-custodial sentence.[79] Lower courts will also enjoy appellate deference when their decisions are appealed. Kent Roach has noted that appellate courts in a variety of jurisdictions have prioritized the seriousness of an offence, leading to deference to lower court incarceration sentences and thereby denuding *Gladue* of much of its promise.[80]

The paradoxical result is that many Aboriginal persons who have been deeply damaged and traumatized by colonialism, who are the most in need of *Gladue's* promise, are cut off from the remedial benefits

78 *Ibid*, para 83–4.

79 Andrew Walsh and James Ogloff, "Progressive Reforms or Maintaining the Status Quo? An Empirical Evaluation of the Judicial Consideration of Aboriginal Status in Sentencing Decisions," *Canadian Journal of Criminology* 50, no. 4 (2008) 491.

80 Kent Roach, "One Step Forward, Two Steps Back: *Gladue* at Ten and in the Courts of Appeal," *Criminal law Quarterly* 54 (2009) 470, 503–4.

intended by *Gladue*.[81] The Supreme Court recently attempted to provide a corrective to this trend in its decision, *R v Ipeelee*, stating that offence bifurcation limiting the applicability of *Gladue* to a small range of less serious offences amounted to "a fundamental misunderstanding and misapplication of both s. 718.2(*e*) and this Court's decision in *Gladue*."[82] Justice LeBel also stated, "The overwhelming message emanating from the various reports and commissions on Aboriginal peoples' involvement in the criminal justice system is that current levels of criminality are intimately tied to the legacy of colonialism."[83] Justice LeBel continued,

> To the extent that *Gladue* will lead to different sanctions for Aboriginal offenders, those sanctions will be justified based on their unique circumstances – circumstances which are rationally related to the sentencing process. Courts must ensure that a formalistic approach to parity in sentencing does not undermine the remedial purpose of s. 718.2(*e*).[84]

Even so, there are parts of *Ipeelee* that may be concerning from an Aboriginal perspective. The Court emphasized that s. 718.2(e) did not amount to a "race-based discount on sentencing."[85] The Court also emphasized that parity, sentencing like crimes to like sentences, remained an important goal of sentencing.[86] The Court also reaffirmed *Gladue*'s statement that the more serious the crime, the more likely that a sentence of incarceration would be appropriate.[87]

And so in *Ipeelee* we have seemingly contradictory messages: the need to consider non-custodial sentences for any Aboriginal accused, no matter how serious the offence, alongside a demand for proportionality. It should, therefore, not be surprising that the trajectory that was observed with respect to *Gladue* continues with *Ipeelee*. At the time of writing, the clear majority of cases that have applied *Ipeelee* have

81 Renée Pelletier, "The Nullification of Section 718.2(e): Aggravating Aboriginal Overrepresentation in Canadian Prisons," *Osgoode Hall Law Journal* 39 (2001) 469, 479–80.
82 *R v Ipeelee*, 2012 SCC 13, para 63.
83 *Ibid*, para 77.
84 *Ibid*, para 79.
85 *Ibid*, para 75.
86 *Ibid*, para 38.
87 *Ibid*, para 84.

continued to use terms of incarceration – with their reasons emphasizing that deterrence and retribution were the most important considerations for the crimes that the Aboriginal accused were charged with – and the circumstances of those crimes.[88] There are cases where courts have applied *Ipeelee* to use a conditional sentence, a term of probation, or a sentence of time served, but these are clearly in the minority.[89]

I do not wish to be understood as mandating that all Aboriginal accused must now receive non-carceral sentences as a matter of course. At the same time, it is worth observing that the sentencing of Aboriginal accused continues to follow a definite trajectory, even in the wake of some pretty strong statements coming from the highest court in *Ipeelee*. The overall framework for Canadian sentencing law remains heavily tilted in favour of deterrence and retribution. This tilt translates into a certain inertia in sentencing decisions such that any statements the Supreme Court provides, whether it is in *Gladue* or *Ipeelee* or any other case thereafter, will have minimal purchase with lower courts.

While sentencing initiatives grounded in a restorative justice process may not guarantee a solution to Aboriginal over-incarceration, it is certain that the legal status quo that emphasizes deterrence and incarceration is part of the problem and not at all any solution. Empirical evidence confirms that longer sentences do not deter crime[90] and that incarceration makes offenders more prone to recidivism compared to probation or conditional sentences.[91] Aboriginal peoples may want to pursue restorative initiatives as a more constructive avenue, but they are severely constrained within parameters set by state law. Section 35 rights may provide an enlarged jurisdictional and legal space within

---

88 See, e.g., *R v Perrot*, 2015 ABCA 209; *R v Lawson*, 2012 BCCA 508; *R v HL*, 2012 MBPC 80; *R v John*, 2012 YKTC 73; *R v Matte* (2012), 111 OR (3d) 791 (CA); *R v Scott* (2014), 116 WCB (2d) 645 (Sask QB); *R v Simon*, 2015 NWTTC 10; *R v Sack*, 2014 NSPC 107.

89 See, e.g., *R v Rockwell*, 2012 MBQB 280; *R v Key*, 2014 SKPC 122; *R v Johnson*, 2012 YKTC 75; *R v FR*, 2012 NWTTC 5; *R v SG*, 2014 ONSC 6309.

90 Raymond Paternoster, "How Much Do We Really Know about Criminal Deterrence?," *Journal of Criminal Law and Criminology* 100, no. 3 (2010) 765.

91 José Cid, "Is Imprisonment Criminogenic? A Comparative Study of Imprisonment Rates between Prison and Suspended Sentence Sanctions," *European Journal of Criminology* 6, no. 6 (2009) 459.

which Aboriginal peoples can use their own laws and traditions to address contemporary problems. But s. 35 jurisprudence does not inspire optimism, either.

An Alternative Conception of Aboriginal Rights

A proposal will now be made to s. 35(1) rights to include Aboriginal self-determination. And, indeed, others have suggested the need for alternative tests.[92] For example, the US Supreme Court recognizes that American Indian tribes have sovereignty to govern themselves. Congress, as a matter of plenary jurisdiction, can pass laws that affect or limit tribal sovereignty;[93] however, individual states cannot pass laws that impinge on tribal sovereignty unless those laws apply to non-Indians living on Indian land or Indians outside Indian land.[94] Senwung Luk and Peter Scott Vicaire suggest that the American plenary jurisdiction doctrine provides a possible starting point for an alternative test in Canada.[95]

The proposal I make is for the recognition of a right of Aboriginal communities to internal autonomy under s. 35(1): the right to govern the conduct of their own members in accordance with their traditional laws and customs. There is the obvious problem that this does not speak to crimes committed by non-Aboriginal persons in Aboriginal communities, or crimes committed by members outside Aboriginal communities, or sorting out jurisdiction for urban Aboriginal communities. How these issues surrounding jurisdiction can be worked out among Aboriginal communities, the federal government, and the provincial governments is beyond the scope of this work. The proposal does, in any event, provide a decent starting point from which Aboriginal communities can try to expand the legal space for realizing their visions of justice.

---

92 Emily Luther, "Whose 'Distinctive Culture'? Aboriginal Feminism and *R. v. Van der Peet*," *Aboriginal Law Journal* 8 (2010) 27.

93 *Worcester v Georgia*, 31 US (6 Pet) 515 (1832).

94 *Oliphant v Suquamish Indian Tribe*, 435 US 191 (1978).

95 Senwung Luk, "Confounding Concepts: The Judicial Definition of the Constitutional Protection of the Aboriginal Right to Self-Government in Canada," *Ottawa Law Review* 41 (2010) 101; Peter Scott Vicaire, "Two Roads Diverged: A Comparative Analysis of Aboriginal Rights in a North American Constitutional Context," *McGill Law Journal* 58, no. 3 (2013) 607.

There is already a firm legal foundation upon which to base this right to internal autonomy: the common law doctrine of Aboriginal rights. Brian Slattery describes the doctrine as follows:

> When the Crown gained suzerainty over a North American territory, the doctrine of aboriginal rights provided that the local customs of the Aboriginal peoples would presumptively continue in force, except insofar as they are unconscionable or incompatible with the Crown's suzerainty.[96]

An example of this is found in the trial judgment in *Connolly v Woolrich*:

> Yet, it will be contended that the territorial rights, political organization, such as it was, or the laws and usages of the Indian tribes, were abrogated; that they ceased to exist, when these two European nations began to trade with the aboriginal occupants? In my opinion, it is beyond controversy that they did not, that so far from being abolished, they were left in full force, and were not even modified in the slightest degree, in regard to the civil rights of the natives.[97]

There are concerns about relying on this doctrine when viewed in isolation. The unconscionability exception that Slattery refers to can imply still imposing Canadian legal standards on Aboriginal communities, at least to some degree. The other exception that Slattery refers to, based upon incompatibility with Crown suzerainty, still implies subordination to state sovereignty, a sore point for Aboriginal academics. Aboriginal rights at common law are indeed subject to legislative modification or even abrogation.[98] However, the genesis of this doctrine precedes the coming into force of the *Constitution Act, 1982*. It is open to the Supreme Court to elevate the common law right of Aboriginal peoples to regulate the conduct of their own members, according to their "customs and usages," to a constitutional right. While constitutional Aboriginal rights are subject to legislative infringement, the infringements must satisfy tests of justification. The elevation of Aboriginal customs and

---

96 Brian Slattery, "Making Sense of Aboriginal and Treaty Rights," *Canadian Bar Review* 79 (2000) 196, 201.

97 *Connolly v Woolrich* (1867), 17 RJRQ 75 (Que SC), 84; upheld on appeal in *Johnstone v Connolly* (1869), 17 RJRQ 266 (Que QB).

98 Slattery, *supra* note 96, 204.

usages to constitutional rights marks an improvement, at least in the sense that legislative interference would have to meet a stricter threshold than would be the case if they remained common law rights.

However, the unconscionability caveat raises some interesting questions that may also be of benefit to Aboriginal communities. The caveat certainly implies that even if Aboriginal communities obtain an enlarged jurisdictional space, that space will not mean a complete severance from the Canadian legal structure. Such would certainly not be to the liking of Taiaiake Alfred, for whom the only satisfactory resolution for Aboriginal peoples is for them to become their own completely independent polities, separate from Canada.[99] Aboriginal self-determination does, however, raise difficult and related questions of whether Aboriginal governance should remain subject to the application of *Charter* rights and freedoms. And there is a definite tension involved. Would the individual rights paradigm of the *Charter* become a colonial imposition that obstructs the collectivist emphasis of Aboriginal legal traditions? Or are *Charter* rights needed to redress potential abuses of power in Aboriginal communities? The former possibility would indeed be an example of Professor Xavier's position that constitutional orders that are ostensibly embracing of diversity are really covers for continued imperialism and oppression.[100]

I have suggested that there is a balance to be reached through the culturally sensitive interpretation of *Charter* rights.[101] I have postulated that Aboriginal community courts can provide a vehicle for that culturally sensitive interpretation of legal rights. Perhaps this illustrates Professor Daly's conception that judicial authority can be diffused away from s. 96 courts to realize greater legal pluralism.[102] I realize that mine will not likely be the final word and that debates over issues such as these will continue.

Justice McLachlin, in her dissent in *Van der Peet*, adopted the common law rights approach by arguing against the majority's emphasis on contact as a temporal cut-off point, instead grounding Aboriginal constitutional rights in continuity between modern practices and Aboriginal

---

99 Alfred Taiaiake, *Peace, Power, Righteousness* (London: Oxford University Press, 2008).
100 Sujith Xavier, ch. 10 in this volume.
101 David Milward, *Aboriginal Justice and the Charter: Realizing a Culturally Sensitive Interpretation of Legal Rights* (Vancouver: UBC Press, 2012).
102 Paul Daly, chap 3 in this volume.

customary laws and practices. Notice that McLachlin also found this approach to be a better reading of the text of s. 35(1).[103] McLachlin's approach may provide a starting point to revisit precedent.

Such an approach would certainly be more to the liking of Ebert, who prefers what he calls a "relational approach." His theory is that the foundation of Aboriginal rights should begin with a recognition of Aboriginal peoples as the prior occupants, who had their own legal systems and traditions and ways of life. The honour of the Crown must take into account that prior occupancy and the laws and ways of life that went with it. The Crown must nurture an equitable relationship with Aboriginal peoples that respects them as the prior occupants. Thus, Ebert hopes, Aboriginal rights are not hidebound to a stereotyped catalogue of cultural stereotypes and have the room to evolve dynamically to meet the evolving needs of Aboriginal peoples.[104] Now I explain more clearly why a new approach is imperative.

Conclusion

As previously mentioned, some would suggest that judicial deference itself amounts to a subjective and substantive choice. More specifically, Jeffrey Staton argues that judicial deference represents a decision to maintain the status quo, often motivated by the desire to avoid a public relations backlash.[105] Daniel Conkle argues that judicial deference is a deliberate choice not to interfere with state majoritarian policies.[106] Such an explanation may indeed underlie Aboriginal-rights jurisprudence, a deliberate choice that says the status quo is preferable. It may be a choice to prevent Aboriginal rights from disrupting that status quo, with one example being to preserve non-Aboriginal access to natural and wildlife resources. Why disrupt the status quo for the sake of a tiny and inconsequential minority?

On that note, my approach may be in disagreement with that of Professor Newman. Both he and I wish for improvement in the social

---

103 *Van der Peet*, *supra* note 2, para 247.

104 Mark Ebert, *supra* note 49, 176–8.

105 Jeffrey Staton, "Constitutional Review and the Selective Promotion of Case Results," *American Journal of Political Science* 50, no. 1 (2006) 98.

106 Daniel Conkle, *Constitutional Law: The Religion Clauses*, 2nd ed. (New York: Thomson Reuters, 2009).

situation of Aboriginal peoples. Where we differ is what we perceive to be the necessary constitutional pathways to get there. Professor Newman's focus is on how the ebb and flow of Aboriginal land title jurisprudence, and its uncertain interaction with property rights, has, from his point of view, troubling implications for destabilizing the constitutional order. What he hopes for is a stabilized jurisprudence that both serves the needs of Aboriginal peoples and cements constitutional stability.[107] I perhaps share that aspiration, but where I diverge is that we are nowhere close to a state of jurisprudence that provides an acceptable foundation for the future. Aboriginal-rights jurisprudence needs to enter a period of fundamental destabilization before it gets to a point where we can even think of rendering it more stable. And, indeed, Professor Kaushal raises the valid point that enlarging the legal space for Aboriginal jurisdiction presents implications of profound destabilization for the constitutional federalist order.[108] That, in my view, is also an acceptable implication of trying to improve the situation of Aboriginal peoples.

If a quaint dismissal of minority aspirations is indeed the underlying explanation, then it must be rejected and cannot continue to justify the current state of Aboriginal-rights jurisprudence. If the underlying assumption is that Aboriginals will continue to remain a tiny minority that can be neglected, that is questionable enough. The assumption is even more fallacious when considering future repercussions.

It is simply wrong to assume that Aboriginal peoples will remain so insignificant a minority that the social problems they face will not have any repercussions for non-Aboriginal Canada. The Aboriginal population as of 2011 was estimated at 1,502,000, representing 4.4 per cent of Canada's population. The Aboriginal population is projected to grow at a rate of 2.2 per cent, compared to a rate of 1 per cent for non-Aboriginal Canadians, over the next twenty years, reaching 1,965,000 to 2,633,000 people by 2036 and representing 4.6 to 6.1 per cent of Canada's population.[109]

The potential repercussions of this growth are staggering. The costs associated with Aboriginal over-incarceration alone should be proof of

107 Dwight Newman, chap 11 in this volume.

108 Kaushal, *supra* note 35.

109 Jean-Dominique Morency et al, *Projections of the Aboriginal Population and Households in Canada, 2011 to 2036* (Ottawa: Statistics Canada, 2015).

that. The cost of keeping a male inmate incarcerated during the 2011–12 fiscal year was $117,788, while the average cost for a female inmate was $211,618. The average cost of probation or a conditional sentence was $35,101.[110] Aboriginal population growth combined with Aboriginal over-incarceration cannot be considered anything less than a looming crisis, with the promise of incredible demands on resources. It is not difficult to anticipate similar repercussions for issues such as Aboriginal over-representation in child welfare apprehensions and Aboriginal underachievement in educational outcomes.

There is, of course, no guarantee that Aboriginal self-determination will necessarily solve the problems. What can be guaranteed is that the status quo will perpetuate or even worsen the problems, and that is simply unacceptable. If judicial deference carries with it the assumption that only Aboriginal peoples will be negatively affected for the sake of preserving an otherwise desirable status quo, that is questionable enough. That is no longer an acceptable justification for judicial deference, if it ever was. Allowing the status quo will entail grave repercussions not only for Aboriginal peoples but for the rest of Canada as well. As John Borrows states, "Furthermore, it should also be apparent that Aboriginal issues are not an inferior field of study but a vital part of Canada's legal fabric. Aboriginal rights are not purely an Aboriginal issue, and they have a great impact on many people's lives."[111] It is time to move the law forward in a more progressive fashion that will liberate Aboriginal peoples from their colonial constraints.

---

110 Public Safety Canada, *Corrections and Conditional Release Statistical Overview: 2013 Annual Report* (Ottawa: Public Safety Canada, 2013), 25.

111 John Borrows, *supra* note 63, 287.

10 False Western Universalism in Constitutionalism? The 1867 Canadian Constitution and the Legacy of the Residential Schools

SUJITH XAVIER

Introduction

My contribution to this edited collection examines the colonial and imperial implications of our modern-day constitutional itch.[1] My argument is that Western universalism is embedded in constitutions, constitutionalism, and constitutionalization.[2] The process of Western universalism, achieved through the various techniques of colonialism and imperialism,[3] can be understood through Antony Anghie's "dynamic of difference."[4] The dynamic of difference is a practice that creates a gap between two cultures, characterizing one as universal, the other as uncivilized. As a consequence, governance and regulatory techniques are developed to transcend this gap.[5]

---

1 Peer C. Zumbansen, "The Incurable Constitutional Itch: Transnational Private Regulatory Governance and the Woes of Legitimacy," in *The Challenges of Global and Local Legal Pluralism: Mediating State and Non-State Law*, ed. Michael Helfand (Cambridge: Cambridge University Press, 2014).

2 This argument is wholly different than Ben Berger's notion of universalism as it relates to the Canadian constitution; see Benjamin L. Berger, "Children of Two Logics: A Way into Canadian Constitutional Culture," *International Journal of Constitutional Law* 11, no. 2 (2013) 319.

3 Edward Said, *Orientalism* (New York: Random House, 1979); Frantz Fanon, *Black Skins, White Masks* (New York: Grove Press, 1952); Frantz Fanon, *The Wretched of the Earth* (New York: Grove Press, 1963).

4 Antony Anghie, *Imperialism, Sovereignty and the Making of International Law* (Cambridge: Cambridge University Press, 2004), 4 [Anghie, *Imperialism*].

5 *Ibid.*

Anghie developed the dynamic of difference by examining the making of international law during the colonial period.[6] Quite simply, he suggests that international law is the handmaiden of colonialism and imperialism. I adopt Anghie's critical insights about the role of international law in imperialism and colonialism. This important insight is relevant in thinking about constitutions, constitutionalism, and constitutionalization in Canada. I focus on the enduring implications of s. 91(24) of the *Constitution Act, 1867* on Indigenous[7] peoples of what is now known as Canada. In laying out this example, I rely on the residential school complex, which was created to remove the "Indian from the child."[8] This argument can, of course, be expanded to include other provisions of the Canadian constitution – namely, s. 35 of the *Constitution Act, 1982*. But this is beyond the scope of this paper as the focus is on the *Constitution Act, 1867*.

The central purpose of this chapter is to highlight the manner in which historic and current practices of colonialism and imperialism shape legal form and practices.[9] I suggest that constitutions, constitutionalism, and constitutionalization encapsulate notions of universalism. In what follows, I outline the recent rise in popularity of constitutions, constitutionalism, and constitutionalization and situate my contributions in this context. From there, I outline Anghie's dynamic of difference. In setting out the process of Western universalism, my focus will be on how international law facilitated the colonial conquest. Incorporating Anghie's

---

6 Antony Anghie, "Finding the Peripheries: Sovereignty and Colonialism in Nineteenth-Century International Law," *Harvard International Law Journal* 40, no. 1 (1999) 3, 4.

7 Throughout this paper, I use the term *Indigenous* as opposed to *Aboriginal*, where appropriate. For more details on the use of *Indigenous* versus *Aboriginal*, see Taiaiake Alfred and Jeff Corntassel, "Being Indigenous: Resurgences against Contemporary Colonialism," *Government and Opposition* 40, no. 1 (2005) 597.

8 Chief Dan Miskokomon (opening welcome delivered at "Our Histories, Our Stories: Moving towards Reconciliation," organized by the University of Windsor Faculty of Law, Walpole Island, 17 March 2016).

9 *Colonialism* is best understood as the creation of foreign rule over territories and peoples in distant parts of the world. *Imperialism*, often used interchangeably with *colonialism*, is the process by which peoples, territories, and their natural resources in the distant parts of the world are exploited. See, generally, Anghie, *Imperialism*, *supra* note 4, 10–1; Michael B. Bishku, "European Imperialism," *Oxford Bibliographies*, http://oxfordbibliographiesonline.com/view/document/obo-9780195390155/obo-9780195390155-0023.xml?rskey=1IArBY&result=1&q=imperialism+#backToTop.

dynamic of difference and Western universalism, this chapter then examines how Western universalism is embedded in constitutionalism at the local and global levels. In the local context, I will explore how the constitutionalization of the Canadian federal dominion over Indigenous people through s. 91(24) demonstrates the dynamic of difference.

Mapping Constitutions, Constitutionalism(s), and Constitutionalization from the Global to the Local

The popularity of constitutions, constitutionalism, and constitutionalization in national, transnational, and international spaces coincides with scholarly reflections on the fact that there is indeed globalization of modern constitutionalism.[10] The rise in comparative constitutionalism is visible through adjudications in which judges rely on interpretative techniques from foreign jurisdictions as a template for their own adjudicatory practices.

The rise in comparative constitutionalism can be credited, rightly or wrongly, to a number of things, including the transition to democracy in different countries.[11] As countries emerge from post-war, post-conflict, and authoritarian contexts, they search for ways in which to structure their institutions, their politics, and their society. Good governance practices are employed by international development agencies as part of an arsenal of tools to support these countries.[12] Some jurisdictions attempt to move forward from a debilitating past marred with mass human rights violations,[13] and, in some instances, these

10 Sujit Choudhry, "Globalization in Search of Justification: Toward a Theory of Comparative Constitutional Interpretation," *Indiana Law Journal* 74, no. 3 (1999) 819, 821.

11 Sujit Choudhry, "Introduction: Integration, Accommodation and the Agenda of Comparative Constitutional Law," in *Constitutional Design for Divided Societies: Integration or Accommodation?*, ed. Sujit Choudhry (New York: Oxford University Press, 2008), 8; Ran Hirschl, *Towards Juristocracy: The Origins and Consequences of the New Constitutionalism* (Cambridge, MA: Harvard University Press, 2004).

12 Terence C. Halliday, "Architects of the State: International Financial Institutions and the Reconstruction of States in East Asia," *Law and Social Inquiry* 37, no. 2 (2012) 265, 272.

13 Sujith Xavier, "Looking for 'Justice' in all the Wrong Places: An International Mechanism or Multidimensional Domestic Strategy for Mass Human Rights Violations in Sri Lanka?," in *Post-war Sri Lanka: Problems and Prospects*, ed. Amarnath Amarasingam and Daniel Bass (New York: Hurst / Oxford University Press, 2015).

countries want to confront individuals who may have participated in the commission of mass atrocities.[14] The transition from a violent past to a peaceful future has been the focus of the dynamic field of transitional justice. Transitional justice seeks to understand how to move forward from periods of acute crisis.[15] The case study relied on in this chapter, Canada's residential school complex as set out in the findings of the Truth and Reconciliation Commission of Canada, exemplifies this dynamic field.

In a similar vein, the rise of global constitutionalism and global constitutionalization is equally important. Global constitutionalism seeks to contend with the modern-day international institutions that make up a dense web of inchoate regulatory actors, norms, and processes.[16] Contemporary global constitutionalism can be traced back to Cicero and the Roman Republic.[17] Some scholars argue that Alfred Verdross and Hans Kelsen were the first international lawyers to embrace the ideas of constitutionalism.[18] Some credit the scholarship of Immanuel Kant and other philosophers of the seventeenth and eighteenth

14 Rama Mani, "Dilemmas of Expanding Transitional Justice, or Forging the Nexus between Transitional Justice and Development," *International Journal of Transitional Justice* 2 (2008) 25; Vasuki Nesiah, "The Trials of History: Losing Justice in the Monstrous and the Banal," in *Law in Transition: Human Rights, Development, and Transitional Justice*, ed. Ruth Buchanan and Peer Zumbansen (Oxford: Hart Publishing, 2013).

15 Ruti G. Teitel, *Transitional Justice* (Oxford: Oxford University Press, 2000); Ruti G. Teitel, "The Transitional Apology," in *Taking Wrongs Seriously: Apologies and Reconciliation*, ed. Elazar Barkan and Alexander Karn (Palo Alto, CA: Stanford University Press, 2006); Paige Arthur, "How Transitions Reshaped Human Rights: A Conceptual History of Transitional Justice," *Human Rights Quarterly* 31 (2009) 2; Nicola Palmer, Phil Clark, and Danielle Granville, *Critical Perspectives in Transitional Justice* (Cambridge: Intersentia, 2012).

16 Peer Zumbansen, "Transnational Law, Evolving," in *Elgar Encyclopedia of Comparative Law*, 2nd ed., ed. Jan M. Smits (Surrey, UK: Edward Elgar, 2012), 898.

17 Douglas M. Johnston, "World Constitutionalism in the Theory of International Law," in *Towards World Constitutionalism: Issues on the Legal Ordering of the World Community*, ed. Ronald St John Macdonald and Douglas M. Johnston (Leiden, Netherlands: Martinus Nihjoff, 2005), 3, 16.

18 Bardo Fassbender, "The Meaning of International Constitutional Law," in *Transnational Constitutionalism: International and European Perspectives*, ed. Nicholas Tsagourias (Cambridge: Cambridge University Press, 2007), 312.

centuries as inspiring the use of constitutionalism in international law.[19] The creation and development of international institutions during the mid-nineteenth century, such as the Danube Commission to regulate international waterways, is emblematic of the ideas expressed in Kant's *Perpetual Peace*.[20]

José Alvarez observed that various social science disciplines have different methods of examining the proliferation of international law and its institutions.[21] The nascent literature on global constitutionalism can be described as an interdisciplinary project that tackles the fast-paced growth of international law and its institutions.[22] International lawyers, political scientists, and other scholars are encouraging the formation of the constitutionalization of international law because of globalization[23] and the fragmentation of international law.[24]

Notwithstanding the unifying aims of global constitutionalism, there remains a tendency to obscure the history of international law and its institutions. Discussions about the organization of various international institutions or the cultural views of global constitutionalism simply ignore the manner in which international institutions were forged

---

19 Martti Koskenniemi, "Constitutionalism as Mindset: Reflections on Kantian Themes about International Law and Globalization," *Theoretical Inquiries in Law* 8, no. 1 (2007) 9, 12; Petra Dobner, "More Law, Less Democracy? Democracy and Transnational Constitutionalism," in *The Twilight of Constitutionalism?*, ed. Petra Dobner and Martin Loughlin (Oxford: Oxford University Press, 2010), 141.

20 Immanuel Kant, *Perpetual Peace: A Philosophical Essay*, trans. Mary Campbell (London: Swan Sonnenschein, 1903).

21 José E. Alvarez, "The New Dispute Settlers: (Half) Truths and Consequences," *Texas International Law Journal* 38 (2003) 405 [Alvarez, "The New Dispute Settlers"].

22 Mattias Kumm et al, "How Large Is the World of Global Constitutionalism?," *Global Constitutionalism* 3, no. 1 (2014) 1, 1; Anthony F. Lang Jr et al, "Interdisciplinarity: Challenges and Opportunities," *Global Constitutionalism* 2, no. 1 (2013) 1; Antje Wiener et al, "Global Constitutionalism: Human Rights, Democracy and the Rule of Law," *Global Constitutionalism* 1, no. 2 (2012) 1.

23 The term *globalization* is used to describe the changes that our global society has witnessed and continues to experience. More specifically, it is considered to be a process of transformation that stretches over several centuries; see William Twining, *Globalization and Legal Theory* (Cambridge: Cambridge University Press, 2000), 6; and Frédéric Mégret, "Globalization and International Law," in *Max Planck Encyclopedia of Public International Law*, ed. Rüdiger Wolfrum (Oxford: Oxford University Press, 2008).

24 Alvarez, "The New Dispute Settlers," *supra* note 21.

and continue to evolve.[25] By disregarding these foundational aspects of international law and its institutions, scholars working in global constitutionalism omit all analysis of how Western values of constitutional arrangements, such as separation of powers, have become the bedrock of their constitutional analysis.

Constitutionalism, as generally understood by constitutional scholars, is the theory associated with the various models of constitutions and norms that permeate any constitutional order. It is the theory of governmental structure, the limits of public power,[26] and the procedures through which public power can be exercised. The key principles of constitutionalism are independence of judges, delineation and separation of the various branches of government, the protection of fundamental rights, and the role of judges in policing the boundaries of public power.[27]

If constitutionalism is the political theory of constitutions, *constitutionalization* can be described as a process born out of the "reconfiguration of the political theory of constitutionalism."[28] Martin Loughlin argues that constitutionalism is being repackaged as Western liberal-legal constitutionalism and presented as a free-standing set of norms[29] that legitimizes our fragmented and globalized social order at all jurisdictional levels. Loughlin states,

> Constitutionalism is no longer treated as some evocative but vague theory, which expresses a belief in the importance of limited, accountable

---

25 Sujith Xavier, "False Universalisms of Global Governance Theories: Global Constitutionalism, Global Administrative Law, International Criminal Institutions and the Global South," (PhD diss, Osgoode Hall Law School, 2015) [Xavier, "False Universalisms"].

26 The term *public power* is specifically used by those advocating for and against global constitutionalism; see Martin Loughlin, "What Is Constitutionalisation?," in *The Twilight of Constitutionalism?*, ed. Petra Dobner and Martin Loughlin (Oxford: Oxford University Press, 2010), 47, 63–8 [Loughlin, "What Is Constitutionalisation?"]; and Neil Walker, "Constitutionalism and Pluralism in Global Context," in *Constitutional Pluralism in the European Union and Beyond*, ed. Matej Avbelj and Jan Komarek (Oxford: Hart Publishing, 2012), 17. The reliance on the word *public* is the subject of a larger debate in critical legal studies; see, e.g., Joseph William Singer, "Legal Realism Now," *California Law Review* 76, no. 2 (1988) 465, 477, 534–5.

27 Loughlin, "What Is Constitutionalisation?," *supra* note 26, 55.

28 *Ibid*, 61.

29 *Ibid*, 61–2.

> government, to be applied flexibly to the peculiar circumstances of particular regimes. It now is being presented as a meta theory which establishes the authoritative standards of legitimacy for the exercise of public power wherever it is located.[30]

This meta-theory of constitutionalism that Loughlin alludes to is intricately connected to past and contemporary practices of imperialism and colonialism. But his arguments, and my own subsequent claims, are not new. Rather, Indigenous scholars in Canada (and in other settler-colonial nations) and scholars from the Global South have sought to interrupt the allure of Western constitutionalism in various ways.

The scholarly debates about the utility of Canadian constitutionalism, in its true, liberal form, are manifold.[31] Indigenous scholars have sought to challenge the application of Western-based legal normativity to their traditional practices and ways of living (a topic I will return to in the following sections). In a similar vein, scholars from the Global South have sought to challenge the Eurocentricity of international law and its institutions. Working under the loose banner of "Third World approaches to international law," scholars have sought to unpack and deconstruct the racial hierarchies embedded in international law and its institutions as the result of colonialism and imperialism.[32] Antony Anghie's work on the creation and evolution of the sovereignty doctrine is pivotal to illustrating the racial hierarchies existing in international law. I have explored elsewhere how theories of global governance – in particular, global constitutionalism – carry these racial hierarchies.[33]

An ancillary intention behind this chapter is to build bridges between the theoretical framings used by scholars writing about the Global South, colonialism, and imperialism and Indigenous scholars chronicling the

30 *Ibid*, 61.

31 John Borrows, *Freedom and Indigenous Constitutionalism* (Toronto: University of Toronto Press, 2016), 12–14.

32 Usha Natarajan et al, "Introduction: TWAIL – on Praxis and the Intellectual," *Third World Quarterly* 37, no. 11 (2016) 1946; James Gathii, "TWAIL: A Brief History of Its Origins, Its Decentralized Network, and a Tentative Bibliography," *Trade, Law and Development* 3, no. 1 (2011) 26.

33 Sujith Xavier, "Learning from Below: Theorising Global Governance through Ethnographies and Critical Reflections from the Global South," *Windsor Yearbook of Access to Justice* 33, no. 3 (2016); Xavier, "False Universalisms," *supra* note 25.

exclusionary nature of the Canadian settler state through constitutionalism. The Faculty of Law at the University of Windsor sits on unceded Anishinabe Territory (as part of the Three Fires Confederacy).[34] As a refugee settler living, writing, thinking/researching, and teaching on traditional Anishinabe Territory, I offer the preceding analysis as a means to connect various bodies of literature and build solidarities. This effort is part of a larger project whose aims are to conceptualize the ways in which arguments about settler colonialism, colonialism, and imperialism have synergies and disjuncture and to decolonize existing governance structures.[35]

Anghie's Dynamic of Difference[36]

The formation of the modern nation state has a significant impact on discussions about the very nature of constitutions, constitutionalism, and constitutionalization. The origins of the nation state, however, are contested; some trace it back to the *Treaty of Westphalia* in 1648,[37] while others date it to the late 1400s.[38] By dating the emergence of the modern nation state to 1648 and locating the event in Europe, there is an erasure of alternatives that existed in the Global South and other parts of the world. This erasure is symptomatic of a broader theme in modern Western history, which neglects the fact that there were, and continue to be, thriving Indigenous and local communities with advanced cultures.

---

34 Val Waboose and Gemma Smyth, "Reflections on Anishinabe Law Camp in Bkejwanong Territory," *Reconciliation Syllabus* (blog), 25 October 2016, https://reconciliationsyllabus.wordpress.com/2016/10/25/reflections-on-the-anishinabe-law-camp-bkejwanong-territory/.

35 Sujith Xavier et al, "Placing TWAIL Scholarship and Praxis: Introduction to the Special Issue of the Windsor Yearbook of Access to Justice," *Windsor Yearbook of Access to Justice* 33, no. 3 (2016).

36 This section draws heavily from chap 1 of my doctoral dissertation; see Xavier, "False Universalisms," *supra* note 25.

37 Anghie, *Imperialism*, *supra* note 4.

38 Arthur Nussbaum, *A Concise History of the Law of Nations* (New York: Macmillan, 1947), 52 [Nussbaum, *Law of Nations*]; Martti Koskenniemi, "International Law and *raison d'état*: Rethinking the Prehistory of International Law," in *The Roman Foundations of the Law of Nations: Alberico Gentili and the Justice of Empire*, ed. Benedict Kingsbury and Benjamin Straumann (Oxford: Oxford University Press, 2010), 297.

Some early scholars of international law, such as Francisco de Vitoria (1480–1546) conceptualized governance mechanisms in the form of specific international law doctrines that facilitated the dispossession of the lands occupied by the original inhabitants of North America. One of these newly formulated doctrines, sovereignty, regulated and continues to regulate relationships between the local inhabitants and the colonizers of the new territories. The emergence of the sovereignty doctrine can be chronicled to the sixteenth century. The development of sovereignty can be ascribed to the scholarship of Vitoria and his assessment of whether the "war of the Spaniards against the Indian aborigines [in the New World] was or was not just."[39]

Some of the animating questions for Vitoria were "Who is the sovereign? What are the powers of a sovereign? Are the [Indians] Sovereigns? What are the rights and duties of the [Indians] and the Spaniards? How are the respective rights and duties of the Spanish and [Indians] to be decided?"[40]

Anghie argues that Vitoria developed the sovereignty doctrine by answering these questions, while focusing on the social and cultural practices of both the Indigenous communities and the Spaniards. In doing so, Vitoria succumbs to the dynamic of difference, which, as stated earlier, is a process that describes how a gap is created between two cultures, characterizing one as universal, the other as uncivilized. Western conceptions of law and legal arguments are then used as techniques to bridge this gap between the superior and inferior cultures.[41]

The Indigenous communities and the Spaniards had different cultures, with two divergent conceptions of governance and ownership.[42] In developing his early conceptions of sovereignty, Vitoria challenged the existing practice of applying divine law to Indigenous communities (or heathens).[43] Subsequently, Vitoria removed the role of the Pope and divine law and replaced it with natural law. Vitoria's argument was that if divine law did not apply to Indigenous communities and they had recourse to natural law, given their political institutions, they were logically already part of a different political and legal order. The central problem was how to bridge the two divergent cultures.

39 Nussbaum, *Law of Nations*, *supra* note 38, 59.
40 Anghie, *Imperialism*, *supra* note 4, 15.
41 *Ibid*, 4.
42 *Ibid*, 16.
43 *Ibid*, 17; Nussbaum, *Law of Nations*, *supra* note 38, 61.

In bridging the cultural gap, or what Anghie terms the "juridical problem of jurisdiction," Vitoria used two techniques: first, he focused on the personality of Indigenous communities; and second, he looked at the application of the universal natural law system.[44] In Vitoria's assessment, the Indigenous communities of the Americas were not barbarians or sinners. Rather, they possessed reason because of their political and social order. The Indigenous communities were able to establish "their own versions of the institutions" found in Vitoria's world because they possessed reason.[45] By making natural law applicable to Indigenous communities, Vitoria extended natural law to the Spanish-Indigenous relationship.[46] Under natural law, the Spaniards had the right to travel, "to sojourn" in Indigenous territory[47] provided that they "did not harm the Indians."[48]

Natural law was used as a means to legitimize a system of interaction between Indigenous peoples and European colonizers as equals. This interaction was characterized as occurring between two parties with equal and analogous understanding of the systems of governance premised on natural law. Yet this natural law was not predicated on an Indigenous understanding of norms of land ownership (i.e., sharing of the land);[49] rather, it was predicated on a Spanish understanding of ownership and governance, and this understanding was taken to be the universal understanding of ownership and governance. It was then used as the basis on which to determine the legality or justness of Indigenous behaviour. Anghie captures the results of resolving the juridical problem of jurisdiction as follows:

> Seen in this way, Vitoria's scheme finally endorses and legitimises endless Spanish incursions into [Indigenous] society. Vitoria's apparently innocuous enunciation of a right to travel and sojourn extends finally to the creation of a comprehensive, indeed inescapable system of norms

---

44 Anghie, *Imperialism*, *supra* note 4, 19.

45 *Ibid*, 20–1.

46 Nussbaum, *Law of Nations*, *supra* note 38, 62.

47 *Ibid*.

48 Anghie, *Imperialism*, *supra* note 4, 20.

49 Aimée Craft, "Living Treaties, Breathing Research," *Canadian Journal of Women and the Law* 26 (2014) 1, 4–7 [Craft, "Living Treaties"]; Craft gives a good description, albeit in the late 1800s, of treaty negotiations between European colonizers and the Indigenous people of what is now Manitoba.

> which are inevitably violated by the [Indigenous people]. For example, Vitoria asserts that to keep certain people out of the city or province as enemies, or to expel them when already there, are acts of war. Thus any [Indian] attempt to resist Spanish penetration would amount to an act of war, which would justify Spanish retaliation. Each encounter between the Spanish and the [Indian] therefore entitles the Spanish to defend themselves against [Indian] aggression and in so doing, continuously expand Spanish territory.[50]

The dynamic of difference is deeply embedded in the structure of contemporary international law. I would argue that it could be extended to other areas of law and legal practice as well. The dynamic of difference can be traced back to the origins of international law and continues to have an effect on the manner in which international law has evolved and continues to function today. More important, for the purposes of this paper, I argue that the dynamic of difference is alive and embedded in constitutions, constitutionalism, and constitutionalization at various levels. In the next section, I will focus on the perpetuation of the dynamic of difference in Canada as part of the Canadian constitutional project.

The Canadian Constitution and Universalism

Contemporary criticisms of the Canadian legal system are increasingly difficult to ignore. In the context of Canadian constitutionalism, there is a burgeoning body of scholarly intervention that traces the encounter between Indigenous people and the settler Canadian state.[51] At the heart of these debates is the notion of recognition. *Recognition* is a fixed idea in constitutional democracies, and it is used as a means of allocating rights to minority communities.[52] Notions of recognition have had

---

50 Anghie, *Imperialism, supra* note 4, 21–2.

51 Mariana Valverde, "The Crown in a Multicultural Age: The Changing Epistemology of (Post)colonial Sovereignty," *Social and Legal Studies* 21, no. 1 (2012) 3; John Borrows, "Indigenous Legal Traditions in Canada," *Washington University Journal of Law and Policy* 19 (2005) 167; Craft, "Living Treaties," *supra* note 49. For a discussion of settler colonialism, see Patrick Wolfe, "Settler Colonialism and the Elimination of the Native," *Journal of Genocide Research* 8, no. 4 (2006) 387.

52 Glen Sean Coulthard, *Red Skins White Masks: Rejecting the Colonial Projects of Recognition* (Minneapolis: University of Minnesota Press, 2014), 25–48 [Coulthard, *Red Skins*].

a significant effect on the manner in which Indigenous communities have sought to regain their sovereignty through the Canadian courts and their reliance on the *Constitution Act, 1867* and the 1982 *Canadian Charter of Rights and Freedoms*.[53]

In his groundbreaking text, *Strange Multiplicity*, James Tully proposes the following to support efforts to reorganize constitutionalism through greater protection of minority rights:

> Perhaps the great constitutional struggles and failures around the world today are grouping towards a third way of constitutional change, symbolized in the ability of the members in the canoe [i.e., multicultural and diverse societies] to discuss and reform their constitutional arrangements in response to the demands of recognition as they paddle.[54]

Moreover, Tully explores how "deeply entrenched roles of constitutional democracies [can] be de-imperialized."[55] He suggests that, in any democracy, people should have greater participation in criticizing, negotiating, and modifying the country's laws.[56] Tully's suggestion and the ensuing development of Canadian jurisprudence is the subject of a deep critique. There are various strands in this critique, and they focus on the emphasis of liberal legalism,[57] notions of sovereignty,[58] the politics of recognition,[59] and the politics of refusal.[60]

---

53 *R v Sparrow*, [1990] 1 SCR 1075, 70 DLR (4th) 385; *R v Van der Peet*, [1996] 2 SCR 507, 137 DLR (4th) 289; *R v Sappier; R v Gray*, 2006 SCC 54, [2006] 2 SCR 686; *R v Powley*, 2003 SCC 43, [2003] 2 SCR 207; *Haida Nation v British Columbia (Minister of Forests)*, 2004 SCC 73, [2004] 3 SCR 511 [*Haida Nation*]; *Taku River Tlingit First Nation v British Columbia (Project Assessment Director)* 2004 SCC 74, [2004] 3 SCR 550.

54 James Tully, *Strange Multiplicities: Constitutionalism in an Age of Diversity* (Cambridge: Cambridge University Press, 1995), 29.

55 James Tully, "Modern Constitutional Democracy and Imperialism," *Osgoode Hall Law Journal* 46, no. 3 (2008) 461, 465–9, 488.

56 *Ibid*, 488.

57 Ruth Buchanan, "The Constitutive Paradox of Modern Law: A Comment on Tully," *Osgoode Hall Law Journal* 46, no. 3 (2008) 495.

58 Taiaiake Alfred, *Peace, Power, and Righteousness: An Indigenous Manifesto* (Oxford: Oxford University Press, 2009).

59 Coulthard, *Red Skins*, *supra* note 52.

60 Audra Simpson, *Mohawk Interruptus: Political Life across the Borders of Settler States* (Durham, NC: Duke University Press, 2014).

Recognition, and the resulting politics, can be characterized as a set of "recognition-based models of legal pluralism" that seek to reconcile the demands for sovereignty by Indigenous groups from settler states like Canada.[61] While these models of recognition tend to be diverse, most often, they encompass some form of delegation of land, capital, and political power from modern settler nation states to Indigenous communities. Simultaneously, the settler courts are the arbitrators of disputes that arise in the manifold contestations that ensue from this delegation. For example, in *Haida Nation*, Canadian Supreme Court Chief Justice Beverley McLachlin articulated the normative foundations of the duty to consult and accommodate Indigenous people.[62] This duty to consult and accommodate, she noted, was rooted in the honour of the Crown.[63]

Since *Haida Nation*, the honour of the Crown and the duty to consult and accommodate have become the normative bedrock that dictate the legitimacy of governmental decisions as they relate to Indigenous rights. Arguably, this methodology outlined by the Supreme Court does not allow for the various Indigenous perspectives that existed during the treaty-making processes across the country. Rather, Indigenous claims have to be adapted and moulded to fit the contours of the Western legal system, as set out in the three-part test to determine when a duty to consult and accommodate arises.[64]

Yellowknives Dene First Nation scholar Glen Coulthard argues that these efforts reproduce colonial and racist state power over Indigenous communities:

> [I]nstead of ushering in an era of peaceful coexistence grounded on the idea of reciprocity or mutual recognition, the politics of recognition in its contemporary liberal form promises to reproduce the very configurations of colonialist, racist, patriarchal state power that Indigenous peoples' demands of recognition have historically sought to transcend.[65]

---

61 Coulthard, *Red Skins, supra* note 52, 3.
62 *Haida Nation, supra* note 53, paras 15–38.
63 *Ibid*, para 16.
64 Aimée Craft, *Breathing Life into the Stone Fort Treaty: An Anishinabe Understanding of Treaty One* (Saskatoon: Purich Publishing, 2013).
65 *Ibid*, 3.

The juxtaposition of the settler state's attempts at recognition and the ensuing negative outcomes alludes to a broader controversy about the manner in which constitutional recognition operates. These types of debates open spaces to think about Canadian constitutionalism as a sovereign's imposition of imperial rule through the lens of the dynamic of difference. In the next section, I explore Anghie's dynamic of difference through the first constitutional provision that allowed the federal government of Canada to regulate the lives of "Indians [*sic*], and Lands reserved for the Indians [*sic*]."[66] I do so in the hope of demonstrating how notions of Western universalism reside in the very heart of the Canadian constitution.

Case Study: Section 91(24) and the Legacy of the Residential Schools

The *Constitution Act, 1867* delineates the various powers of the federal and provincial governments, and s. 91 details the specific powers allocated to the federal government. Its power extends to the regulation of Indigenous people and their respective lands through ss. 24. The historical evolution of s. 91(24) is beyond the scope of this paper. But arguably, the origins of this provision lie in the Royal Proclamation of 1763 and sovereign ownership of Indigenous lands by the British Crown.[67] Section 91 is the basis upon which the federal government enacted the draconian *Indian Act* in 1876. The origins of the *Indian Act* can be sketched back to the *Gradual Civilization Act* of 1857 and the *Gradual Enfranchisement Act* of 1869.[68] In this section, I will use s. 91(24) and

66 S 91(24) of the *Constitution Act, 1867*: "It shall be lawful for the Queen, by and with the Advice and Consent of the Senate and House of Commons, to make Laws for the Peace, Order, and good Government of Canada, in relation to all Matters not coming within the Classes of Subjects by this Act assigned exclusively to the Legislatures of the Provinces; and for greater Certainty, but not so as to restrict the Generality of the foregoing Terms of this Section, it is hereby declared that (notwithstanding anything in this Act) the exclusive Legislative Authority of the Parliament of Canada extends to all Matters coming within the Classes of Subjects next hereinafter enumerated; that is to say, [...] 24. Indians, and Lands reserved for the Indians."

67 *Report of the Royal Commission on Aboriginal Peoples: Looking Forward, Looking Back* (Ottawa: Supply and Services Canada, 1996).

68 John J. Borrows and Leonard I. Rotman, *Aboriginal Legal Issues: Cases, Materials and Commentary* (Markham: LexisNexis, 2012).

the legacy of the residential schools as my case study to exemplify the dynamic of difference.

Aside from the land claim issues arising out of s. 91(24),[69] the federal government enacted the *Indian Act* using its federal powers. In its final report, the Truth and Reconciliation Commission of Canada (TRC) notes that the *Indian Act* defined "who was and who was not an 'Indian' under Canadian law."[70] The TRC draws a direct connection between the *Indian Act* and the assimilationist policy that ushered in the residential schools program, which sought to assimilate the Indigenous population. In this vein, the TRC states,

> Further evidence of this assault on Aboriginal identity can be found in amendments to the *Indian Act* banning a variety of Aboriginal cultural and spiritual practices. The two most prominent of these were the west-coast Potlatch and the Prairie Thirst Dance (often referred to as the "Sun Dance"). Residential school principals had been in the forefront of the campaign to ban these ceremonies, and also urged the government to enforce the bans once they were put in place.
>
> The Aboriginal right to self-government was also undermined. The *Indian Act* gave the federal government the authority to veto decisions made by band councils and to depose chiefs and councillors. The Act placed restrictions on First Nations farmers' ability to sell their crops and take out loans. Over the years, the government also assumed greater authority as to how reserve land could be disposed of: in some cases, entire reserves were relocated against the will of the residents. The *Indian Act* was a piece of colonial legislation by which, in the name of "protection," one group of people ruled and controlled another.[71]

The residential schools initiative started well before the creation of Canada. Its origins can be traced back to the late 1700s.[72] The residential schools sought to separate Indigenous children from their respective

69 *St Catharine's Milling & Lumber Co v The* Queen (1888) UKPC 70, [1888] 14 AC 46; *Calder v British Columbia Attorney General*, [1973] SCR 313, 34 DLR (3d) 145.

70 "The History, Part 1: Origins to 1939," *Final Report of the Truth and Reconciliation Commission of Canada*, vol. 1 (Montreal and Kingston: McGill-Queen's University Press, 2015), 53 [*TRC Report*].

71 *Ibid*, 55.

72 *Ibid*, 51.

communities so that the children could be educated in schools run by religious institutions far away from their families and their respective cultures. Their central mandate was to "break [the children's] link to their culture and identity."[73] Canada's first prime minister, Sir John A. Macdonald, stated the following as a rationale for the schools:

> When the school is on the reserve the child lives with its parents, who are savages; he is surrounded by savages, and though he may learn to read and write his habits, and training and mode of thought are Indian. He is simply a savage who can read and write. It has been strongly pressed on myself, as the head of the Department, that Indian children should be withdrawn as much as possible from the parental influence, and the only way to do that would be to put them in central training industrial schools where they will acquire the habits and modes of thought of white men.[74]

The residential schools complex systematically sought to westernize Indigenous children. In their benevolent attempts to civilize the native, school administrators and school employees traumatized the children through violence, fear, and starvation. In its report, the TRC chronicles the students' experience in detail. For example, the children were not afforded the mainstream education that was available to non-Indigenous students in the same area. Rather, Indigenous students were educated through a bare-minimum curriculum that focused on religious teaching to "counteract the evil tendencies of the Indian Nature."[75] Students were often made to work as a means to generate income for the respective school.[76] These young children were prohibited from using their own native languages.[77] The cruelties inflicted upon them during their time at the schools are countless – ranging from physical violence, sexual violence, and emotional and mental trauma. This was the

73 *Ibid*, 2.

74 *Ibid*.

75 *Ibid*, 73.

76 *Ibid*, 71–7.

77 The language prohibition started at the outset, when residential schools were created. In 1883, Indian Commissioner Edgar Dewdney instructed the Battleford school principal in the following manner: "great attention was to be given towards imparting a knowledge of the art of reading, writing and speaking the English language rather than that of Cree" (*Ibid*, 80).

common experience of the survivors for close to two hundred years. This experience was facilitated and regulated by the Canadian constitution and other relevant legislative mechanisms.

Section 91(24) and the *Indian Act* enabled the creation of the residential schools. The role of the Canadian constitution in this process is emblematic of Canada's dark and brutal colonial past.[78] The TRC's findings demonstrate the lasting impact of the residential schools on the life of Indigenous people. Much more important, the TRC's recommendations illustrate that the residential schools experience continues to cause intergenerational harm to the descendants of residential school survivors.[79]

The haunting legacy of the residential schools illustrates the pervasive nature of Antony Anghie's dynamic of difference. The residential schools were created to bridge the cultural gap between the European settlers of the land and the Indigenous communities. The schools sought to educate the uncivilized savages and turn them into respectable, Western, law-abiding citizens. This process was brutal in all aspects. The school system mechanized the atrocious process of removing the children from their respective families and cultures, far away from their Indigenous traditions and ceremonies. Undoubtedly, this was cultural genocide.[80]

The residential school system demonstrates that the Canadian constitution was used as a means to extend Western universal values to the barbarian, uncivilized Indigenous communities. It is the mechanism through which the Indigenous communities were dispossessed of their culture and their language.

Conclusion

The colonial and imperial histories of settler societies continue to haunt, and have a significant effect on, our contemporary local and global, legal, normative edifices. This chapter argued that notions of Western universalism continue to occupy a central role in how constitutions, constitutionalism, and constitutionalization operate and how they are

78 Jeremy Webber, *The Constitution of Canada: A Contextual Analysis* (Oxford: Hart Publishing, 2014), 225.

79 Amy Bombay, Kim Matheson, and Hymie Anisman, "The Intergenerational Effects of Indian Residential Schools: Implications for the Concept of Historical Trauma," *Transcultural Psychiatry* 51, no. 3 (2014) 320.

80 *TRC Report*, *supra* note 70, 1.

theorized domestically (and globally). In pursuing this argument, I used a distinctly local case study, one that examined the role of the Canadian constitution in creating the residential schools and the significant effect on the lives of Indigenous people. Much more important, the manner in which the *Constitution Act, 1867* facilitated the creation of the residential schools exemplifies the pervasiveness of Western universalism in Canadian constitutionalism. Ultimately, normative conceptions of constitutions, constitutionalism, and constitutionalization, wedded to Western notions of law and in light of colonialism and imperialism, cannot escape their civilizing mission.

The argument that was presented in the above analysis is part of a larger debate about the very nature of law. Law, and legal normativity, is both emancipatory and oppressive.[81] In addition, law has been used as a means to create legal spaces in which local inhabitants were freed and disenfranchised.[82] In this context, irrespective of whether we celebrate or disavow law and its manifold functions, we must contend with its harsh realities. Thus, while my chapter is deeply critical of the role of law (or the Canadian constitution) and views it as a tool of oppression, other chapters included in this collection speak to the emancipatory potential of law. For example, considering notions of jurisdiction[83] or interpretive or institutional pluralism[84] offers the emancipatory potential of the Canadian constitution. But simultaneously, as we move forward, we cannot forget the effects of past practices. There is a need for reform through Indigenous self-government,[85] and this type of reform is part of the recent calls for Indigenous resurgence.[86]

In celebrating Canada's constitution and in generating new arguments about constitutionalism, scholars must be careful not to reify existing structural biases built on notions of Western universalism. If we are truly to search for a better world, our notions of constitutions and constitutionalism must incorporate every perspective, even those with which we are unfamiliar.

81 Patricia Williams, *The Alchemy of Race and Rights* (Cambridge, MA: Harvard University Press, 1992), 164.
82 *Ibid*; Anghie, *Imperialism, supra* note 4, 4.
83 Asha Kaushal, chap 7 in this volume.
84 Paul Daly, chap 3 in this volume.
85 David Milward, chap 9 in this volume.
86 Coulthard, *Red Skins, supra* note 52, 155; Taiaiake Alfred, *Wasáse: Indigenous Pathways of Action and Freedom* (Peterborough, ON: Broadview Press, 2005).

11 The Unstable Scope of Constitutionalized Property Rights in Canada: Public, Indigenous, and Private

DWIGHT NEWMAN*

Introduction

A variety of security crises, economic crises, and legitimation crises in the early years of this century have focused scholars and commentators in new ways on the relationship between the constitution and the political viability of the state and the related phenomenon of the stability of the state's constitutional order.[1] Such issues have, of course, always been a powerful consideration and current in constitutionalism. As John Whyte, one of the éminences grises of Canadian constitutionalism, wrote in a 1997 article, "Political stability is the chief object in constructing the basic framework of the state."[2]

* Professor of Law and Canada Research Chair in Indigenous Rights in Constitutional and International Law, University of Saskatchewan. The first version of this paper was completed while I was a Visiting Fellow in the James Madison Program at Princeton University. I am grateful for the discussion of a draft version of this paper with David Milward and Wade Wright at the "Canada at 150: Frontiers in Constitutional Development" conference, held at Yale University in December 2015. I also thank the editors and anonymous referees for their comments.

1 See, e.g., Philipp Bobbitt, *The Shield of Achilles: War, Peace, and the Course of History* (New York: Alfred A. Knopf, 2002); Robert I. Rotberg, ed., *State Failure and State Weakness in a Time of Terror* (Washington, DC: Brookings Institution Press, 2003); Noel Cox, *Constitutional Paradigms and the Stability of States* (London: Ashgate, 2012); Irvin Studin, *The Strategic Constitution: Understanding Canadian Power in the World* (Vancouver: UBC Press, 2014); John Micklethwait and Adrian Woolridge, *The Fourth Revolution: The Global Race to Reinvent the State* (New York: Penguin, 2014); Daniel A. Bell, *The China Model: Political Meritocracy and the Limits of Democracy* (Princeton, NJ: Princeton University Press, 2015).

2 John D. Whyte, "A Review of Samuel V. LaSelva, *The Moral Foundations of Canadian Federalism*," *McGill Law Journal* 42 (1997) 189, 189.

Given the central place of the protection of property in the roles of the state, the ways in which a constitution interacts with property will, of course, contribute determinatively to that constitution's relationship to political stability, to the stability of the constitutional order, and, ultimately, to the political viability of the state. To say as much is not, as some may suggest, a means of expressing some policy preference concerning slower change but is to identify and consider the implications of one dimension of constitutional statecraft – obviously, ultimately to be considered alongside others as well. It is also to seek to understand, in general terms, the complex interaction of the Canadian constitution and property. This topic has traditionally been under-studied by Canadian constitutional scholars, and, in my approach here, I will deliberately make claims that unsettle some of the established thought of what is too often an intellectually homogeneous academy.

Different constitutional orders have, of course, embodied some significantly differing approaches to property, with some differing choices about constitutionally embedded public, private, and community/Indigenous property rights.[3] That said, Western democratic constitutions have largely tended to follow a particular form, from which Canada has differed in some respects, notably in the failure to constitutionally protect private property, both at Confederation and amid other modifications to property rights in the 1982 constitutional patriation and amendments.[4]

Since 1982, Canada's constitution constitutionally entrenches some reasonably clear public property rights, through provincial ownership of lands and provincial natural resource jurisdiction, and some relatively unclear Indigenous property rights through shifting judicial interpretations of Aboriginal title under s. 35.[5] It does not recognize

---

3 On some of this variety on these particular dimensions, see Jeremy Webber and Kirsty Gover, "Proprietary Constitutionalism," in Mark Tushnet, Thomas Feiner, and Cheryl Saunders, eds., *Routledge Handbook of Constitutional Law* (London: Routledge, 2013), 361.

4 See *Ibid*, 364 (referring to over five dozen constitutions with private property clauses). On the presence of a private property clause in most Commonwealth constitutions, see Tom Allen, *The Right to Property in Commonwealth Constitutions* (Cambridge: Cambridge University Press, 2000). See also Gregory S. Alexander, *The Global Debate over Constitutional Property: Lessons for American Takings Jurisprudence* (Chicago: University of Chicago Press, 2006), 41 (which refers to Canada's constitution on this point as "something of an outlier among the liberal constitutions of the world").

5 I discuss both provincial rights and Indigenous rights at some length in Dwight Newman, *Natural Resource Jurisdiction in Canada* (Toronto: LexisNexis, 2013).

private property rights as these were removed from the constitutional texts under discussion through a series of events.[6]

As I have discussed elsewhere, the decision in 1982 to remove private property from the list of protected rights in the previous *Bill of Rights*[7] that would appear in the *Charter* flowed from a variety of factors. These included certain intellectual currents of the era, worries by some politicians about the constraints on them if private property rights were to receive constitutional protection (many of these being overblown), and some essentially random, chance events.[8] Even today, many Canadian constitutionalists write as if this had been a natural decision in light of worries about potential *Lochner*-style decisions that would strike down Canadian public policy,[9] all the while missing the fact that American scholarship on *Lochner* itself has been gradually revealing much previously unrealized about the case that significantly complicates the old stories about it.[10] But that point is ultimately an aside for present purposes.

In this chapter, I explore the constitutional settlement at which Canada has arrived on property and the prospects for that settlement

6 On this history, see Dwight Newman and Lorelle Binnion, "The Exclusion of Property Rights from the Charter: Correcting the Historical Record," *Alberta Law Review* 52 (2015) 543.

7 *Canadian Bill of Rights*, SC 1960, c 44.

8 Newman and Binnion, *supra* note 6.

9 On the impact of *Lochner* worries, see, e.g., Sujit Choudhry, "The *Lochner* Era and Comparative Constitutionalism," *International Journal of Constitutional Law* 2 (2004) 1. The worry is about something like *Lochner v New York*, 198 US 405 (1905), in which the US Supreme Court seemed to recognize liberty of contract in striking down laws limiting work hours. *Lochner* has, at times, been a commonly invoked spectre in Canadian constitutional argument; e.g., in argument in *Chaoulli v Quebec (Attorney General)*, [2005] 1 SCR 791, 2005 SCC 35, at least four lawyers tried to use *Lochner* to separately challenge what ultimately became the result in the case: Sujit Choudhry, "Worse than *Lochner*?," in *Access to Care, Access to Justice: The Legal Debate over Private Health Insurance in Canada*, ed. Colleen Flood, Kent Roach, and Lorne Sossin (Toronto: University of Toronto Press, 2005), 75, 77.

10 See, notably, David E. Bernstein, *Rehabilitating Lochner: Defending Individual Rights against Progressive Reform* (Chicago: University of Chicago Press, 2011); Thomas Colby and Peter J. Smith, "The Return of Lochner," *Cornell Law Review* 100 (2015) 527. This scholarship has increasingly challenged the traditional consensus that *Lochner* was wrongly decided and contrary to appropriate conceptions of civil rights, with this new scholarship showing its stronger legal roots and its contribution to modern civil rights jurisprudence.

as Canadian constitutionalism moves forward in the coming decades. I will argue that the Canadian constitutional settlement has embedded certain tensions between public and Indigenous property rights and that what is present in the Canadian constitutional settlement, combined with the lack of constitutional protection for private property rights, may well imply future instability.

To do so, I will begin this paper by highlighting some key concepts and themes from the constitutional instability scholarship. I will then characterize the reasonably clear public property rights and reasonably unclear Indigenous property rights that have come to be embedded in the constitutional order, proceeding to examine some tensions between these rights. I will then examine the potential for instability that arises from the lack of constitutional protection for private property rights. I will conclude by arguing that ongoing efforts at a constitutional amendment along these lines can be expected in the decades ahead.

That conclusion, it bears noting, identifies some distinction in the operations of the value of stability compared to the operation of other values. As highlighted in Emily Kidd White's chapter in this volume, some values, like dignity, are susceptible to direct application by the courts in interpreting particular constitutional provisions.[11] By contrast, the value of stability does not have that same sort of application but pertains to a broader architecture of the constitution that factors into various facets of constitutionalism. That said, the value of stability does bear on modes of legal reasoning and may actually challenge some of the ways in which other values are to be applied. Kidd White's defence of highly context-specific judgments, for instance, risks setting the stage for unpredictable judicial activity. However, those particularistic claims are not central to the present argument, which actually looks to the longer-term effects of stability in ways that reach beyond the judicial system as the sole site of constitutionalism.

Constitutional Instability

The literature on constitutions and stability of the political order is multifaceted, so much so that different strands of this literature have sometimes seemed to come close to valuing virtually opposed considerations as contributing to stability. For example, on the one hand, strands of

11 See, e.g., Emily Kidd White, chap 12 in this volume.

the scholarship related to Robert Dahl's stability-related writing have valued the instability of political outcomes and suggested that constitutional systems should not generate permanent winners and losers but facilitate ongoing populist participation in substantive questions, a process that furthers system stability.[12] On the other hand, the writing of William Riker has raised social choice issues with that same political instability to argue for limiting the role of populist determinations essentially to leadership rotations, thus seeking to maintain system stability in virtually the opposite manner.[13]

The present paper seeks to apply considerations from this important literature, while remaining agnostic towards specific contested theories in this literature. It is thus necessary to work from those claims on which this literature is principally in accord. Beginning from fundamentals, then, the constitution, in providing fundamental rules for political action,[14] obviously has significant potential effects on the ongoing stability of the state and has to have order as one of its key purposes.

At an abstract level, a constitutional order will promote stability if it facilitates a constitutional equilibrium, meaning that no sufficiently powerful subgroup has an incentive to defect from the constitutional order; generally efficient social outcomes, clear rules that allow planning, and legal predictability are the relatively basic requirements for any such equilibrium.[15] At a broader level, the constitution needs to be of a character such that it generates support for itself, which requires that it further cohesion, continuity, and legitimation of the state's strategic operations.[16]

To achieve these requirements, particularly over time, the constitution will need to strike a balance between fixed principles and the flexibility to respond to changing circumstances – the combination of the flexibility of democracy and fixity of the rule of law having been one strong way to strike this balance.[17] If the constitution is to

---

12 See, generally, Robert Dahl, *A Preface to Democratic Theory* (Chicago: University of Chicago Press, 1956).

13 See, generally, William Riker, *Liberalism against Populism: A Confrontation between the Theory of Democracy and the Theory of Social Choice* (San Francisco: W.H. Freeland, 1982).

14 Cf. Peter C. Ordeshook, "Constitutional Stability," *Constitutional Political Economy* 3 (1992) 137, 143.

15 Cf. *Ibid*, 150–1.

16 Bobbitt, *supra* note 1, 206.

17 Cox, *supra* note 1, 125*ff*, 236.

maintain its equilibrium, it needs to maintain ongoing support by embodying an ideology that is broadly accepted by the population and adhering rooted to the principles of this ideology,[18] linking back to the basic equilibrium requirements but adding now a dimension of popular legitimacy.

These dimensions are broad characteristics of a constitutional order as opposed to statements about specific features of a constitution. Nonetheless, they may still provide some important guidance for the particular form of a constitution. A constitution that does not support the stability of the state will generate difficulties. So will a constitution that departs from efficient outcomes and clear, predictable rules. Similarly, a constitution that does not foster legitimation for the state's strategic operations or that cannot maintain rootedness in popular ideological legitimacy will also face problems.

As I examine the status of property in the Canadian constitution, I will suggest that some of these criteria are at issue. I will refer particularly to clarity and predictability, legitimation for Canada's strategic operations, and popular ideological legitimacy. One possible result might be gradually building pressures for constitutional amendment in the decades ahead, despite the challenging practical obstacles to such amendment.[19]

Entrenched Public and Indigenous Property Rights in Canada

The 1982 constitutional patriation and related amendments dealt with property in three ways, even if not always fully realized at the time or more recently, and it is worth highlighting these briefly before considering at greater length the nature of entrenched public and Indigenous property rights in Canada. First, the intellectual climate in which constitutional discussions took place made it possible not to provide constitutional protection for private property, and several chance events in the negotiations led to that lack of protection.[20]

---

18 *Ibid*, 236.

19 On constitutional amendment and the obstacles thereto, see, especially, Emmett Macfarlane, ed., *Constitutional Amendment in Canada: The Law and Politics of Part V of the Constitution Act, 1982* (Toronto: University of Toronto Press, 2016).

20 See Newman and Binnion, *supra* note 6.

Second, although the path to including Indigenous property rights was not straightforward in the face of differing levels of opposition by some premiers, Indigenous activism in the decades immediately preceding 1982 culminated in the achievement of s. 35, a constitutional entrenchment of Aboriginal and treaty rights, under which "[t]he existing aboriginal and treaty rights of the aboriginal peoples of Canada are hereby recognized and affirmed."[21] The mixed provincial views led to the text of s. 35 entrenching only *existing* Aboriginal and treaty rights, although the effects of that textual modification have not always been fully elaborated. In any event, the rights contemplated in the context of the s. 35 entrenchment would have included Aboriginal title, already established in the courts in the 1973 *Calder* decision.[22]

Third, although not always discussed as much in some circles, the 1982 amendments would not have obtained sufficient provincial consent without the steps taken to solidify provincial natural resource jurisdiction through the addition of s. 92A to the *Constitution Act, 1867;* more than is often realized, that clause was a dealmaker or deal-breaker.[23] Although s. 117 had entrenched provincial property ownership, and s. 92(5) furthered provincial jurisdiction through the management of public lands, these rights had been denied to several of the western provinces when the provinces were formed. Only a decades-long course of provincial activism led to the belated recognition of provincial ownership of lands in these provinces in the 1930 natural resource transfer agreements.[24] But continued federal incursions and judicial decisions in the 1970s threatened provincial natural resource jurisdiction.[25]

21 *Constitution Act, 1982,* s 35(1). On the mixed Indigenous sentiment on s 35, see Kiera Ladner, "An Indigenous Constitutional Paradox: Both Monumental Achievement and Monumental Defeat," in *Patriation and Its Consequences: Constitution Making in Canada,* ed. Lois Harder and Steve Patten (Vancouver: UBC Press, 2015), 267.

22 *Calder v British Columbia (Attorney General),* [1973] SCR 313.

23 See my discussion in Newman, *Natural Resource Jurisdiction in Canada, supra* note 5. See also J. Peter Meekison, Roy J. Romanow, and William D. Moull, *Origins and Meaning of Section 92A: The 1982 Constitutional Amendment on Resources* (Montreal: Institute for Research on Public Policy, 1985).

24 For the history of that activism, see the excellent Mary Janigan, *Let the Eastern Bastards Freeze in the Dark: The West versus the Rest since Confederation* (Toronto: Penguin, 2013).

25 See, generally, Newman, *Natural Resource Jurisdiction in Canada, supra* note 5.

The provinces thus sought to solidify their jurisdiction in s. 92A, and s. 92A serves as an important legal recognition of, and symbolic capstone on, the public property ownership and natural resource jurisdiction held by the provinces.[26]

Aside from specific lands owned by the federal government,[27] then, provincial land ownership is generally a legal starting point. The nature of that property ownership is reasonably clear, and it also has plenary characteristics. Along with provincial ownership, there is provincial jurisdiction over property and civil rights, with that power also implying that provincial governments may modify the characteristics of property ownership within the province.

They have used that authority in various ways. For example, some provinces have privately held, freehold mineral interests as a result of historical dealings by the federal government before those provinces had ownership of their land. These provinces have tended to try to modify those freehold interests through subtle pressures of royalty and tax regimes to induce the owners to surrender those freehold interests.[28]

But provinces have also altered property rights in more direct ways, such as Alberta's 2010 legislation taking provincial ownership of "pore space" so as to have clear provincial control over any future carbon storage.[29] That provincial taking proceeded explicitly and without compensation. Such an approach was legally possible due to clear provincial jurisdiction combined with the lack of constitutional protection for private property. Together, the constitutionally entrenched provincial ownership of public property and accompanying jurisdiction establish a powerful role for the provinces based on public property ownership.

The nature of entrenched Indigenous property rights is much less clear. The text of s. 35(1), by which "[t]he existing aboriginal and treaty rights of the aboriginal peoples of Canada are hereby recognized and affirmed,"[30] has some opaque features. For example, the addition to the text of the word *existing* was clearly meaningful to the premiers who had

26 *Ibid.*

27 Such lands include national parks, First Nations reserves, and lands used by the Department of National Defence.

28 See discussion in Newman, *Natural Resource Jurisdiction in Canada, supra* note 5.

29 See *Carbon Capture and Storage Statutes Amendment Act,* SA 2010, c 14, s 15.1(1).

30 *Constitution Act, 1982.*

proposed it, but has never received full elaboration.[31] Further constitutional conferences through the 1980s, which were meant to more fully define the contents of s. 35, ended without greater clarity.[32] In the end, the task of elaborating the implications of entrenched s. 35 rights has fallen to the courts, and this process has implied a massive accretion of judicial power in a vitally important policy arena – although the courts themselves have stressed that better outcomes might come from better negotiations between governments and Indigenous communities.

Judicial decisions on the property-related contents of s. 35 have not tended towards clarity or predictability. Taking Aboriginal title as the first main matter at issue, the courts have quite simply struggled with what they are to do with s. 35. The Supreme Court of Canada has three leading precedents on Aboriginal title since 1982: *Delgamuukw* in 1997,[33] *Marshall and Bernard* in 2005,[34] and *Tsilhqot'in* in 2014.[35] The *Tsilhqot'in* decision was seen as revolutionary by many commentators,[36] and it is almost surely proper to recognize it as one of the most important decisions that the Supreme Court of Canada has ever rendered. But, in many respects, the Court simply applied the Aboriginal-title test from *Delgamuukw*, which it restated in an essentially unchanged form (focused on sufficient and exclusive occupation of land before the assertion of European sovereignty),[37] thereby arguably making proper

31 For a view expressing puzzlement at the word, see Peter Russell, "Patriation and the Law of Unintended Consequences," in *Patriation and Its Consequences: Constitution Making in Canada*, ed. Lois Harder and Steve Patten (Vancouver: UBC Press, 2015), 229, 236 (recounting that "[a]t the 2011 Patriation Negotiations Conference, I asked Lougheed about his intentions in having the word 'existing' inserted in the clause. He told me and the other conference attendees that he wanted the rights that were recognized to be those that applied in the contemporary context, without dragging in a lot of history. Given that Aboriginal rights stem from the situation of Aboriginal peoples before the assertion of sovereignty by European powers and from historical treaties, it is not easy to understand Premier Lougheed's thinking.") The word seems, at minimum, to suggest that the 1982 entrenchments do not revive rights that were extinguished before 1982, but it may have further legal effects.

32 See Ladner, *supra* note 21, 279.

33 *Delgamuukw v British Columbia (Attorney General)*, [1997] 3 SCR 1010.

34 *R v Marshall; R v Bernard*, 2005 SCC 43, [2005] 2 SCR 220.

35 *Tsilhqot'in Nation v British Columbia (Attorney General)*, 2014 SCC 44.

36 We reference a number of these in Kenneth Coates and Dwight Newman, *The End Is Not Nigh: Reason over Alarmism in Analysing the Tsilhqot'in Decision* (Ottawa: MacDonald-Laurier Institute, September 2014).

37 *Tsilhqot'in*, *supra* note 35, paras 25*ff*.

the conclusion that it ought in some respects to have been seen as a predictable application of settled law.[38] However, the three-case path of the Court's jurisprudence in this area between 1982 and 2014 makes matters more complicated.

The development of s. 35 Aboriginal-title doctrine did not proceed rapidly after 1982, even though a previous Aboriginal-title decision grounded in common law had been on the books from the 1973 *Calder* decision.[39] It took until 1997 for the Court to pronounce on an Aboriginal-title case under s. 35, and the *Delgamuukw* decision saw it adopting a public law approach that applied the general Aboriginal-rights test from *Van der Peet* to the specific context of title.[40] It thus adopted a test, modified from *Van der Peet*, which was based on sufficient, exclusive occupation before the assertion of European sovereignty.[41] In its 2005 decision in *Marshall and Bernard*, the Court applied this test in the context of a claim in the Maritimes, and it spoke of a standard of intensive use applying,[42] which many interpreted as excluding historically mobile communities from making successful title claims.[43] In *Tsilhqot'in*, however, the Supreme Court overturned the appeal court that had applied *Marshall and Bernard* in this way and granted a declaration of Aboriginal title over lands that the Tsilhqot'in had historically used on a seasonal and migratory basis.[44]

The Supreme Court has not successfully followed a stable, predictable path in its Aboriginal-title jurisprudence. Rather, it has lurched back and forth between different ideas, often without much explanation of why it was doing so. Indeed, considering the trajectory in this area more fully, the *Marshall and Bernard* decision of 2005 actually appeared to suggest that the *Delgamuukw* test would not provide title for a historically mobile community; Justice LeBel mentioned this in a separate opinion at the time, but it seemed to have no effect on

38 This was the view of a few commentators, like Tom Isaac and Robin Junger; see discussion of various commentators in Coates and Newman, *supra* note 36.

39 *Calder, supra* note 22.

40 *Delgamuukw, supra* note 33, paras 134*ff*, applying *R v Van der Peet*, [1996] 2 SCR 507.

41 *Ibid*, paras 138 and 141*ff*.

42 *Marshall and Bernard, supra* note 34.

43 See, e.g., Kent McNeil, "Aboriginal Title and the Supreme Court: What's Happening?," *Saskatchewan Law Review* 69 (2006) 281.

44 *Tsilhqot'in, supra* note 35.

the majority's articulation of the rules in that case.[45] In *Tsilhqot'in*, the British Columbia Court of Appeal applied the *Marshall and Bernard* approach and decided against the title claim.[46] However, the Supreme Court decided in favour of it.

The Supreme Court did not explain the relationship between its approach in *Tsilhqot'in* and its approach in *Marshall and Bernard*. Indeed, it actually relied upon some of the reasoning in the Court of Appeal decision in *Marshall and Bernard* without any explanation of why it was applying a decision it had previously overturned.[47] There are good arguments that the Court reached an appropriate result, one that avoids barring historically mobile Aboriginal communities from any possibility of a title claim. But it reached that result in a manner not in keeping with precedent and without explaining why it had altered precedent. Thus, although *Tsilhqot'in* sets out some major legal statements, its approach to precedent makes the law partly uncertain and leaves the outcome of the next Aboriginal-title claim subject to uncertainty about what the Supreme Court might do on the day it renders any particular judgment. Over a relatively short time – from 1997 to 2005 to 2014 – the Court shifted back and forth in some respects. This probably speaks to the broader conceptual and theoretical uncertainties that affect this whole area of law.

To the extent that it does pronounce a number of key rules on the nature and scope of Aboriginal title, the Supreme Court has not done so particularly clearly, either. For instance, even aside from intriguing suggestions that *Tsilhqot'in* embodies a veiled form of self-government,[48] some features of the *Tsilhqot'in* judgment on simple property issues are very difficult to parse in any determinative manner, sometimes to the significant detriment of Aboriginal communities themselves. For example, where *Delgamuukw* articulated an "inherent

---

45 See *Marshall and Bernard, supra* note 34. I discuss this at some length in Dwight Newman, "Aboriginal Rights, Collective Rights, and Adjudicative Virtues," *Supreme Court Law Review* 70 (2015) 285.

46 *William v British Columbia*, 2012 BCCA 285.

47 See *Tsilhqot'in, supra* note 35, para 39 (adopting the reasoning of Cromwell JA (as he then was) from the Nova Scotia Court of Appeal decision in the case, which looked to a standard of general occupancy previously argued for by Kent McNeil, although many property scholars consider that standard of general occupancy to be extremely difficult to apply in any predictable way).

48 See, e.g., Asha Kaushal, chap 7 in this volume.

limit" on Aboriginal title based on the form of cultural attachment supporting the title claim,[49] *Tsilhqot'in* describes inherent limits on the scope of Aboriginal title based on the inherently collective nature of the ownership it is said to embody. The Court suggests that Aboriginal title is held not only for the present generation but also for future generations and, therefore, that Aboriginal-title lands cannot be used in ways that diminish their value for future generations.[50] This unique limit on the use of particular lands, of Aboriginal-title lands, poses some interpretive challenges and some practical challenges.[51]

The questions that arise include, first, whether this articulation of the inherent limit on the use of Aboriginal-title lands replaces, interprets, and/or supplements the inherent limit in *Delgamuukw*. The Court in *Tsilhqot'in* seemingly could not be bothered to say, with one passage perhaps suggesting that the *Tsilhqot'in* articulation is a specification of the *Delgamuukw* specification but with no real clarity on the point.[52] Second, a further question arises of what this newly articulated limit

---

49 *Delgamuukw, supra* note 33, paras 111, 125–8.

50 See *Tsilhqot'in, supra* note 35, para 15 ("it is group title and cannot be alienated in a way that deprives future generations of the control and benefit of the land"); para 74 ("Aboriginal title, however, comes with an important restriction – it is collective title held not only for the present generation but for all succeeding generations. This means it cannot be alienated except to the Crown or encumbered in ways that would prevent future generations of the group from using and enjoying it. Nor can the land be developed or misused in a way that would substantially deprive future generations of the benefit of the land. Some changes – even permanent changes – to the land may be possible. Whether a particular use is irreconcilable with the ability of succeeding generations to benefit from the land will be a matter to be determined when the issue arises"); and para 88 ("Aboriginal title confers on the group that holds it the exclusive right to decide how the land is used and the right to benefit from those uses, subject to one carve-out – that the uses must be consistent with the group nature of the interest and the enjoyment of the land by future generations").

51 See also my discussion in Dwight Newman, "Indigenous Title and Its Contextual Economic Implications: Lessons for International Law from Canada's Tsilhqot'in Decision," *American Journal of International Law Unbound* 109 (2015) 215; and Dwight Newman, "The Economic Characteristics of Indigenous Property Rights," *Nebraska Law Review* 95 (2016). On appropriate approaches to collective rights generally, see Dwight Newman, *Community and Collective Rights: A Theoretical Framework for Rights Held by Groups* (Oxford: Hart / Bloomsbury, 2011).

52 See *Tsilhqot'in, supra* note 35, para 15: "Negatively, the 'protected uses must not be irreconcilable with the nature of the group's attachment to that land' (*Ibid* [citing here to *Delgamuukw*]) – that is, it is group title and cannot be alienated in a way that deprives future generations of the control and benefit of the land."

actually means and when and how it could be invoked to challenge a particular use of Aboriginal-title lands. In the context of an Aboriginal community that chooses to pursue a particular resource development project, the question arises whether a dissenting part of the community has standing to raise the claims of future generations as well as whether outside environmental non-governmental organizations do.[53] Third, in the context of a particular use of the land, there is the question what types of uses are considered to take away from its usefulness to future generations. So far, we have the unhelpful guidance that "[w]hether a particular use is irreconcilable with the ability of succeeding generations to benefit from the land will be a matter to be determined when the issue arises."[54]

Here, too, the Court is arguably wrestling with an awkward reality that its concepts in this context are caught in some degree of uncertainty, perhaps precisely because they arise from some very challenging attempts to make sense of the establishment of a new state within territories subject to prior land claims. The philosophical examination of the implications remains underdeveloped in the broader literatures as well,[55] and the Court is left trying to wring out some kind of inter-societal doctrine that can satisfy different parties.[56]

In doing so, it may well not want to make definitive conclusions, and there has been strong evidence in its judgments that it considers itself institutionally not well suited to some of the determinations that need to be made. In the powerful, if somewhat textually peculiar, closing

---

53 See our discussion in Coates and Newman, *supra* note 36. See also Newman, "Indigenous Title and Its Contextual Economic Implications," *supra* note 51.

54 *Tsilhqot'in*, *supra* note 35, para 74.

55 Consider Chief Justice Lamer's expression of the point in *Van der Peet* that Aboriginal rights arise from different sources than rights as analysed within the liberal enlightenment: *Van der Peet*, *supra* note 40, paras 18–19. We may not yet have the full texture of the theory under which Aboriginal rights are to be analysed.

56 The conception of s 35 Aboriginal-rights law in Canada as an inter-societal body of law owes much to the classic article by Brian Slattery, "Understanding Aboriginal Rights," *Canadian Bar Review* 66 (1987) 787. There are significant comparisons to be made between Slattery's approach and Vitoria's natural law approach to the interaction of European settler communities and Indigenous communities; the latter is discussed in Sujith Xavier, chap 10 in this volume. However, Xavier's intriguing argument that the patterns of natural law reasoning applied to these interactions inherently override the dynamic of difference with universalized European values may well underplay the consonance of natural law reasoning with many Indigenous approaches to law, with many further questions to be pursued on these issues.

words of *Delgamuukw*, Chief Justice Lamer expressed this point: "Ultimately, it is through negotiated settlements, with good faith and give and take on all sides, reinforced by the judgments of this Court, that we will achieve ... 'the reconciliation of the pre-existence of aboriginal societies with the sovereignty of the Crown'. Let us face it, we are all here to stay."[57] The expressed preference that some of the issues be negotiated by other parties is a recurrent theme and speaks to a mixture of theoretical and institutional challenges. In a culturally and commercially sensitive area, the Court has explicitly suggested that political actors might better make some of the decisions through negotiation.

In his chapter in this volume, David Milward rightly emphasizes that same point in the context of other facets of s. 35 Aboriginal-rights case law than those I am principally considering, going on to argue that the refusal to engage with some questions has a tendency to favour the social status quo.[58] That will be particularly the case in effect where rigid tests apply that attempt to constrain Aboriginal rights, but that effect, arguably, is not sufficient reason to attribute intent to the Court. I find the Court's approach in this area simply less coherent than that theory as some of the ways it has acted have forced significant changes on Canada and even on Indigenous communities themselves.

At the same time that it writes about preferring political negotiation, the Court has nonetheless chosen to make some relatively definitive decisions in this same context, arguably based on its own imagery – and perhaps stereotyping – of Indigenous communities. Notably, even in cases where the Aboriginal communities involved have put claims to fee simple and in cases where Aboriginal communities have introduced evidence of past private Indigenous ownership structures over particular tracts of land, the Supreme Court of Canada has instead chosen to elaborate a doctrine of Aboriginal title that says it is inherently collective.[59] The Court seemingly locks Indigenous communities into a particular image of their landholding practices, even when the culturally traditional practices vary across different communities.[60] Thus, s. 35 has unique constitutional effects on property.

---

57 Delgamuukw, *supra* note 33, para 186, citing *Van der Peet, supra* note 40, para 31.

58 David Milward, chap 9 in this volume.

59 See *Tsilhqot'in, supra* note 35, paras 15, 74, and 88.

60 See discussion in Newman, "Aboriginal Rights, Collective Rights, and Adjudicative Virtues," *supra* note 45.

Property rights entrenched in s. 35 have a further reach than may first be apparent, in several different ways. First, significant areas of the country – not just British Columbia – are subject to existing title claims based on an absence of treaties with surrender clauses, either because of an absence of treaties or the presence of treaties without surrender clauses, both in general and with specific communities. Second, to the extent that treaties may nonetheless seem to resolve title claims in many parts of the country, Indigenous activism will likely call those treaties and their effects into question as it becomes apparent that those communities that settled under historical treaties are now in meaningfully less favourable positions than communities that did not. Thus, in the historical treaty areas of the Prairies, not only have arguments been increasingly raised that the treaties surrendered land only to the "depth of a plough,"[61] but some Indigenous leaders have also begun floating arguments to nullify the effects of the treaties generally, despite a traditionally very strong attachment to them. Given such strong attachment, one may be doubtful that a strategic approach challenging them will prevail among Indigenous polities, but there will at least be arguments for reading them in significantly revised ways, which will be affected by the position of other communities outside treaty areas. That said, the context of treaties is immensely complicated, particularly when many of the historical treaties were entered into by parties with vastly differing world views and perspectives.[62]

Apart from these aspects related to the reach of s. 35 property rights, though, consider that property rights under s. 35 may affect the use of lands that are outside the scope of Aboriginal-title lands. First, the duty to consult doctrine, as judicially developed since 2005, establishes some rights in relation to government action that affects claimed lands,

---

61 See, e.g., Federation of Saskatchewan Indian Nations Executive Communiqué, 9 March 2012 (and thus stating, in this particular use of it, that wildlife and fish are still owned by First Nations, although the subsurface implications are obviously the even larger issue).

62 For an important recent discussion of these historical considerations, see D.J. Hall, *From Treaties to Reserves: The Federal Government and Native Peoples in Territorial Alberta, 1870–1905* (Montreal and Kingston: McGill-Queen's University Press, 2016). Hall's work notably renders more complex some of the standard historical conceptions that continue to affect much legal scholarship (including, in the present volume, the piece by Xavier, *supra* note 56).

including where uncertainty remains about the fate of those claims.[63] To some degree, possibly contrary to its purposes, this doctrine actually creates incentives on the part of Indigenous leaders not to settle issues and even not to talk to government representatives. Consultation applies to a wider scope of territory than will ultimately be subject to title, and communities that may hold a right to be consulted in relation to activities on particular lands will often fare best by negotiating directly with third party stakeholders rather than governments.[64]

Second, some recent cases have raised the possibility that Aboriginal communities may be able to pursue litigation, such as claims in the tort of nuisance, against private landholders whose use of their lands in the vicinity of lands claimed under Aboriginal title could affect the claimed lands, even where there are uncertainties about the fate of the title claims.[65] The management of interim uncertainty that the duty to consult was initially to fulfil has become more and more complex and may have the effect of incentivizing ongoing maintenance of a type of constitutionally entrenched uncertainty.

Although the premiers obviously agreed to s. 35 knowing that it would imply some possibility of Aboriginal-title claims, it is far from clear that they intended to agree to such unclear property rights or to constitutionally entrenched uncertainties. Section 35 obviously responded to certain types of legitimacy deficits in the Canadian constitutional order that Indigenous activism had highlighted. But it has created new challenges to the certainty and predictability of the Canadian constitutional order. In the context of resource development that is of national strategic significance, Irvin Studin has also recently commented that the s. 35 framework is one of the key challenges in Canadian constitutionalism to the state being able to pursue certain types of strategic policy.[66] This point brings us to questions of the

63 See *Haida Nation v British Columbia (Minister of Forests)*, [2004] 3 SCR 511, 2004 SCC 73; Dwight Newman, *The Duty to Consult: New Relationships with Aboriginal Peoples* (Saskatoon: Purich, 2009); Dwight Newman, *Revisiting the Duty to Consult Aboriginal Peoples* (Saskatoon: Purich, 2014).

64 Newman, *Revisiting the Duty to Consult*, *supra* note 63.

65 See, especially, *Saik'uz First Nation v Rio Tinto Alcan Inc.*, 2015 BCCA 154, leave to appeal to SCC denied.

66 Studin, *supra* note 1; see also Irvin Studin, "Reflections on the Aboriginal Question," *GlobalBrief* (24 March 2014); and Irvin Studin, "Confronting the Aboriginal Question," *National Post* (19 August 2015).

interface between constitutionally entrenched public property rights, which would appear to be reasonably clear facets, and constitutionally entrenched Indigenous property rights, which would appear to have relatively unclear facets.

Tensions between Public Property Rights and Indigenous Property Rights

That said, the Court's approach to the main test for Aboriginal title is still relatively precedent-oriented compared to its engagement with precedent on provincial powers to justifiably infringe on Aboriginal title and treaty rights. The latter subject of treaty rights came to the fore just weeks after the *Tsilhqot'in* judgment, in the Court's decision in the *Grassy Narrows*, or *Keewatin*, case.[67] There, aside from resolving the somewhat particular treaty-interpretation question that arose from specific features of Treaty 3 and early boundary alterations in northwestern Ontario, the Court chose to comment on provincial powers to regulate in ways that justifiably infringe on treaty rights. It did so by applying the *Tsilhqot'in* case concerning Aboriginal title to the treaty-rights context to say that provinces may justifiably infringe on treaty rights, just as they may justifiably infringe on Aboriginal title.[68] It did so even in the face of a prior treaty-rights case on point, the *Morris* decision,[69] that it simply chose not to mention in the judgment, thus overturning by sleight of hand what seemed to be a reasonably applicable precedent in favour of the wider application of the *Tsilhqot'in* rule. That decision is arguably quite practical in some respects, and it preserves provincial rights, but it was again not explained by the Court, resulting in meaningful uncertainty about the interaction between provincial public property rights and Indigenous property rights.

In principle, provinces can justifiably infringe on Indigenous property rights when they meet the justified infringement test. This test includes both a proportionality-style test and further requirements, including requirements related to consultation and to a fiduciary-duty

67 *Grassy Narrows First Nation v Ontario (Minister of Natural Resources)*, 2014 SCC 48.

68 *Ibid*, para 53, citing *Tsilhqot'in*, *supra* note 35.

69 *R v Morris*, 2006 SCC 59, [2006] 2 SCR 915.

branch of the test.[70] To this point, the justified infringement tests have been seldom applied or litigated; thus, there is very little case law that interprets the test. As a result, significant legal uncertainties remain about whether the infringement test would be met in particular circumstances.

The Court has not chosen to promote a great deal of clarity on potential interactions between governmental decisions on resource development and entrenched Indigenous property interests. Indeed, in *Tsilhqot'in*, the Court writes as follows:

> Once title is established, it may be necessary for the Crown to reassess prior conduct in light of the new reality in order to faithfully discharge its fiduciary duty to the title-holding group going forward. For example, if the Crown begins a project without consent prior to Aboriginal title being established, it may be required to cancel the project upon establishment of the title if continuation of the project would be unjustifiably infringing. Similarly, if legislation was validly enacted before title was established, such legislation may be rendered inapplicable going forward to the extent that it unjustifiably infringes Aboriginal title.[71]

The passage illustrates the very real possibility of tensions arising between public property rights and Indigenous property rights, signalling that Indigenous property rights could trump public property rights and that very significant remedies could result. The challenge, of course, is that the possibility of such issues arising in future creates a significant degree of uncertainty today. This uncertainty might result in major problems for strategic choices about natural resource development, thereby raising a further complication about the stability-related issues at stake.

At the same time, there is a delicate balance at issue. In making Indigenous property rights meaningful, the Court is, of course, also trying to seek legitimacy for the constitution with Indigenous communities,

---

70 This was first enunciated in *R v Sparrow*, [1990] 1 SCR 1075. On its similarity to *Oakes* and broader proportionality analyses, see Dwight Newman, "The Limitation of Rights: A Comparative Evolution and Ideology of the Oakes and Sparrow Tests," *Saskatchewan Law Review* 62 (1999) 543; Dwight Newman, "Proportionality Analysis: 5½ Myths," *Supreme Court Law Review* 73 (2016) 93.

71 *Tsilhqot'in*, *supra* note 35, para 92.

which would rightfully feel alienated from it were their claims to be ignored or rendered meaningless. The sheer degree of uncertainty, itself problematic in further ways, probably speaks to the Court's own uncertainty as it muddles through some immensely challenging questions. But the potential tensions here are not even the limit of what could be at issue, for another issue being raised as a result of the new Aboriginal-title jurisprudence is the standing of past provincial grants of title to private landholders.

Private Property Rights and Constitutional Instability

The *Tsilhqot'in* judgment, in some respects, does not clarify whether there can be an Aboriginal-title claim against private property. Although there is lower court precedent against such a claim, notably the 2000 Ontario Court of Appeal decision in the *Chippewas of Sarnia* case,[72] some commentators have suggested that the *Tsilhqot'in* judgment itself, in the way it describes the nature of Aboriginal title, in fact implicitly suggests that such title clams would be possible. This is the view, for instance, of John Borrows.[73] And in British Columbia, some Aboriginal-side law firms have been openly publishing articles in which they express the view that there are now Aboriginal-title claims to be put against private property in that province, even if the claims are likely to be resolved through compensation rather than restitution.[74]

In November 2014, the Cowichan First Nation gave notice of an Aboriginal-title claim against Grace Islet, a small knoll in Ganges Harbour, off Salt Spring Island. The First Nation's reason for doing so related to the private landowner's intention to build on a burial site, and the province decided to resolve matters through a purchase of the islet from the landowner and assured the First Nation that it would offer protection to the burial site.[75] But other such claims will be put. In June 2015, two

72 *Chippewas of Sarnia Band v. Canada (Attorney General)* (2000), 195 DLR (4th) 135 (Ont CA).

73 John Borrows, "Aboriginal Title and Private Property," *Supreme Court Law Review* 71 (2015) 91.

74 For just one example, see Rob Miller, "Impacts of Tsilhqot'in Part VI: Effect of Aboriginal Title on Private Property," *MT&Co.* [Miller Titerle] (blog), 3 November 2014.

75 See Wendy Stueck, "British Columbia Pays $5.45 Million for Grace Islet," *Globe and Mail*, 16 February 2015 (noting that the agreement involved was the twelfth time in recent decades that the province had bought land to settle a claim related to what the law considered archeological objects).

Shuswap First Nations declared their claims of Aboriginal title to the proposed Ajax mine site near Kamloops.[76] Environmental assessment processes led to a decision against the project, but the presence of an Aboriginal-title claim added a further legal question and uncertainty for the mining company that was attempting to pursue resource development in the region. And in November 2016, an Aboriginal-title claim was filed to a third of the province of New Brunswick, including areas of private property.

The question that the *Tsilhqot'in* case does not explicitly resolve is what will happen with such claims. Because the claimants strategically carved out of their claim area all privately owned lands, the Court did not adjudicate on this issue. On Borrows's argument, the Court's emphasis on Aboriginal title as a pre-existing legal burden on land that the Crown had acquired with the assertion of sovereignty fit with the argument that any Crown issuance of fee-simple title in areas subject to Aboriginal title was subject to a pre-existing legal claim.

There are, though, reasons not to accept Borrows's argument. The Court's decision, that not only the federal government but also provincial governments may infringe and limit Aboriginal rights, is very significant here. In the trial judgment by Justice *Vickers*,[77] there was a real possibility that the decision precluded a historical provincial extinguishment of Aboriginal title because it suggested that provincial legislation could not impact on Aboriginal landholding – something that was remarked upon by various law firms at the time and that seemed to fit with past statements in *Delgamuukw*. But the Supreme Court's decision says that provinces may regulate Aboriginal-title land and may justifiably infringe Aboriginal title and that these steps cannot be precluded by the doctrine of inter-jurisdictional immunity because the constitution does not contain gaps in matters that neither the federal government nor provincial governments can regulate.

The Court in *Delgamuukw* had suggested that the provinces were unable to extinguish Aboriginal title because such extinguishment needed a particularly clear legislative intent and legislation with a specific intent related to Aboriginal land could not fall within provincial jurisdiction. However, grants of fee simple in British Columbia would not have been

76 The claim was made by the Skeetchestn and Tk'emls te Secwépemc; the KGHM mining company had planned to develop the Ajax mine.

77 *Tsilhqot'in Nation v. British Columbia*, 2007 BCSC 1700.

in federal jurisdiction, either. Thus, the historical approach leads to the sort of legislative vacuum that *Tsilhqot'in* made clear was to be avoided. My view is that *Tsilhqot'in* implicitly suggests that provinces could have permissibly extinguished Aboriginal title before 1982, but past grants of fee-simple interests must now meet the Canadian legal test for extinguishment. However, this is a legal battle that remains to be fought, and there will be serious consequences for Canada, not only from the ultimate result but also from the uncertainty in the meantime.

Again, elements of uncertainty and of issues about Canada's legitimation of its strategic activities arise in the context of interaction between different categories of property rights under the constitution, again raising questions about stability. Further legitimacy questions might arise over time, depending on whether the broader public sees the constitution as ideologically legitimate in entrenching Indigenous property rights, with significant effects on Canada, while not entrenching private property rights that play a significant role in Canadian liberty and Canadian economic development. There are significant reasons to see how property is and is not entrenched in the Canadian constitution might give rise to significant future instability.

Conclusion: Instability Arising

On the criteria, discussed earlier, for the ways in which a constitution can promote more stable equilibrium, the unpredictable ways in which Canada's constitution interacts with property could raise major issues in the decades ahead; this is particularly true in light of the substantial judicial power that has arisen to make very different decisions than those traditionally within the institutional role of the judiciary. Depending on how the courts manage this area of constitutional decision making, and depending on legislative action related to private property, one can foresee situations in which meaningful forces arise in favour of constitutional amendment to restabilize features of the political order in this area.

My argument here has been deliberately focused on property. That s. 35 may bear on jurisdiction and offer arguments for Aboriginal self-government – as referenced in the chapters by Asha Kaushal[78] and by David Milward[79] – presents its own issues for stability that are worthy

78 Kaushal, *supra* note 48.
79 Milward, *supra* note 58.

of extended development. Clarity of jurisdiction can also affect stability, although there are complex things to be said about the nature of stability in a state with a large number of governments. For present purposes, the focus on property raises enough issues and highlights an area where developing judicial approaches raise real prospects of stability challenges down the road.

The present scope of argument does not provide a complete analysis of the probability of constitutional amendment arising from these issues. Major obstacles stand in the way of constitutional amendment in Canada in light of the rigid amending formula.[80] At the same time, the bilateral amending formula offers possible mechanisms for flexibility that allow changes in specific provinces. These mechanisms have already been under political discussion in the context of private property rights.[81] Interestingly, they were actually the subject of discussions by the framers in the context of Indigenous property rights.[82]

If matters related to property develop in a manner that threatens stability, there might well be possibilities in the decades ahead for the bilateral amending formula to serve as an escape hatch from that instability by providing the necessary measure of flexibility in the constitution. At the same time, that possibility of responsive constitutional amendment might motivate both the judicial and the legislative branches to advance prudent approaches to property rights that avoid those issues arising. Property under the Canadian constitution raises some tremendously significant issues, and it might be a source of future pressures, or it might continue to be an example of the rich ways in which Canadian constitutionalism can manage complex issues in prudent ways that avoid more serious conflict.

---

80 See, generally, Macfarlane, *supra* note 19.

81 See Dwight Newman, "The Bilateral Amending Formula as a Mechanism for the Entrenchment of Property Rights," *Constitutional Forum* 21 (2013) 17; Dwight Newman, "Understanding the Section 43 Bilateral Amending Formula," in Macfarlane, *supra* note 19.

82 See Newman, "Aboriginal Rights, Collective Rights, and Adjudicative Virtues," *supra* note 45; Newman, "Understanding the Section 43 Bilateral Amending Formula," *supra* note 79.

12 A Role for Human Dignity under the *Canadian Charter of Rights and Freedoms*

EMILY KIDD WHITE*

Introduction

Since the adoption of the Universal Declaration of Human Rights in 1948,[1] the concept of human dignity has assumed an important place in rights jurisprudence.[2] The Universal Declaration of Human Rights places the concept of human dignity at the foundation of its rights regime, as do both international covenants and a number of domestic constitutions.[3] While the concept does not appear in the *Canadian Charter of Rights and Freedoms*,[4] the Supreme Court of Canada has nevertheless declared that courts must be guided by "respect for the inherent dignity of the human person" as a value essential to a free and democratic society.[5] The concept has been said to reveal "the moral

---

* Assistant professor, Osgoode Hall Law School. The author would like to thank Jeremy Waldron and Christopher McCrudden for discussions on the paper's subject; Richard Albert, Paul Daly, and Vanessa MacDonnell for convening the conference "Canada at 150: New Frontiers in Constitutional Law"; and Howard Kislowicz, Asha Kaushal, Vrinda Narain, and Sujith Xavier for helpful comments.

1 "The Universal Declaration on Human Rights," in *Basic Documents on Human Rights*, ed. Ian Brownlie (Oxford: Oxford University Press, 1994), 21.

2 David Kretzmer and Eckart Klein, eds., *The Concept of Human Dignity in Human Rights Discourse* (The Hague: Kluwer Law International, 2002).

3 The preamble of the Universal Declaration of Human Rights of 10 December 1948 provides, "Whereas recognition of the inherent dignity and of the equal and inalienable rights of all members of the human family ..."

4 Part I of the Constitution Act, 1982, being Schedule B to the Canada Act 1982 (UK), 1982, c 11 [*Charter*].

5 Dickson CJ in *R v Oakes*, [1986] 1 SCR 103, 136. Also cited in *R v Kapp*, [2008] 2 SCR 483, 2008 SCC 41, para 21 [*Kapp*].

infrastructure of the *Charter*, supporting and welding together [its] various freedoms, rights, and obligations."[6] As the Supreme Court has held, all the rights guaranteed by the *Charter* have as their "lodestar the promotion of human dignity."[7]

The Supreme Court has delivered several similarly striking statements concerning the value of human dignity in *Charter* adjudication.[8] Yet precisely what it demands in the interpretation of rights remains a puzzle. Comparative constitutional law scholars have documented wide variation in judicial interpretations of dignity as well as in the case outcomes that engage extensively with the concept.[9] Such variation is also a feature of the Canadian *Charter* jurisprudence.[10] This may be unsurprising. The concept of human dignity has been said to draw from disparate philosophical frameworks, religious ideals, and political histories, spurring vigorous debate along varying lines in the literature.[11] And facets of these contests are analysable in judicial interpretations of the legal concept of human dignity as they emerge alongside a distinctive set of legal debates concerning the nature of evaluative legal concepts and the practices of constitutional interpretation and judicial review.

In light of this variation and contest, focus has been overwhelmingly placed on the difficulty of defining *dignity*, obscuring a number of analysable functions that the concept fulfils in the adjudication of constitutional rights.[12] Addressing this gap, this chapter focuses exclusively on function. In doing so, it develops a theme, noted in the introductory chapter in this volume and interwoven throughout, concerning

---

6 Lorne Sossin, "The 'Supremacy of God', Human Dignity and the Charter of Rights and Freedoms," *University of New Brunswick Law Journal* 52 (2003) 227, 228.

7 *Kapp*, *supra* note 5, para 21.

8 *Law v Canada (Minister of Employment and Immigration)*, [1999] 1 SCR 497; see paras 47–58.

9 Christopher McCrudden, "Human Dignity and Judicial Interpretation of Human Rights," *European Journal of International Law* 19, no. 4 (2008) 655; Erin Daly, *Dignity Rights: Courts, Constitutions, and the Worth of the Human Person* (Philadelphia: University of Pennsylvania Press, 2013).

10 R. James Fyfe, "Dignity as Theory: Competing Conceptions of Human Dignity at the Supreme Court of Canada," *Saskatchewan Law Review* 70 (2007) 1.

11 Christopher McCrudden, ed., introduction to *Understanding Human Dignity*, Proceedings from the British Academy (Oxford: Oxford University Press, 2013).

12 A notable exception is McCrudden, *supra* note 9, which sets out a number of functions that the concept of human dignity has fulfilled in rights adjudication.

the relationship between symbolism and constitutional change.[13] Its contribution is its focus on the role that a specific *Charter* value, itself a symbol, might play in this change dynamic, arguing that the *Charter* value of human dignity can work to establish a broad sensitivity to certain status-based diminutions that occur under the various headings of *Charter* rights.

The chapter sets out three functional features of human dignity as a *Charter* value, with each reliant to a certain extent on the concept's well-documented breadth. For reasons of scope, the paper focuses on the role that human dignity plays as a value in the s. 7 and s. 15 jurisprudence. The three functional features of the *Charter* value of human dignity are that it (1) invites context-sensitive interpretations of rights, (2) resists concrete and criterial definition, and (3) generates contest in the adjudication of *Charter* rights. At times, the paper draws on the comparative jurisprudence of dignity to offer clarity to the account of role on offer. While the chapter's aim is not to defend the *Charter* value of human dignity, nor to suggest that it is sufficient to remedy long-standing indifferences to certain forms of rights violations (economic, for example), this functional analysis illustrates the manner in which a number of consistently raised criticisms lack bite as well as a set of reasons why we should expect the value of human dignity to remain a recurring influence in the adjudication of *Charter* rights.

Human Dignity as a Charter Value

The Backlash over Breadth

A concrete definition of what human dignity demands in the interpretation of rights remains elusive.[14] Across a number of jurisdictions, scholars, practitioners, and jurists have called into question the concept's distinctiveness, utility, and politics.[15] For some, the lack of consensus

---

13 See Richard Albert, Paul Daly, and Vanessa MacDonnell, Introduction to this volume.

14 McCrudden, *supra* note 9; Daly, *supra* note 9.

15 Conor O'Mahony, "There Is No Such Thing as a Right to Human Dignity," *International Journal of Constitutional Law* (2012) 551; McCrudden, *supra* note 9. For example, some have suggested that some conceptions of human dignity are inextricably tied to certain religious understandings that appear to limit rights.

surrounding the concept provides a strong reason for its expulsion from rights jurisprudence.[16]

For others, fluctuations in the concept's juridical use renders it inherently ambiguous,[17] invoked only for the purpose of lending weight to one's political or ethical ideals. Unsettled by the fact that dignity considerations often appear on both sides of a contentious legal debate, some scholars dismiss the term's utility, claiming that it reflects only a given speaker's individual values. A less critical interpretation is that dignity is simply a synonym for other moral principles, such as equality or autonomy.[18]

Many of these broader concerns are reflected in Canadian debates over the meaning of human dignity as a *Charter* value, and concerns are present as to whether dignity offers any analytical or normative purchase in the jurisprudence or whether it, in fact, serves to establish unacceptable limits on existing rights. Precisely what the language of dignity brings to the law, over and above the language of human rights, remains a puzzle. Certain courts have expressed scepticism, including our own Supreme Court, which in 2008 signalled that it intended to stop using dignity as a legal test to reason through discrimination claims under the *Charter,* finding human dignity "an abstract and subjective" notion that proved confusing and difficult to apply, and resulted in additional burdens for rights claimants.[19] It was in *Kapp*[20] that the Supreme Court cited R. James Fyfe, who wrote that the Supreme Court's use of dignity in *Charter* cases "reveals the Court's failure to develop a coherent approach to, or understanding of, dignity. Its use is muddled and inconsistent."[21]

Broad but Not Shapeless

The *Charter* value of human dignity is broad but not shapeless. Some preliminary distinctions clear ground. First, human dignity is

---

16 In the absence of fixed content, the charge runs, the concept of human dignity can be of little use in guiding a court towards the correct reading of a rights case. See, e.g., Fyfe, *supra* note 10; O'Mahony, *supra* note 15.

17 Fyfe, *supra* note 10.

18 Aurel Kolnai, "Dignity," *Philosophy* 51, no. 197 (1976) 252.

19 *Kapp, supra* note 5, paras 19–21. See also *Vilven v Air Canada,* 2009 FC 367, [2010] 2 FCR 189.

20 *Kapp, supra* note 5.

21 Fyfe, *supra* note 10, 2.

frequently listed as a value in the *Charter* jurisprudence without much further use, explication, or argument. The chapter cabins these plainly rhetorical uses. Second, not all references to dignity in *Charter* rights adjudication are references to human dignity, our concept of interest. The explicit or intended pronoun, *human*, matters.[22] This sets aside corporate conceptions of dignity, which would include, for example, the Supreme Court's statements on the dignity of the judicial office in *Yukon Francophone School Board, Education Area #23 v Yukon (Attorney General)*.[23] It also sets aside those references to dignity that refer to personal reputation.[24]

The legal value of human dignity is intended to support a broad and purposive read of the *Charter* rights guarantees. It denotes an orientation of concern and respect towards all human life and establishes a sensitivity to certain status-based diminutions that occur under various rights headings.[25] Justice Iacobucci in *Law* held, "Human dignity is harmed when individuals and groups are marginalized, ignored, or devalued, and is enhanced when laws recognize the full place of all individuals and groups within Canadian society."[26] When legal actors, or subjects, invoke the concept of human dignity, they have in mind what can be construed broadly as an idea about the uniqueness and value of human life, juxtaposed against an idea of how law might infringe upon that value.[27] They are working with a normative picture of what a human life is and what it deserves with respect to the law or, rather, what it demands of law. As Jeremy Waldron writes, "we may say of 'dignity' that the term is used to convey something

---

22 ALMÁSY: "A thing is still a thing no matter what you place in front of it. Big car, slow car, chauffeur-driven car, still a car ..."
KATHARINE: "Love? Romantic love, platonic love, filial love? Quite different things, surely?"
ALMÁSY: "There you have me."
Michael Ondaatje, *The English Patient*

23 2015 SCC 25, para 36.

24 *Blencoe v British Columbia (Human Rights Commission)*, [2000] 2 SCR 307, para 80 on the difference between reputation and the *Charter* value of human dignity.

25 John Rawls has written about the sense of justice in a similar vein; see John Rawls, "The Sense of Justice," *Philosophical Review* 3 (1963) 72.

26 *Law v Canada (Minister of Employment and Immigration)*, *supra* note 8, para 53.

27 Emily Kidd White, "There Is No Such Thing as a Right to Human Dignity: A Reply to Conor O'Mahony," *International Journal of Constitutional Law* (2012) 575.

about the status of human beings and that it is also and concomitantly used to convey the demand that the status should actually be respected."[28]

As Christopher McCrudden writes, although debates abound over the content and history of the concept of human dignity and its role in judicial reasoning, all well-working legal invocations of the concept appear to exhibit a minimum core that "every human being possesses an intrinsic worth, merely by being human ... that this intrinsic worth should be recognized and respected by others, and that some forms of treatment by others are inconsistent with, or required by, respect for this intrinsic worth ... [and that] recognizing the intrinsic worth of the individual requires that the state should be seen to exist for the sake of the individual human being, and not vice versa."[29] This translates into the Canadian context, where Denise Réaume suggests that the *Charter* value of human dignity "is bound up with our attribution of inherent worth to human beings. To ascribe dignity to human beings as a moral matter is to treat human beings as creatures of intrinsic, incomparable, and indelible worth, simply as human beings."[30]

One common thread running through these definitions is that the legal concept of human dignity protects against state action and legislation that treats a human being as less than a human being. The *Charter* value of human dignity is a legal value concerned with political and normative recognition.[31] It signifies a legal commitment to seeing every human life as equal in a deep sense, in the sense of kind or status. The legal value of human dignity offers a form of an argument for the adjudication of *Charter* rights, one that various legal actors will fill out in a myriad of different ways.

---

28 Jeremy Waldron, "Lecture I: Dignity and Rank" (Dignity, Rank, and Rights: The Tanner Lectures at UC Berkeley, April 2009), 3.

29 McCrudden, *supra* note 9, 679–80.

30 Denise Réaume, "Dignity, Choice and Circumstances," in *Understanding Human Dignity*, ed. Christopher McCrudden, Proceedings from the British Academy (Oxford: Oxford University Press, 2013).

31 G.A. Cohen, writing about equality, says something similar about this kind of political and normative recognition: "egalitarians believe not that people's (descriptive) merits are equal, but that people merit equal regard even though their descriptive merits are unequal"; see G.A. Cohen, *Finding Oneself in the Other* (Princeton: Princeton University Press, 2013).

Three Functional Features of the Charter Value of Human Dignity

Interpretations of Human Dignity Are Context-Sensitive

The legal value of human dignity is inchoate, and it generates content through its use in rights adjudication. Its breadth enables judges to interpret rights in ways that that are sensitive to context.[32] This can occur at three levels: at the level of the political community,[33] at the level of the right in question, and, once more, in accordance with the facts and the framing of a particular case.

CONTEXT-SENSITIVITY AT THE LEVEL OF THE POLITICAL COMMUNITY

Dignity, for Christopher McCrudden, "in the judicial context, not only permits the incorporation of local contingencies in the interpretation of human rights norms; it requires it. Dignity allows each jurisdiction to develop its own practice of human rights."[34] Herein lie many of the limits and much of the potential concerning its use. Constitutional courts interpreting the concept of human dignity take into consideration content that is both internal (the constitutional or human rights regime of a specific political community) and external (that political community's historical and social background that led to the recognition of dignity) to the law.[35] Responding to this dynamic, Erin Daly suggests that we should be wary of "lumping together the meanings of dignity that have evolved in dramatically divergent social, historical, and jurisprudential contexts."[36]

While the charge in the literature is often that the concept is irredeemably vague or inchoate, comparative studies on dignity jurisprudence "reveal that courts interpreting the concept of dignity and applying it to concrete factual situations have developed a sense of the concept that is coherent and substantive, and not merely a product of each judge's

---

32 McCrudden, *supra* note 9.

33 Paolo Carozza, "Human Dignity and Judicial Interpretation of Human Rights: A Reply," *European Journal of International Law* 19, no. 5 (2008) 931.

34 McCrudden, *supra* note 9, 720.

35 Aharon Barak, "Human Dignity: The Constitutional Value and the Constitutional Right," in *Understanding Human Dignity*, ed. Christopher McCrudden, Proceedings from the British Academy (Oxford: Oxford University Press, 2013), 361–80.

36 McCrudden, *supra* note 9, 3.

idiosyncratic moral standards."[37] International rights instruments offer thin conceptions of human dignity that require working out at the local or national level.[38] As a matter of empirics, this function is clearly traceable, although the literature is split as to whether the context-sensitivity of human dignity is politically or normatively beneficial.[39] The politics and history embedded in each constitutional system will inevitably inform the interpretation of the dignity value. The breadth of the value provides real interpretative space in the practice of rights adjudication, but its invocation and use will nevertheless hew to the structure of the system and existing interpretations of rights. Political and normative appraisals of the constitutional system will, then, form an essential part of any later assessment of the progressive potential of the value.

CONTEXT-SENSITIVITY AT THE LEVEL OF THE *CHARTER* RIGHT

In *R v Oakes*,[40] the Supreme Court held that human dignity is a value that underlies all *Charter* rights. In *R v Morgentaler*, it found that "human dignity finds expression in almost every right and freedom guaranteed in the Charter."[41] As a *Charter* value, dignity functions as an interpretative device that can extend the purview of existing rights protections to encompass new factual situations where the equal status of an individual or group is called into question. In the context of each right, there will be a different texture to the dignity analysis, including an obligation to engage with the reticulum of legal values, precedents, and legal tests that form part of the analysis associated with that right.[42] James Fyfe has criticized the Supreme Court of Canada for failing to employ

37 *Ibid*, 5.

38 For example, we might think of variations across countries concerning limits to the right of free speech to support the constitutional value of human dignity. One particularly powerful example would be the prohibition by the Austrian Constitutional against holocaust denial (*Verbotsgesetz 1947*, or "*Prohibition Act 1947*"). See also Carozza, *supra* note 33, 932–4.

39 Xavier's contribution to this volume (chap 10) offers a critical lens with which to assess this claim that interpretations of the dignity value are context-sensitive by suggesting the possibility of an underlying, shared logic of colonial law and governance.

40 [1986] 1 SCR 103, 136.

41 [1988] 1 SCR 30.

42 For example, the court has held that "dignity is not the only value underlying s 15. Other values associated with it include freedom and personal autonomy"; see *Quebec (Attorney General) v A, 2013 SCC 5*, [2013] 1 SCR 61, 164.

a principled definition of *dignity* across its *Charter* jurisprudence.[43] The argument misses the mark. The legal value was intended to be worked out with respect to each of the distinctive rights headings. Dignity as an interpretive value will present differently in a s. 7 claim, for example, than it will in a s. 15 claim. Its argumentative form fulfils its function in the context of distinctive rights-based questions.

For instance, the denial of human dignity under s. 7 according to the dissent in *Kindler*[44] (now overturned) concerned questions of physical integrity and infliction of undue pain and suffering in state execution methods, whereas under s. 15, questions about the denial of human dignity often press concerns about social exclusion.[45] Under the equality guarantee in s. 15(1), the value of human dignity "is concerned with the realization of personal autonomy and self-determination." It requires that individuals and groups feel "self-respect and self-worth" under the law[46] and "is concerned with physical and psychological integrity and empowerment."[47] The Supreme Court held in *Law* that "[t]here can be different conceptions of what human dignity means,"[48] finding that the concept was intended to be worked out under each of the various rights headings.

Disparate concerns will be raised under each of the various rights headings, while nevertheless sharing the form of the argument that the governing legal scheme operates to call into question the equal status of persons under the law. There are countless ways that the law might detract from this commitment to equal status, and rights headings as interpreted by the dignity value can serve to pick up some of them. Constitutional values regularly take shape under various rights headings. Arguments are off mark where they aim to undermine the dignity value by pointing to different conceptions of dignity in the jurisprudence.[49]

---

43 Fyfe, *supra* note 10.

44 *Kindler v. Canada (Minister of Justice)*, [1991] 2 SCR 779.

45 *Eaton v Brant County Board of Education*, [1997] 1 SCR 241.

46 *Ibid.*

47 *Ibid.*

48 *Law v Canada (Minister of Employment and Immigration)*, *supra* note 8, para 53.

49 See Jacob Weinrib, *Dimensions of Dignity: The Theory and Practice of Modern Constitutional Law*, Cambridge Studies in Constitutional Law (Cambridge: Cambridge University Press, 2016). His view is that it is not differentiation in the interpretation of dignity that should concern us but rather illiberal interpretations.

CONTEXT-SENSITIVITY AT THE LEVEL OF THE INDIVIDUAL CASE

The legal value of dignity provides a broad platform for the contextual and purposive interpretation of constitutional rights at the level of the individual case as well.[50] The Supreme Court has acknowledged this dynamic. When determining "whether a distinction made on an enumerated or analogous ground is discriminatory, we must examine its context. … In each case, we must ask whether the distinction, viewed in context, treats the subject as less worthy, less imbued with human dignity, on the basis of an enumerated or analogous ground."[51] The s. 15 "analysis involves looking at the circumstances of members of the group and the negative impact of the law on them. The analysis is contextual, not formalistic, grounded in the actual situation of the group and the potential of the impugned law to worsen their situation."[52] In *Law,* Iacobucci J elaborated on the connection between equality and human dignity:

> [T]he purpose of s. 15(1) is to prevent the violation of essential human dignity and freedom through the imposition of disadvantage, stereotyping, or political or social prejudice, and to promote a society in which all persons enjoy equal recognition at law as human beings or as members of Canadian society, equally capable and equally deserving of concern, respect and consideration.[53]

Reflecting on this connection in *Law,* Sophia Moreau suggests that the inchoate value of human dignity assists in the legal recognition of the myriad ways in which differential treatment might violate s. 15's

---

50 The breadth of the legal value of human dignity here might run up against traditional rule-of-law-type concerns regarding predictability, and generality. Macfarlane's contribution in this volume (see chap 2) offers a compelling example of where the Supreme Court's failure to engage in a clear line-drawing exercise resulted in great political uncertainty and helped to precipitate a form of constitutional stasis. This presses a series of related questions concerning whether demands for certainty in law-making might acceptably vary over different areas of constitutional law. See also Newman's contribution to this volume (chap 11) for an illuminating discussion on constitutional instability in the context of public, private, and Indigenous rights to property.

51 *Gosselin v Québec* [2002] SCC 84, para 24, cited also in McCrudden, *supra* note 9, 719.

52 *Quebec (Attorney General) v A, supra* note 42, para 166.

53 *Law v Canada (Minister of Employment and Immigration), supra* note 8, para 51.

commitment to substantive equality.[54] Moreau writes, "there is an advantage in appealing to an ideal as broad and abstract as the idea of human dignity: although this breadth and abstractness do make it more difficult for the ideal to provide concrete guidance, they also leave us better able to recognize the many different ways in which a person can be denied equal treatment and the many sorts of exclusions that can constitute discrimination."[55]

In a separate but related vein, we see that the charge that dignity is vague loses some bite when we consider the great specificity of its use by the parties in particular rights cases. Here *Carter v Canada (Attorney General)*[56] serves as a useful example. It was in *Carter* that the Supreme Court declared the *Criminal Code* provisions pertaining to physician-assisted death to be of no force or effect. The plaintiffs in *Carter* drew upon the concept of dignity to illustrate how the choice to end one's life when suffering a terminal disease empowers individual agency and brings an end to interminable pain. On the other side, a number of disability-advocate groups intervened on behalf of the government's defence of the law. These groups also relied heavily on the concept of dignity, arguing that revoking the ban on euthanasia would send the corrosive social message that a life with significant impairment is not worth living. Regardless of what one might think of the outcome, the case makes clear how the concept of dignity achieves a level of concreteness through the evidence adduced on both sides of the case as the parties describe, through the record, what is important, harmful, or humiliating to them, often in vivid and emotional detail.

The *Charter* value of human dignity denotes a serious interest in lived experiences under the law and a commitment to the careful probing of those evidentiary records that claim that the law has undermined its own commitment to recognizing the equal status of those under its jurisdiction. The concept's breadth enables a context-sensitive

54 Sophia Moreau, "The Promise of Law v. Canada," *University of Toronto Law Journal* 57 (2007) 417.

55 *Ibid*, 417–18. This broadly echoes a concern foregrounded in Narain's contribution to this volume (chap 8). Theoretically framed by critical multiculturalism, critical race feminist theory and postcolonial feminist theory, this chapter explores some of the pernicious consequences that flow from strictly defined legal categories in legal regimes aimed at remedying inequality or discrimination.

56 2015 SCC 5, [2015] 1 SCR 331 [*Carter*].

interpretation at the level of the political community, at the level of the right, and at the level of the individual case.

Interpretations of Human Dignity Are Resistant to Concrete and Criterial Definition

Aharon Barak usefully distinguishes those constitutional orders that establish human dignity as a constitutional right from those that employ human dignity as a constitutional value.[57] A good example of the former is Germany, where violations of the right to dignity are narrowly construed and not subject to proportionality reasoning.[58] There is no free-standing right to human dignity under the Canadian *Charter*;[59] rather, as the Supreme Court reiterated recently in *Kapp*,[60] human dignity is an essential *Charter* value. As a constitutional value, human dignity is broad and largely resistant to concrete and criterial definition.[61] This breadth permits the constitutional value of human dignity to fulfil a variety of functions.[62] For instance, at times it forms the rationale or foundation for a catalogue of rights, and at other times it serves as an interpretative principle for the further explication of particular rights or with respect to the limits placed upon rights in proportionality reasoning.[63]

In this latter role, the value can be dynamic and generative, working to broaden existing understandings of what constitutes a rights violation. As a value concerned with status diminutions, it provides wide ground to argue that an impugned provision devalues, degrades, harms, or marginalizes an individual or group.[64] As George Kateb suggests, "If

57 Barak, *supra* note 35.

58 *Ibid.*

59 "Dignity has never been recognized by this Court as an independent right but has rather been viewed as finding expression in rights, such as equality, privacy or protection from state compulsion"; see *Blencoe v British Columbia (Human Rights Commission), supra* note 24, para 77.

60 *Kapp, supra* note 5.

61 Here the chapter comes into conversation with Newman's contribution to the volume (chap 11). On the subject of constitutional instability, he notes that "the constitution will need to strike a balance between fixed principles and flexibility to respond to changing circumstances." The contribution here is to highlight the role played by the *Charter* value of dignity within this dynamic.

62 McCrudden, *supra* note 9.

63 *Ibid*, 680–1.

64 See, e.g., *Carter, supra* note 56.

we want to think about human dignity we should not remain content with a definition of the term or a short account that fails to acknowledge the idea's difficulty."[65] This is consonant with the broad, purposive, and context-sensitive interpretation of *Charter* rights.[66] When fulfilling this functional role, the *Charter* value of human dignity facilitates a "generous" interpretation of *Charter* rights.[67]

Evaluative legal concepts, like dignity, are purposefully broad, and the task of the judge is to apply them as interpretative guides. As Jeremy Waldron has argued about the interpretation of evaluative terms in legislative schemas, "we should not approach the interpretation of the relevant provisions thinking that [their evaluative character] is some sort of mistake or failure of nerve on the part of the drafters. We should not use the opportunity that interpretation presents to correct or supplant the evaluative character of these terms."[68] Breadth is a regular feature of constitutional values.[69]

One of the functional features of the *Charter* value of human dignity is its responsiveness to context as well as its resistance to concrete and criterial definition. Section 15 provides a good example of this second functional feature at work. Under *Law*, human dignity was presented as a *legal test*, whereby the right to equality guaranteed under s. 15 was violated where the law's adverse distinction had a negative effect on the claimant's human dignity.[70] The analysis had three stages, each aiming at a context-sensitive interpretation of the right:

> At the first stage the claimant must show that the law, program or activity imposes differential treatment between the claimant and others with whom the claimant may fairly claim equality. The second stage requires

65 George Kateb, *Human Dignity* (Cambridge, MA: Belknap Press 2011), ix.

66 In *R v Big M Drug Mart* [1985] 1 SCR 295, Dickson CJ held that the definition of a right should be "a generous rather than a legalistic one, aimed at fulfilling the purpose of the guarantee and securing for individuals the full benefit of the *Charter's* protection" (344), cited in Peter W. Hogg, "Interpreting the Charter of Rights: Generosity and Justification," *Osgoode Hall Law Journal* 28, no. 4 (1990) 817.

67 *Ibid.*

68 Jeremy Waldron, *Torture, Terror, and Trade-Offs: Philosophy for the White House* (Oxford: Oxford University Press, 2010).

69 Ronald Dworkin, *Taking Rights Seriously* (New York: Duckworth Press, 1978).

70 *Quebec (Attorney General) v A, supra* note 42, para 150.

the claimant to demonstrate that this differentiation is based on one or more of the enumerated or analogous grounds. *The third stage requires the claimant to establish that the differentiation amounts to a form of discrimination that has the effect of demeaning the claimant's human dignity.*[71]

The test garnered criticism.[72] Dignity's strength as a *Charter* value (i.e., that it is "capable of recognizing a broad array of different forms of treatment as violations of substantive equality")[73] was its weakness as a legal test (namely, that it "does not give us very detailed guidance on the question of which sorts of treatment violate an individual's dignity, and why").[74] The Court considered human dignity ultimately unamenable to a legal test. Even when guided by detailed contextual factors, it retained an unworkable breadth. In *Kapp*,[75] the Court found the concept to be "an abstract and subjective notion that [was] confusing and difficult to apply,"[76] and, worse still, as a legal test, dignity had proved itself to be an additional burden on equality claimants by issuing a formalism into the s. 15 analysis that was at odds with the established commitment to substantive equality.[77]

In *R v Kapp*[78] and *Withler v Canada (Attorney General)*,[79] the Supreme Court clarified the analytical framework for the s. 15 analysis, finding that "a discriminatory distinction is as a general rule an adverse distinction that perpetuates prejudice or that stereotypes."[80] After *Kapp*[81] and *Withler*,[82] as confirmed in *Quebec (Attorney General) v A*,[83] human dignity remains embedded in the s. 15 jurisprudence not as a legal test but as an underlying constitutional value. Its task is to generate new understandings of how a law might violate the s. 15 equality guarantee through a

71 Established in *Law v Canada (Minister of Employment and Immigration)*, *supra* note 8 (emphasis added).
72 Moreau, *supra* note 54.
73 *Ibid*, 416.
74 *Ibid*, 416–17.
75 *Kapp*, *supra* note 5.
76 *Ibid*, para 22.
77 *Ibid*.
78 *Ibid*.
79 2011 SCC 12, [2011] 1 SCR 396.
80 *Quebec (Attorney General) v A*, *supra* note 42.
81 *Supra* note 5.
82 *Supra* note 79, para 161.
83 *Supra* note 42.

status-based diminution of an individual or group. As an interpretive value underlying the *Charter*, human dignity can serve an exploratory function, seeking to root out the various ways in which existing laws might diminish the equal status of individuals and groups. A criterial account of the s. 15 test can never quite settle as the dignity value is routinely invoked to extend the purview of the right to encompass new factual situations that raise the structural problem of a dignity violation. We can trace this functional feature of dignity at work in the Supreme Court's evolving discussions on stereotype and prejudice, as laid out in the recent case of *Quebec (Attorney General) v A*.[84] The s. 15 test was described there as follows:

> [A] court analyzing the validity of a claim that s. 15(1) has been infringed must address the following questions: (1) Does the law create a distinction based on an enumerated or analogous ground? (2) Does the distinction create a disadvantage by perpetuating prejudice or stereotyping?[85]

The legal value of human dignity, with its sensitivity to status diminutions and commitment to equal concern and respect for all persons under law's authority,[86] sets the scope for the s. 15 enquiry in this case. The Court held that a law is discriminatory if it "has the effect of perpetuating or promoting the view that the individual is less capable, *or* less worthy of recognition or value as a human being or as a member of Canadian society."[87] This is an articulation of the legal value of human dignity that acknowledges its broad enquiry into an existing law's effect on the worth or status of the claimant, formulating the wrong of prejudice as its denial of a fundamental equality of status to persons under the law.

This is not to say that the dignity value always serves this function well in judicial reasoning or that the Court has made use of the dignity value even where it appears engaged by the case before it. Given the functions outlined in this chapter, it will be important to explore those instances where the Court appears impervious, or even actively

---

84 *Ibid.*

85 *Ibid*, para 185.

86 *Ibid*. The Supreme Court refers to Dworkin, *supra* note 69, 272–3: "Government must not only treat people with concern and respect, but with equal concern and respect."

87 *Law v Canada (Minister of Employment and Immigration)*, *supra* note 8, para 51, also cited in *Quebec (Attorney General) v A*, *supra* note 42, 192.

resistant, to invocations of the dignity value in a rights case. In their contribution to this volume on the s. 15 *Charter* jurisprudence on immigration status, Arbel and Myrdahl show how courts have exhibited a stubborn, if not pernicious, resistance to exploring the dignity value in this area of law.[88] The chapter demonstrates how the rigid adherence to the criteria of immutability as the test for analogous grounds under the s. 15 tests serves as a bulwark against a substantive interpretation of the equality right in line with the *Charter* value of human dignity. This tension is exposed, as the authors show, through evidentiary records that document the claimant's lived experiences of discrimination.[89] As argued further on in this chapter, the dignity value should operate to pick up precisely this kind of evidence. And yet the structure of the s. 15 enquiry, as the authors argue, stands in the way of an interpretation of the right in line with the dignity value.

The value of human dignity also animates the s. 15 focus on prejudice. The Supreme Court citation to Denise G. Réaume is illuminating in this respect:

> A legislative distinction based on prejudice denies a class of persons a benefit out of animus or contempt. It directly connotes a belief in their inferiority, a denial of equal moral status. Legislated prejudice denies a benefit for the sake of causing harm to those denied. It thus treats members of a group as loci of intrinsic negative value, rather than intrinsic moral worth. Such treatment not only deprives them of the concrete benefit at issue, but also, through doing so, treats them as unworthy of basic human respect.[90]

What is clearly unacceptable, says the Court, would be the law "establishing a hierarchy of worth based on prohibited grounds of discrimination, such as sex or sexual orientation."[91] A hierarchy of worth clearly undermines the legal commitment to human dignity.

---

88 See Arbel and Myrdahl's contribution in this volume (chap 14). They write, "Rather than explore the broad, underlying notions of substantive equality – such as anti-discrimination and human dignity – the Court has instead adopted a rigid approach that does not meaningfully analyse the relationship between personal characteristics and equality that s. 15(1) strives to protect and that is far removed from the principles outlined in [the] Andrews [decision]."

89 *Ibid.*

90 *Quebec (Attorney General) v A, supra* note 42, para 195.

91 *Ibid*, para 197.

The Court also notes that a hierarchy of worth might be communicated even where the legislation appears to be neutral but, in fact, draws on characteristics of a dominant group to define a legal category. In such cases, the law still might operate to send the corrosive social message that "others are not equally entitled to participate in society and its enterprises, and are not equally members of its institutions."[92] Serving this function, the value of human dignity works to expose the myriad ways in which stereotypes and prejudice threaten the state's attribution of equal human status to persons under its legal authority. The Supreme Court's reasoning in *Kapp* and *Withler* used the dignity value to push for depth and nuance in its analysis of prejudice and stereotype and to construct a framework that might encompass the complex of ways that stereotyping and prejudice violates human dignity. The structure of the dignity value motivated a broad understanding of the status-based threats posed by stereotyping and prejudice beyond the practice of overt, negative stereotyping and prejudice.

Moved by the dignity value to capture relevant instances where the law might undermine the equal status of persons, the Court constructed the legal category of *reverse stereotyping* to capture those cases where the governing legal regime, in setting what it takes to be a neutral standard, nevertheless establishes reduced classes of citizenship through its failure to take into account the actual needs of persons or groups.[93] Here the *Charter* value of dignity, as interpreted through the s. 15 protection, illuminates how laws that rely on inaccurate understandings of an individual or group are arbitrary and demeaning.[94] The *Charter* value of dignity here functioned to press and reconstitute the framework of what constitutes stereotyping under the law.

While it is outside the bounds of this paper to offer reasons as to where and how the dignity value comes to play a substantial, or even determinative, role in individual *Charter* cases, focusing on this functional feature of the dignity value allows us to see how it has been used in some of the *Charter* jurisprudence to continually shift and rework the s. 15 analysis.

---

92 *Ibid*, para 198.

93 *Ibid*, para 199.

94 *Ibid*, para 298.

Interpretations of Human Dignity Generate Contest

A third functional feature of the *Charter* value of human dignity is that it generates contest. This paper focuses on two aspects of this contest-generating function. First, human dignity generates legal contests over its subject matter. The legal value of human dignity engages with deep political questions.[95] Second, the legal value of human dignity generates contest precisely at the point where existing rights protections appear to run out. The legal value of dignity functions as an interpretative device to clarify or extend the reach of rights, so its work is inevitably done on the contentious margins of a legal question. It is, then, a function, not a failure, of the legal value of human dignity that it picks up on political questions about how to live together under law.[96] This section works through these two facets of dignity's contest-generating function in the *Charter* jurisprudence before charting two trends in *Charter* adjudication that respond to this feature of dignity.

TWO ASPECTS OF THE CONTEST-GENERATING FUNCTION OF THE *CHARTER* VALUE OF HUMAN DIGNITY

A Contest over Subject Matter. In the adjudication of rights, dignity's subject matter is generally highly contentious. The concept is invoked, across a number of jurisdictions, in cases of deep personal and political significance, on questions concerning cruel and unusual punishment, physician-assisted death, the right to life, and the provision of basic goods, for example.[97] The *Charter* value of human dignity invites a contest over whether an impugned provision can be depicted as diminishing the equal status and respect owed to all human beings in a democratic polity such as Canada. In Canada, the concept of human dignity is consistently raised in rights cases concerning "psychological

---

95 White, *supra* note 27.

96 Judicial interpretations of human dignity can, of course, fail to meet their own value-based commitments. Judicial interpretations can defy their own logic, be ironic or pernicious, or fail to accord with other legal values. Nothing in this identification of this function of the value in the adjudication of *Charter* rights aims to undermine political, normative, or legal assessments of the legal value of human dignity.

97 For a categorization of the various areas of law in which the concept of human dignity is regularly invoked, see Daly, *supra* note 9.

integrity, physical security, privacy, personal autonomy, professional reputation, and personal affiliation or group identity"[98] and in cases pertaining to the right to equality and non-discrimination.

All this is charged political ground. It is for this reason that Christopher McCrudden has argued that the concept of human dignity in international human rights instruments was never reflective of a universal consensus on human rights. It serves rather as a "theoretical placeholder" and not as a marker of substantive agreement.[99]

A Contest Where the Rights Run Out. A second facet of this contest-generating function is that the value of human dignity is invoked in *Charter* cases where existing rights protections do not appear to encompass the legal questions before the Court. This paper addresses three different sorts of reasons for this. Dignity is invoked as a *Charter* value where (a) the legal question occurs under a rights heading that is not particularly well defined, (b) the legal issue appears to place two different sets of rights in conflict with one another, and (c) the harm or injury caused by the legislative scheme or government act is difficult for the Court (for good or ill reasons) to ascertain. Under each of these three scenarios, the value of dignity operates as a focal point for contestation.[100]

Dignity is frequently invoked where rights protections have not been extensively worked out. Often this occurs under the headings of the so-called positive rights. For example, under the South African constitution, where the civil and political rights protections are fairly well defined, the value of dignity operates most extensively under the less worked-out social and economic rights provisions.[101] The same is true in Canada, where dignity features prominently as an interpretive aid in the s. 15 jurisprudence.[102] As is the case in South Africa, Canadian judges use, at times, human dignity as an interpretive value to extend the purview of existing equality rights.[103]

98 Sossin, *supra* note 6.
99 Carozza, *supra* note 33, 941.
100 Narain's contribution to this volume (see chap 8) rightly presses the question whether demands for equality are best managed through the courts.
101 Barak, *supra* note 35.
102 Réaume, "Dignity, Choice and Circumstances," *supra* note 30, 546.
103 Rory O'Connell, "The Role of Dignity in Equality Law: Lessons from Canada and South Africa," *International Journal of Constitutional Law* 6, no. 2 (2008) 267.

The broad value of human dignity can also become a site of contestation between existing rights commitments. This function of dignity is reflected in an often-raised criticism that the value appears regularly on both sides of a legal issue. For instance, in the deeply contested terrain of abortion rights, dignity considerations are routinely invoked on behalf of both the pregnant woman and the fetus.[104] The same is true regarding debates on the death penalty and hate speech, where dignity considerations are invoked on behalf of the victim, the accused, and also the state.[105]

Réaume illustrates this dynamic at play in cases where the value of autonomy seems set against socio-economic conditions that detract from individual choice.[106] She writes, "governments tend to understand dignity as simple respect for choice, and when that seems implausible, they shift to patronizing people as incapable of choice. … Against this, advocates for disadvantaged groups try to direct our attention to whether the conditions of choice are adequate to support dignity."[107] Here the breadth and normative force of the concept of dignity generates a contest between these competing rights, and the result is a push for a nuanced reconciliation. It is then, in a sense, off the mark to criticize the value for operating on both sides of a legal case, when its function is to offer the form of an argument in the face of these already existing tension points between rights.

This contest-generating function of dignity is, at times, even set against generally accepted theories of rights and the role of courts in upholding rights guarantees. This tension is analysable in the s. 15 jurisprudence, where dignity arguments often appear to press for positive obligations on behalf of the state to secure the protection of essential human dignity. As Moreau writes, "For whatever it is to treat individuals as full members of society possessing equal status, it must, in at least some circumstances, involve giving them access to certain important opportunities or resources – not just because denying them access to

104 Jeremy Waldron, *Dignity, Rank, and Rights* (New York: Oxford University Press, 2012).

105 Jeremy Waldron, "2009 Holmes Lectures: Dignity and Defamation: The Visibility of Hate," *Harvard Law Review* 123 (2010) 1596.

106 Réaume, "Dignity, Choice and Circumstances," *supra* note 30, 539.

107 *Ibid*, 540.

these opportunities would send a demeaning message about them, but because the opportunities or resources themselves are necessary for full and dignified participation in society."[108] Although successful strategic uses of the dignity value by rights claimants will likely build modestly on existing interpretations of rights, Moreau rightly points to the progressive potential, perhaps even radical potential, that is embedded in the very form of the dignity argument.

Human dignity plays an interpretative role not only where the right in question is not fully worked out but also where the harm or injury caused by the rights infringement is not easily detectable. One early example of this function of dignity occurred in the jurisprudence on intentional infliction of nervous shock.[109] Where harms are obvious to the Court, and easily translatable into a rights violation, the value of dignity will not be needed to aid the argument, aside perhaps from its added rhetorical emphasis. But where the harms are not obvious to the Court, nor easily translated into the language of rights, the value of human dignity can be used as an interpretative aid to illustrate the way in which a law violates its own commitment to recognizing the equal status of persons.[110]

It is here that the argumentative structure of a dignity claim bears relation to the category of expressive harms.[111] The value of human dignity sets up a contest as to whether the impugned law harms, devalues, marginalizes, or degrades an individual or group. We see the effects of this contest in the so-called evidentiary turn in the adjudication of constitutional rights. The value of human dignity can function to amplify the value-laden picture of human equality underlying *Charter* rights, and this function takes on a particular significance in cases where the harms or wrongs alleged under the legislative scheme are not obvious to the Court, directing it to make a sombre and sustained enquiry into the evidence alleging the dignity violation.

---

108 Moreau, *supra* note 54, 416.

109 Denise Réaume, "Indignities: Making a Place for Human Dignity in Modern Legal Thought," *Queen's Law Review* 28 (2002) 61.

110 John Gardner, "Discrimination as Injustice," *Oxford Journal of Legal Studies* 16 (1996) 353.

111 Elizabeth Anderson and Richard Pildes, "Expressive Theories of Law: A General Restatement," *University of Pennsylvania Law Review* 148 (2000) 1503, cited also in Tarunabh Khaitan, "Dignity as an Expressive Norm: Neither Vacuous Nor a Panacea," *Oxford Journal of Legal Studies* 32 (2012) 1.

TWO TRENDS FOLLOWING THE CONTEST-GENERATING FUNCTION OF THE *CHARTER* VALUE OF HUMAN DIGNITY

Two argumentative tendencies follow from dignity's contest-generating function in the *Charter* jurisprudence. Both are products of a long-running historical development in constitutional interpretation emphasizing the role of legislative impact in determining constitutionality.[112] The Supreme Court has repeatedly stressed impact in determining the constitutionality of an impugned law. When ascertaining the law's impact on an individual or group, dignity's breadth presents as an especially useful platform for two sorts of argumentative strategies. The first concerns the use of comparative law and evidence; the second, the generation of a formidable evidentiary record detailing harm, degradation, and humiliation.

Comparative Evidence. Comparative constitutional and human rights scholars have documented how the concept of dignity is especially amenable to the practice of judicial borrowing.[113] *Judicial borrowing* refers to the practice of judges drawing on like-seeming cases from jurisdictions that they consider relevant. While there may not be one consistent definition across or even within jurisdictions, "the concept of human dignity, in virtue of its purchase on universality, serves as a common currency of transnational judicial dialogue and borrowing in matters of human rights."[114] The concept of dignity invites comparison between rights protections in other regimes and, also, at the international level. Dignity serves as a platform for judicial borrowing in *Charter* rights adjudication, most particularly with respect to the rights-limiting proportionality reasoning. In *Carter,* for instance, questions over dignity generated extensive comparative evidence regarding those regimes in which physician-assisted death was permissive. Much of the focus of this evidence was on the s. 1 minimal impairment test.[115]

112 See Arbel and Myrdahl, *supra* note 88.

113 Christopher McCrudden, "Using Comparative Reasoning in Human Rights Adjudication: The Court of Justice of the European Union and the European Court of Human Rights Compared," vol. 15 of the *Cambridge Yearbook of European Legal Studies* (Cambridge: Cambridge University Press, 2012–13).

114 McCrudden, *supra* note 9.

115 *Carter, supra* note 56, paras 103 and 104. See also *Canada (Attorney General) v Bedford,* 2013 SCC 72, [2013] 3 SCR [*Bedford*].

Following what has been labelled the "empirical trend in constitutional jurisprudence,"[116] dignity questions frequently come down to questions of or, rather, contests over evidence.[117] We saw the legal value of dignity used in this way in *United States v Burns*,[118] which concerned the question whether extradition without assurances to death-penalty states violated the *Charter*. Fourteen paragraphs of the judgment were dedicated to the recitation of international and comparative practice on assurances in extradition requests,[119] and this was considered a central enquiry into the s. 7 principles of fundamental justice.[120]

Evidentiary Records of Indignity. A further trend is related, and it follows from the legal value of human dignity's function of inviting contest over the content of *Charter* rights. The legal value of human dignity motivates the collection of comparative evidence for submission in a *Charter* rights case as well as testimony aimed at documenting realities anathema to dignity's commitment to equal human status. Evidence that clearly and strikingly documents the pain, harm, humiliation, or degradation experienced by a claimant or group under a law is powerful evidence that the law violates an existing right as interpreted by the dignity value.[121]

---

116 Kerri Froc, "Chaos Theory," *CBA National* (blog), Canadian Bar Association, 4 July 2014, http://nationalmagazine.ca/Blog/July-2014/Chaos-theory.aspx?feed=blogs, citing *Carter, supra* note 56 and *Bedford, supra* note 115 as examples of this trend.

117 Paul Daly documented this trend: "*R. v. Smith*, 2015 SCC 34 is the latest in a series of cases in which the Supreme Court of Canada has struck down a regulatory regime or decision as unconstitutional based on trial-level findings of fact that harm had been caused to individuals in violation of the *Charter* guarantee of 'security of the person'"; see Paul Daly, "An Age of Facts? R. v. Smith, 2015 SCC 34," *Administrative Law Matters* (blog), 23 June 2015, http://www.administrativelawmatters.com/blog/2015/06/23/an-age-of-facts-r-v-smith-2015-scc-34/.

118 [2001] 1 SCR 283, 2001 SCC 7.

119 *Ibid*, paras 79–93.

120 *Ibid*, para 512. The Court cited Justice Lamer in *Re: B.C. Motor Vehicle Act*, who expressly recognized the role of international law in elucidating the scope of the principles of fundamental justice. "[Principles of fundamental justice] represent principles which have been recognized by the common law, the international conventions and by the very fact of entrenchment in the Charter, as essential elements of a system for the administration of justice which is founded upon the belief in the dignity and worth of the human person and the rule of law."

121 See Arbel and Myrdahl, *supra* note 88 for the ways in which detailed evidentiary records put pressure on the restrictive s 15 test by detailing precisely how the

The case of *R v Morgentaler*,[122] wherein the Supreme Court of Canada struck down s. 251 of the *Criminal Code*, offers us a good example of this dynamic. Section 251 then required that all women seeking an abortion in Canada obtain a certificate of permission from a therapeutic abortion committee of an accredited or approved hospital (specified under s. 251(4) of the *Code*). Evidence brought before the Court showed that the wait times and overall difficulty in obtaining a certificate resulted in women having to undergo later-term abortions. Evidence was also presented that later-term abortions were more dangerous and psychologically traumatic for women. Drawing expressly on the concept of human dignity, the Court held that the provision in question infringed s. 7 of the *Charter*. Central to this argument was the detailed, painful, and, at times, horrifying evidentiary record of the practice with these vivid accounts serving an epistemic function, flagging for the Court the precise ways in which the provision violated the dignity of the claimants.

This is the argumentative strategy that we are seeing in the s. 7 jurisprudence. There are, of course, other argumentative strategies that might follow from dignity's contest-generating function. Reva Siegel has argued how the conception of dignity-as-autonomy was crucial for the decriminalization of abortion in the United States and Germany.[123] Siegel has shown how an argumentative strategy that emphasized autonomy and choice was distinct from the turn to painful and arresting evidence that was relied upon in *Morgentaler* to emphasize the dignity-violating status of s. 251 of the *Criminal Code*.

A further example of the role the evidentiary record plays in establishing a dignity violation occurred in *Kindler v Canada (Minister of Justice)*,[124] a case heard by the Supreme Court of Canada regarding an extradition request from the United States for an accused person who would face the death penalty, at that time considered an infringement

"restrictive understanding of the immutability requirement translates into a framework for equality that too often looks to applicants' choices rather than the dynamics of discrimination they suffer." It is the commitment to substantive equality girded by the dignity value that structures this argumentative strategy.

122 *Supra* note 41.

123 Reva Siegel, "Dignity and the Duty to Protect Unborn Life," in *Understanding Human Dignity*, ed. Christopher McCrudden, Proceedings from the British Academy (Oxford: Oxford University Press, 2013), 509.

124 *Supra* note 44.

of the *Canadian Charter of Rights and Freedoms*. (The case was later overturned.) The dissent in this case employed the following terms when discussing human dignity: *desecration*,[125] *outrages of dignity*,[126] *demeaning*,[127] and *repugnant*.[128] Also interesting is the fact that the dissent used this section of the judgment to paint vivid descriptions of the victim's potential suffering, describing the painful and horrifying aspects of various execution techniques. While the majority opinion appeared to dryly consider the rights and obligations of the state vis-à-vis the accused, Justice Sopinka, writing for the dissent, included a particularly visceral and shocking account of an execution.

> In the chamber now, he was strapped to the chair. The cyanide had been prepared, and was placed beneath his chair, over a pan of acid that would later react with the cyanide to form the deadly gas. Electrocardiographic wires were attached to Daniels' forearms and legs, and connected to a monitor in the observation area. This lets the doctor know when the heart stops beating.
>
> … In an instant, puffs of light white smoke began to rise. Daniels saw the smoke, and moved his head to try to avoid breathing it in. As the gas continued to rise he moved his head this way and that way, thrashing as much as his straps would allow still in an attempt to avoid breathing. He was like an animal in a trap, with no escape, all the time being watched by his fellow humans in the windows that lined the chamber. …
>
> Then the convulsions began. His body strained as much as the straps would allow. He had inhaled the deadly gas, and it seemed as if every muscle in his body was straining in reaction. His eyes looked as if they were bulging, much as a choking man with a rope cutting off his windpipe. But he could get no air in the chamber.[129]

The next paragraph in the judgment concludes, "The death penalty not only deprives the prisoner of all vestiges of human dignity, it is the ultimate desecration of the individual as a human being. It is the annihilation of the very essence of human dignity."[130]

---

125 *Ibid*, paras 51, 81, and 94.
126 *Ibid*, para 82.
127 *Ibid*, para 83.
128 *Ibid*, para 85.
129 *Ibid*, para 88.
130 *Ibid*, para 89.

The passages illustrate how the emotions of horror, revulsion, and empathy are handmaiden to legal interpretations of human dignity. The majority of the Court spoke nothing of pain and horror, choosing to emphasize rather the rights and duties of the state regarding extradition. The dissent, however, drew regularly on the concept of dignity, while hitting us again and again with passages that invoke horror and revulsion (the baking of the brain, the repeated attempts at electrocution, the duration of the electrocution process, etc.), pressing the question of the acceptability of the practice.

In each of these cases, it is not just evidence of harm, degradation, and humiliation that is placed on record, but social science evidence legitimating the experience of law's impact on the claimant.[131] Evidentiary records are growing ever more extensive in the adjudication of constitutional rights, and they are replete with social science evidence and expert reports that aim to augment[132] the harm, degradation, and/or humiliation described by the claimants.[133]

Defining the content of the concept of human dignity is difficult, but understanding a practice as being harmful, degrading, or humiliating is less abstract.[134] Descriptions of this sort serve an epistemic function

131 Paul Daly commented on this mix: "There is a lot of blood and a lot of numbers in these cases," *supra* note 117.

132 Elaine Scarry suggests that compassion can be generated either through an engagement with narratives or with statistics. "Statistical compassion" is generated by the presentation of social science findings, and "narrative compassion" is generated by personal accounts of hardship; see Elaine Scarry, "Speech Acts in Criminal Cases," in *Law's Stories: Narrative and Rhetoric in the Law*, ed. Peter Brooks and Paul Gewirtz (New Haven, CT: Yale University Press, 1996).

133 Emily Kidd White, "Till Human Voices Wake Us: The Role of Emotion in the Adjudication of Dignity Claims," *Journal of Law, Religion and State* 3 (2014) 201.

134 For example, South African constitutional scholar Edwin Cameron illustrates how the experience of humiliation and degradation suffered under apartheid pressed upon the question of discrimination based on sexual orientation. Cameron's argument is that this experience of indignity made it easy to see clearly, resulting in South Africa adopting the first constitution to expressly outlaw discrimination based on sexual orientation and one of the first to extend equal rights to marry to lesbian and gay couples. See Edwin Cameron, "Dignity and Disgrace, Moral Citizenship and Constitutional Protection," in *Understanding Human Dignity*, ed. Christopher McCrudden, Proceedings from the British Academy (Oxford: Oxford University Press, 2013), 467.

calling judicial attention to certain descriptions of law's impact.[135] They can serve to demand, capture, and sustain judicial attention.[136] These have their natural home under s. 7 arguments, but because this is such a powerful and vivid way to use the form of the dignity value, we can also expect to see these sorts of arguments, and evidentiary records, developing under other rights headings, including s. 15.[137]

Conclusion

Charter litigants draw on the legal concept of dignity to make a particular sort of argument. The *Charter* value of human dignity invites a contest over whether the impugned provision can be depicted as undermining the equal status and respect owed to all human beings in a democratic polity such as Canada. The value of human dignity engages fundamental normative and political questions about human flourishing, security, economics, and harm. Dignity is concerned with the legal recognition of an equal human rank or status.[138] The legal value of human dignity is a commitment to "treat human beings as creatures of intrinsic, incomparable, and indelible worth, simply as human beings."[139] A violation of essential human dignity occurs when the equal human status of a person or group is called into question.

While the difficulty of defining dignity has persisted since its introduction into the *Charter* jurisprudence, the Supreme Court has held unequivocal support for its role in rights adjudication. This chapter has aimed to provide a functional account of the *Charter* value of human dignity. It has argued that the *Charter* value of human dignity functions

---

135 Avishai Margalit, "Human Dignity between Kitsch and Deification," in *Philosophy, Ethics, and a Common Humanity: Essays in Honour of Raimond Gaita*, ed. Christopher Cordner and Raimond Gaita (Routledge, 2011): "My claim is that we understand the internal sense of respect for humans as humans basically through the negative sense of not treating humans as humans" (10).

136 In *Carter*, *supra* note 56, e.g., one particularly salient line of evidence brought by the claimants was the myriad of extraordinarily painful ways in which persons took their own lives in the absence of physician-assisted death. Central among these arguments were accounts of the agony of self-starvation.

137 *Quebec (Attorney General) v A*, *supra* note 42. In this case, the s 15 argument concentrated, in part, on the vulnerability of, and the harm caused to, those denied social security benefits over a certain age.

138 Waldron, *Dignity, Rank, and Rights*, *supra* note 104.

139 Réaume, "Dignity, Choice and Circumstances," *supra* note 30, 540.

to invite contextual interpretation, resist concrete and criterial definition, and generate contest in rights adjudication. It has offered a portrait of the legal value's dynamic nature, its stubborn breadth, and its generative potential in *Charter* rights jurisprudence. It has not aimed to sidestep its structural flaws. While the emphasis in much of the literature concerns the difficulty of defining the legal concept of human dignity, the three functional features of dignity operate alongside open questions of the value's impact on substantive rights. It is under the *Canadian Charter of Rights and Freedoms* that we work through the fundamental political and moral questions of how to live together under law. These are not the sorts of questions that can be worked out once. The value of human dignity will continue to play a significant role in the adjudication of *Charter* rights. At its worst, the value compounds, elides, or moves too slowly against the structural inequalities built into Canadian constitutional law. At its best, the legal value is as broad as the country is wide, serving, for legal subjects, as an inexhaustible, fertile ground for its living-tree constitution.

13 Is the Permanent Campaign the End of the Egalitarian Model for Elections?

MICHAEL PAL*

Introduction

Canada's federal politicians compete for office according to rules that reflect an egalitarian model for elections. The basic contours of the egalitarian model are well established. Donations to parties and candidates are limited, and spending by political actors during election campaigns is capped at relatively modest levels. The virtues of the egalitarian model are apparent in light of the failure in the United States to regulate the excessive influence of money in politics.[1] The Canadian approach to regulating money in politics has been lauded as a success for its creation of a level playing field.[2]

The egalitarian model rests on firm constitutional ground despite the undoubted costs it imposes on freedom of political expression. The Supreme Court of Canada has never disputed the formula that spending money to advance political views counts as speech. Limiting how individuals, parties, and interest groups can spend money to express themselves politically is a serious breach of one of the most fundamental

* Associate Professor, Faculty of Common Law, University of Ottawa, mpal@uottawa.ca.
I would like to thank the editors of this volume, the anonymous reviewers, Richard Pildes, Mark Jarvis, and Matthew Mendelsohn for their comments. The feedback of the participants at the December 2015 symposium at Yale Law School was extremely helpful and I would like to thank Howie Kislowicz and Noura Karazivan in particular for their close reading of the chapter.

1 Eric Lichtblau, "F.E.C. Can't Curb 2016 Election Abuse, Commission Chief Says," *New York Times*, 2 May 2015, http://www.nytimes.com/2015/05/03/us/politics/fec-cant-curb-2016-election-abuse-commission-chief-says.html?_r=0.

2 Colin Feasby, "*Libman v. Quebec (A.G.)* and the Administration of the Democratic Process under the Charter: The Emerging Egalitarian Model," *McGill Law Journal* 44, no. 1 (1999) 5 [Feasby, "Egalitarian Model"].

freedoms. In a series of cases, however, the Court has upheld limits placed for egalitarian reasons. The Court has developed, nurtured, and expanded the egalitarian model to ensure a level playing field.

Despite this notable achievement, cracks have emerged in the foundation of the model in light of shifting political behaviour. Politics has moved towards a "permanent campaign," characterized by high degrees of partisanship, politicization of government decision making, and the continuous use of campaign tactics such as negative advertising, among other features. In Canada, the permanent campaign has manifested itself in a variety of ways that exploit regulatory gaps in existing electoral rules, particularly the fact that spending caps apply only during the formal election period. The October 2015 election was the costliest in Canadian history. It was defined by pre-writ spending on negative advertisements, a proliferation of interest groups (known as *third parties*) such as HarperPAC and Engage Canada spending large amounts of money, and partisan gamesmanship about the length of the election. The move towards a permanent campaign threatens to eclipse the effectiveness of existing electoral laws and undermine egalitarian values.

This chapter asks whether the much-lauded egalitarian model can survive the onslaught of the permanent campaign.[3] It does not attempt to offer a full-fledged defence of the virtues of egalitarian values[4] in comparison to libertarian ones. That is well-trod ground.[5] The chapter

3 Jennifer Smith and Gerald Baier addressed this question in 2012, although the permanent campaign has evolved significantly since then: "Fixed Election Dates, the Continuous Campaign and Campaign Advertising Restrictions," in *From "New Public Management" to the "New Political Governance,"* ed. Herman Bakvis and Mark Jarvis (Montreal and Kingston: McGill-Queen's University Press, 2012). Leonid Sirota considers the viability of the egalitarian model with regard to third parties in "Third Parties and Democracy 2.0," *McGill Law Journal* 60, no. 2 (2015) 253.

4 Various aspects of the approaches to equality present in Canadian constitutionalism are investigated in this volume, including as a component of human dignity in Emily Kidd White (chap 12), as it pertains to migration in Efrat Arbel and Eileen Myrdahl (chap 14), and as a value in religious freedom jurisprudence in Howard Kislowicz (chap 6).

5 Feasby, "Egalitarian Model," *supra* note 2; Colin Feasby, "Freedom of Expression and the Law of the Democratic Process," *Supreme Court Law Review* (2d) 29 (2005) 237, 277–82; and Colin Feasby, "Constitutional Questions about Canada's New Political Finance Regime," *Osgoode Hall Law Journal* 45, no. 3 (2007) 513 [Feasby, "Constitutional Questions"]. Christopher Manfredi and Mark Rush are sceptical of the egalitarian model in *Judging Democracy* (Peterborough, ON: Broadview Press, 2008), 97–117. Yasmin Dawood argues that Canada's egalitarian model has gone too far in "Democracy and the Freedom of Speech: Rethinking the Conflict between Liberty and Equality," *Canadian Journal of Law and Jurisprudence* 26 (2012) 293.

instead focuses on how new forms of political behaviour strain the current regulatory model. It considers whether election laws can be reformed to effectively regulate money in politics, while being consistent with protection for freedom of political expression.[6] I argue that the egalitarian model can be adapted to meet these new challenges, but that this will require enhancing its regulatory ambit and addressing the accompanying constitutional issues.

This chapter proceeds as follows. The next section outlines briefly the major planks of the egalitarian model and the jurisprudence, finding it to be consistent with the *Canadian Charter of Rights and Freedoms*. It is followed by details of the emergence of the permanent campaign in Canada and its corrosive impact on the effectiveness of current electoral rules. Various reforms are then proposed so that a level playing field can be ensured despite the move to a permanent campaign. The centrepiece of this set of proposals is the imposition of a spending limit for a defined period of time in the pre-writ period. These proposals raise constitutional questions about harms to freedom of political expression. The next section analyses the constitutional issues involved in adapting the egalitarian model to address the permanent campaign. I conclude that pre-writ spending limits can be designed in a constitutionally compliant fashion. The final section then analyses recent federal legislation, which takes tentative steps in the direction of pre-writ regulation, and considers its constitutionality.

Canada's Electoral Ecosystem and the *Charter*

The Main Features of the Egalitarian Model

The rules composing the egalitarian model can be set out relatively briefly.[7] They consist of spending limits on major political actors during the campaign period, caps on donations to candidates as well as political parties, and disclosure requirements. Canada's electoral regime has

6 The egalitarian model applies to judicial reasoning, but also to the exercise of legislative and executive authority. For the development of constitutional norms outside the courts, see in this volume Wade K. Wright (chap 4) and Mary Liston (chap 1) with regard to the executive.

7 For a history, see Feasby, "Constitutional Questions," *supra* note 5.

emerged as one of the most egalitarian in the world[8] since its implementation in 1976.[9] The 2015 election saw a spending limit for parties running candidates in all ridings of just under $55 million, which was more than double the $21 million permitted in 2011.[10] The larger scope for party spending was made possible due to amendments introduced by the *Fair Elections Act*[11] and the decision of the government to call an eleven-week campaign instead of the traditional five-week one. For candidates, the limit varies according to riding population, with a maximum of approximately $270,000.[12] The limit for third party spending during the campaign was just under $440,000 nationally and no more than approximately $9,000 in any one riding.[13]

A central feature of the spending provisions is that they are time-limited. Political parties, third parties, and candidates face spending restrictions only from the issuance of the writ until election day. Canada's rules on spending are egalitarian, but they are exclusively focused on the campaign period and do not apply in the pre-writ period. Parties, candidates, and third parties can, therefore, spend unlimited amounts before the official start of the campaign. With respect to spending, the egalitarian model as conceived of in Canada is best understood as campaign period regulation.[14]

---

8 Fred Fletcher and André Blais, "New Media, Old Media, Campaigns, and Canadian Democracy," in *From "New Public Management" to the "New Political Governance,"* ed. Herman Bakvis and Mark Jarvis (Montreal and Kingston: McGill-Queen's University Press, 2012), 152–4; and Andrew Geddis, "Liberté, Égalité, Argent: Third Party Election Spending and the Charter," *Alberta Law Review* 42, no. 2 (2004) 429.

9 Feasby, "Constitutional Questions," *supra* note 5.

10 Elections Canada, "Final Expense Limits for Registered Political Parties 42nd General Election, October 19, 2015," http://www.elections.ca.

11 SC 2014, c 12 [*Fair Elections Act*].

12 The limit in most ridings in 2011 was considerably less, at $92,000; see Elections Canada, "Final Expense Limits for Candidates 41st General Election," http://www.elections.ca.

13 *Canada Elections Act*, SC 2000, c 9, s 350. The baseline limit is $150,000 per election, with no more than $3,000 per riding, subject to increases for inflation and to campaigns longer than thirty-seven days. This resulted in limits of $188,250 nationally and $3,765 per riding in 2011.

14 On campaign period regulation, see Samuel Issacharoff, "The Constitutional Logic of Campaign Finance Regulation," *Pepperdine Law Review* 9 (2009) 373. The donation limits apply continuously.

Donations to political parties, candidates, electoral district associations, and leadership contestants are also capped, although there is no limit on what these entities can raise. Contributions are capped at $1,500, subject to a yearly increase of $25.[15] Corporate and union donations, which were a staple of federal politics until recently, have been banned outright. The Conservatives famously eliminated the direct per vote subsidy that had been introduced by the earlier Liberal government, and it was the subject of one of the disputes leading to the prorogation of Parliament in 2008.[16] Parties and candidates, however, still receive significant amounts of public money through reimbursement of portions of their election expenses and indirectly through tax credits provided to donors.[17]

Third parties operate under a different regime.[18] Third parties spending over a minimum threshold of $500 during a campaign must register with Elections Canada. Registration requires the disclosure of a relatively minimal amount of information. *Third parties* are defined as any group other than a candidate, registered political party, or electoral district association. As with political parties and candidates, they are subject to spending limits only during a campaign. Unlike those entities, however, they can receive donations in unlimited amounts. This raises the risk that third parties could be used as vehicles to evade the contribution limits imposed on political parties. Funds from foreign or anonymous donors may not be used for election advertising expenses.

---

15 *Fair Elections Act, supra* note 11.

16 The most comprehensive set of studies on the party subsidy is Lisa Young and Harold J. Jansen, eds., *Money, Politics, and Democracy: Canada's Party Finance Reforms* (Vancouver: UBC Press, 2011).

17 James Fitz-Morris, "MPs, Failed Candidates Set to Get Tens of Millions in Rebates from Taxpayers," *CBC News*, 9 November 2015, http://www.cbc.ca/news/politics/canada-election-2015-candidates-reimbursements-1.3300510. See Harold J. Jansen and Lisa Young, "Cartels, Syndicates, and Coalitions: Canada's Political Parties after the 2004 Reforms," in *Money, Politics, and Democracy: Canada's Party Finance Reforms*, ed. Lisa Young and Harold J. Jansen (Vancouver: UBC Press, 2011); Richard S. Katz, "Finance Reform and the Cartel Party Model in Canada," in *Money, Politics, and Democracy: Canada's Party Finance Reforms*, ed. Lisa Young and Harold J. Jansen (Vancouver: UBC Press, 2011).

18 *Canada Elections Act, supra* note 13, s 349–62.

The Supreme Court of Canada's Egalitarian Jurisprudence

The Supreme Court has, in a series of cases, outlined the constitutional contours of the egalitarian model[19] and recognized the costs that it imposes on political expression. The cases also, however, uphold the constitutionality of rules that create a level playing field for democratic competition for state power. The Court's initial move in this direction was in *Libman v Quebec.*[20] The Court struck down restrictive rules operating during the Charlottetown Accord referendum that prevented individuals not associated with either of the official Yes or No campaigns from spending any significant amount. The Court held, however, that egalitarian rationales were legitimate state objectives under s. 2(b) and s. 1 of the *Charter* and could justify limiting political speech to "preserve the confidence of the electorate in a democratic process that it knows will not be dominated by the power of money."[21]

Harper v Canada[22] expanded the initial statement from *Libman* by upholding caps on third party spending in federal campaigns. These rules had received judicial disfavour in earlier decisions from lower courts.[23] Stephen Harper, as head of the interest group the National Citizens' Coalition, challenged the restrictions on third party spending as violations of s. 2(b). In a 7–2 decision, the majority of the Court built on *Libman* to articulate an egalitarian rationale for the limit. Unregulated third party spending, in the majority's view, risked allowing moneyed interests to capture the political conversation to the exclusion of other perspectives. It held that the rules in the *Canada Elections Act* concerning third parties were legitimate restrictions on political expression as they embodied the principle that all voices should be heard. The dissent viewed the permitted amount of spending as being so low as to create an unconstitutional "virtual ban" on third party participation.[24]

19 Feasby, "Egalitarian Model," *supra* note 2. See also *Thomson Newspapers v Canada*, [1998] 1 SCR 877.

20 [1997] 3 SCR 569.

21 *Ibid*, 597.

22 2004 SCC 33.

23 *National Citizens' Coalition v Canada (AG)*, (1984) 32 Alta LR (2d) 249 (QB) [*Harper*]; and *Somerville v Canada (AG)*, (1996) 184 AR 241.

24 *Harper, supra* note 23 *per* the dissent, para 35. The Supreme Court upheld the registration requirement for third parties in the British Columbia provincial election

In *R v Bryan*,[25] the Court pushed this approach even further and endorsed a right to equality of information. The decision upheld a rule banning the early transmission of election results before the polls had closed in all areas of the country.[26] Along with staggered voting hours, this rule guaranteed that voters in British Columbia would not have information about election results from the East Coast when casting their ballots. The Court held that the ban infringed freedom of expression, but upheld it because it furthered the goal of informational equality.[27]

In *Figueroa v Canada*,[28] the Court struck down rules that discriminated against small political parties.[29] The law required that a party field fifty candidates to qualify for registered party status, which granted the right to list the party name beside the candidate's on the ballot, to be able to issue tax receipts for donations made between elections, and to be permitted to transfer funds from the candidate to the party.[30] The Court's decision can be understood as insisting on the equality of political parties.

The Permanent Campaign and Changing Political Behaviour

The egalitarian model outlined in the previous section is now under threat from the permanent campaign. The *permanent campaign* as an understanding of political behaviour was initially developed in the United States.[31] It refers to a series of connected phenomena

---

statute in *BC Freedom of Information and Privacy Association v British Columbia (Attorney General)*, [2017] 1 SCR 93, aff'ing 2015 BCCA 172 (*BC FIPA*). The case is an important one for upholding the constitutionality of mandatory registration rules. In my view, mandatory registration for third parties should be seen as constitutional when imposed in the writ period, as in *Harper* and *BC FIPA*, or during the pre-writ period.

25 2007 SCC 12.

26 See Michael Pal, "Democratic Rights and Social Science Evidence," *National Journal of Constitutional Law* 32 (2014) 151; Christopher D. Bredt and Margot Finley, "The Supreme Court and the Electoral Process," *Supreme Court Law Review* (2d) 42 (2008) 63.

27 Despite its constitutionality being upheld in *Bryan*, the *Fair Elections Act*, *supra* note 11, did away with the rule.

28 2003 SCC 37 [*Figueroa*].

29 A constitutional challenge to the minimum level of popular support required to qualify for political party funding (since discontinued) was rejected in *Longley v Canada (AG)*, (2007), 88 OR (3d) 408 (CA).

30 *Figueroa*, *supra* note 28, paras 3–8.

31 Sydney Blumenthal, *The Permanent Campaign* (New York: Simon and Shuster, 1982).

in contemporary politics, including the erasure of any distinction between campaigning and governing, with political parties operating in a similar fashion both during and between elections. The permanent campaign is characterized by partisan government decision making driven by public opinion polling, negative advertising against opponents, the politicization of the public service to further the partisan interests of the government, the concentration of power in the central organs of government and political staff, and an emphasis on message discipline.

The existence of the permanent campaign is well recognized in Canada.[32] It is a cross-national phenomenon, and it now also defines politics in Australia, the United Kingdom,[33] and the United States,[34]

---

32 Fletcher and Blais, *supra* note 8, 151; Tom Flanagan, "Political Communication and the 'Permanent Campaign,'" in *How Canadians Communicate IV: Media and Politics*, ed. David Taras and Christopher Waddell (Edmonton: Athabaska Press, 2012) [Flanagan, "Political Communication"]; Tom Flanagan, "'Something Blue': Conservative Organization in an Era of Permanent Campaign" (address to the Canadian Political Science Association, 3 June 2010); Tom Flanagan and Harold J. Jansen, "Election Campaigns under Canada's Party Finance Law," in *The Canadian Federal Election of 2008*, ed. Jon H. Pammett and Christopher Dornan (Toronto: Dundurn Press, 2009); Peter Aucoin, "New Public Governance in Westminster Systems: Impartial Public Administration and Management Performance at Risk," *Governance* 25, no. 2 (2012) 177, 186; Smith and Baier, *supra* note 3; Jonathan Rose, "Are Negative Ads Positive? Political Advertising and the Permanent Campaign," in *How Canadians Communicate IV: Media and Politics*, ed. David Taras and Christopher Waddell (Edmonton: Athabaska Press, 2012); and Tamara Small, "E-ttack Politics: Negativity, the Internet, and Canadian Political Parties," in *How Canadians Communicate IV: Media and Politics*, ed. David Taras and Christopher Waddell (Edmonton: Athabaska Press, 2012), 183–4.

33 Aucoin, *supra* note 32, 185; Peter Van Onselen and Wayne Errington, "The Democratic State as a Marketing Tool: The Permanent Campaign in Australia," *Commonwealth and Comparative Politics* 45, no. 1 (2007) 78; Nick Sparrow and John Turner, "The Permanent Campaign: The Integration of Market Research Techniques in Developing Strategies in a More Uncertain Political Climate," *European Journal of Marketing* 36, no. 9/10 (2001).

34 Norman Ornstein and Thomas Mann, eds., *The Permanent Campaign and Its Future* (Washington, DC: American Enterprise Institute / Brookings Institute, 2000); Catherine Needham, "Brand Leaders: Clinton Blair and the Limitations of the Permanent Campaign," *Political Studies* 53 (2005) 343; Kathryn Dunn Tenpas and James A. McCann, "Testing the Permanence of the Permanent Campaign: An Analysis of Presidential Polling Expenditures, 1977–2002," *Public Opinion Quarterly* 71, no. 3 (2007) 349.

among others. The move to a permanent campaign has been shaped by the existing rules on campaign finance and the presence of minority governments.[35] The cross-national nature of the trend, however, strongly indicates that it will remain an enduring feature of Canadian politics even in a time of majority governments.

The permanent campaign has manifested itself in a number of ways in Canada, and they collectively undermine the effectiveness of the rules regulating money in politics. These instances include (1) a shift to political spending in the unregulated, pre-writ period; (2) the changing role of third parties; and (3) manipulations of election timing and campaign length.

The Campaign Period and Pre-writ Spending

The centrepiece of the egalitarian model is the cap on spending by political parties and candidates during an election campaign. The combination of a heavily regulated campaign and entirely unregulated pre-writ period, however, creates incentives for political actors to shift their spending to the time before the official campaign commencement. Parties with access to resources beyond what they are permitted to spend during the campaign have a natural outlet for their money. The parties began engaging in pre-writ spending in large amounts in the 2008 election and continued in 2011 and 2015.[36]

Given that advertising on television is one of the largest expenses for parties, the focus of pre-writ spending has quickly become what is colloquially called the "air war." The move to pre-writ negative advertising is now an ongoing feature of Canadian political life. The Conservative Party notably ran television advertisements against Liberal leaders, including the "He's Just Not Ready" claim against now Prime Minister Justin Trudeau. The Liberals and the New Democratic Party (NDP) have also joined the pre-writ air wars with negative advertisements of their own. The move to pre-writ spending gives the party with the greatest resources a decided advantage. It can shape public opinion by bombarding the airwaves with negative advertisements that, if effective, can damage the image of opposing candidates.

35 Flanagan, "Political Communication," *supra* note 32. (I thank Richard Albert as well for pointing out the importance of minority governments to this dynamic.)

36 *Ibid.*

The existence of a fixed election date has likely contributed to the growth of pre-writ advertising. Fixed-date elections were introduced federally by legislation in 2007,[37] although the 2015 election was the first that occurred according to schedule. The fixed-date legislation may have the virtue of decreasing the government's discretion around when to call an election, but it adds certainty as to when pre-writ advertisements can be deployed to their maximum effectiveness in the lead-up to the statutorily mandated election day.[38] All the parties could run negative ads in the months before the start of the 2015 election, knowing that they would not count against the spending limit for the impending campaign and that they would reach their audience at an opportune time.

The move to pre-writ spending for one of the most expensive features of electioneering – namely, advertising – undermines the egalitarian model. While all parties face the same expenses limit during a campaign, the ability to dispense funds just before the campaign begins on advertisements with the potential to change public opinion provides an advantage to the parties with the largest war chests. Given the fundraising advantages of incumbency, this loophole will often work to the benefit of the governing party. Parties can easily thwart egalitarian regulations by shifting their resources to the pre-writ period. Perhaps the most surprising thing about the move to pre-writ spending is that it took so long for the loophole to be exploited.

The Permanent Campaign and the Changing Role of Third Parties

The role of third parties participating in elections[39] attracted renewed attention in 2015 with the emergence of high-profile groups such as

---

37 *Canada Elections Act, supra* note 13, s 56.1(2).

38 There is a robust debate in the political science literature about when voters make up their minds, sometimes framed as "Do campaigns matter?" At least half of voters tend to make up their minds during the campaign, with significant increases over time in the size of this group of late deciders; see Patrick Fourner et al, "Time-of-Voting Decisions and Susceptibility to Campaign Effects," *Electoral Studies* 23 (2004) 661, 675–6. Strong partisan identification is the leading determinant for why the rest make up their minds earlier.

39 See Geddis on the evolution of third party rules, "Third Party Election Spending," *supra* note 8; and Sirota for a more recent account involving the role of new technologies and third parties, *supra* note 3.

Working Canadians and HarperPAC. Working Canadians was a combination of NDP and Liberal partisans, along with labour unions, dedicated to advertising to defeat the Conservative government. HarperPAC supported the Conservatives, although it disbanded before the election after being criticized by the party in whose very interests it was purportedly acting. These were the two most prominent ones, but a record 113 third parties registered in 2015.[40]

Third parties have exploited the same gap as the political parties by shifting their spending to the unregulated pre-writ period. During this time, not only the spending caps but even the registration requirements that apply during the campaign period are inapplicable. Voters faced third party advertisements before the 2015 campaign, but they had little to no information about where the funding for these groups was coming from or in whose interests they were operating.

The rise of third parties raises the specific problem of coordination with political parties as a means of flouting the caps on spending by and donations to political parties. Both Working Canadians and HarperPAC were run by political operatives who had previously served at a high level within the parties themselves. Policing coordination between third parties and political parties is notoriously difficult.[41] It seems likely that some of the corporate and union money that can no longer be donated to political parties is now flowing to interest groups.

The permanent campaign has ushered in a more powerful role for third parties. The *Harper* dissent was correct in viewing existing laws as providing a near monopoly on communications within the campaign period for political parties. Third parties have often participated in federal elections, but their impact has generally been minimal.[42] Their

---

40 Elections Canada, "Registered Third Parties 42nd General Election, October 19, 2015," http://www.elections.ca.

41 For example, see Alexandra Jaffe and Kailani Koenig, "Fiorina Super PAC Tests Legal Limits of Campaign Coordination," *NBC News*, 17 September 2015, http://www.nbcnews.com/meet-the-press/fiorina-super-pac-tests-legal-limits-campaign-coordination-n428056. See Michael Pal, "Third Party Political Participation and Anti-Collusion Rules," Canadian Public Administration 61, no. 2 (2018) (forthcoming).

42 Andrea Lawlor and Erin Crandall, "Understanding Third-Party Advertising: An Analysis of the 2004, 2006, and 2008 Canadian Elections," *Canadian Public Administration* 54, no. 4 (2011) 509.

degree of participation in 2015 implies that enhanced influence for third parties may be the new norm.

A more robust role for third parties raises both opportunities and threats for political parties. The HarperPAC example is illustrative. On the one hand, parties may stand to benefit from increased spending by interest groups, particularly on advertising. HarperPAC explicitly mimicked the Conservative Party's messaging. Working Canadians served a similar mission on the left, although it remained agnostic between the NDP and the Liberals. On the other hand, parties are at risk of losing control of their campaign. HarperPAC disbanded after a rebuke from the Conservative Party that the name might confuse voters about the boundaries between the official campaign and the interest group.

One of the consequences of the government's decision to launch the lengthy election campaign was that the spending limits for third parties kicked in earlier than expected. By adhering to the fixed date, but putting in place a longer election period, the campaign started earlier than it would have under an election of regular length. The relatively strict limit on their spending that applied during the campaign, even under the elevated amount of approximately $440,000 permitted by the *Fair Elections Act*, effectively removed third parties as players able to move votes in any significant number.

Election Timing and Campaign Length

The election on 19 October 2015 was the longest and most expensive campaign in modern history, which had significant ramifications for electoral fairness. A relevant background factor is the presence of fixed election dates, which were introduced in 2007 to put in place regular elections every four years. The immediate consequence was seen to be the removal from the executive of the traditional power in parliamentary systems to determine the timing of elections. The authority to set the election date has been used strategically by governing parties seeking to ensure that an election occurs at the most favourable possible time.[43]

The Federal Court ruled in *Conacher v Canada* that the fixed-election-date legislation did not and could not displace the governor general's

43 A recent example was Prime Minister Jean Chrétien calling the 2000 election shortly after Stockwell Day was elected leader of the opposition Canadian Alliance.

prerogative power over the calling of elections.[44] Given the convention that the governor general acts on the advice of the prime minister, the executive retains significant discretion over election dates, even with the legislation in place. Prime Minister Harper applied this authority in calling early elections in 2008 and 2011. Fixed election dates promised much as a potential constraining force on prime ministerial authority and partisan-minded chicanery regarding timing, but have delivered relatively little.

The length of the 2015 election – eleven weeks – is the most recent iteration of an attempt to evade the strictures of Canadian campaign finance law within the relatively weak constraints of the fixed-election-date legislation. Campaigns have traditionally lasted just over five weeks, or approximately thirty-seven days, although they have frequently deviated from this number.[45] A lengthy campaign historically meant that parties had to spread the same resources over an expanded period as the spending limit remained constant. Parties with money to spend did not gain any partisan advantage, from the point of view of campaign finance, from a longer election period. The *Fair Elections Act* altered the status quo. It introduced a multiplier so that the longer the campaign period, the higher the spending limit. The result in 2015 was an unprecedented $55 million spending limit.

The early election call in August 2015 that resulted in the eleven-week campaign undermined the egalitarian model in several ways. First, it raised the possibility that not all the three major parties would be able to spend the maximum. The Conservatives, Liberals, and, for the first

---

44 *Conacher v Canada (Prime Minister)*, 2010 FCA 131. See also Adam Dodek, "The Past, Present and Future of Fixed Election Date Legislation in Canada," *Journal of Parliamentary and Political Law* 4 (2010) 215; Adam Dodek, "Fixing Our Fixed Election Date Legislation," *Canadian Parliamentary Review* 32, no. 1 (2009) 18; Andrew Heard, "*Conacher* Missed the Mark on Constitutional Conventions and Fixed Election Dates," *Constitutional Forum* 19, no. 1 (2010) 129; and Christopher Alcantra and Jason Roy, "Reforming Election Dates in Canada: Toward an Explanatory Framework," *Canadian Public Administration* 57, no. 2 (2014) 256. S 56.1(1) of the *Canada Elections Act*, *supra* note 13, is explicit that the governor general's discretion to dissolve Parliament remains in place. The *Charter* requires elections at least every five years, s 4(1).

45 See Bruce Deacham, "78 Days? The Long and the Short of Canadian Campaigns," *Ottawa Citizen*, 3 August 2015, for a concise summary: http://ottawacitizen.com/news/politics/two-down-76-to-go-the-longest-election-campaign-since-we-first-re-elected-john-a.

time, the NDP had all done so in 2011. Second, it provided an element of surprise. The *Fair Elections Act* gained royal assent in June 2014, but the increase in the spending limit in the instance of a longer campaign was not well recognized until months later.[46] Third, the significantly higher spending limit risked undermining fair competition in future elections. Even if able to spend the maximum in 2015, parties might have exhausted existing resources or gone into debt. In a minority government scenario with another election quickly following the October vote, they may have faced a financial disadvantage. The outcome was a majority government instead, but this result was far from certain when the campaign began. The lengthy campaign may have produced advantages for voters as they had a longer time to scrutinize candidates. Yet the consequences for the egalitarian model were troubling.

Regulating the Permanent Campaign

The challenges posed by the permanent campaign to a level playing field are numerous and robust. Given the prevalence of similar trends in other democracies, it seems unlikely that they are transitory. Political actors have demonstrated that significant loopholes exist in the current legal regime. The permanent campaign as waged in Canadian electoral politics has undermined the egalitarian model and stands as a significant threat to its continued viability.

In this section, I address whether a new set of rules can be crafted to enhance the likelihood of achieving a level playing field in light of the permanent campaign. I advocate here for an approach that centres on extending spending restrictions beyond the campaign period to encompass the lead-up to an election. To be effective, this approach also requires some corresponding amendments to the third party regime to prevent attempts at regulatory avoidance. I will argue that this is the most promising avenue for preserving a level playing field in light of the particular operation of the permanent campaign in Canada. I also recommend setting a legal limit on campaign length to end the

46 *Canada Elections Act*, *supra* note 13, s 430(2), as amended by the *Fair Elections Act*, *supra* note 11, s 86. Alice Funke first highlighted this issue in "Re-up-UPDATED: How a Little-Noticed Clause in the Fair Elections Act Up-Ends All Conventional Election Timing Speculation," *Guide to the Pundits Guide* (blog), 15 January 2015, http://www.punditsguide.ca/2015/01/how-a-little-noticed-clause-in-the-fair-elections-act-up-ends-all-conventional-election-timing-speculation/.

gamesmanship that occurred around the 2015 vote. These proposals raise constitutional issues, which will be addressed in the next section.

Regulating the Pre-writ Period

Re-establishing a level playing field will be impossible without addressing the shift in spending by political actors to the pre-writ period. A portion of the pre-writ period should be governed by the same rules capping spending as exist during a campaign, to re-level the field. With the prevalence of pre-writ spending, the campaign expenses limit encapsulates only a portion of the actual amount dispensed on fighting an election. Campaign finance laws need to capture a broader set of the election-related expenses incurred by parties and third parties. The fixed date has exacerbated the effects of the permanent campaign, but it also provides an opportunity to set a true ceiling on spending, working backwards from election day.

Other jurisdictions have taken this approach to regulating election spending.[47] The experience of the United Kingdom is especially instructive. The United Kingdom limits political party spending in the year before an election.[48] The year-long limit has proved to be an effective tool for furthering egalitarian values. It ensures a level playing field for the parties not only from when the writ is drawn up and Parliament is dissolved but also during the time of the unofficial campaign, in the months leading up to an anticipated election. It captures most of the spending that we would plausibly count as entailing election-related expenses. Like Canada, the United Kingdom now has fixed-election-date legislation.[49] Before the introduction of the fixed-term legislation, the spending cap in the year leading up to an election was a floating one. It applied retroactively from the time an election was called according to the whims of the government of the day. With a fixed election date, parties can now know with greater certainty when the limits will kick in.

---

47 Some Canadian jurisdictions have adopted various pre-writ restrictions on political parties and interest groups; see Smith and Baier, *supra* note 3, 133–45.

48 *Political Parties, Elections, and Referendums Act*, 2000, c 41. See Keith Ewing, Jacob Rowbottom, and Joo-Cheong Tham, eds., *The Funding of Political Parties: Where Now?* (London: Routledge, 2012).

49 *Fixed Term Parliaments Act*, 2011, c 14.

As with the Canadian campaign period model, the UK approach still generates incentives to shift spending outside the regulated zone to evade the spending limit. Because the restrictions apply in the year leading up to election day, however, these incentives are blunted. The unregulated period is sufficiently far away from ballots being cast that spending at that juncture is much less likely to have an impact on the intentions of a significant portion of the electorate that is open to persuasion.[50] A spending limit applying in each year is another option, although one that is fraught with greater constitutional risk, as will be considered in the next section.

Applying the United Kingdom's approach to Canada would mean capping spending for relevant entities for a significant time period before a fixed election date. The establishment in the United Kingdom of a year as the relevant period provides a plausible lead time by which to capture expenses likely related to the upcoming election. If an election occurred earlier than expected, the cap would operate retroactively to capture all past party spending during the period, as it did in the United Kingdom before the introduction of the *Fixed Term Parliaments Act*. Parties, candidates, third parties, and electoral district associations would need to be captured by the spending limit. Otherwise, political actors could simply avoid the reach of the spending limit by shifting their activities to the auspices of an unregulated entity. Parties will still undoubtedly move some spending to the pre-regulatory period, wherever it is set. Yet voters are less likely to be paying attention to negative advertising far out from an election. Work will need to be done to appropriately set the exact amount of the spending limit to make sure that there is no virtual ban on the participation of any particular type of political entity.

Pre-writ restrictions on third party spending would have to be crafted with consideration of viable enforcement of the rules and recognition of constitutionally protected freedom of expression. An option for regulating pre-writ activities by third parties would be to subject their spending to a limit only if it is an "electioneering" expense, rather than "issue-based" spending.[51] Most spending by third parties remains on advertising. Issue advertising advances the third party's views on

50 See Fourner et al, *supra* note 38.

51 See Colin Feasby, "Issue Advocacy and Third Parties in the United Kingdom and Canada," *McGill Law Journal* 48 (2003) 11 for a discussion of these terms.

a topic of public interest, such as the environment or natural resource development. Electioneering messages are those that expressly advocate on behalf of a party, candidate, or issue with which a party or candidate is closely associated.[52] Such a regime could allow unlimited spending on issue-based advertising by third parties that was of general benefit to public debate, but regulate their attempts to influence voter intentions about particular parties or candidates. It would therefore catch fewer types of third party expenses and intrude less obviously into the freedom of expression of interest groups.

The central problem with this approach, however, is enforcement. The distinction between what counts as issue-based versus advocacy advertising is a fine one, and it is, in practice, difficult to sustain. Drawing a distinction for regulatory purposes among types of speech or advertising would create significant incentives for third parties to try to mask electioneering as issue-based participation.[53] Election administrators and courts overseeing the scheme would have the nearly impossible task of parsing the content of political messages by third parties.[54]

Eliminating Partisan Manipulation of Campaign Length

The potential for partisan abuse of campaign length must also be addressed. There has been no fixed timeline for a campaign in federal politics. Just as with the introduction of the fixed election date, a set campaign length would reduce the discretion of the governing party and enhance equality among electoral competitors.

The regulatory response here should be twofold. The *Fair Elections Act* should, in this respect, be undone by reimposing a fixed spending limit that does not vary, regardless of the length of the campaign. This would eliminate the financial benefits of a lengthy campaign for a governing party with a monetary advantage. This reform should be accompanied by an introduction of a set campaign length, outlined in legislation. Whether it is thirty-seven days or some longer amount is less relevant than the existence of a rule regarding campaign length.

---

52 *Ibid.*

53 Feasby, *supra* note 51, compellingly sets out the problem of "sham issue advocacy," which is really electioneering for or against a politician or party, 45–52.

54 The development of norms by an administrative agency, such as Elections Canada, is a theme explored by Paul Daly in chap 3 of this volume.

The key is that the parties have a common understanding of when the campaign will occur, thereby preserving the level playing field that the *Fair Elections Act* undermined.

The ability to extend the official campaign period, as the government did for the 2015 election, reflected the exercise of discretionary authority for what appeared to be partisan purposes. Setting a fixed campaign period and eliminating the spending limit escalator would reduce opportunities for manipulation of this type.

Other Considerations

There are two additional options that should be flagged as worthy of consideration. New rules on pre-writ spending and campaign length do not address the existing contribution limits. The *Fair Elections Act* increased the amount that could be donated to parties and candidates, and this potentially augmented the influence of high-end donors.

In my view, however, the contribution limits are functioning well. The limits are comparatively quite low, even after the *Fair Elections Act*, and apply year-round; thus, there is no unregulated pre-campaign period for donations. Corporate and union donations are already banned. All three major parties now rely primarily on small contributions from a large number of donors rather than large contributions from a small group of wealthy individuals, corporations, and/or unions.

The other potential egalitarian reform could be to reintroduce the party subsidy.[55] This would be an appropriate course of action if the goal were to pursue a more radical extension of the egalitarian model rather than preserve its gains. Any reintroduction of a party subsidy would have to take into account the flaws in the previous system, which favoured the larger parties that had received substantial numbers of votes in the previous election.[56] The significant public support already given to parties and candidates directly through rebates and indirectly through tax credits would seem to make a return to the public

55 F. Leslie Seidle, "Public Funding of Political Parties: The Case for Further Reform," in *Money, Politics, and Democracy: Canada's Party Finance Reforms*, ed. Lisa Young and Harold J. Jansen (Vancouver: UBC Press, 2011) considers this issue in depth.

56 Michael Pal, "Breakdowns in the Democratic Process and the Law of Canadian Democracy," *McGill Law Journal* 57, no. 2 (2011) 299, 337–8.

subsidy less relevant. If the donation limit were lowered, however, re-implementing a party subsidy would be one way to compensate.

The Constitutional Dimension

The proposed reform to regulate pre-writ spending is more intrusive of freedom of political expression than existing rules and raises questions as to its constitutionality. Legislating on the length of a campaign and reimposing a static spending limit pose no similar serious questions. Would a pre-writ spending limit be constitutional under the approach articulated by the Supreme Court in *Harper*?

Given the Court's commitment to the egalitarian model and the clear need for enhanced regulation to address the evolution of a permanent campaign, pre-writ spending limits of a reasonable length and amount should be understood as legitimate limits on freedom of political expression. There are undeniable trade-offs between the effective regulation of money in politics, however, and upholding freedom of political speech. A pre-writ spending limit would admittedly stretch the constitutional commitment to a level playing field, given the more extensive restrictions on political expression that it would entail. A restriction on political spending in the year leading up to an election, however, should be seen as being consistent with the reasoning of a majority of the Supreme Court of Canada in *Harper*.

To address this constitutional issue, it is first worth putting *Harper* in comparative perspective. *Harper* occupies the proverbial Canadian middle ground between the two more extreme approaches in the United States and the United Kingdom to the constitutionality of limiting political speech. The United States Supreme Court famously, in *Citizens United v FEC*,[57] struck down a ban on corporate and union spending in the lead-up to an election under the First Amendment. In doing so, it ruled that the prevention of either corruption or the appearance of corruption was the only legitimate state rationale for limiting the right to free political speech.[58] The goal of ensuring a level playing field had previously been viewed favourably by the Court in

---

57 558 US 310 (2010).

58 See, from a now large literature, the influential work of Samuel Issacharoff, "On Political Corruption," *Harvard Law Review* 124 (2010) 118 [Issacharoff, "Corruption"].

some decisions,[59] but a majority in *Citizens United* decisively rejected this line of cases. The Court instead ruled that egalitarian values cannot be pursued in attempts to regulate political speech. Given the Court's approach to the First Amendment, there is little remaining scope for restrictions on the role of money in politics in the United States, save for rules on disclosure,[60] unless a viable anti-corruption rationale can be established.

The jurisprudence of the European Court of Human Rights, in reviewing rules in the United Kingdom on interest group spending, provides a sharp contrast. The United Kingdom sharply limits spending by these groups. In *Bowman v United Kingdom*,[61] the European Court upheld quite draconian restrictions on interest group participation. More recently, in *Animal Defenders International v United Kingdom*,[62] the Court upheld a total ban on political advertisements on television and radio by interest groups, even though it applied outside the campaign period. This jurisprudence represents a clear defence of egalitarian values.

The Canadian law at issue in *Harper* was much less intrusive than those in the United Kingdom considered in *Bowman* and *Animal Defenders*. The reasoning in the Canadian and United Kingdom cases clearly accepted the egalitarian rationale for limiting freedom of political expression, in contrast to *Citizens United*. The unsolved issue in Canada is how much of an imposition is permitted. The majority in *Harper* found that electoral fairness was undermined by third party spending in large amounts,[63] but did not set more specific parameters.

Extending the spending limit to the pre-writ period is undoubtedly a greater intrusion into freedom of political expression than the law at issue in *Harper*, although applying it to the year before an election is less restrictive than if a permanent spending limit were in place. It expands the time period where political speech is restricted and captures a greater quantity of speech directly related to the election. This

59 *Austin v Michigan State Chamber of Commerce*, 494 US 652 (1990); and *McConnell v FEC*, 540 US 93 (2003).

60 Issacharoff, "Corruption," *supra* note 58.

61 [1998] ECHR 4.

62 (2013) 57 EHRR 21. See Tom Lewis, "*Animal Defenders International v United Kingdom:* Sensible Dialogue or a Bad Case of Strasbourg Jitters?," *Modern Law Review* 77, no. 3 (2014) 460.

63 *Harper, supra* note 23, paras 80–2.

may be problematic, given how protective the Court has been of political speech. The Court understands political expression as standing at the heart of the s. 2(b) guarantee and has held that it must be accorded the maximum amount of protection possible.[64]

Yet a rule restricting pre-writ spending simply extends the constitutional logic in *Harper* in a responsible fashion. *Harper* adopted a realistic account of the influence of money and advertising in politics. The limits on political and third party spending were responses to the increasing flow of money into politics and the growing influence of radio and television advertising. Pre-writ spending limits should be seen in a similar light: as regulatory reactions to changes in how politics is actually conducted. Pre-writ limits respond to the shifts in political behaviour stemming from the reality of the permanent campaign.

Pre-writ limits also hold true to the long-standing commitment to egalitarian values in the case law. The purpose of pre-writ limits would be to ensure a level playing field. As long as the total amount of spending permitted were still within an acceptable range to allow for true participation by parties, interest groups, and candidates, even if the period of time being regulated were longer, there would be no distortion of the process in favour of any particular entity. Such a rule would ensure equality among political competitors to give voters the confidence that the democratic process was open to all. A move from election period regulation to oversight of pre-writ spending would further the goal of electoral fairness endorsed not only in *Harper* but also in *Libman* and *Bryan*.

For the sake of comparison, a spending limit that applied in every year would be less likely to find constitutional favour.[65] Imagine a limit of $25 million per year for parties, for example. If political speech is at the core of s. 2(b), it is harder to see a court upholding ongoing and continuous restrictions. A pre-writ spending limit that kicks in only as an election is in sight would be less impairing of freedom of expression. A year-long pre-writ limit harms the freedom of expression of those with significant resources only to the extent that is necessary to achieve the egalitarian goals that informed *Harper*.

---

64 *Ibid*, para 66, *per* the majority, and paras 2 and 11, *per* the dissent.

65 Leonid Sirota writes, "A permanent restriction on individuals or civil society groups wishing to speak out – and wishing to spend money on speaking out – on political issues, parties, or candidates would surely be considered draconian"; see "Democracy 2.0," *supra* note 3, 256.

Harper also permitted limits on spending in the campaign period, even though this is when political speech is at its most valuable. A reform of the type I am proposing covers a longer time period by targeting spending plausibly related to the election campaign, whether occurring before or during the official campaign. Pre-writ spending, however, could be seen as entailing lighter protection by s. 2(b). Speech made at a distance from election day is arguably less central to the democratic process than that occurring during the official campaign itself. If the Court were willing to accept the need to limit political expression during an election, when it is arguably at its most important, then pre-writ limits would not be a drastic departure, but consistent with the egalitarian model's gradual evolution.

Pre-writ restrictions on interest group spending received disfavour from the British Columbia courts in two recent cases, *Reference re Election Act (BC)* (*Reference*)[66] and *British Columbia Teachers' Federation v British Columbia (Attorney General)* (*BCTF*),[67] which are relevant to a discussion of the reform of federal rules. In *BCTF*, the British Columbia Supreme Court and then the Court of Appeal struck down legislation limiting third party advertising in the sixty days before the official start of the provincial election period. The province responded with a spending cap to apply during the forty days before the campaign commencement. The British Columbia Court of Appeal disapproved of even this more narrowly tailored legislation in the *Reference*. The view of the British Columbia courts appears to have been that *Harper* should be read narrowly, as permitting only election period restrictions. Pre-writ spending restrictions are outside the ambit of what *Harper* envisioned, on this view.

The British Columbia courts failed to give effect to the legitimacy of egalitarian regulation of the permanent campaign. The legislation restricting pre-writ spending by interest groups accompanied the introduction of fixed election dates in the province.[68] The courts ignored the fact that the move to fixed dates provided incentives for third parties, like teachers' unions, to shift their advertising to the pre-writ period.

The *Reference* and *BCTF* also misread the Supreme Court in *Harper*. The British Columbia courts understood the result in *Harper* as turning

66 2012 BCCA 394.

67 2009 BCSC 436 aff'd 2011 BCCA 408.

68 *Reference*, *supra* note 66, para 10.

on the fact that the federal third party rules restricted spending only during the official election period. It is true that because the rules applied only during the official campaign, the *Harper* majority viewed them as less intrusive than if in force more broadly. Yet this was not the decisive factor for the Supreme Court. *Harper* ruled on the constitutionality of the federal third party regime during a period of political behaviour that did not include pre-writ spending in any significant amount. There was no relevant time period other than the campaign for the Court to consider. Reading *Harper* as permitting only election period restrictions misunderstands the political circumstances informing the Court at the time, before the full emergence of the permanent campaign.

The British Columbia *Reference* states that "[i]interfering with the freedom of political expression must then be justifiable only where there are the clearest and most compelling reasons for doing so."[69] This statement correctly envisions freedom of political expression as worthy of the highest protection from the courts and the constitution. In my view, however, ensuring the viability of the egalitarian model fits within the need to limit political expression only for the "clearest and most compelling reasons." As the Supreme Court recognized in *Harper,* without a level playing field for elections, we risk allowing money to dominate politics.

The *Elections Modernization Act* – Bill C-76

Bill C-76, the *Elections Modernization Act,*[70] would make amendments related to many of the issues discussed in this paper. Introduced in April 2018, the bill at the time of writing had passed Second Reading, been referred to Committee, and appears likely to be passed in substantially similar form before the October 2019 federal election. It would impose far-reaching changes to the *Canada Elections Act*. In regard to the permanent campaign, it would (1) introduce a maximum campaign length, (2) introduce pre-writ spending limits, and (3) expand the list of regulated third party activities in both the pre-writ and the writ periods.

69 *Ibid*, para 25.

70 Canada, Parliament, House of Commons, "An Act to amend the Canada Elections Act and other Acts and to make certain consequential amendments," Bill C-76, 42nd Parliament, 1st Session, 2015–18. (2nd Reading, 23 May 2018).

Overall, the bill would make a very positive contribution, although it could have gone further in defence of egalitarian values.

The bill would restrict but not eliminate discretion over the length of the campaign. It would set a range of thirty-seven to fifty days for the campaign.[71] The spending limit would still increase if the campaign went longer than thirty-seven days.[72] Its provisions would provide advance notice to all parties as to the earliest and latest possible starts of the formal campaign and the resulting possible variance in the spending limit. The bill would, therefore, meaningfully limit the most problematic potential manipulations of election campaign length by a government. It would, however, still provide some discretion for a government to expand the length of the campaign and therefore also to increase the spending limit if such a move brought some anticipated partisan advantage.

The legislation would also introduce pre-writ spending limits for third parties and political parties. Political parties would be able to spend up to $1.5 million, and third parties $1 million, subject to an inflation adjustment.[73] The pre-writ period would begin on 30 June of an election year.[74] Working backwards from the fixed election date of 21 October 2019, the pre-writ period would run from the end of June until the beginning or middle of September, depending on whether the official campaign was closer to thirty-seven or fifty days. The introduction of a pre-writ regulatory period is very welcome, although it is likely to be over too short a time period to truly transform the permanent campaign. Given the fixed election date in late October, the pre-writ period would also only cover the late summer, when most Canadians seem unlikely to be paying close attention to federal politics.

The new restrictions would also expand the scope of third party activities that are captured by the rules. Not just advertising but also other "partisan activities"[75] would be subject to spending limits, for the first time. Both the pre-writ and the writ period spending limits would cover advertising as well as other partisan activities of third parties. Partisan activities are defined to specifically include door-to-door

71 *Ibid*, s 47.

72 *Ibid*, s 263, amending s 430(2) of the *Canada Elections Act*, *supra* note 13.

73 *Ibid*, s 349.1(1). See s 348 and s 349(4) for the inflation adjustment that brings the initial amount of $700,000 to $1 million.

74 See the definition of *pre-election period*, *Ibid*, s 2(7).

75 *Ibid*, s 222(3).

canvassing and telephone contact with voters and would likely also encompass "get out the vote" operations.[76]

The most constitutionally suspect aspects of Bill C-76 are the pre-writ spending limits and the expansion of the scope of third party activities subject to them. I have advanced in this chapter a general argument that reasonable pre-writ restrictions should be seen as constitutional. In my view, the pre-writ restrictions on third parties and political parties in C-76 should be seen as passing *Charter* scrutiny.

The bill addresses constitutional concerns in three main ways. First, the pre-writ period is limited in length. This fact causes policy concerns as it reduces its effectiveness. Advertising of unlimited dollar value can still occur before 30 June in an election year. The intrusion on freedom of expression, however, is reduced in comparison to a longer pre-writ period of six months or a year. Further, the House of Commons usually does not sit in July and August. The pre-writ period is therefore unlikely to restrict third parties from criticizing elected representatives in the process of carrying out their legislative duties, which was a concern in the British Columbia litigation.[77]

Second, the spending limits on third parties appear to be rationally connected to the length of the regulated period and the amount permitted in the official campaign. The $1 million pre-writ limit on third parties can be spent over approximately two months. C-76 would increase the amount that third parties can spend during the official campaign, on political advertising but also partisan activities, to $500,000. The limit applying in the two-month pre-writ period would therefore be double the amount permitted in the just over a month-long official campaign period, if the campaign is thirty-seven days.

Restrictions on political party activity in the pre-writ period are less constitutionally controversial than those on third parties. Political parties are highly regulated in many ways already. The pre-writ spending limit for political parties is in any case quite generous, which should mitigate constitutional concerns.

---

76 *Ibid.*

77 The "Charter Statement" released by the minister of justice on C-76 directly supports this interpretation of why 30 June was chosen as the start date. Minister of Justice, "Charter Statement – *Bill C-76,*" tabled 8 May 2018, http://www.justice.gc.ca/eng/csj-sjc/pl/charter-charte/c76.html.

Third, while the pre-writ spending limit would capture more of the "partisan activities" of third parties, it would cover less advertising than in the writ period. The pre-writ limit would cover the newly defined practice of "partisan advertising," rather than "election advertising," which sets out what advertising is caught during the campaign period.[78] The difference between the two is that while election advertising during the official campaign includes communications on issues "associated" with a candidate, leader, or party, such messages would not be captured in the pre-writ period.[79] The restrictions on expression in the pre-writ period would, therefore, be less intrusive than during the campaign.

It seems inevitable that these aspects of C-76, particularly the restrictions on third party partisan advertising and partisan activities during the pre-writ period, will be the subject of a constitutional challenge. In my view, while the content of the bill goes beyond what was specifically contemplated in *Harper,* it should be seen as constitutional. The bill takes a relatively conservative constitutional approach. By limiting the length of the pre-writ period, as well as by applying high spending limits, the pre-writ rules are much less intrusive than they could be otherwise. They also appear to be narrowly tailored to respond to the now well-documented changes in political behaviour that undermine the egalitarian model, such as third parties carrying out activities beyond advertising. If anything, the bill could have been even more aggressive in regulating the pre-writ period in defence of egalitarian values.

Conclusion

The permanent campaign seems to be a permanent feature of Canadian electoral life. The egalitarian model reflected in the *Canada Elections Act,* and endorsed by the Supreme Court of Canada on multiple occasions, has been put at risk by the move to a permanent campaign. The permanent campaign as manifest in Canada has exposed the loopholes in the existing legal regime. Pre-writ spending, strategic manipulation of campaign length, and an evolving and more robust role for third parties challenge the continuing viability of the egalitarian model.

78 See the definition of *partisan advertising* in C-76, *supra* note 70, s 2(7).

79 *Ibid.* See the phrase "otherwise than by taking a position on an issue with which any such person or party is associated."

The model needs to be updated to take into account these shifts in political behaviour. Reforms establishing a spending limit not just during the official campaign but also in the lead-up to an election, as well as mandating campaign length, would go a long way to re-establishing the egalitarian model. A cap on spending in the pre-writ period would likely stretch the Supreme Court of Canada's willingness to limit political expression in the furtherance of egalitarian goals. The underlying attempt to ensure a level playing field and the narrow tailoring of the proposed new rules to the time immediately preceding a campaign should be seen as answering these constitutional concerns. If the courts are not willing to countenance restrictions on pre-writ spending, the permanent campaign will mean the end of the egalitarian model of elections in Canada.

14 Immutability, Immigration Status, and the Limits of Equality Protection

EFRAT ARBEL AND EILEEN MYRDAHL*

Introduction

It is well established that s. 15 of the *Canadian Charter of Rights and Freedoms* was designed to ensure a generous reading of equality rights and to reverse the restrictive interpretation of equality that had dominated under the *Bill of Rights*.[1] In giving meaning to s. 15(1), the Supreme Court of Canada has sought to balance the *Charter*'s equality guarantee with the recognition that making distinctions is central to governing.[2] To this end, the Court limits the scope of s. 15(1) to claims of discrimination based on the grounds enumerated in the section and grounds that are analogous to these. As originally formulated, the grounds analysis was designed as a way to understand discrimination: it was to be the looking glass through which courts could analyse the discrimination

* Efrat Arbel is assistant professor at the University of British Columbia Peter A. Allard School of Law. Eileen Myrdahl is an articled student in Vancouver. Our thanks to the volume editors and conference participants for their helpful comments on earlier drafts of this chapter.

1 See, e.g., *Andrews v Law Society of British Columbia* [1989] 1 SCR 143 p 170 [*Andrews*]; Leslie A. Pal and F.L. Morton, "*Bliss v Attorney General of Canada:* From Legal Defeat to Political Victory," *Osgoode Hall Law Journal* 24 (1986) 141, 156; Claire L'Heureux-Dubé, "The Changing Face of Equality: The Indirect Effects of Section 15 of the Charter," *Canadian Woman Studies* (1999) 1. Section 15(1) reads, "Every individual is equal before and under the law and has the right to the equal protection and equal benefit of the law without discrimination and, in particular, without discrimination based on race, national or ethnic origin, colour, religion, sex, age or mental or physical disability."

2 *Andrews*, *supra* note 1, 175; *Quebec v A* 2013 SCC 5 [*Quebec v A*], para 141.

that s. 15(1) prohibits.[3] In time, however, the grounds analysis has come to operate less as a way to understand discrimination and more as a hurdle that claimants must overcome for their experiences of discrimination to be made legally comprehensible. As a result, the analysis has distanced s. 15(1) from the underlying goal of substantive equality that it purports to protect.

In *Corbiere v Canada*, the Supreme Court explained that two criteria are required to recognize a new analogous ground under s. 15(1): historic discrimination and immutability.[4] While the historical discrimination requirement has been applied in a straightforward manner, the immutability requirement has been subject to both controversy and criticism.[5] In this chapter, we build on this criticism by pointing to key problems with courts' interpretation of the immutability requirement in recent case law. To elucidate these problems, we survey cases in which courts have interpreted the immutability requirement to deny claims based on the ground of immigration status. Since immigration status is a core category through which the federal and provincial governments seek to incorporate permissible distinctions made in one context (immigration) into other areas of law (e.g., health care), these cases are particularly apt to illustrate the problems with placing a requirement of immutability at the heart of the grounds analysis.

More broadly, as Asha Kaushal argues in this volume, the nature of Canadian diversity is changing, and these changes are closely tied to immigration.[6] Since discrimination claims on the basis of immigration status are likely to proliferate, these cases present opportunities to

---

3 *Andrews, supra* note 1, 179–80.

4 *Corbiere v Canada (Minister of Indian and Northern Affairs)*, [1999] 2 SCR 203 [*Corbiere*], para 13.

5 See, e.g., Rosalind Dixon, "The Supreme Court of Canada and Constitutional (Equality) Baselines," *Osgoode Hall Law Journal* 50 (2013) 637; Joshua Sealy-Harrington, "Assessing Analogous Grounds: The Doctrinal and Normative Superiority of a Multi-variable Approach," *Journal of Law and Equality* 10 (2013) 37. For additional critiques of the concept of immutability as applied in law, see, e.g., Jessica A. Clarke, "Against Immutability," *Yale Law Journal* 125, no. 2 (2015) 32; Emily R. Gill, "Beyond Immutability: Sexuality and Constitutive Choice," *Review of Politics* 76 (2014) 93; Carl F. Stychin, "Essential Rights and Contested Identities: Sexual Orientation and Equality Rights Jurisprudence in Canada," *Canadian Journal of Law and Jurisprudence* 8 (1995) 49. See also Justice L'Heureux-Dubé's dissent in *Corbiere*, discussed *infra*, notes 77 and 78.

6 Asha Kaushal, chap 7 in this volume.

rethink existing frameworks of constitutional thinking to better enable the realization of the *Charter*'s substantive equality guarantee.

While the case law on immigration status is mixed, more often than not, Canadian courts have rejected immigration status as an analogous ground, demonstrating a tacit resistance to viewing it as a marker of "suspect decision making or potential discrimination."[7] We focus on three such cases: *Irshad (Litigation guardian of) v Ontario*, *Toussaint v Canada*, and *Doctors for Refugee Care v Canada*.[8] We argue that these cases point to two troubling tendencies in judicial interpretations of immutability: first, the tendency to pay insufficient attention to factors that constrain an applicant's choice in relation to her immigration status; and second, the tendency to narrowly fixate on the perceived inalterability of the applicant's status over time. In the result, courts too often reject equality claims at the first stage of the s. 15(1) analysis and never reach the stage where they can engage in the sort of fine-grained analysis of discrimination that Emily Kidd White envisions in this volume.[9] In critiquing these tendencies, we advocate for an approach that is grounded in context, one that more meaningfully considers both an applicant's lived experience and the broader dynamics of discrimination she suffers. Such an approach, we suggest, has the potential to reshape the s. 15(1) analysis to better meet contemporary challenges and more effectively realize the goal of substantive equality.

---

7 As the Supreme Court of Canada explained in *Corbiere*, *supra* note 4, the "enumerated and analogous grounds stand as constant markers of suspect decision making or potential discrimination. What varies is whether they amount to discrimination in the particular circumstances of the case" (para 8).

8 *Irshad (Litigation guardian of) v Ontario* (2001), 55 OR (3d) 43 [*Irshad*]; *Toussaint v Canada* 2011 FCA 213 [*Toussaint*]; *Doctors for Refugee Care v Canada*, 2013 FC 651 [*Doctors for Refugee Care*]. The Supreme Court of Canada has never been asked to recognize immigration status as an analogous ground. It refused leave in both *Irshad* and *Toussaint*, where lower courts had declined to recognize immigration status as an analogous ground. While the Harper government appealed the Federal Court's decision in *Doctors for Refugee Care*, the appeal was dropped with the election of the Trudeau government in 2015 and its restoration of the Interim Federal Health Program as of 1 April 2016. See Stephanie Levitz, "Liberals Formally Drop Lawsuit over Refugee Health Care Cuts," *Globe and Mail*, 16 December 2015, http://www.theglobeandmail.com/news/politics/liberals-formally-drop-lawsuit-over-refugee-health-care-cuts/article27780258/.

9 Emily Kidd White, chap 12 in this volume.

Our analysis proceeds in three parts. First, we briefly lay out court jurisprudence on the purpose of s. 15(1) and the justification for, and development of, the analogous grounds analysis. Second, we illustrate the problems with this approach through a discussion of the three cases noted above. We conclude by arguing that the courts' use of the grounds analysis exposes the limits of s. 15(1)'s equality guarantee: the grounds analysis both fails to recognize how discrimination operates and makes it more difficult to recognize even egregious state conduct targeting vulnerable groups for inferior treatment as discrimination. Both legally and symbolically, s. 15(1) operates as the gatekeeper that separates discriminatory distinctions from the distinctions that must necessarily be drawn in the process of governing. When courts institute a system of gatekeeping that makes certain state discrimination effectively permissible, they send a signal that these forms of discrimination are not "repugnant" and are, by implication, not really discrimination at all.[10]

The Promise of "Unremitting" Equality Protection: The Analogous Grounds Analysis

The grounds analysis has been subject to surprisingly little challenge since it was introduced in *Andrews v Law Society of British Columbia*, a 1989 case in which a British citizen and permanent resident in Canada challenged the Law Society of British Columbia's restriction on non-citizens practising law in the province.[11] There, Justice McIntyre stated that s. 15(1)'s purpose was "to ensure equality in the formulation and application of the law" and to promote "a society in which all are secure in the knowledge that they are recognized at law as human beings equally deserving of concern, respect and consideration."[12] McIntyre J further made clear that s. 15 protected substantive equality. In other words, it would not be enough for the law to treat everyone the same (formal equality) if doing so imposed "burdens, obligations, or disadvantages" on, or withheld "opportunities, benefits, and advantages" from, individuals based on their personal characteristics.[13] Although

10 In *Andrews, supra* note 1, McIntyre J noted that "discrimination reinforced by law is particularly repugnant" (172).

11 *Ibid.*

12 *Ibid*, 171.

13 *Ibid*, 174–5. Although the Court has been steadfast in its commitment to substantive equality, its analyses sometimes veer very close to formal equality. See, e.g., Margot

the Supreme Court has since come to diverge on how to conceive of the s. 15(1) test, the goal of substantive equality has remained unchallenged and still lies at the core of the provision.[14]

While the Court's commitment to substantive equality is expansive, it must be viewed in the context of its much narrower understanding of what s. 15(1) seeks to prohibit. The Supreme Court clarified the s. 15(1) test most recently in *Quebec v A*, stating that to establish a s. 15(1) violation, an applicant must prove (1) that the government has made a distinction based on a ground that is either enumerated in, or analogous to, those listed in the section and (2) that the distinction's impact on the individual or group results in discrimination by creating a disadvantage or perpetuating a stereotype or prejudice.[15]

In its application, therefore, s. 15(1) extends only to claims of discrimination experienced on the basis of the enumerated grounds of race, national or ethnic origin, colour, religion, sex, age, and mental or physical disability, or on grounds found to be analogous to these. In establishing this approach in *Andrews*, McIntyre J explained that the grounds operated as an expression of the discrimination that s. 15(1) prohibited.[16] Put another way, the grounds analysis provides courts with the necessary guideposts by which to determine what discrimination means. As Justice McIntyre further explained, the grounds must be interpreted in a "broad and generous manner" to provide both a "continuing framework for the legitimate exercise of governmental power" and a mechanism to enable the "unremitting protection" of equality rights.[17] This approach, he noted, not only best accorded with the definition of discrimination that he had laid out,

---

Young, "Blissed Out: Section 15 at Twenty," *Supreme Court Law Review* 33 (2006) 45; Jennifer Koshan and Jonnette Watson Hamilton, "Meaningless Mantra: Substantive Equality after *Withler*," *Review of Constitutional* Studies 16 (2011) 31.

14 See, e.g., *Quebec v A*, *supra* note 2, comparing the differences between the majority and dissent.

15 *Ibid*, para 324. Once a violation of s 15(1) is found, the burden shifts to the government to prove that the violation is demonstrably justified under s 1 of the *Charter*.

16 *Andrews*, *supra* note 1, 179–80. See also William Black and Lynn Smith, "The Equality Rights," in *Canadian Charter of Rights and Freedoms*, ed. Gérald-A. Beaudoin and Errol Mendes (Markham, ON: LexisNexis Butterworths, 2005), 925, 962. In contrast, Rosalind Dixon argues that the focus on enumerated and analogous grounds is a compromise between those seeking a broad equality guarantee and those wanting to limit the equality guarantee; see *supra* note 5, 644.

17 *Andrews*, *supra* note 1, 174–5 (citations omitted).

but also effectively balanced s. 15 and s. 1 and protected against "the trivial and vexatious claim."[18]

While the legal test for determining analogous grounds has changed very little since *Andrews*, the Court's overall approach to this determination has shifted over the years. As Rosalind Dixon demonstrates, in its initial years of applying the test, the Court's approach was relatively broad and generous, allowing for the recognition of various grounds as analogous.[19] Over time, however, the Court has moved towards a more formalist analysis, which focuses on the common denominator of the enumerated grounds – necessarily a much more limited scope, given the variety of the list.[20] The Court's formalistic approach to the grounds analysis emerged with the release of *Corbiere*, where the majority entrenched immutability as the test for recognizing analogous grounds. Writing for the majority, Bastarache J and McLachlin J (as she then was) held that the common denominator of the enumerated grounds was that they were traits that were "immutable or changeable only at unacceptable cost to personal identity."[21] They further described the enumerated grounds as "legislative markers of suspect grounds associated with stereotypical, discriminatory decision making," which distinguished trivial from non-trivial equality claims.[22]

18 *Ibid*, 182. Under Canadian law, for a constitutional violation to be found, the applicant must first show a violation of a *Charter* provision, after which the burden shifts to the government to prove that the violation is demonstrably justified under s 1 of the *Charter*. The s 1 test, outlined in *R v Oakes*, [1986] 1 SCR 103, as supplemented by subsequent case law, prescribes that a violating law will be upheld under s 1 only if it relates to a pressing and substantial legislative objective that warrants overriding a constitutionally protected right and if the means chosen for its implementation are reasonable, proportionate, and impair the right as minimally as possible.

19 For a complete discussion, see Dixon, *supra* note 5. (In addition to recognizing citizenship as an analogous ground in *Andrews*, the Court recognized a few other analogous grounds in the years after the *Andrews* release – namely, sexual orientation in *Egan v Canada*, [1995] 2 SCR 513 [*Egan*], marital status in *Miron v Trudel* [1995] 2 SCR 418, and off-reserve residential status in *Corbiere*, *supra* note 4.)

20 *Ibid*, 646–55. Indeed, rather than deploy the heterogeneous nature of the grounds enumerated in s 15(1) to broaden equality protection to a diverse range of claimants, the Court has instead referenced this heterogeneity to deny claims.

21 *Corbiere*, *supra* note 4, para 13.

22 *Ibid*, paras 7, 11.

In the *Corbiere* framework, immutability is understood to apply to characteristics that are either "actually immutable," such as race, or "constructively immutable, like religion."[23] It is important to note that the scope of what is considered "like religion" is limited to characteristics that "the government has no legitimate interest in expecting us to change to receive equal treatment under the law."[24] Despite these guidelines, the Court never truly explains what immutability means in the context of the grounds analysis or why it should play such a central role in the s. 15(1) test.[25] As Joshua Sealy-Harrington's analysis persuasively demonstrates, this has left the *Corbiere* test "replete with conceptual ambiguities."[26] Nevertheless, the Court has confirmed that immutability remains at the core of the grounds analysis.[27]

In the years since the Court identified immutability as essential to the grounds analysis, it has not recognized a single new ground as analogous.[28] Notwithstanding its stated commitment to a broad and generous reading of equality rights, the Court has adopted an increasingly inflexible approach to this branch of the s. 15(1) test, exhibiting what Dixon describes as a "surprising degree of formalism at the level of constitutional reasoning."[29] Rather than explore the broad, underlying notions of substantive equality – such as anti-discrimination and human dignity – the Court has instead adopted a rigid approach that does not meaningfully analyse the relationship between personal characteristics

23 *Ibid*, para 13.

24 *Ibid*.

25 For an analysis of why courts identify immutability as central to the equality analysis, see Clarke, *supra* note 5 – suggesting, *inter alia*, that the immutability analysis is "premised on the moral intuition that discrimination against those who are blameworthy is fair" or on the "unstated assumption that the law should create incentives for good (or efficient) behaviour by allowing discrimination on the basis of certain bad (or costly) choices."

26 Sealy-Harrington, *supra* note 5.

27 In *Quebec v A*, *supra* note 2, Abella J, for the majority on s 15(1), noted that "*by definition*, analogous grounds are 'personal characteristic[s] that [are] immutable or changeable only at unacceptable cost to personal identity'" (para 335; emphasis added).

28 For a complete analysis, see Dixon, *supra* note 5. In *Corbiere*, *supra* note 4, the Supreme Court cautioned against adopting "formalistic straightjacket[s]" (para 12). The rigid application of the immutability requirement is at risk of becoming one such straitjacket.

29 Dixon, *supra* note 5, 639.

and equality that s. 15(1) strives to protect and that is far removed from the principles outlined in *Andrews*.[30] In practice, the post-*Corbiere* analysis focuses on the mutability of the claimant's "choice," without considering how underlying dynamics of discrimination constrain or inform that choice. Too often, the analysis is reduced to a judicial assessment of whether a claimant's choices make him sufficiently worthy of protection in the eyes of the law. In the context of the "immigration status" cases, the grounds analysis has constrained, rather than broadened, the scope of equality protection extended by s. 15(1).

The "Immigration Status" Cases and the Challenge of Immutability

While the s. 15(1) case law involving immigration status is inconsistent, most courts have been stern in their refusal to recognize the ground as analogous.[31] Three recent decisions – *Irshad (Litigation guardian of) v Ontario, Toussaint v Canada,* and *Canadian Doctors for Refugee Care v Canada* – stand out in particular.[32] Each of these cases involved a s. 15(1) claim made by non-citizen claimants who had been denied access to health care. All three claims failed at the first branch of the s. 15(1) test on the basis that immigration status could not be recognized as an analogous ground. These decisions illustrate the core problem with the grounds analysis that we referenced above – namely, the judicial tendency to interpret immutability without adequately considering a claimant's lived experience or the broader dynamics of discrimination to which she is subject.

Toussaint v Canada illuminates the problems with the courts' current preoccupation with choice in determining whether a ground can be regarded as immutable and therefore recognized as analogous.[33] The

---

30 *Ibid.*

31 Indeed, in *Fraser v Canada*, [2005] OJ No 5580, para 78, the Ontario Superior Court of Justice stated clearly that whether immigration status was an analogous ground had not been settled. See, e.g., *Jaballah, Re*, 2006 FC 115, para 80, where the Federal Court recognized immigration status as an analogous ground (involving a challenge to a provision of the *Immigration and Refugee Protection Act*, which was found to be unconstitutional under s 15(1)).

32 *Irshad, Toussaint, Doctors for Refugee Care, supra* note 8.

33 The focus on choice is common in the case law. As the Supreme Court explained most recently in *Quebec v A, supra* note 2, para 343, choice "may be an important

case involved a s. 15(1) claim by a woman who had been denied medical coverage because she had overstayed her visitor's visa. Throughout her first seven years in Canada, she had worked and earned enough to sustain herself, but when her health began to deteriorate and she could no longer work, she applied for health coverage – first under the Ontario Health Insurance Plan and later under the Interim Federal Health Program (IFHP).[34] She was denied coverage under both programs. During this time, she also sought to regularize her status by applying for permanent residency.[35] Unable to afford the application fees, she applied for a fee waiver, which was refused, and her application was consequently never considered.[36]

Ms. Toussaint advanced a claim *inter alia,* under s. 15(1) of the *Charter*, on the basis that the decision to deny her coverage under the IFHP discriminated against her because of her immigration status.[37] The Federal Court of Appeal rejected her claim on the basis that immigration status could not be recognized as an analogous ground. The Court reasoned that Ms. Toussaint's immigration status – which it defined as "presence in Canada illegally" – was the product of personal choice and thus within her capacity to change. The Court's analysis on this

---

factor in determining whether a ground of discrimination qualifies as an analogous ground," per Abella J (for the majority on s 15(1)). The Supreme Court of Canada has also deployed narratives of choice to deny equality claims based on enumerated grounds. See, e.g., *Hodge v Canada,* 2004 SCC 65; *Nova Scotia (AG) v Walsh,* 2002 SCC 83; *Gosselin v Québec,* 2002 SCC 84. For further discussion, see also Sonia Lawrence, "Choice, Equality and Tales of Racial Discrimination: Reading the Supreme Court on Section 15," *Supreme Court Law Review* 33 (2006) 115; Young, *supra* note 13.

34 *Toussaint, supra* note 8 at para 2.

35 *Ibid*, paras 4–6.

36 *Ibid*, paras 4–7.

37 *Ibid*. The applicant also sought judicial review of the decision to reject her application for coverage under the Interim Federal Health Program, and she advanced a claim under s 7 of the *Charter,* which guarantees the right to "life, liberty and security of the person and the right not to be deprived thereof except in accordance with the principles of fundamental justice." Notably, the applicant did not seek to have immigration status recognized as an analogous ground at the Federal Court. See *Toussaint v Canada,* 2010 FC 810, where the court stated that it was "not for the Court in *Charter* cases to construct arguments for the parties or advance them on their behalf. Given the applicant's failure to argue that 'immigration status' was an analogous ground, the applicant's s.15(1) argument must fail" (para 82).

point was scant and unambiguous. Citing *Corbiere*, it held simply that "presence in Canada illegally" was a characteristic that not only could Ms. Toussaint change but that the Canadian government also had a "legitimate interest" in expecting her to change.[38] The Court held further that the Canadian government had a "real, valid, and justified interest in expecting those present in Canada to have a legal right to be in Canada."[39] It concluded that Ms. Toussaint's immigration status could not be characterized as "immutable or changeable only at unacceptable cost to personal identity" and that her claim could not succeed.

In its fixation on the mutability of the claimant's status, the Federal Court of Appeal did not consider how the claimant – a poor and marginalized woman with severe medical conditions and precarious legal status – was constrained in her ability to choose a different course of action.[40] It also did not consider either the claimant's reasons for remaining in Canada without a permit or her exhibited willingness to change her status but inability to do so.[41] Rather than analyse how her social positioning might constrain her choice, the Court approached Ms. Toussaint as a liberal, autonomous subject whose agency was not impeded by societal or legal structures. This approach, unmoored from an actual engagement with how dynamics of discrimination operate in practice, tells a skewed story.[42] As Sonia Lawrence notes in her analysis of race-based claims under s. 15(1), such an approach almost certainly tells a different story than the story of discrimination that those who are its targets would tell.[43] It fails to recognize that the details of one's immigration status affect almost every aspect of one's life in Canada:

---

38 *Toussaint, supra* note 8, para 99.

39 *Ibid.*

40 Notably, *Doctors for Refugee Care, Irshad,* and *Toussaint, supra* note 8 were released before *Canada v Bedford,* 2013 SCC 72, in which the Supreme Court of Canada engaged with the meaning of *constrained choice* in its s 7 analysis. For an analysis of how the *Bedford* decision might impact the conclusions reached in *Doctors for Refugee Care,* see Naomi Moses, "'Seeking the Protection of Canada': Applying *Bedford's* Section 7 Principles to the *Canadian Doctors* Decision," on file with author.

41 *Toussaint, supra* note 8, para 4.

42 Lawrence, *supra* note 33, 128.

43 *Ibid.*

where one may live, where or if one may work or go to school, the health care one receives, and every aspect of one's interactions with the government and the law.[44]

The Ontario Court of Appeal adopted a similar approach in *Irshad (Litigation guardian of) v Ontario,* where it refused to recognize immigration status as an analogous ground on the basis that the applicants' status as non-permanent residents of a province was not immutable.[45] One of five applicants in the case, Raja, was a child immigrant whose permanent disability made him inadmissible under Canadian immigration law. Through an exercise of ministerial discretion, Raja was given an indefinite temporary immigration permit, which in turn made him ineligible for provincial health care benefits due to his "temporary" residence in Ontario.[46] In finding that his immigration status was mutable, the Ontario Court of Appeal noted that it was open to the minister of citizenship and immigration to grant Raja the permanent residency that would make him eligible for the health care benefits at issue.[47] Notwithstanding the fact that he could not exercise choice without the minister's approval, the Court did not recognize such constraints as legally relevant.

44 *Corbiere, supra* note 4, para 13. Indeed, most migrants have significantly *less* control over their immigration status than any individual has over, e.g., their marital status, which the Court has recognized as an analogous ground. For documentation of the current and historical discrimination of immigrants in Canada, see, e.g., Andrew Baldwin, Laura Cameron, and Audrey Kobayashi, *Rethinking the Great White North* (Vancouver: UBC Press, 2011); Sherene H. Razack, *Casting Out* (Toronto: University of Toronto Press, 2008).

45 *Irshad, supra* note 8, paras 135–6.

46 *Ibid*, para 56. The applicant's father had refugee status in Canada, which meant that the family could not simply return to their country of origin. Since the applicant was only eight years old when he entered Canada, and also had a severe and permanent disability, it would not have been reasonable to expect his family to leave him behind (as, indeed, Canada acknowledged by granting him a discretionary permit).

47 *Ibid*, para 139. *Irshad* is cited by subsequent case law as a precedent for the rejection of immigration status as an analogous ground; see, e.g., *Doctors for Refugee Care, supra* note 8, paras 865–7. But it should be noted that discrimination based on immigration status was not argued in the case. The quality of reasoning on this matter in *Irshad* is particularly poor, but the case is also a weak example of courts' treatment of equality claims based on immigration status as the Ontario Court of Appeal did not have the benefit of submissions on the issue. Compare *Jaballah, Re, supra* note 31, where the Federal Court accepted that differential treatment among immigrants constituted discrimination on an analogous ground.

Had the Court engaged with this claim by reference to broader dynamics of discrimination, it would have been able to analyse the immutability of Raja's immigration status along multiple axes of difference: in view of his social positioning, age, and disability. Such an approach would not only have better reflected his lived experience but also have better accorded with the thrust of the Supreme Court of Canada's s. 15(1) case law. In its early decision in *R v Turpin*, for example, cautioning against reducing the s. 15(1) analysis to a "mechanical and sterile categorization process," the Court held that the analogous grounds analysis must be made "in the context of the place of the group in the entire social, political and legal fabric of our society."[48] To the extent that it failed to consider the factors that informed Raja's choice, this approach obscured from view the broader dynamics of discrimination, which, as Janet Halley argues, were the "normatively important thing to notice."[49] Indeed, analysing the applicant's choice contextually and by reference to these dynamics would have forced the Court to contend more fully with the claim before it and, perhaps, to recognize the extent to which Raja's choice was fundamentally constrained.

In addition to its narrow treatment of choice, the Court held in *Irshad* that immigration status could not be recognized as immutable because it was subject to change over time. Contrasting Raja's disability with his immigration status, the Court concluded that while the former was inalterable, there was "no basis in [the] record" for concluding that the latter would stay fixed should the minister decide to exercise his discretion.[50] In support of this conclusion, the Court emphasized that four of the five applicants in the case, who were non-permanent residents at the time the litigation started, had acquired permanent residency by the time the appeal was heard.[51] Since their status had changed, the Court reasoned, it could not be regarded as immutable. By implication, therefore, neither could Raja's.

48 *R v Turpin*, [1989] 1 SCR 1296.

49 Janet E. Halley, "'Like Race' Arguments," in *What's Left of Theory*, ed. Judith Butler et al (New York: Routledge, 2000). See also Janet E. Halley, "Sexual Orientation and the Politics of Biology: A Critique of the Argument from Immutability," *Stanford Law Review* 46 (1993–94) 503.

50 *Irshad*, *supra* note 8, para 136.

51 *Ibid*.

This tendency to interpret the immutability requirement as necessitating proof of inalterability over time – also exhibited by the Court in *Toussaint* and *Doctors for Refugee Care* – is misguided. Neither *Andrews* nor *Corbiere* required courts to find that the trait at issue could *never* change for it to be immutable, only that the discrimination experienced by the claimant as a result of that trait would exist for a long time.[52] The courts have long recognized this with age – the fact that one's age will eventually change does not diminish the discrimination one suffers as a result of one's age at any given time.[53] As Lebel J noted in *Quebec v A* (in dissent), the "concept of immutability … is not synonymous with eternity" – immutable traits can still "change or disappear … especially where they are related to customs or social behaviour that could change."[54]

Moreover, the mere fact that one's immigration status might, at some point, change does not detract from the discrimination one experiences before that change. Take, for example, the case of *Andrews*: the fact that Mr. Andrews acquired Canadian citizenship in the course of his appeal did not diminish the discrimination he had suffered as a non-citizen at the material time, nor did it render his status as a non-citizen mutable in the eyes of the Supreme Court of Canada. Indeed, *Andrews* recognized that citizenship was immutable not because it was inalterable over time, but because it was "typically not *within the control of the individual*" to change, suggesting that it was the control of the individual that was relevant for the purposes of the immutability analysis, not the inalterability of the trait at issue.[55] This approach also accords with *Corbiere,* which states that the thrust of the analogous grounds analysis "is to reveal grounds based on characteristics that *we cannot change* or that the government has no legitimate interest in expecting us to change to receive equal treatment under the law."[56]

The courts' misguided search for inalterability over time not only strays from *Andrews* and *Corbiere* but also replicates the problems associated with the comparator group analysis, now firmly rejected by the Supreme

52 Respondents' Memorandum of Fact and Law, *Canada v Doctors for Refugee Care et al,* Court File No.: A-407-14 [Respondents' Memorandum], para 98.

53 We are grateful to Audrey Macklin for this insight; see also *Ibid.*

54 *Quebec v A, supra* note 2, para 182.

55 *Andrews, supra* note 1, para 67 (emphasis added); see also Respondents' Memorandum, *supra* note 52.

56 *Corbiere, supra* note 4 (emphasis added).

Court of Canada in *Withler v Canada*.[57] There, writing for the Court, Justice Abella and Chief Justice McLachlin cautioned against "converting the inquiry into substantive equality into a formalistic and arbitrary search for the 'proper' comparator group."[58] Instead, they emphasized the need for an "approach that looks at the full context," underscoring that it was the goal of substantive equality that must be the foremost concern in analyses of discrimination under s. 15.[59] *Withler* cautions against adopting an approach that allows the comparator group analysis to determine the outcome of the case without sufficient attention being paid to the allegations of discrimination raised by the claimant.[60] This critique applies equally to the grounds analysis: when a s. 15(1) claim is made on grounds that are not recognized as analogous, the analysis stops before it has substantially engaged with the discrimination at issue.

The Federal Court's recent decision in *Doctors for Refugee Care v Canada* highlights the logical inconsistencies that flow from making the analysis of discrimination so wholly dependent on the establishment of an analogous ground. This case involved a challenge to changes made to the IFHP – a federal health program in place since 1957 that provided basic, life-saving care to refugees, asylum seekers, and other non-citizens.[61] In 2012, the minister of citizenship and immigration

57 *Withler v Canada*, 2011 SCC 12 [*Withler*]. Before *Withler*'s release, the s 15(1) test mandated the identification of a "comparator group," against which the test was to be evaluated. The Court rejected this approach in *Withler*, stating that a "formal analysis based on comparison between the claimant group and a 'similarly situated' group, does not assure a result that captures the wrong to which s.15(1) is directed. ... What is required is not formal comparison with a selected mirror comparator group, but an approach that looks at the full context, including the situation of the claimant group and whether the impact of the impugned law is to perpetuate disadvantage or negative stereotypes about that group" (para 40).

58 *Ibid*, para 2.

59 *Ibid*, para 40.

60 *Ibid*, para 56. Notably, *Withler* also cautions against deploying the comparator group analysis to overlook the realities of intersectional grounds of discrimination (paras 56–9, 63).

61 *Doctors for Refugee Care*, *supra* note 8, para 58. For the sake of brevity, we refer to the migrants covered by the IFHP as *refugees*, but this is imprecise. The program covers protected persons; refugee claimants and rejected refugee claimants; victims of human trafficking granted temporary resident permits; persons granted permanent residency due to public policy, or under humanitarian and compassionate grounds, and who receive income support; foreign nationals and permanent residents detained under the *Immigration and Refugee Protection Act*.

introduced drastic changes to the program, which slashed health care coverage to all refugees and denied coverage for some.[62] The 2012 cuts to the IFHP effectively created a hierarchy among refugees, providing descending levels of health care based on a convoluted scheme that allotted different levels of care to different groups of refugees depending on how "worthy" of assistance the government perceived them to be.[63] The applicants challenged these changes as unconstitutional under ss. 7, 12, and 15 of the *Charter of Rights and Freedoms*.

In July 2014, the Federal Court allowed the claim, declaring that the 2012 changes amounted to "cruel and unusual treatment" and violated s. 12 of the *Charter*.[64] Mactavish J also found that certain of the 2012 changes – namely, the denial of health care coverage to refugees from countries identified by the government as Designated Countries of Origin (DCOs) – violated s. 15(1) by discriminating against DCO claimants on the basis of their national origin, an enumerated ground.[65] Reasoning that the 2012 changes made a distinction between DCO claimants and non-DCO claimants that served to "marginalize, prejudice, and stereotype refugee claimants from DCO countries," put "their lives at risk and [perpetuate] the stereotypical view that they are cheats and queue-jumpers," and "perpetuate the historical disadvantage suffered by members of an admittedly vulnerable, poor and disadvantaged group," she found that these changes violated s. 15(1) and could not be upheld.[66]

Justice Mactavish declined, however, to find that the changes made to the IFHP *as a whole* violated s. 15(1).[67] That is, while she was willing to find that the DCO/non-DCO distinction was discriminatory because it treated *some* refugees as less deserving of health care than others, she

62 When justifying the cuts, the minister's spokesperson explained that the changes were designed to prevent "illegal immigrants and bogus refugee claimants" from receiving "gold-plated health care benefits that are better than those Canadian taxpayers receive," despite the fact that there was no factual evidence that such a discrepancy existed under the old IFHP (*Ibid*, para 56). See also *Ibid*, para 620, finding that there was no "inequality in the health care system between Canadians and refugees and asylum seekers."

63 For an overview of the 2012 changes, see *Ibid*, paras 57–87.

64 *Ibid*, paras 689–91.

65 *Ibid*, paras 849–51.

66 *Ibid*, paras 837, 850–1.

67 *Ibid*, paras 860–72.

was not willing to find that the changes violated s. 15(1) because they treated *all* refugees as less deserving than non-refugees. Justice Mactavish arrived at this conclusion on the basis that the ground proposed by the applicants – that of immigration status – could not be recognized as analogous. Acknowledging that the case law on this point was "mixed," she relied on *Lavoie v Canada* to find that the prior rejection of immigration status as an analogous ground by the Federal Court of Appeal and Ontario Court of Appeal in *Toussaint* and *Irshad* could not be judicially revisited.[68]

Mactavish J concluded that while the 2012 changes were discriminatory to the extent that they treated DCO claimants most egregiously, the program as a whole was not discriminatory. This conclusion ignores the ways in which her factual findings about the punitive and life-threatening nature of the 2012 changes applied not just to DCO claimants but also to all claimants impacted by the cuts. In her analysis of the DCO/non-DCO distinction, she pointed to the prevalence of historical stereotypes of "undesirable" immigrants – rooted in racism, xenophobia, and fears of economic competition, criminality, and terrorism – and the perpetuation of these stereotypes through rhetoric that labelled DCO claimants "bogus."[69] Yet as shown by both the general justifications for the program and the complex, sliding scale of benefits instituted, it was not only DCO claimants who were labelled undesirable and whose lives were put at risk by the 2012 changes to the IFHP. Thus, although a broad group of refugees had been captured both by the perpetuation of stereotype and prejudice and by the harm of inadequate health care caused by the 2012 cuts, the Court found that only a subsection of the group had been subject to unequal and unconstitutional treatment. This discrepancy does not flow from the facts of the case but from the refusal to recognize immigration status as an analogous ground. In the result, Justice Mactavish never analysed whether the 2012 cuts – as applied to refugee claimants as a whole – amounted to discrimination.

---

68 *Ibid*, paras 856, 868–98, citing *Lavoie v Canada*, [2002] 1 SCR 769 [*Lavoie*]. Arguably, this proposition is incorrect. The Supreme Court's findings in *Lavoie* that, once identified, an analogous ground need not be established again in subsequent cases, applies only where an analogous ground has already been recognized. Nothing in the jurisprudence precludes future courts from revising prior courts' findings that a specific ground is not analogous.

69 *Doctors for Refugee Care, supra* note 8, paras 837–8.

When the grounds analysis is applied in this manner, it too often entails a "formalistic and arbitrary search"[70] for characteristics that come dangerously close to an "I know it when I see it" approach. This approach risks favouring claims that are legible within existing understandings of what discrimination means and privileging protection for groups that fit such understandings. As Richard Delgado writes, "the more analogous a current case strikes us to a previous one in which our intuition was clear, the more likely we are to dispose of it in similar fashion."[71] This approach is fundamentally limited: it risks blinding courts to forms and grounds of discrimination that do not neatly fit into the categories of protection that s. 15(1) already safeguards. It also risks replicating some of the shortcomings that Kidd-White identifies in her analysis of s. 15(1) in this volume – namely, interpretations that are acontextual and criterial in nature.[72] Rather than serving as a guidepost by which to determine what discrimination means and how it operates, the grounds analysis operates as a hurdle that claimants must overcome for their claims to be substantively considered. In the result, the grounds analysis obscures, rather than illuminates, how discrimination operates in practice.

The courts' reluctance to recognize immigration status as an analogous ground does more than point to the limits of the *Charter*'s equality guarantee. Framing immigration status as a "constant marker" of suspect decision making would also pose broader legal and conceptual challenges for Canadian courts. Legally, since immigration status is a means by which the Canadian government draws distinctions through law, recognizing it as an analogous ground would force the courts to recognize that *any* equality rights claim based on immigration status must pass the first stage of the s. 15(1) test and attract constitutional scrutiny.[73] Conceptually, such an approach would force the courts to

70 *Withler, supra* note 57, para 2, where the Court rejected a "formalistic and arbitrary search for the 'proper' comparator group."

71 Richard Delgado, "Four Reservations on Civil Rights Reasoning by Analogy," *Columbia Law Review* 112 (2012) 1883, 1897.

72 White, *supra* note 9.

73 While legally challenging, such an approach would be doctrinally sound: as *Lavoie* instructs, the first branch of the s 15(1) test is not designed to constrain the provision to cases of genuine discrimination. That is the task of the second branch of the test, and it "should not be pre-empted"; see *Lavoie, supra* note 68, para 41.

contend with the fact that, by design, Canadian immigration law is fundamentally unequal: it singles out both immigrants and refugees for inferior treatment precisely because of their immigration status.[74]

Viewed in this light, the courts' reluctance to recognize immigration status as an analogous ground not only reflects core problems with the immutability analysis but also alludes to broader structural problems with Canadian rights protection. This reluctance points to the uncomfortable reality that the Canadian government treats immigrants and refugees as less worthy of basic rights protection and that our legal system views it as normatively justified in doing so. Such a conclusion not only exposes the limits of s. 15(1)'s equality guarantee but also poses a challenge to the vision that Canada has proclaimed for itself as welcoming and generous in its treatment of immigrants and refugees, and as a world leader in rights protection.

The Supreme Court of Canada has called s. 15 the *Charter*'s "most conceptually difficult provision," noting that equality is an "elusive concept" that "lacks precise definition."[75] As the last few decades of *Charter* law have shown, there is nothing inherently more elusive about equality than about other rights protected in the *Charter*: for instance, "life, liberty and security of the person" are all potentially broad and elusive concepts, yet the Court has wrestled with them to give them meaning. The great difficulty at the heart of s. 15 is not that equality is an elusive concept or that discrimination is hard to define. It is that equality claims challenge the courts to contend with some of Canada's most difficult realities and subject some of our most entrenched distinctions to constitutional scrutiny. Such claims are difficult because they force us to contend with the limits of both our constitutional promises and our understanding of Canada as a rights-protecting nation.

---

74 As Catherine Dauvergne explains, for those who stand at the periphery of the nation, state protection is granted not as a matter of right, but as a matter of compassion in the case of refugees or economic expediency in the case of immigrants. She conceives of this through concentric circles: "The closer one is to belonging to the nation, the more rights one has in the migration realm"; see Catherine Dauvergne, *Humanitarianism, Identity, and Nation: Migration Laws in Canada and Australia* (Vancouver: UBC Press, 2005), 171. See also Shauna Labman, "Globalizing Rights and Going Wrong: The 'Right' Path to Refugee Protection," *Journal of International Law and International Relations* 5, no. 2 (2009) 141, 145.

75 *Law*, *infra* note 76, para 2.

Conclusion: The Failed Promise of Equality Protection

Until she joined the Court majority in *Law v Canada*, Justice L'Heureux-Dubé was the lone voice on the Supreme Court of Canada critiquing the enumerated and analogous grounds approach to s. 15(1) protection.[76] In *Corbiere* (with Gonthier, Iacobucci, and Binnie JJ concurring), her dissent articulates a more complex analysis of potential analogous grounds, suggesting that immutable characteristics are just one possible way to show that a ground for discrimination is analogous to those enumerated in s. 15(1), and that each element of s. 15(1) must be analysed using a purposive and contextual approach.[77]

In analyses of potential analogous grounds, this would mean that a number of indicators could be considered, but none of them would be required to show discrimination.[78] In *Egan v Canada*, L'Heureux-Dubé J noted that the enumerated grounds are "particular applications and illustrations of the ambit of s. 15. *They are not the guarantee itself*."[79] Arguing that giving meaning to *discrimination* through an analysis of enumerated and analogous grounds – as McIntyre J did in *Andrews* and as the Court has done subsequently – is an indirect way of understanding discrimination, L'Heureux-Dubé J preferred giving an independent meaning to *discrimination* and developing s. 15(1) jurisprudence accordingly. She warned that the standard of analysis "must not be so broad or vague as to risk undermining in practice the very purposes that s. 15 is intended to further."[80]

---

76 *Law v Canada (Minister of Employment and Immigration)*, [1999] 1 SCR 497 [*Law*]. For analysis, see Daphne Gilbert, "'Time to Regroup': Rethinking Section 15 of the Charter," *McGill Law Journal* 48 (2003) 627. But see Margot Young, "Travels with Justice L'Heureux-Dubé: Equality Law Abroad," in *Adding Feminism to Law: The Contributions of Justice Claire L'Heureux-Dubé*, ed. Elizabeth Sheehy (Toronto: Irwin Law, 2004), 287, 289, where she argues that the Court in *Law* accepted some of L'Heureux-Dubé J's analysis from *Egan, supra* note 19, in the test it developed for s 15(1), notably by its focus on human dignity. While Young (and L'Heureux-Dubé J herself; see Gilbert, 632n288) describes this as a success for Justice L'Heureux-Dubé, Gilbert describes it as a compromise among divergent views on the Court, 629. For present purposes, *Law* represents the point at which L'Heureux-Dubé J stopped critiquing the enumerated and analogous grounds approach.

77 *Corbiere, supra* note 4, para 60.

78 *Ibid.*

79 *Egan, supra* note 19, 542 (emphasis in original).

80 *Ibid*, 542–3.

L'Heureux-Dubé J's warning was all too prescient. The current approach to s. 15(1) upholds a limited vision of equality in Canada and one that is at odds with the values of the *Charter* explored in this volume. Its restrictive understanding of the immutability requirement translates into a framework for equality that too often looks to applicants' choices rather than the dynamics of discrimination that they suffer. With the courts' current fixation on finding immutability through narratives of choice and demonstrated inalterability over time, the grounds analysis fails to operate as a means of illuminating discrimination and too often operates instead as a signifier of worthiness. In the result, it creates a broad legal sphere in which the state is permitted to target specific groups, such as immigrants and refugees, for inferior treatment without this being understood as constitutionally suspect.

The cases analysed here offer an opportunity not only to reflect on where we have been but also to consider how our constitutional protections can and should evolve to more effectively extend the "unremitting protection" that s. 15 purports to guarantee. Section 15(1) holds out the promise of the better, more equal, and just Canadian society. The framework within which equality claims are analysed not only delineates the operational space of discrimination in Canada but also directs public ideas about what discrimination is and how it operates, and it signals to marginalized groups the extent to which the courts are willing to protect them.[81] As Margot Young writes, "Court pronouncements speak loudly, legitimating certain visions of society and de-legitimating others."[82] Put another way, s. 15(1) is at once a vehicle through which Canadian courts can advance equality and a vehicle through which Canadians can imagine – and aspire towards – a more just and equal society.

As Kaushal's analysis in this volume notes, the composition of Canada's population is shifting. With new demographic pressures and a growing influx of immigrants and refugees arriving at Canada's borders every day, cases involving discrimination claims on the basis of

81 *Ibid*. As Justice L'Heureux-Dubé maintains, the Court's substantive equality jurisprudence has enabled Canada to break with a long Western history of seeing a discriminatory state of affairs as the natural order of things; see L'Heureux-Dubé *supra* note 1, 2.

82 Margot Young, "Social Justice and the Charter: Comparison and Choice," *Osgoode Hall Law Journal* 50 (2013) 669, 671.

immigration status will continue to bring new dynamics of inequality before the courts. Such cases test our constitutional commitment to equality rights and also remind us that equality goals are not just substantive but also symbolic, not just remedial but also aspirational: we need them precisely because our current systems of law and governance do not provide equal benefits and protections to all.

Backing equality goals with the force of law is important because, as the Supreme Court of Canada has recognized, political and other processes have often failed marginalized and denigrated groups.[83] Courts must put in place a system capable of recognizing and redressing discrimination claims advanced by claimants whose personal traits may not neatly fit within current understandings of immutability and whose choices may be constrained. To do otherwise would be to further diminish the "unremitting protection" of equality rights that s. 15(1) purports to guarantee.[84] In immigration status cases, it would be to deprive both immigrants and refugees of meaningful consideration under s. 15(1).

---

83 *Andrews*, *supra* note 1, 152.
84 *Ibid*, 175.

Contributors

Richard Albert, William Stamps Farish Professor of Law, The University of Texas at Austin, School of Law

Efrat Arbel, assistant professor, University of British Columbia, Peter A. Allard School of Law

Paul Daly, senior lecturer in public law, University of Cambridge, Faculty of Law

Noura Karazivan, associate professor, Université de Montréal, Faculty of Law

Asha Kaushal, assistant professor, University of British Columbia, Peter A. Allard School of Law

Emily Kidd White, assistant professor, York University, Osgoode Hall Law School

Howard Kislowicz, assistant professor, University of Calgary, Faculty of Law

Mary Liston, assistant professor, University of British Columbia, Peter A. Allard School of Law

Vanessa MacDonnell, associate professor, University of Ottawa, Faculty of Law (Common Law Section)

Emmett Macfarlane, associate professor, University of Waterloo, Department of Political Science

David Milward, associate professor, University of Victoria, Faculty of Law

Eileen Myrdahl, articled student

Vrinda Narain, associate professor, McGill University, Faculty of Law

Dwight Newman, professor of law and Canada Research Chair in Indigenous Rights in Constitutional and International Law, University of Saskatchewan, College of Law

Michael Pal, associate professor, University of Ottawa, Faculty of Law (Common Law Section)

Wade K. Wright, assistant professor, Western University, Faculty of Law

Sujith Xavier, assistant professor and director, Transnational Law and Justice Network, University of Windsor, Faculty of Law

Index of Cases and Statutes

Canada

Constitutional

Statutes and Regulations

Codes

Bills and Statutes – Provinces and Territories

Regulations

Cases

Other Jurisdictions

International Instruments

Cases – European Union

Cases – United Kingdom

Cases – United States

Codes – New Zealand

Codes – United Kingdom

Constitutional – Austria

Constitutional – United Kingdom

Statutes – United Kingdom

Index of Names

General Index

www.ingramcontent.com/pod-product-compliance
Lightning Source LLC
LaVergne TN
LVHW090800070826
844660LV00022B/1044
* 9 7 8 1 4 8 7 5 2 3 0 2 2 *